GW00359361

Evacuees and
Crabapple Trees

Sheila Newberry was born in Suffolk and spent a lot of time there both before and during the war. She wrote her first 'book' before she was ten – all sixty pages of it – in purple ink. Her family was certainly her inspiration and she was published for most of her adult life. She spent forty years living in Kent with her husband John on a smallholding. She had nine children, twenty-two grandchildren and twelve great-grandchildren. Sheila retired back to Suffolk where she lived until she passed away in 2020.

Novels by Sheila Newberry

Angel's Wish
A Winter Hope
Bicycles and Blackberries
Far From Home
The Canal Boat Girl
The Forget-Me-Not Girl
The Gingerbread Girl
The Girl with No Home
Hay Bales and Hollyhocks
Hot Pies on the Tram Car
The Meadow Girls
The Mother and Baby Home
The Nursemaid's Journey
The Nursemaid's Secret
The Punch and Judy Girl
The Winter Baby
The East End Nurse
The Girl by the Sea

Sheila
NEWBERRY

Evacuees and Crabapple Trees

ZAFFRE

First published in the UK by Dales Large Print as *Come You on Inside,
Dancing in the Street, Knee Deep in Plums, Seven Pounds of
Potatoes Please and Who Stirs the Porridge in the Pot*
This edition published in 2024 by
ZAFFRE
An imprint of Zaffre Publishing Group
A Bonnier Books UK Company
4th Floor, Victoria House, Bloomsbury Square, London WC1B 4DA
Owned by Bonnier Books
Sveavägen 56, Stockholm, Sweden

A CIP catalogue record for this book is
available from the British Library.

ISBN: 978-1-80418-549-0

Also available as an ebook

1 3 5 7 9 10 8 6 4 2

Typeset by IDSUK (Data Connection) Ltd
Printed and bound in Great Britain by Clays Ltd, Elcograf S.p.A.

Zaffre is an imprint of Zaffre Publishing Group
A Bonnier Books UK Company
www.bonnierbooks.co.uk

Sheila's family would like to dedicate this book to her.
An inspiring mother, grandmother and great grandmother
who had a gift for telling stories.

A foreword by Rosie Goodwin

Welcome to the wonderful memoirs of Sheila Newberry. Sheila was the author of over twenty bestselling novels and I'm sure as you read on you will discover, as I did, that her life was just as intriguing as her amazing stories. I felt very honoured when I was asked to write a foreword for these memoirs, as I was a great fan of Sheila's books, although sadly I never got to meet her in person. I am told by people who did know her personally that she was a wonderfully kind and loving soul and that comes across very much in this book. As I began to read, I was amazed to discover how alike Sheila and I were in many ways. For instance, I loved English at school, but like Sheila I was useless at maths! Sheila wrote her very first book at school in purple ink, whereas I always tended to be writing short stories and poetry. I was also always surrounded by children, although many of mine were foster children, whereas Sheila had nine of her own!

Sheila begins her memoirs in 1939 when she was just seven years old and had spent six weeks in an isolation hospital after being very ill with scarlet fever, and from the first page I was enthralled. Such brilliant names are mentioned: Aunty Rum, Dolly and of course her beloved Pekingese, Waggles, who was a surprise present to welcome her home. All names worthy of appearing in one of her books! Sheila's writing is so descriptive that she brings the characters and the stories to life and you can almost imagine being there. There followed a fun-filled week spent with family to help her convalesce in a little bungalow perched right on a cliff edge in California, Norfolk, with crumbling steps that led down to a golden beach.

The family owned an Austin 7 and every year during the August break they would travel from their home in a London suburb to stay with Dolly in her little cottage in the small village of Fordlea, Suffolk for their summer holidays. Idyllic!

Sheila goes on to describe the terrifying crump of gunfire, the menacing drone of enemy planes and the screaming of bombs dropping dangerously close to their home during the war years. How terrifying it must have been for people to live through! Her home was damaged during one of these raids and she was evacuated with all of her pets, including Waggles of course, to Aunt Dolly's house. There's another thing we had in common, a love of dogs and animals.

Thankfully Sheila survived the war and soon after she met her husband John at a dance in Streatham and from then on, they were inseparable. As I read on it became obvious that they were soulmates. They married and within six years had five children. Soon after they bought their first home, Crabapple Cottage, on a smallholding in Kent. What a wonderful name, although the real thing left a lot to be desired. It was terribly run down and there was no heating or indoor bathroom. Imagine how hard it must have been for them, but Sheila and John set to and made it into a lovely home for their family, adding four more children to their brood along the way. John worked away from home for some of the time and Sheila chipped in to earn extra money doing anything she could. Hop picking, strawberry picking and potato picking to name just a few. A truly remarkable woman.

When the children were growing up, they began their next venture, a little corner shop, and once more Sheila put all her efforts into it, although sadly it never turned into the resounding success they had hoped it would be.

Some years later they bought a Chapel, which once again required complete restoration. I wonder where she got her energy from. Nothing seemed to phase her and throughout all this she was still finding time to write her brilliant stories. Many of the short stories were published in magazines and her children, like mine, were weaned on stories she wrote for them.

Sheila's first novel was written on an old typewriter that John bought for her and was published when she was quite late on in life, and a total of over twenty books ended up on the shelves. What an achievement. As her children grew, she was proud to see them all make their own way in life, although as you read you can feel her sadness as each of them flew the nest. It comes across very clearly that she was incredibly proud of each and every one of them. And then there was finally time for John and Sheila to have some quality time together – until the grandchildren started to come along that was – and then it seems she was as taken with them as she had been with their parents. Sheila had a total of nine children, twenty-two grandchildren and twelve great-grandchildren. Christmas shopping must have been very busy for her! Throughout this book the deep love she felt for her family shines through. They must be so very proud of her, and rightly so. Sadly, Sheila passed peacefully away in January 2020.

So now you are in for a treat. I'm sure you will all enjoy reading these wonderful memoirs just as much as I did. Sheila had such a remarkable way of bringing her characters and her stories to life and we are all very grateful for the lovely legacy she left behind through her novels.

So rest in peace lovely lady and know that you and your stories are very loved and you will live on in them.

Rosie Goodwin xxx

Contents

Part 1: Come You on Inside
1939–1942

1	Come You on Inside	3
2	'Friday Night is Amami Night'	10
3	Christmas at the Swan	15
4	Full of Spring	23
5	Wholly Holy	30
6	Festive Laments	36
7	The Tides of March	43
8	Summer Ripe	51
9	Fare Ye Well Together	58

Part 2: Dancing in the Street
1942–1951

10	The Homecoming	67
11	Bread Buns and Big Girls	72
12	Disraeli and Me	77
13	Glycerine, Greens and Gristle	84
14	Sealing Wax and Other Crafts	90
15	Dodging the Doodlebugs	96
16	All Those Begats and Shakespeare Too	102
17	Dancing in the Street	108
18	Donkeys, John Bull and Tangos	115
19	Life Itself is a Roller-Coaster	121
20	Moments of Glory	126

21	Down Among the Dead Men	133
22	Twelfth Street Rag	140
23	Black-Eyed Susie	146

Part 3: Knee Deep in Plums
1962–1970

24	Knee Deep in Plums	153
25	Everyone Calls, Dawn to Dusk	159
26	Frozen Apples, Frozen Pipes and Festive Fires	165
27	Who Lives Down the Lane	172
28	Dear Sister Susie	179
29	Piano, Pets and Pests	186
30	The House that Ben Built	193
31	Mumps, Mopes and Moggies	200
32	In and Out the Orchard	207
33	Bramleys by the Bushel	215
34	Come In, Number Nine	223

Part 4: Seven Pounds of Potatoes Please
Mid 1970s

35	Seven Pounds of Potatoes, Please	233
36	From the Crossroads	236
37	We'll Fill the Shelves	239
38	Early Doors	243
39	Old Cat, Young Dog and Roaming Tortoise	247
40	Concorde and Kites	251
41	Good Old Bachelor Boys	255
42	Platform Shoes and Lightning Strikes	259
43	What Can You Do With a Gallon of Ice-cream?	262
44	Maff and the Big Bar of Chocolate	265
45	Sunken Sugar	269
46	Going Out	272
47	The Little Shop Can Save Your Bacon	276
48	Then the Wall Fell Down	279
49	Goodbye	284
50	A Moving Experience	288

Part 5: Who Stirs the Porridge in the Pot?
Early 1980s

51	Who Stirs the Porridge in the Pot?	295
52	Happy Days are Here Again	300
53	Feathers Flying and Adorning	306
54	You Can't Teach an Old Dog New Tricks	311
55	Boys and Girls Come Out to Play	316
56	Wedding Bells	321
57	No Cup of Tea for Rosy Lee?	326
58	'Gorillas', Grapes and a Ticket to Rye	331
59	The Bash Street Lot	336
60	On the Leslie 'Gateau' Trail	341
61	A Family Crisis, Followed by Two Summer Weddings	348
62	Well, There's Kids – and Kids . . .	353
63	Putting on Our Parts	359
64	Merv the Midnight Grocer	365
65	A Writer's Companion	371

PART 1

COME YOU ON INSIDE

1939–1942

CHAPTER 1

Come You On Inside

Sunday morning, a polite tap on the back door, and Auntie Rum from the cottage next door came into the kitchen. Molly turned off the crackling wireless and Dolly filled the kettle from the pail in the pantry. She lit the gas ring in the hearth, with the familiar hiss and plop.

'Do sit down Auntie Rum. This is it then,' Dolly said.

'This is it,' echoed Auntie Rum. She sat down heavily, the black bentwood rocker creaking, resting her forearms on the table covered with the red chenille cloth with its bobbled fringe. I sat opposite, busy with my colouring book; Jassy beside me in her high chair, chewing on a rusk.

Auntie Rum smiled at my solemn face. 'Being good, and quiet, I see.'

I nodded. 'Shush!' they said, 'we want to listen to the news . . .'

* * *

In the spring of 1939, when I was seven, I spent six weeks in an isolation hospital, very ill with scarlet fever, coming home to much fussing and affection. My dreams had come true: there was a lovely surprise, a fluffy Pekingese puppy called Waggles.

In June, my convalescence was boosted during a happy, sandy, fun-filled week with my parents, Molly and Jim, and my brother David, together with Molly's sister Dolly, her husband Ross, and their small daughter Jasmine, at California in Norfolk. We stayed in a bungalow perched right at the cliff's edge, with crumbling steps to the golden beach below. The lanes around were ablaze with Californian poppies.

At the beginning of the long school holiday in August, Molly, David and I, plus the pup, left our home in a London suburb and went by coach, which was an ordeal for me due to my travel sickness, to stay with Dolly and Ross in their little cottage in the village of Fordlea in Suffolk, not far from the coast. Nothing unusual about this; we did this every summer.

My father joined us one weekend and crammed us all into the Austin 7 for an outing to the grandparents who lived near Southwold. It was a day for eating juicy greengages; watching out for wasps, and feeding pennies into the amusement machines on the pier. We spent the next afternoon, Sunday, sitting under the cedars edging the village cricket field, only half-aware of the crack of bat against ball and white clad men, some quite advanced in years, whooping like boys. Later, Jim told David and me that he was going away, but not for too long, he hoped – he hugged us tight, then drove off.

Molly went back to our house for a few days. She returned with a trunkful of clothes, a box of books and favourite toys. I certainly didn't mind our prolonged stay in Suffolk – I loved the cottage, the village and the lush countryside, but I was puzzled, and the grown-ups were too pre-occupied to explain. I missed my father, wondering why he had gone to Somerset, wherever that was. Letters arrived daily for his 'dearest Molly', with amusing notes enclosed for David and me.

Each morning now I awoke at first light, slipping out of the hollow in the big feather bed I shared with my mother, creeping over to the low window to look out over the garden. There was a creaking, groaning sound, a gushing, a clanging. Uncle Ross at the pump, filling the water pails for the day. As he carried the buckets back to the cottage, Tiger, the half-Persian ginger cat, weaving in and out of his legs, the milkman arrived, going under the covered way with his churn. I listened for the clinking of the measuring jug as he dipped it into the milk and filled the array of jugs on the shelf. He covered each jug with its beaded cotton cap and then chatted to Ross while he was shaving in the washhouse adjoining the kitchen. There was no bathroom here, as at our own home, with hot water from the popping gas geyser, no real kitchen with gas stove and water on tap, no inside lavatory with Izal toilet roll to be stealthily unwound to collect the picture cards; only the washhouse with its copper, and zinc bath, the open fire in the living room, with the gas ring in the hearth, and the privy round the corner of the property with its scrubbed wooden box, strong smell of carbolic, *Daily Mirror*s cut up for-the-use-of hanging on a loop of string from a nail, and old parish magazines to read, piled on a shelf. In winter, after-dark visits to the Library, as it was known, necessitated much dressing up in coats, boots and gloves, always accompanied by a flickering torch and sometimes an umbrella.

Now it was September, and Molly seemed to have forgotten that the long holiday was almost over, and that we must return home to go to school. Still, it would be nice, I thought, if we were still here for my birthday, on the fifth . . .

* * *

Miss Rumbelow, known to us as Auntie Rum, was tall and angular with a face both plain and handsome; she had prominent teeth, all her own; soft, wrinkled skin; bright eyes behind gold-wire glasses and silky, sparse white hair pulled back into an untidy bun fastened with crinkly, black hairpins which she shed all over the place.

She seemed very old to me, compared to my slim, pretty mother, with her short, wavy golden hair, near-sighted eyes framed with tortoiseshell glasses, fashionable in a cotton dress patterned with huge scarlet poppies, silk stockings and court shoes. And to my aunt, shorter, rounder, but just as vivacious. Dolly had a mop of beautiful red curls, as did her daughter; she had blue eyes and freckled bare arms. Despite the differences in their colouring and height, the two were often mistaken one for the other. They were the middle pair of four lively sisters, the two nearest in age. Even their names fitted together, I always thought, Molly and Dolly. Yet Molly had married before she was twenty and gone off confidently to live in London, while Dolly had remained close to the family home and wed a local chap. Both husbands were shortish, slight, dark-haired and musical, with a gentle sense of humour. They got on very well, too.

I observed and listened as the women talked. Dolly poured dark brown tea into the orange and green patterned Woolworth cups. We had a tea-set like that at home, too. She fished out a tea-leaf with her thumb, passed the cup to Auntie Rum.

'You don't want to meet a dark stranger, do you, Auntie Rum?'

Molly lit a cigarette, taking short, nervous puffs. She screwed up her eyes against the smoke.

'Jim says we should stay on here. It's safer. The whole department went West last week. They've been ready for it, for months.'

'It'll be a squeeze, but we'll manage,' Dolly smiled, fingering the pretty black and gold tea caddy which Ross had brought back from one of his trips around the world.

She had waited patiently five years for him to settle down, and since his marriage he worked with his brother, delivering cattle-feed by lorry to local farmers. Memories of Ross's years at sea were all around the tiny living room. The guitar on the shelf, carved wooden curiosities, a rice paper fan, gleaming brass, embroidered cushion covers. I liked especially the wooden bird which pecked up a cigarette in its beak from a box which sprang open when a knob was pressed.

'What is *it*?' I ventured at last.

'War, ducky,' said Dolly. 'That nasty old Hitler has gone too far. We've been listening to the Prime Minister on the wireless this morning. You're going to stay with Uncle Ross and me for a while and you children can go to school here, next week.'

'All of us?'

'You and David and your mum. Your dad's got to stay in Bath. He'll come up when he can. You like it here, don't you?'

I thought about it. We came 'home' as Molly called it, at every opportunity, the family ties were very strong. I knew that my parents had 'come back' so that David and I could be born in Suffolk, in my case, only just in time, as I was a premature baby. I'd often heard the tale of Molly eating shrimps while jolting along in the Austin, not liking to make a fuss. Perhaps that's why I was allergic to shellfish. But I wished that Jim could be with us, too.

Ross and David came in, with a trug full of earthy potatoes and fresh vegetables from the garden. David had his pockets full of small golden plums.

'Dinner! Good gracious!' Dolly exclaimed. 'We hadn't given it a thought . . .'

'Heard the church bell . . . this is it, then,' Ross said.

'This is it,' Dolly said. 'But let's enjoy today, eh?'

* * *

It was my birthday; early on it seemed a clouded, disappointing day. The postman had let me down this year, it seemed – there were no cards on the front door mat. There were hand-delivered ones from the family here, of course, but no presents yet.

Dear Auntie Rum came in as usual to ask if she could help. She and Molly tackled the breakfast washing-up in the pantry, while Dolly bathed Jassy by the fire. I sat hunched in the armchair with my book, while David rolled tiny flour and water balls for bait, on a tray on the table. He was going fishing in the nearby pond, with another boy. I wasn't allowed to tag along in case I disturbed the fish!

'Someone's got a long face, I see,' observed Auntie Rum, looking at me as she passed a nice soft towel to Dolly before she scooped the splashing toddler from the tub.

'It's my birthday, Auntie Rum,' I said miserably.

'Is it now, my dear? However did I forget it? I'll find you something when I go back, eh? Sit on my lap for five minutes and tell me all about it . . . you don't want to worry about that old war, it'll all be over soon . . .'

Later, we went down the sun-baked path between the neat rows of glossy-leaved cabbages and onions spread out, past the riot of roses round the lawn, sprinkled with fading petals like confetti, past the chickens scratching and quarrelling in the dirt in their run, and through the gap in the hedge by the pump, into an almost identical garden. The two cottages leaned comfortably together, with matching, blinking, small windows.

A giant tabby cat lay stretched across the whitened back step at Auntie Rum's, purring faintly, claws unsheathed, tail gently waving as I bent to stroke it.

The furniture in the living room was angular and straight-backed like its owner. A hard commode chair stood stiffly in a corner. The stick hooked round one arm was a reminder of Auntie Rum's late father who'd sat there, tucked around with rugs. Auntie Rum had nursed him for many years after her mother died and remained smiling and happy despite all the hard work involved.

'Some woman, that Miss Rumbelow,' they said in the village. Elderly spinster that she was, she had an affinity with children which she retained well into her nineties. She owned both the cottages and from the day they arrived treated the young couple next door as her family, and although her frequent visits were sometimes at inconvenient times, they had great affection and respect for her. She could despatch a rat with a thump of a spade, resuscitate aged chickens by shaking them upside down vigorously and then administering black treacle; she cured the egg-pecker with a crafty, mustard-filled egg and reared chicks under a mop head; she nursed the sick and helped the poor unobtrusively and her life was so full you could see that she could never have found the time to marry.

Auntie Rum poked behind the clock and discovered a bar of Nestlé Milk Chocolate.

'Here you are, then. And let me look in my box.'

We dipped in the box, which still had a faint whiff of long-gone cigars; strings of beads with faulty clasps, jet and amber, trickled through my fingers.

'Jet was fashionable as a mark of respect after the old Queen died,' Auntie Rum mused.

To me, the glittering beads were shaped like black teardrops. I replaced them quickly.

'The amber,' she continued, 'came from our own beaches, I shouldn't wonder. After a high tide's the best time to look for it.'

There was a cameo brooch, with pin missing, and a background of brilliant blue.

'Butterfly wings,' she told me.

'How cruel! How could they?'

At last she located a small rolled-gold tiepin with a mobile green bead.

'A young man gave me this a long time ago. You have it.' I was to treasure this for many years, but like Auntie Rum, I never wore it.

From a high shelf came a thick pile of *Girl's Own* papers, within a leather cover.

'I'll have them back when you've read them. I've had these nearly sixty years now. But mind you don't read them on a Sunday. I never did.'

But I knew I would. How could I help it?

Ross popped home for lunch, with a rabbit he'd been given. He hung the poor thing up on a hook on the pantry door. I tried not to look at it. His Old English sheepdog cross Rover was at his heels. The two were inseparable. David was back from fishing, his bait all gone, guarding jealously two minute roaches in a jar of water.

Molly set the table and Dolly went to the outhouse to fetch the shepherd's pie from the oven there. There was pink blancmange and red jelly for afters because it was my birthday. They toasted me with fizzy lemonade, which tickled my nose.

In the afternoon we went blackberrying, going through the gate at the bottom of the garden into a paddock and across further fields. We were armed with walking sticks and baskets, and the pushchair went bumping over the ruts. We opened and closed gates, skirted the bullocks, and stroked the noble heads of the pair of Suffolk Punches when they came to greet us. And there were the bushes, laden with fruit, literally falling into our eager hands.

I had insisted on wearing my birthday present from my parents. The pink taffeta party dress gained purple stains from the berries, but I was happy again.

What was war? It wasn't here in Suffolk, with Molly and Dolly giggling like girls.

* * *

We went back to paste sandwiches for tea, chocolate biscuits and a lovely pink and white iced cake, brought out from its hiding place. Little Jassy was entranced with the candles. She was undressed ready for bed, and she smeared chocolate and cake down her clean white cotton nighty. Dolly took it in her stride, as Molly had my frock.

The gas light, sighing softly, gentle to sit under as the evening closed in, and the family drew closer together. My birthday cards, set out neatly on the mantlepiece, said *Happy Birthday to You*.

CHAPTER 2

'Friday Night is Amami Night'

'Why did you have to show off again?' David asked, as we dropped down into the gully from the bank, crunching noisily through a carpet of dry leaves. We were on our way home from school, choosing the longer way home along the old high road because we were on our own, sauntering past the church and turning left by the village hut, a long wooden building, where all the local social events took place.

In winter and spring, water flowed through the gullies, concrete lined trenches, whirling hedge clippings and twigs through the dark tunnels which appeared at intervals. Even now, these tunnels were damp, smelly and slimy, and not nice to crawl through. We were not supposed to do so, but, of course, we did.

I looked at David's cross, freckled face. He was only sixteen months my senior, but took seriously his role of older brother, responsible for a dreamy younger sister. He had the family auburn hair, I was very fair like Molly. Our brown eyes were from Jim. These dark eyes, he said, were a legacy from his Spanish grandmother, and I had learned to use this as a defence when children at school noticed my fleeting squint.

'I didn't!' I retorted. It was true, I hadn't meant to show off. It was Miss House who had unwittingly caused a barrier between me and my classmates on my first day in the local school, and thus embarrassed David, wanting to remain as inconspicuous as possible.

I had been put in the first classroom with the infants and lower juniors, while David had joined the older children in the headmaster's class.

Miss House stood with her back to the smudged blackboard, dusting the chalk from her small, plump hands, before picking up a book from her high desk. She had lazy-lidded eyes and glossy black hair in a knot in the nape of her neck, and a beautiful bell-like voice. She called for silence.

'Books open at the first page. New girl, will you begin reading please?'

I was seated on a long form between two hefty girls. The table before us was pitted and scarred, the inkpots jammed with blotting paper. I didn't have a book, but, on a nod from the teacher, one girl obligingly pushed hers over. I began to read, soon happily absorbed in the story, not noticing Miss House's lifted hand at the end of the first page, signalling the next reader to take over. I gathered speed and eloquence and read on and on, undisturbed until the end of the first lesson. With a start, I looked up and saw the hostile, stony faces around me.

Miss House swept over, beaming. 'Now, children,' she cried, 'this is the way you should all read. With expression, fluency and enthusiasm. Class dismissed. New girl, you come with me. I would like Mr Todd to hear you read.'

I felt a sharp pain on my ankle as the girl next to me aimed a swift kick, and the girl on my other side, wrenched the book from my hands.

'Show-off!' they hissed.

Tears prickled my eyes. It was unfair, I was a compulsive reader and made good use of the lending library back home, reckoning to read one book while still in the library, a second on the way home, occasionally bumping into a lamp-post, and another book that same day, returning the next day for another set of books. Of course, these were only short books, some with lovely pictures, but I had almost worked my way through the children's section.

So, I read from one of the top-class books to a smiling Mr Todd. He immediately decided that I should be promoted to his class for lessons, but I encountered further unfriendliness from the bigger children.

Two days later, to my shame, and their satisfaction, my 'brilliance' was discovered to be one-sided, when I failed dismally in a rudimentary arithmetic test, so it was back to Class One to jeers from both sides.

'Cockney!' they taunted out in the playground. I wasn't sure what that meant.

'I'm not!' They circled round me.

'You come from London, don't you?'

'Not London, no—' But what did it matter if I did? I was bewildered at their jibes.

'*Cockney!*'

I tried to conform. I read only the required single page in a low, monotonous voice. I brought an Oxo-tin filled with grit for hopscotch; I shared my coloured pencils; I laughed at myself when my attempts at knitting and sewing looked pathetic beside the accomplished handwork of my classmates. My pixie-hood was destined to become a potholder, my cotton gingham apron a duster. I offered my sweets. By the end of the first week I even had a couple of friends. One, in particular, Mary the Co-op manager's daughter, also new to the school. And a large girl called Farje (short for Marjorie, I think) mothered me and cushioned me against the playground knocks.

But today I had 'showed-off' again. The school inspector came and looked at a selection of our work. He called on me to read my latest composition aloud to the assembled school, and congratulated me on a piece of imaginative writing.

In the playground later David exchanged punches with a boy who had mimicked his sister, and had a puffy eye to show for it, but he was naturally resentful that I should again have been singled out.

Now, I suddenly decided: 'I'm going to see Uncle Ross.'

'We're supposed to go straight home!'

'I don't care. I'm going to ask if I can go out with him in the lorry tomorrow.'

'I am, too!' David wriggled through the tunnel and clambered out of the gully, running ahead of me.

The big garage and store was just up the road. We arrived there, panting and dishevelled, skirting the patches of oil between the parked lorries, scrambling up the wooden ladder onto the storage deck. It smelled mealy and musty up there, the heavy sacks of grain and pellets piled high. The cobwebs were thick on the rafters, the dust motes were dancing. David picked up a square of cattle-cake and chewed the edge. He made a wry face and threw it at the overhead beam. Uncle Ross's brother, Chas, whom we called Uncle too, even though strictly, he wasn't, had fixed a swing up here for his children, who were weekly boarders at school, and their friends, which included us. Once I'd swung so high I had cracked my nose on the beam and suffered an awful nose-bleed. But I was only six then; I'd learned my lesson.

'There's a mouse!' David yelled, as one streaked past us and disappeared in a gap between two sacks. I squealed in fright, and a familiar voice called up to us: 'Hey! What are you two doing up there?' It was Uncle Ross, loading sacks onto the back of his lorry, making ready for an early-morning start.

'Can I? Can I?' we chorused in unison. Uncle Ross flipped a penny and I called, 'Heads!' quickly, because David and I suspected it was a two-headed penny, and so I won the toss, and the short ride to a local farm to make a delivery next morning.

Molly and Dolly were just finishing up in the washhouse. There was a delicious smell of chutney. 'Stir 'em in. Add a bit of meat to it,' was Dolly's teasing battle cry as the wasps dive-bombed and she batted them away with her wooden spoon. They had been stoking the copper all day for baths that evening and our lunch had been boiled beef and dumplings cooked in the big black pot which sat on top of the bubbling cauldron. Dolly scraped the gravy from surplus dumplings and served these with a dollop of golden syrup for pudding. This didn't quite disguise the hint of onion. This afternoon they'd been chopping green tomatoes, apples, onions and adding sultanas sugar and spices to the chutney.

Later, Dolly said: 'You children can write the labels and stick them on the jars.' We enjoyed doing this while the washhouse was re-arranged for bath night. I wrote 1939 on the labels except for a couple on which I put 1839, and couldn't stop giggling.

It was growing dark by the time the ablutions were over. The youngest went first, and the next in line had a topping-up of hot water. Dolly added soap flakes to swish into bubbles and huge towels warmed by the fire enveloped us children before we were carried into the living room to be dried.

It was late evening before Molly and Dolly had finished mopping up the brick floor of the washhouse and Ross had baled out the bath, bucket by bucketful. We children sat together in the big chair in the alcove by the fire, reading the *Rainbow* comic, friends again. Jassy was already asleep upstairs in her cot, the puppy in his basket. Rover sprawled out on the rag rug and I wriggled my bare toes in his soft, grey fur.

Ross often made toasted cheese for supper, which we loved. He toasted bread on a fork, then cut thick pieces of cheese to cover each slice. These were placed on a tin plate under the fire grate. The smell of the melting cheddar and the cindery taste was bliss to David and me tonight. It didn't give us nightmares!

It was also Amami night for the ladies, who had washed their hair with soft water from the butt, straining off the creepy crawlies, and who now sat rubbing each other's damp locks dry. They were pyjama and dressing-gown clad, too.

When the greasy plates had been stacked and put to soak in a bowl in the pantry, we drank our milky cocoa, and Ross settled down to play his guitar. He had sensitive hands, well-cared for, in spite of his job. I watched, fascinated, as he bent his dark head, plucking at the strings, making soft, vibrating, melodious chords.

'Comb my hair?' Dolly asked me, leaning back in her chair. I perched behind her, inventing weird and wonderful styles with a wire-bristled brush and a steel comb. Dolly closed her eyes blissfully. My mother didn't enjoy these grooming sessions and asked Dolly if she realised what she was going to look like in the morning! Or didn't she recall how she'd been caught out with little bows all over her head, just like Topsy in the story, when the Parson called unexpectedly last week?

David sat on at the table, sandpapering the balsa wood pieces of the latest aeroplane kit, Molly's steel knitting needles clicked busily while her ball of wool rolled across the floor. The only time she was without her knitting was on the beach; her sister would not allow it!

'Little old lady passing by' and 'There's a little grey home in the West,' we sang.

The feather beds were warm and welcoming, the candle flickering lopsidedly in the saucer was comforting. I was asleep before Molly crept in beside me. David slumbered, too, in his narrow bed at the other end of the long, narrow bedroom.

I didn't know it then, of course, but Molly's tears wet her pillow as she cried for her husband, hearing the low voices of Dolly and Ross the other side of the lath and plaster wall. She cried because of the uncertainty of the future, because she had been happy that day. And she cried for us, her children, because she could only let the tears fall when we were asleep.

CHAPTER 3

Christmas at the Swan

Our grandparents lived about eight miles away. As small girls, just before and after the Great War, Molly and Dolly had led a carefree and happy existence, well-fed and cared for mainly by their own grandma, who lived with them, as their parents were both in business. Nanna and Grandad to us, Isabella and Ernest were the Guv'nor and the Missus of the Buck Inn, adjacent to which Ernest had built a modern butcher's shop. They were both busy from dawn to midnight. There was music there, too. The children sometimes lay in bed listening raptly to their father playing the nostalgic songs of the Great War on his banjo, which hung on the bar wall. He invariably ended his repertoire with 'I'll Take You Home Again Kathleen', a reminder of his Irish origins.

While Ernest was away in the war, having been called up although over forty, Isabella bravely attempted to carry on with both businesses, although by then she had a new baby, Tilly. That made five children at home, although by the end of the war the two oldest, Emma and Frank, had left school and were working.

During that difficult time, Isabella drove the pony and trap miles to deliver orders from the shop, endeavouring to cope with all the heavy tasks at the Inn, with help from fourteen-year-old Frank before and after work, because even the older men of the village were needed for the war effort. Eventually, sheer exhaustion forced her to close the shop, and after the war it had taken some years for her husband to build up his trade and reputation again.

In 1935 they left the Buck and returned to the Swan Inn in the next village, now a private dwelling, where Isabella had been born. She enjoyed providing bed and breakfast accommodation, for touring cyclists. Ernest took over a butcher's shop across the road, and was now struggling with wartime shortages once again.

Molly had been an intrepid cyclist as a young girl, and Jim's first sight of her had been of her tousled curls and glowing cheeks, as she sped, no hands, down a steep hill towards the Buck, shooting through a gap she'd made in the hedge, jumping off the bike, before it careened into the privy. He was thirty, about to begin a quiet country break, staying at the inn, and she was only twelve, but he fell in love with the place, and much later, of course, with Molly. When she was grown up, he married her. It was a real romance, everyone said.

Now Molly had taken up cycling again, on a great black monster of a bike, with sit-up-and-beg handlebars, belonging to Ross. She and Dolly pedalled the long, dusty miles once a week, to see their parents.

Auntie Rum looked after Jassy and made a midday meal for David and me, and Ross, if he was in the vicinity, as he was now travelling much further afield delivering vital foodstuffs for the war effort.

After school in the later afternoon, we'd be impatient for the cyclists to return home, their legs wearily turning the pedals, their carriers laden with goodies. Sometimes fresh fish for supper, caught by our Uncle Frank; sausages made to our grandad's secret recipe; sweetbreads and soup bones; eggs from the pet duck; *Comic Cuts*, Grandad's favourite, for the children, and balls of wool for knitting.

It was dark not long after we arrived back. David and I were busy each evening making Christmas presents. A huge woolly ball for Jasmine, a kettle-holder for Dolly, a long tube of French knitting became a tie for Jim. We made calendars for relatives and friends from old Christmas cards, a raffia bracelet for Molly and a spill box for Ross. We must've used a gallon of flour and water paste.

Early in December there was the school Christmas party. Numbers had swelled with the arrival of 'real' evacuees (soon to depart, when it was realised how vulnerable the village was, being so near the coast) and now it was Us and Them, and suddenly we were counted among Us and life became easier at school. Auntie Rum had opened her home and heart to one of these evacuees, as had Uncle Chas and his family.

'And I've got *you!*' Dolly said fondly. 'Aren't I lucky?' We thought we were, too.

The party was held in the village hut on a Friday afternoon. We walked in pairs from the school, first the girls, followed by the boys, with the headmaster leading the way, and Miss House bringing up the rear.

As we filed into the hut, we were greeted by the Squire and his wife, each holding a leather money bag. The girls were required to bob their knees, then we were rewarded with a shiny new sixpence by the Squire's lady, with a gracious smile. The boys had to shake hands with the Squire before receiving their gift.

'Happy Christmas!' they chorused in turn. 'Thank you very much.'

This all seemed very old-fashioned to me, but I tied my sixpence in a corner of my hanky and before the afternoon was out, I'd lost it.

Long trestle tables were laden with unexpected good things, egg sandwiches, buttered Suffolk rusks, split in two, tinned fruit in jelly, iced biscuits, and in the centre of the top table was a giant fruit cake, dark, rich and yet to be cut. Each child had a small poke bag of boiled sweets beside their plates.

Miss House played the off-key piano with panache and we laughed and sang and marched to the 'Grand Old Duke of York' and chopped our linked hands with a will as others dodged through in 'Oranges and Lemons'.

This was the last Christmas party of plenty, for rationing was about to hit us all hard.

* * *

Christmas was spent, as always, with our grandparents. This year, there was no excited packing of cases and long journey by car from Surrey. No 'tsking' from Isabella over her wan little granddaughter Shummy, as the family called me, pale and sickly-smelling. Last year, she'd exclaimed over my skinny frame:

'That child's too fussy, Molly; she needs a-feeding up, come you here; I'll soon sweeten you up with a flannel and nice, warm water . . .'

Uncle Ross took us children, the luggage and the box of Christmas presents over in his lorry on Christmas Eve afternoon and Molly and Dolly cycled over as usual.

Ernest was at the open door to greet us. He had been watching out for the lorry from his shop. He was a giant of a man, with a shock of white hair and a ruddy face, with lively blue eyes and a bristling Lord Kitchener moustache, tinged with ginger. His arms hugged us tightly as he lifted each one of us aloft for a kiss, and I closed my eyes and tried not to wince as the fierce moustache prickled my face.

'Hull-oo there! What-ho my old sugar-lumps! Come you on inside. I'll carry the little 'un, give you her to me. Where's those girls? Still a-pedalling?'

We went through the square hall, with the mounted horns above the mirror; we solemnly hung our coats on the hallstand. We admired the shelves of ornaments including the weather house (the old lady was always out, rain or shine), the goldfish circling endlessly in its round globe, with a tiny roach, a present from David, trailing in its wake. On one wall was a great picture entitled 'The Charge of the Light Brigade'. Our great-great grandfather was there, Ernest told us with pride.

'My dad was a real hero; he was an officer in the London Fire Brigade and he lost his life after a terrible fire. I was only a child and my youngest brother Frank, who went to Canada as a young man, wasn't even born. Our dear mother brought us all up by Dad's example and we all did well.'

There was a short flight of stairs into the living room, formerly the 'snug', warm, dark and cosy, with shiny leather armchairs, rag rugs, pegged by the sisters as girls, and the big table already set for tea. The big black kettle steamed on the stove, and the pictures hung in rows on every wall.

Isabella came bustling in from the pantry, tiny beside her husband. She was plump and pretty, with half-moon glasses and soft brown hair which curled all over her head. We children had heard the story of how she'd had her hair cut short, long before it was the mode. Just after the Great War, our grandparents had travelled by pony and trap to Lowestoft market. It was dusk as they returned home and as they crossed a bridge, still a few miles to go, the pony stumbled and Isabella, dozing under a rug, hands in her lap, was thrown out on to the road, falling heavily on to her shoulder. Shaken and cross, she refused to get back into the trap, so they walked and walked, leading the pony until they came to a place they knew. Isabella was given brandy and a sling and was finally persuaded to ride the rest of the way home.

In pain, she struggled to undress herself; being defeated by the brand-new chemise she had sat up sewing, trying her eyes, the night before, to wear on her day out. Ernest, standing by, not daring to say a word, was finally ordered to help. The younger daughters, shushed by their grandma, peeped round the door to see their father, exasperated, taking a pair of scissors and slitting the garment right up the back and easing it off.

Although she could not have lifted her arms to pull the chemise over her head, Isabella's wrath was to be heard all over the house and she often sighed over the spoiled garment.

Next day, when the doctor called, he found her collar bone was broken, and after a few days of trying to comb her long hair, Isabella had suddenly decided, 'Cut it all off!' Ernest did as he was told. Unlike the chemise, she never regretted her shorn locks.

'Just time for a cup of tea,' Ross told Isabella. 'Not finished my deliveries yet. I'll be back this evening.' He drank the scalding tea with the dash of milk, and was gone.

I watched in fascination, as Ernest lifted his huge cup with the special rim to accommodate his moustache. The cup was embellished with a stern coronation picture of King George V and Queen Mary. Ernest drained it in several great gulps.

We children ate bread and butter and sponge cake, sandwiched with plum jam, and sipped tea from our smaller cups because it was so strong.

We were still at the table when Molly and Dolly arrived, wheeling their bikes along the cobbled yard at the back, to leave them in the old cart-shed where the wheels and harness were hanging oiled and saddle-soaped as if awaiting the return of the long-gone pony. Dolly wore a pair of Ross's old trousers, belted tightly and cycle-clipped. They unwound the scarves from round their glowing faces and stood warming up by the fire, girlish and giggling as they always were with their family.

I shared my chair with the cat, Toby the tail-less, with battered ears and a tremendous purr. The inevitable spaniel, fat and affectionate, always named Susie, sat expectantly near the children's end of the table, waiting for the crumbs to fall.

This was a house to daydream in, I thought: full of secrets, with little-used rooms to explore. There was the cosy sitting room, with crackling fire and velvet-covered feather cushions in the vast chairs. The polished piano, with glass case containing the taxidermist's art, at which I could not bear to look.

Tilly, our pretty blonde youngest aunt was newly married but home again because her husband had joined the army at the outbreak of war, had decorated this room with sprays of holly and twisted crepe paper chains and lanterns; every year the same trimmings came down in their box from the attic, the dust was blown off and the old favourites were pinned in their usual place.

The room on the other side of the passage lacked the warmth and family feeling of its partner. This was called the library; it was dark and musty, with shelves crammed full of books. Although I felt a trifle nervous when alone in this room, I was usually to be found in there, books spread along the shiny hard length of the leather covered chaise longue, my back to the ancient piano with the dumb yellow keys because that too had a glass case on top . . . When Jassy was a little older, she became my companion in there.

There were no children's books in the library, but many of the classics and some thrillers and westerns; however, my favourite was the newest book there, the *Film Book* of 1937, which had obviously belonged to Tilly. I puzzled over the picture of Cicely Courtneidge, dressed in men's clothing, with a pencilled-in moustache, but thought the portrait of Marion Davies, protégée of William Randolph Hearst the U.S. newspaper magnate, beautiful, because she was swathed in soft, white furs. I read the potted biographies avidly.

Bedrooms were in unexpected places, on half-landings up short flights of stairs, but the bedrooms used by visiting family were at the top of the house. David and I shared a bedroom with our mother; my little bed was at the sloping end of the room, right by the window. When it was moonlight, the old Saxon church opposite was illuminated with a ghostly glow and even the curtains could not shut out the feeling that it was *there*. Over Molly's bed was hung a picture of a sleeping child with an angel hovering over her. A mother watching over her little one, so the text told. I found this picture upsetting and sometimes dreamed about it.

The marble-topped washstand had a matching rose-patterned bowl, jug, soap dish and hair-pin holder. Hidden discreetly in a cupboard below was a chamber pot.

The bedroom next door at that time was unused, but on the dressing table was another curiosity, an enormous chocolate Easter egg with Parma violet flowers, preserved for many years in its transparent box. Last summer, my brother and I had succumbed to temptation. We had scraped a sliver of chocolate from the base of the egg with David's penknife. The chocolate was greyish and crumbly. It tasted foul. Probably we were not the first grandchildren to try it!

There was a gilt-framed portrait of a red-haired baby in here, and we guessed this was probably the little brother who sadly passed away when Molly and Dolly were tiny girls, and before Tilly was born.

The end bedroom was occupied by Dolly, Ross and little Jassy. In here was a grand brass bed. At her age, Jassy was fascinated by the glass cases full of beautiful birds, ranged along one wall, but I wished they were alive and flying free.

* * *

We all joined in the Christmas Eve preparations. Isabella was busy in the pantry, rolling out soft, white pastry made with goose fat, while Frank, who was unmarried and lived at home, plucked the latest bird for tomorrow. This would be cooked in the bakery oven next door, slowly overnight and during Christmas morning. There was a huge ham to cover with breadcrumbs. The best glasses and china were taken into the scullery to be washed. This stone-walled annexe to the pantry smelled of ammonia and Pears soap, and here the buckets, mops and brushes lurked in every corner. I associated the deep sink with soda and greasy water, and the sore red hands of the females of the house.

'Would you like to stir the jellies?' Tilly asked us children, as we sampled the mince pies. She was shyer than her sisters, wonderfully artistic and with a passion for animals and plants. In the yard was housed her aviary of exotic pigeons and the pet duck, Peggy, which she shared with Ernest. This duck had been intended for a Christmas dinner a few years back, but had escaped because of its engaging personality. Ernest kept a record of all the eggs it ever laid, to produce in self-defence, if ever Isabella looked at it speculatively.

Our grandad was the first to bed, even before Jassy. We knew he'd hang up his stocking and that it would be full of toys like our own – these he would give to us later when we had tired of, or broken, ours.

'I'll never get to sleep, will you?' I whispered to David when we lay in our little beds at last, with our snowy pillow cases pinned to the bed-posts.

'I know who Father Christmas really is,' David said mysteriously, but he wasn't telling.

Downstairs, a door banged and voices were raised in laughter and greeting. We crept along the landing to the top of the stairs.

'Is that you, Father Christmas?' we called down daringly. The voices broke off.

Then a deep voice, slow and good humoured. ''Course it is, but I'm not a-going to come up them stairs until you go to sleep.'

'What are you doing down there?' Me, prompted by David.

'Just havin' a little owd drink and waiting for you to get back to bed!'

'Merry Christmas!' we called. 'We're going now – promise! Hurry up!'

* * *

It was still pitch dark. I had been awake for some time and now I scrambled to the bottom of the bed and felt for the pillow case. It

21

bulged promisingly. Satisfied, I dived back into my warm hollow and waited for the first light of Christmas morning.

A shrill whistle cut through the silence, seeming to slice through the cold, morning air. Grandad was opening his stocking!

'Mummy, are you awake, can we open our stockings now?'

I was already feeling inside mine, fingers groping past the parcels to the tangerine, chocolate pennies wrapped in gold paper, and the walnut, from the tree in the Swan garden, in the very corner. All permitted Christmas morning sampling before breakfast. A torch flickered, David plumped on the bed beside me, heaving his own heavy sack between us.

Voices from the big bed, a match flared, and the lamp was lit. The soft yellow light haloed two heads on the pillows – our father was home for Christmas! Presents abandoned, we children threw back the bedclothes and rushed over for hugs and cries of 'Happy Christmas!'

A rattling of cups on a tray and Isabella appeared, her glasses and little gold earrings glinting. 'Something to warm you up. Happy Christmas to you all.' Molly and Jim's tea was a special Christmas morning treat, it had a dash of whisky added; I took a sip and made a face, I thought it tasted horrible.

We were all together for the first Christmas of the war and that was all that mattered.

CHAPTER 4

Full of Spring

With numb white fingers barely able to grip the chewed wooden pen holder, I scratched laboriously with the spluttery steel nib: January, 1940. It was a grey world both inside and outside the village school. Children sat huddled in overcoats, balaclava helmets or pixie hoods, wound round with scarves. The only warm area was around the tortoise stove. Miss House positioned her desk right beside it, and for once we were eager to take our books up to her for correction or comment, and to warm our chilly behinds surreptitiously as we leaned over the desk. Sighing breaths hung as smoke in the air and now and again when chattering teeth and audible shivering stirred the silent studying too much, Miss House would jump to her feet and exhort us:

'Stand up! Feet apart, arms outstretched. Bend to the right! Bend to the left! Elbows, bend, circle right, circle left, circle both. Shake hands! Stamp feet! Touch your toes, feet together. Arms down. Sit! Now get on with your work.'

At break time there was another ordeal for me to face. The boys had arrived at school early and prepared a long, icy slide in the play-ground. The bigger boys and girls slid down this with ease, as if wearing invisible skates. I was not athletic like my brother. I got off to a jerky start and slid most of the way ignominiously on my bottom. My navy-blue knickers were soaked and I spent an uncomfortable morning, sitting in class on them, chilled to the marrow.

After lunch at home, I pleaded not to go back, there was no visible path, just a wide blanket of snow. I wanted to stay with Jassy, sitting on her potty before the fire, wrapped snugly round with a blanket, with an egg-cup full of currants as a treat. I secretly wanted to go on reading

Dolly's library book, the latest Pearl S. Buck, with its enthralling background set in China. It was easy enough to locate these books, kept away from the children, not because of their content but because they might be spoiled – the adults didn't want a fine from the library. The books were always tucked away in the same place – under the cushion in the armchair.

Molly was sympathetic, but firm. She and Dolly had spent an exhausting morning battling with the washing, poking in the copper with the soapy stick, pushing the heavy, sodden flannelette sheets and cumbersome underwear through the mangle, finally hanging it out without a hope of it drying.

Now, Ross's long johns hung frozen stiff and 'invited' Molly and Dolly to dance with them later in the warm living room, until the garments subsided limply as they thawed out. The sisters sang, as they stepped around the furniture, the dance tunes of their youth. The baby's nappies had to be dried out in the oven. There was still the copper to bale out, the brick floor of the outhouse to scrub, beds to make up.

They really couldn't be doing with me at home. So I trudged back, dodging the snowballs, head down, mittened hands in my pockets, dreading the slide and school. But in the playground the slide was forgotten. Those who had stayed because they had too far to go home at lunchtime, had rolled two enormous snowballs and made a wobbly snowman. He had stones for eyes, nose and buttons, a spare cane for his walking stick and a scarf donated by one of the hardy Connor children (some of the bigger boys were rumoured to sleep in the hay-loft at home and were much envied by those who had to sleep in a proper bed) who didn't seem to worry about the bitter cold. Now the game was to throw snowballs at the snowman, to try to dislodge his head from his body. My mittens were soon packed hard with ice and like the others I threw with all my might.

Great excitement during the afternoon! The siren was heard for the first time since the day war was declared, when there had been a false alarm. This was a practice, Miss House explained. The classes filed out quickly and in an orderly fashion, climbed over the school wall and were shepherded up the short cut to the hut. This was the normal fire drill procedure, there were no air-raid shelters as yet.

At home, the cellar had been prepared as a refuge. I'd only ventured down there once: there were steep steps down into a dark cavern, smelling of damp and pungently of wrinkling apples in boxes.

Ross made a connecting door between the two cottages, so that in an emergency, Auntie Rum could come through from her little square hall into the one next door and join her friends in their cellar. Now her visits were even more regular, she came through the parlour, but she always tapped politely on the living room door before entering. Molly and Dolly were still smiling sheepishly about a recent visit.

Ross, tired after returning from a delivery to London, was in the tin tub by the fire, quite late in the evening.

'Don't go out, Molly – it's too cold in the front room,' Dolly said. 'I'll screen him off with the clothes horse and you can keep the paper up in front of your eyes.'

Dolly sat darning, the paper rustled, Ross relaxed, roasting pink on one side and letting the soap melt in the bottom of the tub. The kettle was ready for topping-up.

The usual discreet knock was heard and Molly called out jokingly: 'Come in, Auntie Rum!' Dolly grinned, having seen Molly tap on the door. To their astonishment, Ross leapt out of the tub, knocked over the clothes horse and ran into the pantry, bolting the door. He eventually emerged, very cross, camouflaged with damp tea-cloths to hysterical laughter from the women.

Wiping her eyes, Dolly asked: 'Why on earth didn't you stay put?'

It took Ross a while to see the funny side, but Molly said she was sorry and wouldn't play tricks again.

* * *

The cold seemed to go on forever; Ross was often away now, delivering essential food supplies all over the country.

The sisters delayed going to bed as long as possible, allowing the children to doze off in the armchair and the baby to sleep in the big pram in the corner of the room. Finally, the dreaded moment came, the stone hot water bottles had been placed in the beds, the candles were lit, the fire dying down. We undressed by the last embers and then put on more than we had taken off – flannel pyjamas, old jumpers, saggy cardigans, thick bed socks. I shared a bed with Dolly when Ross was away; we clung together, both chilly mortals with bad circulation, shivering under the weight of bedclothes that were heavy without heat. It was a winter of red sore noses, chilblains and little cheer.

* * *

Spring came suddenly. Water gushed down the gullies. I felt full of energy, pleased to run errands to the shops or to neighbours. Dolly was a devotee of the Co-op, where small change whizzed back and forth in the shuttle and despite the diminishing array of goods, a small army of cheerful girls, fresh out of school, with names like Honor, Hope and Joy, scurried back and forth, flipping over bales of cloth to measure by the brass yard at the edge of the long counter; slicing cheese with a wire, bacon with a lethal looking knife; making neat blue packets of sugar; and easing on new shoes with a tortoiseshell horn.

I liked the little shops best, and one in particular: this tiny cubby hole was attached to the pub and only opened on Saturday mornings. Pip, the publican's dark-haired daughter, served sweets in deftly twisted paper pokes; she was patient and smiling, understanding the need for making a penny and sweet ration go as far as possible.

Pip helped her brother and parents care for her motherless little niece and nephew, beautiful children with springy dark curls, red apple cheeks deeply dimpled. Several of the village's maiden ladies took an interest in these children too, especially Connie, a sister of Uncle Chas's wife, Maggie. Connie lived two cottages down the street from Dolly and Ross. Connie often invited me to join her on her perambulations with Ann and Paul. I suppose she was in her late thirties then, tall, with prematurely grey wavy hair, clipped back from a smooth face with expressive dark eyes.

In her teens Connie had contracted consumption and her gentle, scholarly father had built her a wooden Swiss-style chalet at the end of the garden, so that she might live in isolation, but be treated at home. She survived the cold and prescribed fresh air of two winters before she finally emerged, healthy after her long ordeal. But maybe that wasn't how she saw it – the chalet was crammed with the books she had studied during that time, and she was passionately interested in birds and all wildlife. She now disliked being confined indoors and worked away in her lovely garden. She went for long hikes, usually accompanied by her nieces, Sally and Meg, the same ages as David and me, when they were home at weekends and holidays, and now, me. Meg and I soon became great friends as well as honorary cousins. Connie had a small dog, lively and brisk like herself, wary at first of strangers. He enjoyed fetching sticks for us. 'More!' his pricked ears seemed to tell us, whenever we paused. Our Waggles was more of a lap dog; he preferred being wheeled around in a doll's pram!

Connie, like Auntie Rum, was a great 'helper'. Only once did she upset me – the day she tried to teach me, as she had so many other children, to ride a bicycle. Her method was simple and had always worked until then. We went along a quiet back lane. I was assisted on to the saddle, the bike held steady, then Con let go and allowed the bike to run down a gentle incline towards a patch of grass. She ran behind me, ready to yell 'Brake!' However, my lack of balance saw me veering off course and tumbling off into a bed of nettles. I stumbled to my feet, shocked, to see the fallen steed's wheels still spinning madly and Con panting towards me, calling, 'Get back on! It's the only way!' as if I had fallen from a horse. I ran straight home to be comforted by Molly, and later Con came round to 'make up'. That was easy to do, because I liked her so much and she was upset, too. Riding a bicycle was a closed subject between us thereafter.

There was another shop in a village several miles away to which we once paid a visit. We set off early one mild morning: Molly, Dolly, Jassy in her pram, David, me and Con, with Ann, and Paul in his pram. We picked wild flowers on the way. 'It'll soon be cowslip time,' we said.

The reason for this trek was there was a rumour that the shop-keeper had discovered a stock of pre-war cotton dresses, pinafores and canvas shoes – long out of fashion, but to be sold without the need for clothing coupons. It was not surprising that this treasure trove had long been forgotten, for the shop was crammed with a jumble of goods, aniseed balls alongside mothballs, bootlaces beside the bacon: any request took some time to fulfil, necessitating much searching.

'Fancy that!' the shop lady would exclaim, astonished, uncovering some unexpected item. There was always a long queue of people waiting to be served, but fortunately a low wall outside to sit on.

I didn't think much of the garishly patterned coarse woven pina-fores that Molly and Dolly were so pleased with at four-and-eleven-three each, but I was quite happy with the button-over canvas shoes with tiny Mickey Mouses all over them. David refused to have a pair but was given an odd piece of elastic for his catapult. 'Perished,' the shop lady said, twanging it. 'But it gives a bit.' A liberty bodice was popped discreetly in the bag for Jassy and Con bought us all colouring books. The shoppers seemed very pleased with themselves and set off for home and a nice cup of tea.

Gathering cowslips was our next expedition. We walked up towards the level crossing, each carrying a basket. The meadow beyond was a sheer carpet of gold, the scent of the flowers powerful and intoxicat-ing. I knelt down carefully, trying not to crush the delicate flowers, so I could breathe in the scent close to.

Our fingers were unstoppable, the baskets filling fast, but fortu-nately, we seemed to have made no impression on the golden meadow.

We walked slowly back as if dreaming. The fragrance lingered for hours; even after washing my hands, I could cup them round my nose, close my eyes and imagine myself back in the cowslip meadow. Auntie Rum and Con were kept busy with wine-making.

* * *

I was never as keen on fishing, lacking the patience of David, who would spend hours with rod and jar. There were ponds in all the meadows beyond the cottage.

'Look!' my friend Mary said one day in hushed tones, parting some reeds edging one of the bigger, murkier ponds.

I saw a nest with eggs in it.

'They're moorhen's eggs,' Mary continued. 'You can eat them.'

I made a face, but I didn't stop Mary from slipping her hand in the nest and removing one of the eggs. We stroked it. It was still warm.

We hurried back to Mary's home, feeling guilty, and went out into the garden. Behind the shed, Mary lit a small fire of twigs and placed a somewhat rusty old frying pan on top. We waited a few minutes, then Mary cracked the egg into the pan. It was addled. We put out the fire and buried our awful secret, tears in our eyes, vowing never to touch another bird's egg . . .

* * *

Mary and I joined the Brownies. Our Brown Owl was young and her name was Diana, although we did not call her that. We all adored her. She had tawny hair and boundless enthusiasm. I never learned to tie a reef knot but I enjoyed the paper chases and animal tracking, the occasional meetings at Brown Owl's home, where she let us play with her collection of soft toy animals – I liked particularly the little white cat with green glass eyes and stiff whiskers. I wished it belonged to me!

When I found a baby bird fluttering feebly on the ground during one of my walks, I ran home to change into my Brownie uniform and carefully placed the tiny fledgling in my breast pocket, then went round to show it to Diana.

She took the bird gently from me and placed it in a little box lined with wisps of cotton wool. 'I'll look after it for you,' she told me reassuringly. She knew what I did not: the little bird had lost its struggle to survive.

Some other baby birds were more fortunate, in fact they unexpectedly thrived. A local farmer was culling the weakest chicks from his large flock and gave me half-a-dozen of these 'as pets'. Dolly was doubtful, but she kept the chicks in their box by the fire for several days. There was only one mortality; five little chicks became fine hens and proved a very useful addition to our elderly hens, when they commenced laying.

I liked to feed 'my' hens personally, until one day when I opened the sack of grain to dip into, a mouse jumped out, and corn was spilled everywhere and I ran indoors shuddering and shrieking.

* * *

Molly was becoming restless, the war seemed remote, she decided to take us back to our home near Croydon. We arrived just in time to see the Battle of Britain being fought in the skies overhead.

CHAPTER 5

Wholly Holy

November, 1940

The dining table was oak, solid and well-made; we four youngsters lay huddled together on a mattress beneath it. Molly and her good friend May, mother of the other two little boys, lay back in easy chairs, awake but not talking.

Pin-point flashes of light pierced the room despite the blackout. We heard the *crump* of gunfire, the menacing drone of heavy planes, followed by the screaming of bombs. It was like grim background music to a flickering film.

The front door opened, banged, and May's husband Will, an air-raid warden, carrying his bucket and stirrup pump, was in the hall, calling out: 'Can't stop! Incendiary two doors up – here's a visitor for you, Molly.'

It was Ross. He hugged us all, his face white and lined with fatigue, eyes sunken and bleary from many hours relentless driving.

'Why didn't you let us know?' he asked reproachfully, while May brewed tea and we children called out excitedly to him, while being cautioned to stay right where we were.

Molly wiped her eyes. It was the first time she'd wept since we had been bombed out almost a week previously. The story spilled out.

'We were all in the kitchen . . . on a mattress on the floor . . . there was the usual raid – Jim had just arrived unexpectedly . . . we thought he was coming on Saturday morning, but he said he'd had a feeling he should come that night after work. He had a terrible journey, was stopped several times coming through London.

'As he joined us on the mattress, there was a terrific bang! That was close, we thought, as the kitchen door caved in, the place was full of smoke and choking dust and the wardens came rushing in to find us. The bomb had come right down the dividing wall between our house and next door. We were all taken up to the church hall and stayed there overnight, then we came here to May's . . . Jim had to go back to Bath after a couple of days. We were going to let you know of course, but we had to make sure our worldly goods were secure first.'

'You can guess what I thought when I saw your house with the top storey gone and the windows boarded up,' Ross said. 'I didn't know what to do, it was such a shock. Then a policeman came up to tell me I couldn't park the lorry in a prohibited area. He told me you were here. Thank God you weren't hurt.'

At first light we were roused and dressed. Molly hugged David and me and cried again. We sat beside Ross in the cab of the lorry, piled around with hastily gathered together possessions, and, of course, our pets. The dog still looked very grey instead of white, because he'd been in the dining room on the night we were bombed out and so much soot came down the chimney, he'd been covered in it although, like us, mercifully unhurt. There was also the goldfish bowl and our pair of budgies in their cage.

Ross tried to persuade Molly to come too, but she refused. 'I've still got things to take care of here – Jim'll be down again in a day or two to help me, then he'll bring me to you by car, if he can get enough petrol, or I'll take the train. Please don't worry – I'm only thankful you're taking the children out of all this. Give Dolly and Jassy my love, and tell Mother and Dada they're not to worry!'

Around breakfast time we stopped and Ross opened the old Oxo tin and shared out his corned beef sandwiches. I'd been too excited to feel sick, and we ate hungrily and drank sweet tea from our uncle's flask.

We sang on our way, the darkness and fear of the past weeks lifted magically as we saw fields and trees and drove through small villages. 'She'll be coming round the mountain – she'll be wearing pink pyjamas – she'll be eating kippers and marmalade – she'll be riding six white horses . . . when she comes!' Ross did some impressive yodelling, his party piece, after prompting from us, then we slept, sagging among the parcels, while Ross's hands remained steady on the steering wheel.

* * *

Dolly was entertaining Auntie Rum when we arrived at the cottage and Jassy was cutting up an old magazine on the table. In the six months we'd been away, she'd become a little girl, no longer a baby.

We opened the back door and stood there, feeling strangely shy, while Dolly and Auntie Rum stared at us wonderingly, then it was embracing, kisses, followed by tears and explanations. While Ross drove the lorry back to the garage, David and I talked.

'Our school was closed,' I told them, 'so we had to pay half-a-crown each a week to attend a little private school, in the front room of an old retired teacher's house, mornings only. Mummy said the equipment left much to be desired – we had ancient desks, a wonky globe of the world, and hardly any books.'

'We had daily spelling tests and we had to keep reciting our tables, and the only exciting thing was spinning the globe when the teacher's back was turned,' David said.

He showed off his collection of shrapnel and described the dog-fights in the sky: '*Eeow!* Down came the enemy plane with black smoke from its tail – he went round and round and *round* – then we saw a parachute, then another one . . .'

'We slept under the stairs next-door for a bit,' I chimed in. 'I used to read Mabel Lucie Attwell to their little boy. Then they built themselves a shelter like a wigwam indoors, from a plan in the *Daily Mirror*, and that saved *them* when the bomb fell.'

'Now, you can forget all *that*,' Dolly told us firmly. 'It's good to have you back. We've missed you. Oh, Jassy, what *have* you done!'

While we'd been talking, young Jasmine had cut a large hole in the tablecloth!

* * *

It was reassuring to find everything the same and we were soon back at school. Miss House told us that her cousin, a concert pianist, had stayed on in London, despite the bombing, and with other musicians was giving lunchtime concerts to packed audiences.

Paper being in short supply, the old slates were brought out for the smaller children once more. The big girls made a delicious-looking milk pudding, substituting soap flakes for tapioca.

'You mustn't eat it,' warned Miss House, 'but you'll know how to cook it, after the war.'

I thought you would probably foam at the mouth if you did try it. But it did look tasty.

* * *

'We're all going to church this Sunday,' Dolly said firmly. 'We've got a lot to thank God for. We've got a new parson—'

'Why have you gone all red, Auntie?' David asked.

I sympathised. Blushing was a family blight among the females. 'She isn't!' I insisted.

'Talking about the new parson?' Ross asked, with a sly grin, popping in with a precious paper bag of brown sugar (sweepings from the lorry). Dolly marched into the pantry to put the sugar in a jar.

Ross sat warming his hands by the fire for a few moments. 'Did she tell you about the church cleaning?' he teased.

Dolly came back in, as he said that. 'Oh well,' she said, resigned, 'they'll find out on Sunday anyway, and if I don't tell them, you will!' She perched on the arm of Ross's chair and he slipped his arm around her waist and gave her a squeeze.

'The ladies of the church drew up their cleaning rota and they asked me if I'd care to join them – quite a surprise as it's usually the same old lot and they call you a stranger 'til you've been here about twenty years – well, I went along with my bucket and scrubbing brush and waited for my orders. They gave me that big, carved pew right at the front. It looked pretty mucky to me, so I gave it a good old go with Vim and plenty of hot water and had a cup of tea while I waited for it to dry.

'Oh, no! Something terrible had happened – that old pew had dried up a ghostly off-white. I'd scrubbed all the varnish off! All the ladies were staring and muttering. I really had a go with the old polish, but it was no use, that pew stuck out like a sore thumb. I went home and had a good old cry.

'Next Sunday I hardly dared show my face in church – it *was* red that day, I can tell you, and I guessed they were all pointing out my awful mistake and saying who was responsible . . . The service went right over my head, until I heard the parson say: '*And this is the holiest pew in the church*, and it is to be left as it is, because it is a real labour of love . . .'

We couldn't wait to see the holiest pew.

* * *

When I opened the back door on Sunday morning to let the cat in, I was horrified to see a poor rabbit lying on the door mat. The cat purred loudly and I scolded him: 'You bad cat! Auntie, look what Tiger's brought home!'

'I'm afraid that's what cats do.' She looked at the trophy reflectively. 'It'll make a pie and eke out the meat ration. Auntie Rum'll see to it, and we'll share it with her.'

'I shan't eat it!' I declared.

David was persuaded to take the rabbit round to Auntie Rum's.

'Don't bring it through here!' I shrieked.

The coat-stand in the little hall had a compartment for Sunday gloves, prayer books and headscarves. I wore my best coat, with the pockets sewn up, to prevent me putting my hands in them. We could hear Auntie Rum on her side, making ready too, but we would part company when we reached the church, because Auntie Rum was Chapel and this was further up the main street.

'Hello, you're back again, I see,' Mr Rudd observed, handing David and me a hymn book each. His son, Tommy, was in the choir, hair shining with brilliantine. Farje gave me a friendly pinch on the leg as we walked past her, while we stared, fascinated, at the holiest pew, which was already occupied.

Dolly ushered us into a side pew where she hoped to escape notice and sat Jassy between herself and me. Jassy was solemn faced, warmly clad in a yellow coat, bonnet and leggings with many buttons and elastic under the instep. David fidgeted with the hassocks. My collection penny rolled under the pew in front and he retrieved it for me.

The parson knelt in silent prayer for some time before he addressed the congregation.

'He was invalided out of the army. He's the youngest parson we've had here, he lives with his mother, he's not married . . .' whispered Dolly.

He was tall and dark, with a deep, powerful voice. There was a watchfulness, a waiting, apparent among those who knelt, heads bowed. When it happened, I felt cold and fearful. Like a gramophone record with the needle stuck in a groove, the beautiful voice intoned over and over again: 'Make clean our hearts within – within – within –'

Tense, we knelt on, as he continued: 'Within – within – *within* us.' A sigh, and the parson continued as if unaware what had happened. The congregation relaxed, but everyone was aware this could recur. I prayed fervently that it would not.

During the sermon the parson turned toward the side pew and addressed his thoughts to Dolly and her family. His gaze was almost mesmeric.

He took both my hands in his when we came up to him after church.

'Goodbye and God bless you.' Then he asked my name; repeated it.

We didn't speak of what had happened, but even at my age I knew that I had met an extraordinary person.

* * *

Molly returned by train, and we walked in the winter drizzle to the little station, with the pram to transport her luggage. The steam cleared and there she was, slender in her green woollen suit with the fur tippet round her shoulders. She rubbed at a smut on her face. She looked very tired and pale.

'I had to sit on my case in the corridor most of the way, the train was packed with troops. I was smoking, we all were, and someone jogged my arm and the cigarette fell down inside my blouse . . . I had to press it to me, to put it out – oh, it does hurt!'

Once home, a nasty burn was revealed and Molly wiped her eyes as Dolly, concerned, spread on Vaseline and applied pink lint. She said, 'It's an awkward place to bandage, dearie.'

'A cup of tea and an aspirin – that's all I want . . .'

We children were quiet; we were bursting with questions but our mother's exhaustion and pain had communicated itself to us.

* * *

It was time to prepare for Christmas once more. Dolly sat cutting up remnants of mustard-coloured parachute silk to make pyjamas and Molly was sewing something from red felt. I was busy with a cardboard doll which I had drawn and cut round. Most things could be used again, like empty packets of Force Flakes, our breakfast cereal. From sugar paper I produced a selection of gaily coloured clothes – my crayons were wearing out! This was my present for Jassy. David painstakingly plaited bracelets from odd lengths of plastic-covered electrical wire. My efforts at this were lumpy; his, neat.

Ross hoped he would be able to take us over to the grandparents as usual. We hadn't seen them since our return, and the weather had been too bad for cycling.

The magic would surely return and the war would fade away when we heard our grandparents welcome us with, 'Come you on inside.'

CHAPTER 6

Festive Laments

Ross slumped in his chair by the fire, ashen-faced, red-eyed. We children sat quietly at the table, seemingly absorbed in our craft work, but glancing surreptitiously at our uncle from time to time. The grey, hairy dog who always lay at his master's feet on the rag rug, was missing. Rover's thick leather lead still hung on its hook by the fireplace, rarely used for the old sheepdog was trained to heel. He was full of tricks, which we loved to watch – the sugar lump or dog biscuit placed carefully on his nose, the command, 'Throw!' – the tidbit tossed in the air and caught neatly in the soft mouth – the patient waiting for the word 'Eat!' A polite paw offered to us to shake . . . Rover had been Ross's friend and constant companion for years before and since his marriage.

I knew why he had gone. The old dog had suddenly become unpredictable. He had flown at, and nipped, a pedlar who had surprised him in the garden. A complaint had been made to the village bobby. He was a great friend of Ross, but he had to caution vigilance. Yesterday the dog had bitten Jassy, fortunately not badly, when she had gone up to him and put her arms trustingly around him.

'*You've got to do it, Ross* . . .' This morning he had taken the dog out early. Much later, he returned alone.

I'd never seen a man cry before; Dolly hugged him and Molly rushed to make him tea. Warning glances were directed at us.

'I threw the ball, he chased after it, stood there, waiting for me to say "come", his tail was going . . . then the vet arrived. After a while I stroked him and told him I was sorry, then I picked him up, brought him back and put him where we decided.'

We woke several times during the night to hear poor Ross sobbing.

* * *

Molly, perusing the latest letter from Jim, twenty-odd pages in close, copperplate writing, was overjoyed at unexpected good news. She had to tell us, right away.

'He'll be home for Christmas, two days before, he hopes – a whole week off! He'll be able to run us over home. The bombing's been very bad in Bath, but is any city safe? Shall I ask Auntie Rum if the girls can sleep next door, for a night or two?'

Auntie Rum's spare bed had a big dip in the centre.

She explained: 'When my father was so ill, a stout nurse stayed over-night. She broke the spring! Keep to the sides and you'll be all right.'

Jassy and I found ourselves constantly rolling into the dip and becoming stuck, all night long. I began a long-running serial story about a one-legged chick called Hoppo, and kept my little cousin awake for hours. 'Don't stop!' she would plead, when I paused to yawn. Later, I learned that Dolly and Ross had to keep this story going for years!

* * *

The Austin 7 drew up to the pump in the yard and Isabella came rushing out, hands all floury as usual from Christmas baking, to greet us.

'Here you all are then. Come you on inside. You'll freeze out here, together.'

Ernest didn't seem his normal cheerful self.

Isabella whispered to us: 'He's been shedding a few tears – his lad at the shop passed away yesterday . . . he'd just wasted away, it's so sad. His poor mother . . .'

It reminded her of her own lost child. 'I couldn't find any holly with berries this year, for little Ernie's wreath. It needs that touch of colour.'

The house was certainly full this Christmas, there were two land girls billeted here, Ivy and Rose; the former slight, dark and reticent, the latter, blooming like her name, with a thatch of peroxided hair. Rose obviously had her eye on our Uncle Frank, but he had wisely invited his long-standing girlfriend Hester to stay.

Frank, much to his chagrin had been classed medically unfit for the army because of flat feet. There was a carpenter in every generation of the family, and this was Frank's trade. He was part of a team who did all the maintenance and building work on a large estate. These men were all hand-picked, and many carried on the tradition within their own family. In Frank's case, he had followed on from an older cousin Joe, who went to Canada – that's why Frank was known as 'Joe' on the estate!

There was also another lodger, who had to share a room with Frank while we were there. He was a dashing young man called Herbie, herdsman on a local farm. Now Ernest had several to call each morning at dawn, not just, 'Boy Frank – you awake? Rise up now!' but, 'You girls – that's half past five, you know!' And, repeated several times before there was a response: 'Herbie! What about them poor old cows? *They* don't know you got to bed so late last night!' Herbie was a noted (or more accurately, a notorious!) ladies' man . . .

There were more tears from young Tilly, who'd recently returned to her little cottage almost next-door, but was staying at home over Christmas. She had been working up north to be near her husband for a few months before he was posted overseas. She had transferred to war work in this area. She missed Sam terribly because they had been childhood sweethearts before they married, and now they had been forced to postpone having a longed-for baby.

I wasn't aware of that, of course, but I did know, from 'listening in' as my mother called it, that Dolly and Ross had also decided not to add to their family, until 'after the war'. I'd sort of hoped my own parents would present me with a little sister, but this didn't seem so important now, because I had Jassy to play that role for me.

I did have the feeling that this Christmas would not be like the last one. However, there was my father to sit close to, and listen to; I loved to hear all about the mischief 'the girls' had got up to in their youth.

'Why don't you tell her a few home-truths about a boy called Jim!' Molly said tartly, catching us at the story-telling.

* * *

A giant, golden-crusted giblet pie sat square in the centre of the Christmas Eve lunch table; floury potatoes and sprouts picked with the frost on them were ladled into serving dishes, the blue and white patterned ones which had belonged to my great grandma Emma, whom I could remember well. She was ninety-five when she passed away.

The menfolk were supposed to be having 'a little stroll' but Isabella suspected that they were in the White Lion just down the street, and she sent me to fetch them.

The little village had three pubs (there had been four when our Swan was in business) and there were also two big busy grocery shops; one small, poky 'front room' shop which sold sweets, tobacco and goose eggs (because the owner had a pair of geese!); a bakery, two butchers and a post-office. Being on the main route to Southwold meant good passing trade, and the village flourished.

I was allowed in the dark, low-ceilinged hall of the pub and glimpsed my grandfather and my dad at the centre of a merry crowd.

'A glass of cherryade for my little old sugar-lump!' Ernest ordered, and I was smuggled in and set on a three-legged stool in a corner, and given a frothy bright red concoction to drink which seemed to owe more to almonds than to cherries. I gained a pink moustache in the process. Then I ran home to say they were coming. I was spared the giblets, 'the girls' had guessed I wouldn't like those, so I had pie crust and vegetables.

Isabella scolded them: 'Your dinner'll be cold, serve you all right, we've had ours.'

'You'll be getting enough sweet things tomorrow,' Tilly said later, bringing in rusks, a slab of hard cheese wrapped in muslin and a bulbous jar of dark brown pickled onions.

'Your mother,' Jim told David and me, as he speared a monster onion, 'had a very nasty experience once with a pickled onion . . .'

Molly laughed ruefully, sitting down for a moment with a drying cloth and a bundle of washed knives and forks.

'I needed my tonsils out, the doctor said, and Mother took me to Lowestoft hospital in the trap. It was the afternoon before I was laid on a table, given a little old whiff of gas, and they whipped 'em out. Well, I came round and was worrying that it was getting dark, because Mother had no lights on the trap. So, they told her she could take me home. I was still all whoozy when they wrapped me in the blanket.

'"All that fuss about a light," Mother said, "I borrowed a lamp, of course, from where I left the pony and trap. But you're a brave girl, I must say . . ."

'I was feeling hungry when we arrived home, but Mother said to wait – have a little lie-down and recover yourself. When you're twelve you're always hungry and you *can't* wait, so I sneaked into the pantry and right in front of me was a jar of pickled onions just like this one. My favourites! I picked out the biggest one I could find and put it in my mouth. The vinegar ran down my raw throat, I was in agony, so I spat the onion in the sink, and tears trickled down my face.

'Mother saw me dancing about but I couldn't make a sound, my throat was so sore. She thought I'd been punished enough, so she didn't say anything about it. She got me a glass of water, and helped me back to bed.'

'Poor old Mummy!' I exclaimed. I could almost feel the pain myself. Years later, Molly would tell me that Isabella had waited anxiously all day at the hospital because the last time she had been there, was when her little son died . . .

We youngsters were in bed when Ross arrived, and it was not long before Molly and Jim crept quietly into the room our family were sharing. They undressed by candlelight, and got into bed. I wondered if Father Christmas had been yet, but was too drowsy to find out.

Later, I awoke suddenly to hear raised voices. Frank and Herbie were coming up the stairs.

'Come along old lad, it won't do no good crying about it tonight. They couldn't do anything else, you know that. Drink that little drop of whisky, that'll make you feel better . . .'

'Quiet, you boys,' Ernest called. 'You'll wake everyone up.'

A door closed. I wondered why Herbie was home so late; Isabella had been worrying at supper-time, wondering where he could be, but Ernest suspected he had been out celebrating or chasing the girls. Frank had been despatched to find him; he'd come back later to report that Herbie was not in his usual haunts.

* * *

When I unwrapped my sixth slim diary, I couldn't help feeling sorry for myself. However, there was one small present remaining, and to my relief and delight I discovered a shiny round silver watch with a red leather strap, coiled in a box lined with matching velvet. This was my parent's special present and a gentle reminder that I really should learn to tell the time.

'Don't wind it,' my dad warned. 'I'll show you how to do that later. Is it ticking? I wound it last night.' It was, and I watched, entranced, as the second hand flew round. David, too, had a watch, and under cover of his blankets in his little bed beside mine, he stealthily rotated the winder.

Jassy bounced in, dragging her heavy pillowcase, leaving a trail of torn wrapping paper. The joy of Christmas revived, as I helped her take out her presents, one by one.

Our dear grandad wound up his clockwork donkey and let it jerk across the breakfast table. Its string tail whizzed round and round until it cannoned into the salt pot. Tilly hastily threw salt over her left shoulder.

There were boiled eggs for David, Jassy and me; deftly topped by Ernest's sharp knife, with toast cut into thin fingers.

'Do eat all that up, else it'll be bread and pull-it, next time,' Isabella smiled, putting out the plates for the delicately curling slices of tender pink ham.

I mused: 'Bread and chicken, what's wrong with that?'

I peeked at the unfamiliar faces round the table. Ivy and Rose, yawning, back from the early milking on the farm, still in their green jumpers, breeches and heavy socks, their hair in steel curlers beneath scarves tied turban-wise to be combed into Christmas afternoon frizz. Hester, pale-skinned, pale-haired, sat shyly toying with her breakfast, self-conscious about the ring glinting on her finger. She was waiting for Frank to join her at breakfast, to make the news official.

Frank was out in the yard, cheerfully whistling as he pumped icy cold water over his head and shoulders. Of Herbie there was no sign, nor of Dolly and Ross.

Ernest told us: 'Ross kept Dolly awake talking about his poor old dog – I said to them, when I took them their tea, "Have you a lie-in, we'll keep an eye on Jassy."'

Christmas dinner for the children was eaten in the sitting room to ease the congestion downstairs. We had great fun blowing down the speaking tube still set in the wall, and calling down our 'orders'. Tilly dashed backwards and forwards between the two rooms. We finished much earlier than the grownups, and I asked if I might take Jassy out for a short walk.

The saga of Hoppo continued as I pushed Jassy along and we went further than I'd intended.

'Look!' Jassy cried, pointing. In a pocket-sized cottage garden there was an evergreen massed with huge crimson berries.

I stared at it, remembering the wreath, with its lack of colour. I hesitated, then opened the gate, and Jassy and I went up the path. I knocked on the door . . .

We arrived back in time to find Isabella and Ernest putting on their coats ready for the long walk to the churchyard in the other village, near the Buck Inn.

Isabella's eyes sparkled with tears and she rubbed at her glasses fiercely while our grandad swung his sugar-lumps up in his arms for a prickly kiss.

He said, 'There'll be a few over to go in my lad's wreath, too. Have you got the basket ready, Bella, for his poor old mother? We can drop that off along our way.'

* * *

That evening we sang round the piano, played by Jim, with the usual duet by Molly and Dolly, 'The Skater's Waltz'. We were warmed by ginger wine and full of Christmas cake. Even Hester became flushed and sang sweetly in a trembly soprano; Jassy dropped in action, sleeping on the hearth rug. As the songs became nostalgic there was a low sobbing from Herbie, left alone in a corner.

'Poor old Pansy, poor little Blossom,' he moaned.

'Uncle Frank, what's the matter with Herbie?' I whispered.

'All his cows were put down yesterday, foot and mouth disease. Poor old Herbie, he loved them cows like sweethearts. He has no job to go back to, now, either. He knew all them creatures by name.'

'Poor old Daisy, poor old Bluebell,' Herbie choked.

Through the night, the lament continued. And others shed tears, too.

CHAPTER 7

The Tides of March

Every Friday afternoon the whole school straggled up to the hut for country dancing. The infants waited their turn in the little store room and I was asked to keep them quiet, with a story. Black-eyed Bill the pirate, swash-buckled his way through a long-running, rambling serial. If the little ones became restless, I employed different accents as I enacted all the parts and the plot became more incredible and gory.

Mr Todd listened in one day and called me out to re-tell the tale to the older children. Surrounded by disbelieving faces, I floundered and completely dried up.

'I can't remember anymore!' I cried.

Dolly had heard about the story-telling, too.

'The old caretaker tells me he always puts his ear to the wall when you're going on about Black-eyed Bill and that it makes his Friday afternoons.'

Embarrassed, I couldn't continue with the stories in the old unselfconscious way and they gradually fizzled out. But around this time, I really began writing in earnest. Finding enough paper, in these times of shortages, to keep up with my output, was the problem. The reverse side of wall-paper from an old pattern book; the backs of greetings cards; carefully slit envelopes. Dolly and Molly were always asking around, 'Any spare paper for Shummy's scribbling?' Someone even kindly cut the yellowing fly-leaves from some discarded books for my use.

'You'll get lead poisoning!' Molly warned, as I chewed my pencils. I did indeed get a purple tongue from an indelible pencil once.

It was nice to curl up in the chair in the alcove by the fire, with my feet snug in the beaded moccasins which Molly had contrived from the red felt, my pencil flying away but finding it difficult to keep pace with my thoughts.

Molly and Dolly swept and dusted around me and let me get on with it.

'You can tell that young Jassy's going to be just the same,' Dolly remarked wryly.

* * *

The first signs of spring this year were not outside, but indoors as cupboard doors were flung wide, drawers opened and contents pulled out and sorted through; paintwork washed down; rugs taken up and whacked with a carpet beater in the garden; buckets clattered around filled with hot water and knobs of harsh soda; old garments past the very last darn were pounced on for washing clothes, or padding for sore, flattened knees.

'I feel absolutely filthy,' Dolly sighed after one particularly hectic morning. 'I think I'll have a bath after the children go back to school after dinner. There's enough hot water still in the copper.'

As she lay soaking thankfully, she heard the side gate open and the Parson strode past the wash-house, glancing in at the uncurtained window. All Dolly could do was to subside beneath the soapy water, face matching her fiery hair. The Parson raised his hat politely, called, 'Good afternoon!' and beat a hasty retreat.

We children fell about laughing when Dolly told her rueful tale.

'Serves you right for having a bath out of hours, instead of being ready to serve afternoon tea to visitors,' Molly said unsympathetically, dodging a wet cloth thrown at her.

While turning out, the sisters discovered a parcel full of odd pieces of knitting. Before she was married, Dolly had worked at a place called the HomeKnit.

'We used to be given these bits – pieces cut off during the tailoring – and some samples,' Dolly mused. 'I couldn't see much use for them, but now . . .'

They sat patiently unravelling the fine wool, making frequent joins where the stitches had been cut. They wound small, tight balls to ease out the crinkles. Multi-coloured garments, Joseph's coats, grew on their fast-clicking needles.

I was curious to know more about the HomeKnit.

'Well,' Dolly explained, 'I stayed on at home after your mum got married. Dada didn't want me to get a proper job, but I became tired of just helping Mother with the housework. Then I heard about this new enterprise starting up at Southwold – they were advertising for girls to work the knitting and sewing machines – they made up all the latest fashions: jumper suits, long coats, dresses, bathing costumes; our garments went to all the top London shops. We were quite famous – rather like Chanel, in France!

'I loved working there and I made lots of friends. The problem was, although I was nearly twenty, Dada wouldn't hear of me going out dancing with them, on Saturday nights. So I used to go to bed early, and once Tilly was asleep, I opened the window, slid down the drain pipe, collected my bike from where I'd hidden it round the corner, then I pedalled like mad into Southwold!'

'Didn't you get found out?' I wanted to know. I could picture Dolly in evening dress, satin-slippered feet whirling the pedals round.

Dolly laughed. ''Course I did! Tilly woke up one evening and went to tell our grandma that I wasn't in bed. Dada was waiting to catch me when I got back at eleven.'

'Weren't you allowed to go again?'

Dolly's red hair gleamed in the gas light. Her blue eyes flashed. 'Put it this way; I went out the front door in future,' she said firmly.

* * *

Movement was restricted in and out of Southwold, but one day when Ross had to make a delivery there, Dolly and I went along for the ride. 'You'll meet one of my old HomeKnit friends,' she told me.

We ducked down when Ross was stopped at the checkpoint, but a pass was slapped on the windscreen and Ross drove us to a little street just off the front, where a row of fishermen's cottages crowded together against the North Sea blasts. He left us there while he was working.

The beach was sadly deserted, cut off by cruel tangles of barbed wire, the bathing huts boarded up, their paint peeling. The sea rushed urgently at the pebbles and the pier was heavily fortified.

Before the war we had loved to wander round the town, with its busy shops, the lighthouse, brightly painted houses with curiosities in their gardens, including gaudy ships' figureheads. I recalled again the greengages we had bought on our last visit, which tasted like nectar; the shilling's worth of pennies which had provided an afternoon's entertainment on the machines on the pier. Once, I had even struck lucky with the grabber crane. At the last minute, the coveted prize fell from its slippery jaws, and only a handful of brilliant green sweets rattled out into the drawer.

'You can't eat those, they look disgusting and you never know how old they might be.' Molly had taken them away from me.

However, my favourite machine was the fortune-teller. In a glass-fronted box a waxen-faced traveller sat, scarved and beaded, with a pen in her patient hand. You dialled your birth date, shoved in your penny, the pen dipped and began to scratch at the paper. The machine whirred and hummed, finally stopped and out came a little printed card. How many times had I asked the traveller to tell my fortune, and each time the message was always the same. Somehow, it still came as a surprise.

'You remember my young niece, Shummy?' Dolly said now, to her friend's mother. 'She was one of my baby bridesmaids.'

We were welcomed into a neat little parlour with its half-curtain across the window to shut out the view from the street. There was no front garden, just a neat square at the back, with a rockery fashioned from broken crockery, fitted in like a puzzle: a jutting pink teapot spout, a cracked willow plate, thick brown earthenware, half a bone-china saucer, with a gilded rim.

The family were all at home. Pearl, Dolly's friend, tiny, black-haired and vivacious, with a daughter almost as tall as herself, just my age. Pearl's mother was small and trim, too, wrapped around with a big apron, a relic of her fish-gutting days. Pearl's father sat chewing reflectively on his pipe stem, nut-brown and lined from many years' exposure to the elements. His thick hair was liberally sprinkled with grey as if grains of sea salt still clung to it. He said little, but smiled and listened to the women's chatter.

'Stay to dinner,' Pearl's mother insisted. 'Chicken broth, there's aplenty.'

I sat in silent despair over my piled-up plate, but I ate as much as I could, and was relieved to see that Pearl's daughter Hazel, couldn't finish her portion either.

'What time is Ross a'coming for you?' Pearl asked as they supped tea from giant cups after tackling the washing-up. 'Only we were going to the pictures – we always do, Saturday afternoons.'

Dolly thought we would be back in good time if we went to the early performance. I was excited, I hadn't been to the cinema since before the war. Then only to carefully selected Shirley Temple films or Walt Disney cartoons.

The picture house was packed with men in khaki, girls with elaborate hairstyles, children fidgeting in the front row, too close to the screen, so their heads had to be tilted back. I liked to be near the screen, because I couldn't see from the back; anyway, Dolly could only afford the cheapest seats, having not anticipated this outing.

'Don't put your head against the back of the seat,' Dolly cautioned, ensuring even stiffer necks.

The picture was unsuitable for children, frightening even. I can recall fragments of it to this day. The story was about a 'poison pen' letter writer and the upset caused in a small community. At the end the culprit was revealed, a spell-binding performance by Flora Robson. The climax was electrifying and gave me a few nightmares afterwards.

'Better not tell your mum, I think, what the film was about,' Dolly said, worried.

We hurried back to Pearl's house, to find Ross waiting and impatient to leave: 'We don't want to get caught here in a raid.'

'Lucky girl, going to the pictures – did you enjoy it?' Molly asked me when we arrived home.

I said yes, because I didn't want to get Dolly into trouble.

* * *

The weather was mild and the long walks were resumed. We went several times to the cowslip meadow to see if the flowering had begun. There were still plenty of primroses. David and I discovered an old willow tree bending low over a little stream bordering the meadow, and we spent many happy afternoons climbing along its trunk, pulling at loose pieces of bark to reveal scurrying insect life hidden beneath. We parted the dipping leafy fronds to look at the water below. David fished there sometimes and I waved at the trains as they steamed past the far end of the meadow. I liked to think someone might be waving back. We named our secret place 'Chris and Crusty' and even hauled Jassy up behind us and wedged her in between two stout branches.

We saved six large eggs to hard-boil and decorate for Easter and painted one egg each with a pattern and name of another. I chose to give my egg to Ross. Dolly fetched out the special egg cups, saved from pre-war Easters, shaped like elephants, ducks or donkeys with a hole in the top for the egg to sit in. The silver apostle spoons were taken from their case and laid ready. No chocolate eggs this year, but after lunch, a special treat: pancakes served with Welfare orange juice, concentrated and strong-tasting.

Isabella had invited me to stay for a week over the break to provide companionship for my cousin, Laura, five years my senior, the only daughter of Emma, Molly and Dolly's eldest sister. It was in Emma's home in Ipswich that both David and I had been born, Emma being an experienced mother of five. She was a very calm and sweet-natured person. Unfortunately, we didn't see as much of her as we would have

liked, as her husband was in the Royal Navy, and she could not afford
the train fare for so many. Laura was special to Molly and Jim, not
only because she was their goddaughter, but because Molly had been
with Emma when Laura was born.

Emma's husband was at sea and Molly, just seventeen, celebrating
her engagement to Jim with a weekend at Ipswich, had been sharing
Emma's bed when her sister went into sudden labour.

'I hardly knew where babies came from,' as Molly said once to
her friend May, not aware that I could hear. 'But I had the sense to
whip back the bedclothes and catch the tiny baby, which had the cord
wrapped round its neck. I had the presence of mind to ease the baby
free and to do what Emma told me to make the baby cry . . .'

Laura was still petite and dainty with silken golden hair, a beautiful face and a bubbling sense of fun. She was a great favourite with the
grandparents.

'Here it is, Shum,' Laura giggled, pointing out a particular tomb-
stone as we read the inscription in the churchyard one day. I squinted
my eyes. It was a rhyme about a man who had insisted on cutting his
toenails on a Sunday, so, of course, had expired.

In the field beyond the church were some donkeys, which we girls
liked to feed. Two children, of about eleven or twelve, often regarded
us over the fence. They smiled and nodded but didn't speak.

'Why are they like that?' I was puzzled.

'Their parents were first cousins,' Laura said knowledgeably.

'But so are we.'

'Yes, but *we're* not married!'

* * *

'W.I. this afternoon,' our grandma told us, bustling busily about.
She wore her best dress with tight corsets beneath, court shoes and
shiny silk stockings. She had applied pink face powder liberally and
was skewering a feathered hat to her curls with an enormous sharp-
pointed hat pin. 'A girl's best friend, do they say . . . Would you girls
care to come along?'

Isabella was president of the W.I. and was quite clearly in charge.
When she swept in, the ladies sat down meekly and then rose again at
her command to sing 'Jerusalem'.

This was a knitting for the troops afternoon and there was much
winding of wool, turning of heels and patterns passed round for balaclava helmets. Laura and I were put to work sorting through books

and tying them up into parcels of six. The biggest teapot I had ever seen provided endless cups of tea, sugar, milk and tea being provided by members.

On the walls of the meeting room were faded sepia pictures, rather fly-blown, of glassy-eyed cricket teams, arms stiffly folded, with unsmiling, whiskered faces, and Sunday School Treat photographs with little girls in Holland dresses and black stockings, with long curls tied back in satin bows, and crisp, lace-edged best pinafores. The boys wore knickerbockers and long knee stockings, highly polished boots and stiff, high collars.

'That's your mother along of me,' said one of the ladies, pointing. 'She was a lively girl all right! We had a long walk to school, you know, and I used to keep watch while she nipped in the turnip field and pulled one up. We rubbed the mud off and chewed it the rest of the way.'

'She still likes turnips,' I told her. 'She eats them peeled like apples, but she often says they taste best with the dirt on.'

'Ah, they taste a whole lot nicer that way,' she sighed.

I had a wobbly tooth – Laura had the answer. When we were back at the Swan, she fetched a reel of cotton, tied one end round the annoying wobbler, and the other end to the door knob.

'You stand still, and I'll slam the door,' she counselled.

Like a coward, I ran like mad as Laura did so, and the tooth remained hanging on its thread.

'Like to try my remedy?' Ernest asked, sitting down to listen to the wireless and to another cup of tea.

'He pulls out his teeth – and mine – with pliers,' Frank said with a grin.

I shuddered. 'No fear!'

There was an unexpected visitor that evening. The touring cyclists sign was still outside, but there had been no holidaymakers since August, 1939. Isabella answered his knock at the front door. Usually visitors just walked in, the door was never locked.

We heard her talking to someone in the hall. She called to Ernest. We children followed behind, curious to see who it was. A young man, wearing baggy drill shorts, long, thick socks and sandals, an open-necked shirt and Fair Isle pullover was requesting a bed for the night.

'I told him we've a pretty full house just at the moment,' Isabella said doubtfully.

'There's the couch in the library,' offered Ernest. 'Can't manage bacon for breakfast, but it's getting dark and chilly. Come you on inside and have some supper with us.'

'Thank you,' the young man smiled. He wheeled his bicycle into the hall. Neatly rolled on the carrier was an oilskin cape round a small bundle of clothes. Fastened to the handlebars was a box containing an enamel mug and a water bottle.

After tea, we helped our grandma to lay out blankets and pillows on the hard couch.

'He wants to turn in early,' Isabella said.

'I reckon he's a spy,' Laura whispered to me when we were in bed. 'He didn't have much luggage, did he, and what would anybody be doing on a cycling holiday in a prohibited area in the War? Did you see all those maps he's got in the pocket of his oilskins? I think he's got a foreign accent too, that's why he didn't speak much.'

'Uncle Frank told Grandad he might be Polish,' I whispered back.

'*Might* be . . . but *he* didn't say so, did he?'

By the time we were up in the morning, the cyclist had gone, leaving a neatly folded ten-shilling note on the table. Even Ernest hadn't heard him leave. Frank was for telling the village bobby, 'just in case'; Laura and I wondered if the cyclist had really been there at all . . .

CHAPTER 8

Summer Ripe

At any time of the year in this lush countryside there was always something to be had for free, and great enjoyment to be had in the gathering. From cowslips to Christmas evergreens, blackberries to bullaces, gleaning corn to picking chestnuts, bulrushes to fir cones, mushrooms to crab apples, rosehips to . . . wild strawberries, my favourite fruits.

The wild strawberries grew along the railway line, near the cowslip meadow. Baskets were carried as a token gesture, but hardly any of the fruit reached home – the temptation was too much. The tiny, sweet berries almost melted away on the tongue, like liquid sunshine. The stains on our fingers remained for days.

Shelling peas in the garden for Sunday lunch, and scattering them when sighting a fat, wriggly maggot; picking poppies; blowing dandelion clocks, or fairies as she called them, for Jassy; drying lavender to pack into tiny, unevenly stitched bags; pounding on rose leaves to make dark brown 'scent', I daydreamed the sun-soaked summers away.

We children were unaware that our stay in the country was drawing to a close. The bombing had long since ceased. Our house was ready for reoccupation. Time for us to go back to Surrey. We were old enough now to realise what being at war meant; we, like our parents read the papers avidly and listened to the news, which was full of the conflict overseas.

* * *

The long school holidays began. David and I were enjoying a week at the Swan. We went with Tilly one sizzling day to the water meadow where long ago the old Earl of the estate where Frank worked had decreed a diving board be fixed over the natural swimming pool. We were joined by most of the village youngsters who dived or jumped in the water, shrieking and playing exuberantly like puppies.

David and Tilly joined them; this was where Tilly had learned to swim as a child. I wandered away, my feet sinking now and again in the soggy, bright green turf. Suddenly, I was enveloped in a great whirling mass of dancing, dazzling blue butterflies. I stretched out my hands in delight and wonder and felt a frantic fluttering against my palms. Then the butterfly fluttered away. Later, when I looked at my hands, I could discern the faintest smudge of blue.

Tilly, in her HomeKnit swimming costume, heavy with water, stretched out to dry on the grass. I sat beside her, dabbling my toes in the water because I couldn't yet swim like David. I heeded Tilly's warning that the river was deep and treacherous in places, and didn't venture in.

Isabella was busy as usual; she had an old school friend and her son staying, too. This lady was remarkable for being the mother of twenty-two children and for giving all her daughters flower names. She lived with her youngest son, a contemporary of Frank's. Aunt Moss, as we called her, told us proudly that her Albert was a concert pianist.

'Be careful of your hands,' his mother cautioned him frequently.

I had met Aunt Moss before; I had endured being cuddled on her satin-covered lap, when I was too big for that, with my face pressed uncomfortably close to her bosom, and a prickly brooch dangerously near my eyes. As the plump fingers stroked my hair, Aunt Moss's husky voice would whisper in my ear: 'I'll remember you, when I go . . .'

Go where? I puzzled.

There was more room for guests, the land girls having departed, one to join the A.T.S., 'to see a bit more of life', and the other had married the farmer they'd worked for. 'She played her cards right,' as some said.

But on this occasion, Aunt Moss had been taken ill during her stay, and was upstairs in our grandparents own big bed.

At teatime, Albert brought down a dish of overripe strawberries.

'She doesn't feel up to these. She wanted Shummy to have them.' He watched while I ate them, not liking to leave the mushy bits.

That night I was in agony with nettle rash and Tilly dabbed on cooling calamine with cotton wool. Fortunately, my parents arrived the next morning, to stay for the weekend, and afterwards to take us children back to Dolly's. I clung to my dad, feeling very out of sorts. They'd brought Jassy with them, which cheered me up.

We went up to see Aunt Moss, who lay against mounds of pillows. Her long, improbably auburn hair clung damply to her neck, and she beckoned me to come closer. I heard the familiar whisper, fainter now, 'I'll remember you when I go . . .'

* * *

The garden at the Swan was beyond the cobbled yard. It meandered down to a gnarled walnut tree. Beyond was a water meadow – to get into it you first had to hack your way through a fearsome mass of nettles. David and I had only tried this once, and had to be anointed with vinegar to ease the stings.

Well-turned plots of rich, black soil were edged by dozens of upturned glass bottles and jars, some of them going back sixty years or more. Frank carried on the family tradition. Behind the old privy with the 'bottomless pit' – 'Watch out!' as David warned me, enormous raspberries grew profusely. 'That's no wonder,' as Frank pointed out.

Flowers rioted among the vegetables, every pocket of earth was utilised. Two stout green mossy posts supported the flapping washing line, held high by a forked prop.

Early one morning I followed Frank down the path, when the dew still glimmered on the bushes and the fine cobwebs trembled in a soft breeze.

'I wish you wouldn't do it, Uncle,' I said anxiously, as his dung-coloured corduroy clad legs disappeared through a gap in the hedge into the garden next door.

He returned with an armful of tender pink-tipped rhubarb. 'He pinches my cabbages and I pinch his rhubarb,' he said. 'He knows and I know. That's it.' And he winked.

It was not a garden to play in, like Dolly and Ross's, I thought. There was no lawn to laze on; spades and forks leaned at the ready and weeds were twitched out as soon as they reared their heads.

The womenfolk being preoccupied with Aunt Moss and the daily visits of the doctor. Jim took us young ones out for long walks each day, reminiscing about the family as we looked in at the Buck where Molly's family had grown up, the little school the girls had attended, and the church where he and Molly had married.

'It was only used for occasional weddings and so on then, and we had to walk across the meadow to it, and we got soaking wet feet. Photographers didn't come to the church then – we had to dress up again in our wedding clothes a month or so later, and go into Southwold to the studio there to have pictures taken.'

Jim's family on his mother's side had originated from Cornwall, but his father's family had come from this part of Suffolk, hence Jim's great affection for it. His parents had both been born on the Isle of Sheppey into naval families and he had lived there until he was seven.

'This is where we threw our case over the hedge: we'd come by train and bus as far as we could get on our first visit home after we were married, and written to Grandad asking him to meet us with the pony and trap. They were living on a remote farm then, while waiting to move to the Swan.

'It was pitch dark, no Grandad, so we started walking – we had about six miles to go. The case got heavier and heavier, and Molly said, "Throw it over there, and we can collect it in the morning." Just then we heard someone coming and we felt quite guilty; it was only a cyclist whose lamp had gone out. We struck a bargain with him – if he would wheel our case on his bike, we would get his lamp fixed at Grandad's and something to eat to help him on his way.

'So we walked the last stretch together and Nanna and Grandad were really surprised to see us, because they hadn't had our letter.'

I loved my dad's stories.

* * *

We arrived back to find the house in a turmoil. Isabella had received word that troops would be stopping off in the village that afternoon, and as she was involved with the W.V.S. as well as the W.I., she and her band of helpers were to provide refreshments.

We all helped; Isabella produced a key, and a little cupboard above the short flight of stairs was unlocked and the biggest tin of spam I had ever seen was brought forth from its hiding place.

David and I were despatched to the bakery to fetch dozens of newly baked rolls, and were rewarded with a large slice of soft, moist gingerbread, the baker's speciality.

The rolls were split, margarine spread, the spam cut skilfully by Ernest. Cakes appeared from all around the village, sponges were sliced into twelve, trays were used instead of plates. From the secret cupboard came hoarded tea and sugar – Isabella's black cash-box was opened and ten shillings extracted to purchase milk.

Cups, saucers and plates arrived in boxes on the doorstep; neat piles of red-bordered tea-cloths were fetched from the linen cupboard.

Ernest shut his shop for the afternoon and opened up the shuttered warehouse next door. Now the busy brooms sent the dust flying, then trestle tables were set up and covered with white sheets. Finally, the food was laid out. Huge urns bubbled frantically and an array of tea-cups marched along a makeshift counter.

Jim fixed up a dartboard on one wall, and the men wheeled over the old piano. We children arranged jam jars of flowers and painted a big banner declaiming WELCOME!

We waited impatiently and finally, at almost five o'clock, we heard the rumbling of the first trucks. Young men in khaki jumped down, stood hesitantly looking around the village street. The doors were flung wide and Jim thumped out 'Pack Up Your Troubles . . .' and the young soldiers were ushered enthusiastically within.

I carefully carried over cups of tea and handed out the Spam rolls. The soldiers seemed more in need of the tea than food, as if too tired to eat, but they drank many cups of tea.

'Care to play darts with me?' a young soldier asked me. My first dart went wide and hit the wall and the second dropped and stabbed my toes through my sandal. I kept a smile on my face, everyone had to look happy today.

There was much singing, the air became hazy with cigarette smoke, the tables were cleared for impromptu dancing which spilled over into the street. Dear Tilly was much in demand as a partner, being so sweet-faced, young and blonde.

Suddenly they were gone, and a new battalion took over to tackle the washing-up. Isabella was obviously weary but pleased that the whole operation had gone so smoothly.

'I'd best hurry back to see to my dear friend,' she said, eager to tell Aunt Moss how we had fed 'the five thousand'.

* * *

The old house sighed and fidgeted the nights away like an aged person with a chronic wheeze, but this night there were other stealthy movements. Doors opened and closed, slippered feet shuffled along the corridors, the stairs creaked, low voices conversed earnestly. I lay half-awake, not really aware of what was happening, but I started up in bed as I heard the urgent rapping on the bedroom door. Molly was out of bed immediately, and came over, laying me down and bidding me not to wake Jassy, who was sharing my bed. Then she went to join the mystery caller.

Jim hastily pulled his top clothes on over his pyjamas. Then he, too, disappeared.

The front door banged, footsteps pounded and echoed down the street.

All was quiet for a time and I was drifting into an uneasy sleep when there came a heavy tread on the stairs. A little later, Jim came back quietly into the bedroom, looked down at me and Jassy, then bent to tuck us in more securely.

I had to ask. 'What's wrong, Daddy?'

'Oh, nothing for you to worry about, old dear. Goodnight, see you in the morning.'

Over breakfast, the muted tones puzzled me as I encouraged Jassy to eat up her porridge, when she would rather have had an egg.

'Pneumonia, the doctor said . . .'

'Completely wore out . . .'

'Where's Mother?'

'I should say, send a telegram, first thing Monday morning . . .'

'Has anyone asked Alice to come to help out?'

By the fire, despite the promise of another scorching, sultry day. Albert sat, rubbing his delicate hands together, as if he felt chilled. His aesthetic face was unshaven, his expression remote. Family, in passing, squeezed his frail shoulders, stood by him for a moment, but said nothing.

Only Jim sat at the table with me, after Tilly took Jassy off to be washed and dressed. David had gone out in the garden with Frank. But Jim, too, was preoccupied. He appeared to be writing a list on a piece of paper. Others came and went, then Tilly appeared with Jassy and told me to amuse her.

'Be good girls! Pity,' she added to Jim, 'that the children had to be here, at this time. But we weren't to know, were we?'

I wanted to ask: 'What's happened?' But I had already guessed the answer. So I said instead: 'Can I take Jassy for a walk this morning?'

'That's a good idea,' my father said, clearly relieved.

So, soon after, we two, hand in hand, set off, along a familiar path past a cluster of houses, and then flat fields on either side. We went across the bridge and then through the dappled sunlight and shade afforded by the huge trees on either side of the road which leaned towards each other as if they'd been blown by the wind. There was not a soul in sight; just the vast parkland of the estate. When we reached the crossroads, we hesitated. Perhaps we ought to turn back, I thought.

'Which way shall we go, Jassy?' I asked.

'I want to go home.' Jassy had sensed the atmosphere, too.

'It's a long way – I'm not sure you can walk that far . . .'

'I can!' Jassy's lower lip trembled. 'I want to see Mummy.'

'All right. But you mustn't grizzle if you get tired. I'll tell you a story, shall I? They'll probably ask us to walk back this afternoon, though.'

'This is the right way,' Jassy told me. I was notorious for having no sense of direction. We ambled along confidently and the stories of magic and fairies, which Jassy loved, spilled forth.

We stopped just once, when we reached the outskirts of the village, having walked about seven miles. We had reached a farmhouse, and there was the farmer's wife, hanging out washing in the garden, with a clothes peg in her mouth. She came to the gate to see what we wanted.

'Please can we have a glass of water?' I asked politely. 'We've walked over from our grandparents – it was a long way . . .'

The farmer's wife had recognised Jassy. She didn't give us water, she sat us down on kitchen chairs in the garden, poured us long glasses of fresh milk, and gave us currant buns, still warm from baking.

'Aren't your feet sore?' she asked us.

We shook our heads. But we both had very fair skin and we were red from exposure to the sun. We said goodbye and thank you, and walked on. Suddenly, despite the rest, we both felt very tired. It was a real effort to walk that last, long mile.

Dolly was laying the table for lunch when we arrived. She could hardly believe the evidence of her eyes. 'How on earth—?'

'We walked,' I said simply.

We were made to rest on our beds, while Dolly ran down to the pub on the corner to make a phone call to the pub near the grandparents.

'It's best for you to stay here,' she told us, on her return. 'Luckily they hadn't missed you. Poor Aunt Moss passed away last night, and everyone's rushing around in circles.'

Suddenly, it all made sense to me. 'When I go,' Aunt Moss had said. And she'd sounded as if she was expecting it, and that it was the most natural thing in the world.

CHAPTER 9

Fare Ye Well Together

Before we left Suffolk, there was the village fete.

'"The Old Woman who Lived in the Shoe", that's it!' We spread newspaper on the table, Auntie Rum produced a big cardboard container. I rinsed the muddy mixings from my paint box, Molly drew some experimental shapes and Dolly sharpened her dressmaking shears.

Jassy wheeled her doll's pram, once mine, up and down the garden path while she waited. The pram was crammed full of toys as befitted the nursery rhyme.

The giant shoe took shape and was finally fitted round the pram, completely disguising it, so that the 'children' peeped out of the cutout windows and poked their heads cheekily through the chimneys. David laced the two sides together with string brushed black with shoe-polish, then we all stood back to admire the results of our ingenuity and hard work.

'Quick! Now for Jassy, we've only an hour before we go . . .'

Auntie Rum had been sewing a long skirt from blackout material and Molly had improvised a mob cap from a piece of flowered cotton from the rag-bag. A shawl, fastened together with a safety pin, and a pair of lensless glasses, completed the outfit.

I'd been busy with my own fancy dress costume – DRESSED FOR ALL OCCASIONS stated the placard on my back.

I wore a wellington boot on one foot and on the other, a plimsoll; a scarf with a straw hat; a pyjama jacket over shorts; and carried an umbrella and a tennis racquet.

'Don't forget,' Dolly reminded me, 'go straight to the clothes stall – Connie says there is a pair of nearly new Clarks sandals that might be your size. They'll go quickly, so you make sure you're the first to try 'em on!'

We met up with other fete goers on our way, the ladies wearing their best summer dresses in hectically flowered crepe, with precious silk stockings (Molly had darned hers 'invisibly', with a hair plucked from her own head) and high heels. Their hair was rolled fashionably round a band or neatly tucked back in a snood. The older women all wore hats. Some of the younger ones had a platinum streak in their hair at the front, stealthily applied with a toothbrush dipped into a saucer containing peroxide. Dolly and Molly had used their hoarded Tangee Natural lipstick and Dolly had borrowed a brown wax crayon from me to emphasise her fair eyebrows.

'You've drawn one higher than the other,' her sister told her tactlessly.

The air was heavy with mingled scents as they walked: Devon violets, attar of roses, cloying Papier Poudre.

The fete was being held in the grounds of the Big House and was to be opened, naturally, by the Squire's lady. I went straight to the clothes stall as instructed, and joined the queue, while the opening phrases were intoned:

'So pleased you could all come ... please make this occasion an outstanding success ... all proceeds to the Red Cross ... wonderful bargains ... I now declare this Grand Summer Fete well and truly OPEN!'

Like Cinderella I waited my turn to try on the coveted sandals. Auntie Con winked at me, contriving to cover them with a voluminous skirt, while I inched nearer.

Whenever I took my own children, in later years, to buy new shoes, I always recalled that special fitting. The sandals were in brown leather, with a simple cross-over strap leaving the toes free, and when on, they proved a perfect fit, and so comfortable that I wore them almost non-stop for the rest of the summer.

'Sixpence, please,' whispered Auntie Con.

To our delight, Jassy won the first prize for her fancy dress. I rather wished I had not chosen to wear such contrasting footwear for my costume. Dolly won a beautiful china doll, long treasured by someone in the village, in the Name Me competition. The doll, of course, was named Jasmine! David was an easy winner in the hundred yards in the school races; to my shame, I only came second when running, by mistake, in a younger age group!

The Red Cross contingent made a fuss of Jassy and me, for not long ago we had made lots of lavender bags and gone round the village to sell them in aid of the Red Cross, as our war effort. (I must now confess, after all these years, that when we ran short of lavender, we bumped up the filling with scented cotton wool.) These good ladies were kept very busy administering first aid to casualties of wasp stings – the stall crammed full of sticky buns and toffee apples was the cause of this invasion. Plants and produce wilted and became sad in the shimmering heat. Dolly was one of the stung, but she did not seek treatment.

'Well, would you? If you'd sat down on a wasp when you were talking to the Parson? Ooh, it is painful, cheeky thing stung me right through all my clothes. They're really spiteful this year, dopey from eating too much fruit.'

Miss House fussed over winding up the gramophone, becoming agitated when the music slowed down during the country dancing. Most of the boys had slunk off and the big girls had to double as partners for the little ones. I found myself being whirled round by an energetic Farje, who despite her plumpness, was light on her feet. By then I'd had the sense to change into my new sandals.

We staggered home laden with prizes and bargains. I'd won a bottle of Daddies Sauce on the hoopla, which pleased my brother, and I'd purchased for threepence an old-fashioned portable escritoire, with a lined drawer for writing paper, a tray for sand and a china inkwell. Ross had won two shillings on Hitting the Hammer and Dolly and Molly had an armful each of out-of-date dresses to unpick and make-over. David had spent his sixpence for winning his race on a jar of jam.

Mused Molly: 'Looks all sugary on top – I wonder how old it is?'

'I feel sick . . .' I said suddenly as we neared home. And I was.

After being put to bed, I woke again at twilight and Ross came in, his kind face concerned, carrying a tray.

'You missed your tea. So I made you a nice piece of toast, and I sneaked a bit of butter, instead of marg.' He sat on the end of my bed and watched me eat. 'Feel better now, old dear?'

Molly bustled in, with a glass of hot, sugared milk, followed by Dolly, Jassy and David. They squeezed beside Ross on the bed.

'How's the invalid?' they asked.

It was almost like a party, I thought, all the family around and caring about you when you felt poorly. We chatted about the afternoon's events, and finally I lay back, my stomach settled, and slept again, to wake, feeling much better in the morning. My writing box had been placed on the bedside table, and someone had filled the drawer with writing paper.

* * *

'Run and borrow Auntie Rum's stick and a couple of baskets,' Dolly said after lunch. 'We'll pack up some tea and call for Auntie Connie, she might like to bring the children along. There should be a fair few blackberries ripe after all this sun, and I've boiled up some old muslin nappies for the bramble jelly.'

'I see Mrs T has picked her cultivated blackberries,' twinkled Auntie Con, with a sly glance at us children, as we all made our way through the long grass, skirting the cowpats and shooing the curious cows.

We still felt guilty about picking the most perfect blackberries we had ever seen, which hung over into the meadow from a cottage garden a few doors along from Dolly's. As we ate our spoils, an irate voice berated us:

'You lot! Them blackberries is for a special order! Get on out of it!'

Molly was quiet, enjoying the walk, the heady air, but she was also thinking of her own home and wondering when she would break the news to us that we were going back sooner than we expected.

She'd written to Jim:

Jassy needs a room of her own and Dolly is thinking of having another baby. The schools at home have finally reopened and I know you feel there's more chance of the children taking the scholarship there. It's tiring for you coming up here to see us, too. 'All quiet on the Home Front' now, as they say . . .

There was such an abundance of fruit that we didn't know where to begin picking. We dashed along the bushes, filling our baskets, getting scratched arms and legs, squashing the overripe berries which fell, underfoot.

'Let's eat our tea in the old garden.' Auntie Con led the way, climbing over the stile into the next field and going toward a group of gnarled old fruit trees. There had once been a little cottage on this site, but all that remained now was the garden. Flowers had seeded and re-seeded and struggled for existence among the high grass. There was evidence of a rockery, and the big stones served as useful seats. The trees were bowed down under the weight of unpicked apples, plums and pears; the fruit was small and hard, and, as we soon discovered, tasteless.

We ate our jam sandwiches, throwing the crusts to the birds. Canterbury bells, ants crawling up my leg, the rough stone I sat on, the disappointing golden plums, the unreal sensation of sitting in a garden which should not be there, the brimming blackberry baskets – all these things were stored in my memory.

'Why?' I asked tearfully later. 'Why can't I stay here while you and David go home?'

Molly was hurt. She hadn't realised just how attached I had become to my 'second family'.

'Remember Granny Thomas?' Dolly asked suddenly. We were all sitting in the little front room that evening, basking in the late sunlight which beamed through the windows.

'Yes, of course I do.' Molly was still glancing reproachfully at me. If I had said, 'Can't we *all* stay here, a bit longer?' it would have been different, but . . .

'Who was Granny Thomas?' I asked, still sniffing.

'She wasn't really a granny – well, perhaps she was, but not *our* granny. Mother used to visit the workhouse regularly when we were still at the Buck, to cheer up the poor old souls there, and one day she found Granny Thomas among the elderly ladies – they were cruel in those days, they used to separate married couples you know. "I never thought I'd come this low," Granny said, crying. The old dear had worked so hard all her life, she was widowed young. Mother remembered her being grateful for the used tea-leaves her employers gave her. She was a proud old lady and no trouble to anyone. I don't know what happened to her family, or even if she had one, but to her it was shameful to end up in the workhouse. "Pack your things," Mother said, "You're coming home along of me!" And she did. We fitted her in, in our family, and she lived on for a good few more years and when she went, it was like losing one of us.'

'Dear old Granny,' Molly said fondly.

'Play the guitar, Uncle Ross,' I wheedled. He fetched it, and we sang as we so often did, with golden light streaming in on us, and sentimental tears not far away.

* * *

It was my birthday, and I was going home that afternoon. Jim had arrived late the night before, and the car was already packed with our things.

I had made the rounds of goodbyes. I saved Auntie Rum until last, knowing she would be with the family to see us off.

Auntie Con cleared her throat. 'Come back soon. Meg will miss taking you out on the back of her bike.'

I didn't tell her that on the last occasion, Meg had sung out at the top of a hill: 'Hold tight! Close your eyes!' And she freewheeled all the way down, no hands.

I would miss my tomboy friend and honorary cousin. I had never dared to emulate her party trick – riding bareback on their house cow, holding on to the horns, like handlebars.

Mary was sad. 'I don't suppose I'll ever have another friend like you,' she said dolefully. Her mother presented me with a bag of broken Co-op biscuits for the journey and picked a fragrant bunch of flowers for my mother.

There was a cluster of children in the Jubilee seat, a favourite meeting place for the young. 'Goodbye!' they called good-naturedly and then seemed to forget me instantly, absorbed in their talking and games.

I called at Mr Todd's, and he shook my hand and wished me well. 'I shall say I knew you, when you're famous,' he joked.

'Please say goodbye to Miss House for us,' I requested. She was away.

The parson was in his garden.

'Goodbye! I'm going home today,' I called out shyly. He came to the gate and regarded me thoughtfully. 'But you'll be back, won't you?'

I nodded. I couldn't know that we would indeed be back after the flying bombs devastated London and the suburbs. But that was in the future. We would welcome into our home a young mother with a baby girl. And they'd stay with us for a long while, just like old Granny Thomas did at the Buck. I would attend a big new school with inspiring teachers. But best of all, eventually my father would come home, and we would be a real family unit again . . .

The Austin 7 shook and rumbled into life. We waved until we'd turned the corner. As dear Grandad always said:

'Fare Ye Well, Together.'

PART 2

DANCING IN THE STREET

1942-1951

CHAPTER 10

The Homecoming

Molly, our mum, David and I returned to Surrey in 1942. We had been bombed out in November, 1940, after witnessing the Battle of Britain in the skies overhead. The past two years had been spent in Suffolk with my aunt Dolly and her family, while our father remained in Bath with the Admiralty personnel who had been evacuated there at the beginning of the war.

* * *

We travelled by train, having to stand most of the way in the corridor, to Liverpool Street Station, which was crowded with men in uniform, laden with heavy kitbags. We queued for what seemed hours for a bus home, were driven through ravaged London streets and were relieved when the windows misted up with fine rain, obscuring our view. As usual I began to feel sick, and my head drooped on to Molly's shoulder to rest against her fox fur tippet, which smelled of mothballs. The black beady eyes of the fox (what a horrible fashion this was) were frightening, though I was no longer a baby, but at that moment I was too nauseous to care.

Our house had been patched up, with temporary ceilings, new windows and doors. There was an odour of neglect, of damp: silver fish scuttled across the floors; books left piled on the shelves, old friends which I immediately turned to, had rust marks on pages and corners nibbled by mites, or maybe mice. To me, this didn't feel like home anymore. Although it was early September, we all felt chilled. There was a recent fall of soot in the hearth, a reminder of the aftermath of the bomb, when our little white dog was black with coal dust.

The first thing Molly did was to put on one bar of the electric fire in the living room. We weren't due a delivery of coal yet. Shivering, but not complaining, we made toast, scorching slices of bread left over from the journey, and drank tepid tea from the flask. We had brought a few provisions with us, but although the electricity had been restored, as yet there was no gas: Molly couldn't use the New World cooker as she'd intended – she'd looked forward to this, after managing with a gas ring in the hearth in the cottage – nor could she light the geyser for a bath.

There were beds to make up, cases to unpack. That was our homecoming.

The grandfather clock under the stairwell, damaged by the blast, no longer chimed, but it was still there. We glanced in the front room before climbing the stairs to bed. The carpet was rolled up under the window, the settee and chairs shrouded in dust sheets. The piano, which Jim's parents had given him and Molly as a wedding gift, had survived. All these familiar things had been in storage until Jim paid a brief visit to the house the previous week to see them reinstalled. He'd endured hours of driving, some of it in the blackout, after calling in on us at Dolly's to pick up the heavy trunk and a couple of cases of clothes. I knew something was up, but we were sent to school as usual, and only saw our dad briefly. I think Molly was afraid I would make a fuss, for Dolly was like a second mother to me, little Jassy like a sister, and I loved country life, although, of course, I missed my father.

Now, we paused by the harmonium in the hall. David and I looked at each other, each wanting to be first to pull out all the stops.

'Not tonight children,' Molly sighed.

The last time we slept in our house, I remembered, we lay between our parents, on a mattress on the kitchen floor, for Jim had arrived home unexpectedly that night, listening to the thunder of the ack-ack guns and the drone of enemy planes overhead. Tonight, we would be in our own beds.

The new bedroom suite Molly had been so proud of had been smashed to pieces when my parents' bedroom received the full impact of the bomb. Jim had acquired a double bed for their room from somewhere, but otherwise it was empty of furniture. David and I had our single beds in the back bedroom, his with the Cambridge blue bedspread, mine draped in Oxford blue, as we were rivals in the Boat Race. The Edwardian wardrobe and dressing table had been painted pink by Molly to 'freshen them up' just before the war. The wardrobe had an open compartment for 'hats', ideal for me to keep my own books. I would unpack them from their box first thing tomorrow, I promised myself.

Molly turned the little nightlight low. She bent over each bed to kiss us goodnight. 'Nice to be home, isn't it . . .'

I murmured, 'Yes, Mummy,' because I knew that was what she wanted to hear.

* * *

Many of the neighbouring houses remained boarded up: the Motts next door were still away. We'd come home because my brother had a place at a grammar school in Croydon in September, and I was due to sit the scholarship next spring.

The schools had finally reopened, three years after they were closed, following one or two false starts. Things were quiet on the Home Front. Our local school had small classes, few teachers, as the majority of children evacuated at the outbreak of war had not returned. Some had lost their homes: the rubble had been cleared, but gaps between the houses had created little overgrown alleyways for us curious children to explore. Before the war, we'd not been allowed to play in the street, nor during our first homecoming, just before the Blitz, as Molly deemed it too hazardous. In Suffolk we had roamed freely.

Now, the only danger of being 'run over', as Molly put it, was from the occasional bicycle or highly unlikely, by a runaway milk-man's horse, if the horse was startled when rooting in his nose-bag outside a customer's house. Cars were a rare sight these days due to the shortage of petrol and the fact that most drivers between eighteen and forty, except for those in reserved occupations, were serving in the forces. The only women about were mothers of young children and the elderly. Those with children over ten years old were drafted into war work . . .

At first I didn't venture far from home – just across the road to where there was a large blank wall, known as *Henry's*, where I practised playing with a couple of old tennis balls, a game called *Sevenses*, which required bouncing the balls and chanting in a sing-song way: *Goering is Boring! Goebbels throws snowballs!* were two of the 'calypsos' of the day. I was not alone, but it wasn't a team game. The girls who joined me were newcomers, Londoners, as empty houses were requisitioned for the homeless at this time. The relentless thump of the ball against the wall drove the bald man who worked in the court-yard beyond (at what, we never discovered) to appear from round the side of the house to shout furiously, 'Clear off!' We never answered him back, but ran away, with the balls stuffed up our knickers. We would return in a day or two. Our mothers didn't discourage us, as they could see us from the upstairs windows.

I still missed the countryside, the walks across the meadows, the glimpses of wildlife – but I was adapting slowly. There were few dogs around now, for many of these had been taken to the vets and put to sleep at the beginning of the war, when the evacuation had commenced, and again, when the bombing led to many stray ownerless animals. Cats were everywhere, often thin and abandoned, and I adopted a black tom whom I named Timoshenko after a prominent Russian of the time. We still had our Pekingese, Waggles, though the only walks he enjoyed were in my dolls' pram, and I was getting too old for that. David had his white mice in the garage: he sold the offspring at 6d. each, but after hiding them in his desk at school, had been told to cease trading. Despite the mice doing tricks, like balancing on a string between chairs, I didn't care to hold them as I didn't like their long, pink tails, and their incontinence. Timoshenko blinked his golden eyes, and purred on my lap, while waiting his chance. Plain old house mice were opportunists, too. David soon had 'rare' brown and white mice which were much prized by the local boys. His money box was soon far heavier than mine.

Our semi-detached end-of-row house, with attached garage, was part of a small suburban estate built between the wars, off a pleasant green lane of rather grand Edwardian houses and Victorian villas, where it was rumoured there were still parlour maids and gardeners. Our street, like the others on the so-called white collar estate, was named after a famous general of the Boer War. It was convenient for all the amenities. It was a ten-minute walk to the clock tower, the high street with that wonderful store, Woolworths, and the Pavilion, known to all as the 'Pav', our local cinema. This was next to the municipal swimming baths. Turn right at the Clock and you came to the mainline station to London. Further down was the library, which due to my new-found freedom, I was able to visit most days. I usually began reading the first of my two books on the way home, often bumping into a lamp-post or someone hurrying to catch a tram, when I would be sternly reminded: 'Look where you're going!' I recall reading poems aloud as I walked along, 'Fair Imogen' was a favourite: why hadn't my parents called me that? I loved the name.

I met an elderly lady further up our road who invited me in for biscuits and a glass of milk. 'Do you like Westerns?' she asked. I hadn't read one, but I'd seen *Hopalong Cassidy* at the Pav, also *The Lone Ranger* and heard his call: 'Heigh ho, Silver!' to his horse. I was thus introduced to the novels of Zane Grey, who roamed the Wild Frontier. Miss W lent me all the books in turn.

Molly preferred the travelling library, which called once a week. For tuppence a book, she chose half a dozen novels by her favourite authors like Pearl S. Buck. The bookman staggered up the path, carrying these, and then spread his selection halfway up our stairs, chatting to Molly while she inspected the books. He was a little man with a 'pencil' moustache, and a mouthful of brown stained teeth, due to puffing an evil-smelling pipe. He looked at me as if he wished I would vanish, and reminded me: 'I do not have books for children.' I would sneakily read these love stories when I got a chance, retrieving them from under the cushion in Molly's chair when I had exhausted my own library books. They had titles like *A Woman's Way, Stormy Petrel* and *Thursday's Child*. I knelt by the chair, with my face close to the printed pages and read every word. I was in a world of my own, so Molly said.

CHAPTER 11

Bread Buns and Big Girls

We had our own parade of local shops on the way to the school, where I was about to join The Big Girls, divided from The Big Boys by a high fence. The children spied on each other through the knotholes.

At the end of our row of houses was the police station, surrounded by a low brick wall. It was a ritual for me to walk along the top of this wall, before jumping down to cross the road to the baker's shop on the corner.

Before the war I could just remember the lovely cakes always on show in the window: now, there was a tray of bread buns which cost a penny each; you could count the currants, and once I found only three – and the National loaf, greyish rather than white. Molly had brought us up on brown bread before the war, but I thought longingly of soft white bread and real butter, of the special treat of a thick crust cut from the crusty loaves still available in the village baker's.

Skirting the off-licence, where on special Sundays we bought a bottle of Tizer, we came to the corner tobacconist's, run by two sisters who lived with their brother, who worked in London but sometimes served customers on a Saturday morning. All three were middle-aged and kindly. Kit was the younger sister, who Molly and her friend May agreed, 'has become rather skittish, since the war. Did you see the bow in her hair?' Kit kept packets of Players under the counter for any servicemen who might be on leave. Molly and May exchanged local gossip with Kit while she passed over their 'Five Craven A, please.'

We bought our sweets from a shop called Bob's. Mrs Bob (I don't think that was her name) helped us juggle our sweet coupons. After biting off the stem of my liquorice pipe, I looked at the selection of second-hand magazines and comics spread on the counter. These were sold for a penny each, and if you returned them in good order, you were given a halfpenny in return. The comics were sold again at the original price. I wonder how many times they changed hands? Mrs Bob saved me copies of the *Girls' Crystal*, which cost tuppence, having more reading matter.

I loved those magazines and the serials, and unlike the comics, didn't part with them. As toys were in short supply, Mrs Bob took a small commission from selling hand-knitted soft toys – kangaroos in striped wool were a favourite, because in the pouch was a tiny knitted Joey. There was also the occasional wooden train or bricks in a box on wheels, made by a grandad. Mrs Bob kept things under the counter too, like lemonade powder, which she measured by the spoonful into poke bags she fashioned herself from pieces of newspaper. We dipped a forefinger in the acid crystals and licked blissfully – gaining a bright yellow tongue in the process. Ice-cream wafers, soft and tasting rather unpleasant, for ice-creams had long ago disappeared, were fourteen a penny. We were always hungry, so they filled us up. Cough sweets were not rationed, but tasted horrible when the sugar coating was sucked off.

Halfway up the parade was the shop where you could buy newspapers and stationery. This shop was busiest on a Sunday, when the other shops were closed, as the proprietors were Jewish. We bought coloured pencils, pencil sharpeners and boxes of paint from Mrs Morris. When I was older, I bought deckled-edged writing paper with envelopes lined with blue tissue, and a bottle of purple ink. I had many pen friends. I also spent my pocket money once on a pencil sharpener, which had a blade like a guillotine, which was confiscated almost immediately by Jim next time he was home, as a dangerous object.

Set back was the greengrocer's – where there were lengthy queues for vegetables on Saturday mornings. I stood with Molly, listening to the artless chat of young factory workers with their hair still in steel curlers under turbans, which they combed into a frizz later, for Saturday night dances in the church hall. I was reminded of the land girls billeted with my grandparents, who sounded the same. They went to the dances in pairs; men were in short supply, so the taller of the two girls would 'lead' the shorter in a waltz or quickstep. It was either Victor Silvester on the wind-up gramophone, or a cheerful matron thumping on the piano.

The fruit-and-veg sisters were Amazons, over six-foot tall, and cheerful, decanting potatoes with small clods of earth into our baskets with a smile. They lifted great boxes with ease. They had taken over from their brothers when they joined up. I couldn't remember what bananas tasted like, there were none available nowadays, but an orange was an occasional treat, cut in two between my brother and me. We had fun making 'false teeth' from the pith. When we had colds, Molly would poke a hole in an orange, and insert a precious sugar cube. 'Suck the juice,' she told us, 'and you'll soon feel better.' Eggs were another rare treat, we missed the ones we'd collected warm from the nest, with a stray feather clinging, in the country. Dried egg, mostly scrambled, was not the same at all.

On the other side of the road, the shops were less interesting, though Molly lingered in all of them at times, while I fidgeted and wished we were in Mrs Bob's shop. There was the chemist, who mixed potions and lotions and dispensed free advice on our ailments. Boxes of Dr Williams' Pink Pills intrigued me. Did they taste like cachous? There was liquorice there too, but it was hard and bitter and used as a laxative. Chilblain ointment was sold in little round cardboard boxes. It didn't work though, as we discovered when we anointed our itching toes.

The grocery shop was like a long, dimly lit cavern, with dusty sacks, boxes of biscuits, mouse traps, a wire cheese cutter and scissors to cut the coupons from our ration books. Some things, like tinned fruit, were on 'points', and sugar was measured into stiff blue bags with the tops turned over. The grocer, Mr Noble, so an older resident told us, had started out with a stall on the pavement, between the wars. He was cheap and cheerful then, and he still did his best for the regular customers despite all the shortages. Molly called in there most days after she met me from school for one or two items, like Force flakes, Fairy soap, and Typhoo tea. I pointed out the jars of salmon and shrimp paste, my favourite spread at teatime.

We usually just looked in the window of the draper's shop, but one afternoon we stepped inside to the pealing of a bell. I was hopeful Molly would buy something today so I could watch the little cash container whizzing along the wire overhead to the cashier's desk. Back it would come with the change, often a farthing for most prices ended in 'eleven-three', the pence and farthings after the shillings.

Molly had received a letter from Dolly that morning and we were delighted when she told David and me at breakfast that her sister was coming the following day to stay – 'just for a day or two.'

'Oh, goody, is Jassy coming?'

'Not this time, Auntie Rum next door is looking after her.'

Now, Molly took the letter from the bag and read out from a list.

Miss Winterbourne opened drawers below the counter and placed some small items on the counter. A pink knitted matinee coat, matching leggings, bonnet, bootees and mittens. Baby clothes. Molly counted the money in her purse. 'Have you a little cotton nighty?' Dolly had sent some coupons, it seemed.

'One's not much use,' said Miss Winterbourne, who though she was unmarried was conversant with infant needs. 'I've a pre-war one that's shop-soiled. I'll throw that in, shall I?'

I was curious. Who on earth were these things for? Was Dolly having a baby? A thought struck me: Wouldn't it be wonderful if I was going to have a little sister at last! But then I realised, you don't know what a baby will be, boy or girl, until it's born, and Mummy hasn't said anything to us . . .

All Molly said, as we walked home with our parcel, neatly tied with string, was, 'While Dolly's here, we're going to see a friend in London, who has just had a baby. Don't worry, we'll be back before you arrive home in the afternoon from school.'

* * *

I was adapting to the routine in The Big Girls, as David was his new school. He had to leave earlier than me in the mornings to catch a bus from the Clock, and in the evenings he had homework awaiting his attention in his satchel. At night, he often woke me up when he came to bed, for he stayed up later than me, as he recited his Latin verbs. 'Hic, Hoc, Hec' – I pulled the covers over my ears.

My new teacher, Miss Lancaster, was very stern. She had a profile as described in the Zane Grey Westerns: a hooked nose and jet-black hair swept back into a tight knot in the nape of her neck. I felt apprehensive whenever she fixed her gaze on me, in the front row. The first day I joined her class, she swooped down on me, long forefinger jabbing at my copy work.

'You! Why are you printing? You should be doing joined-up writing by now!'

'We – only did printing, at my last school . . .' I faltered.

'Ridiculous!' With a pencil she drew curves between all my letters. 'Follow that, and don't let me see that infantile printing again!'

My neighbour whispered: 'Loops on your g's and y's – look at mine.' But it wasn't as easy as that, as I soon discovered.

I was in the top class, and Miss L was determined that every child should leave The Big Girls able to read and write. Some had problems due to evacuation, a few were naturally slow. Miss L picked out a team to coach the less able: as I tried to remain inconspicuous after being exposed as one who couldn't do joined-up writing, I was surprised to become one of the pupil teachers. The girl who sat next to me, Anne, was also appointed. I helped two girls, and Anne took charge of two boys. Both Anne and I found it a very rewarding experience and talk about it still.

I made another lifelong friend in The Big Girls' class, a vivacious small girl called Maggie, with beautiful dark red hair flowing down her back. She has to this day an infectious husky giggle, and suffered from chronic asthma, but she was full of fun, we had a lot in common, both loving books, writing and painting.

However, around this time, I found difficulty in reading what was written on the blackboard, despite being so close to it. Goodness knows why I didn't tell anyone, but others who developed short sight around the same age have told me they kept this worry to themselves, too. I recall whispering to Anne, 'Can you tell me what Miss Lancaster has written for us to copy?' and Anne looking at me as if I'd lost my marbles. 'What is this world if full of care, We have no time to stop and stare,' she hissed.

'No talking!' barked Miss Lancaster.

Yet at this time, as much later I discovered, the fierce Miss L kept every one of my compositions to encourage the next generation or two of Big Girls in creative writing. When I learned that, I wished I had been privileged to know her better . . .

* * *

Back to Dolly's visit: and again, I heard about this years later – she and Molly visited their young friend Lily in a Salvation Army Home for Mothers and Babies. Lily had become pregnant while working in London, the soldier responsible turned out to be married, and Lily had just given birth to a baby daughter. The kindly people who cared for her and helped her through it all, thought that adoption was the best option. Lily agreed, but when she saw her baby she knew she could never part with her. 'I could leave here,' she cried, 'but I haven't anywhere to go . . .'

Molly followed her mother's example, who took an old friend home after visiting her in the workhouse. She wrote to Jim, and by return post was told, 'Yes, old dear, let them come to you. Lily will be company for you, while I am away . . .'

A week later, I came in from school to find Molly and Lily together, with baby Jenny in a rush basket. Jenny was, of course, dressed all in pink!

CHAPTER 12

Disraeli and Me

September, 1943

I was no longer a Big Girl. I felt very small indeed on my first day at my new school.

There were Big Girls everywhere, and quite a few in my class, it seemed. Big Girls in gymslips and school ties, whereas Molly had decided it was still warm enough for me to wear a summer dress. Before the war, the girls had worn dresses in fine cream-coloured tussore, material which was no longer available. Molly did her best with more substantial cotton, in beige. Such a light shade was totally impractical for school wear. The dresses were too short when she finished sewing, so she lengthened them with false hems. I inherited David's navy gabardine mackintosh, which could be buttoned on either side, but I was conscious it had been worn by a boy before me. We could choose between a pudding basin hat or a beret: I opted for the latter which lasted my entire school days. I intended to jump on it, when I left school, but Jim appropriated it to protect his bald head when painting the house.

A class photograph of the new intake of girls was taken by a teacher. I am among 'the shrimps' at the front, recognisable by my untidy mop of blonde hair. A note was sent to my mother: 'Girls should have short hair, or restrain long hair.' Thereafter, I wore bunches, tied firmly with ribbon, and for years after I left school my hair parted down the middle at the back, where Molly's comb had made a groove. At least I escaped having cropped hair, unlike my friend Maggie, now divested of her crowning glory. I cried with her, for her loss. I was glad though to have Maggie with me as, although she was even smaller than me (she still is petite), she gave me a nudge when I indulged in too much daydreaming. The other girl from our old school was Anne, who soon established herself as top of the class. Anne was also sporty, which helped her popularity, and she looked out for me when larger girls teased me about always missing the ball in games. This was because I couldn't see it until it passed my nose.

I chose which school I wanted to go to when the 11+ results came through – it was always called the scholarship then. As an insurance against not passing (my half-joined-up writing was a drawback) I also sat the entrance exam to a fee-paying girls' school. I overheard my parents, when Jim had a rare weekend at home, discussing what economies would have to be made if I were to go there, and this worried me. It was a well-established school; David was thriving in the companion boys' school, which had a very good reputation for academic success. I said firmly that I didn't want to go there, but not the reason why. I rejected the offer of a bicycle as a reward for success (I already knew I would never make a cyclist) and asked instead for a puppy! Poor old Waggles had had an untimely end when someone threw chicken bones into our garden and he gobbled them up. Jim's landlady's dog had just had a litter of pups, and so I was given my first little Jack Russell. I called her Dinkie. I wasn't aware then, that my parents received several letters from the exclusive school, asking them to change their mind. Apparently, the Head had been impressed by an essay I wrote (entirely from my imagination) about the thrills of an aeroplane trip from Croydon Airport! However, I never regretted the choice I made.

Pupils who had been evacuated with my new school at the beginning of the war were gradually trickling back. Others who joined Class 1 were a year or two older having come home to take the scholarship later, at thirteen instead of eleven. Teachers, too, appeared during my first term, including 'Auntie' who had been further delayed by breaking her collarbone. I think Maggie and I were disappointed at first, because we had enjoyed a stand-in form mistress, a jolly gym teacher who we all admired, in her green Grecian tunic. She taught us country dancing too, and like the amusing Joyce Grenfell song, when she partnered you, it was embarrassingly 'bust to bust' – or should I say chest, for all the skinny Lizzies? The curvaceous teacher departed to a boys' school with some alacrity. I imagine she was even more popular there.

AEC, that middle-aged lady with curly, dark hair, and two pairs of glasses which she invariably mixed up, ribbed lisle stockings, sensible laced-up shoes and tweedy costumes, soon won us over. She was the kindest teacher I have known; she was rarely cross, and her English lessons were inspiring. She really was like everyone's favourite 'aunt'.

Our school was modern, and well-equipped, although not in a very salubrious area. We had to run the gauntlet of youngsters from the housing estate who bombarded us with snowballs in winter, trying to dislodge our hats as we walked down the road to the school. Woe betide any girl seen by a teacher not wearing her hat. That was punishable with a discredit mark against your name.

There was a grand Assembly Hall with a curtained stage and piano, where the music teacher, who closed her eyes when she touched the keys, swayed back and forth on her stool, as she played the hymns. Faces were red when the school song was announced on special occasions: 'St Patrick's Breastplate' – any sniggers were quelled by the stern Head.

Until I had my first pair of glasses, I was frequently lost within the school – it seemed so vast. There were quadrangles outside the class windows, long corridors and stairs leading upwards on one side to the Science Lab and on the other to the Art Room. There was a wing which housed the Domestic Science room; off that was the library. Stairs led to a flat where girls learned how to make beds, clean the bath and shine silver, with pink gritty paste on a saucer. The flat was used by teachers on fire-watch duty at various times during the war. Beyond this complex was the dining hall and the kitchens where I became reluctantly acquainted with school dinners . . .

There were junior and senior cloakrooms, a staff room, from which billowed smoke from many cigarettes, each time the door opened; the Head's study, and a well-equipped gymnasium. Later, showers were installed – purgatory to me and others. We never had enough time to dress before the bell shrilled. The lost property box (items were sold end of term) brimmed with towels, knickers and socks.

Outside was the field, partly given over to Dig for Victory, and a shelter which had been erected at the beginning of the war in the games area, where only the netball posts remained.

The jolly gym teacher was replaced by a much sterner individual. She took a dislike to me almost immediately. I'd enjoyed country dancing sessions, despite being almost smothered by the jolly one's bust at times. The only thing the two teachers had in common was the Grecian tunic which hung loosely on Miss GT's lean figure. She came silently into the hall on that first day carrying a bunch of wooden swords. I was blamed when my insecurely thrust baton at the end of the sword dance caused the shield which was held aloft to fall apart and my fellow dancers to scatter.

'Your name?' Miss GT commanded. I murmured a reply. 'I shall remember that,' she intoned ominously. And she did, to the day I left the school . . .

I resumed dancing classes on Saturday mornings in the Applegarth Hall, near my home, with a glamorous lady called Joan – known professionally as Cherry. Joan had been involved in a horrific car accident at the beginning of the war, and was unable to return to the stage. She always had hopes of discovering a young prodigy; however, although most of her pupils loved tap dancing and the routines, very few rose on their points. Joan's mother played the piano with great gusto. Molly no doubt breathed a sigh of relief that I wasn't stuck at home with my nose in a book, but I still feared every lesson, in or out of the school gym, with caustic comments on my ineptitude from Miss GT.

I wasn't the only one with defective eyesight. Class 1 had a Medical in the Sick Room in the middle of our first term. Our mothers were summoned to attend. We were used now to the indignity of parading in our fleece-lined brown knickers and vests, for this was our sports garb, in the gym and in the field. It was a cold day, I recall, and there was much exaggerated shivering. My fingers were numb and white as they always were in chilly weather. When my name was called, I was measured in height and girth, weighed, and the size of my feet was noted. Girls with large feet got extra clothing coupons; unfortunately, mine were too small.

Then came the dreaded eye test. I gazed intently at what appeared to be a blank chart on the wall. 'Read down as far as you can,' I was instructed. I screwed up the uncovered eye. 'H' I guessed. 'T', the nurse prompted. The other eye was uncovered. Well, I did get the 'T' right, this time.

The doctor was furious with my poor mother. 'Didn't you observe this child is half-blind?' It was a tactless thing to say.

Poor Molly had tears in her eyes. 'She's always reading – she never said . . .' She turned to me: 'Why ever didn't you tell me you couldn't see properly?'

I had no answer for that. I felt I was being admonished for something I couldn't help.

Shortly afterwards, there were half a dozen girls wearing glasses, including both my friends, though they only needed them for reading. Molly made sure I had attractive frames, for which I was grateful. Two other memories are stirred by recalling that humiliating eye test: I had drops in my eyes at the clinic, which took ages to wear off. I went to the sweet shop – and cannoned into the iron struts of the blind, being cleaned by the owner, and nearly knocked myself out ... However, the other memory makes me smile. 'The first thing I did after I got *my* glasses,' Molly said, 'Was to go to the Pictures. I couldn't believe how clearly I could see the screen ... I'll take you this Saturday afternoon to the Pav.'

This was an unexpected treat. I didn't have to peer from the front row in the cinema, but sat a few rows back. The film was A.J. Cronin's *Hatter's Castle*, with James Mason menacing in the lead role. There was a seduction scene, and poor Molly kept whispering in my ear, 'Can you see all right?' and me answering, 'Yes Mummy, *perfectly!*'

* * *

The subjects I liked best at school were English Language and Literature with dear Auntie; Art, with Helen who wore fishnet stockings and blue eyeshadow, another unconventional young woman, who was a friend of FF, she who made History come alive; French, with Mademoiselle, who suffered from catarrh and taught us to roll our r's, while looking in a hand mirror – 'gargle, girls, gargle!' she encouraged; Geography – except I never could tell Africa from India, you must admit they are both pear-shaped! I once had top marks for writing about the Eskimos, illustrated with an igloo. However, Mademoiselle made me rub out the doodles I drew in my French book, while FF didn't comment on the picture of Archimedes in his tub, exclaiming, 'Eureka – I haf found it!' although another teacher who saw it, reproved me with 'You rude girl!' I wanted to ask why it was rude, I wasn't aware of the double entendre.

Subjects I did not shine in: Sewing: I could never manage a thimble, and my efforts were always spotted with pinpricks of blood – we spent our first year making our Cookery/Science overalls. (These subjects were not studied until our third term.) I always felt it was unfair that the material, available in patterns of blue or orange, was given out by eye colour – thus, I didn't get my preferred blue, but the less popular orange, as it went with brown eyes. 'Me, too!' said Maggie, but she could at least sew beautifully.

AEC sighed over my feeble efforts in Maths. I could do mental arithmetic all right, but fractions, algebra and geometry were not my cup of tea. I couldn't comprehend why she had chosen two such different subjects in which to specialise. The only time I had a glimmering of hope maths-wise was when the Head Mistress, a lofty being of whom I was very nervous, took us for geometry one day and I suddenly realised that

I knew what she was talking about . . . HM didn't give praise readily, she was the mistress of 'put down', but it was a pity she gave up teaching for administration.

Music lessons: these were taken around the piano in the Assembly Hall. I soon learned to mime when we sang, because again I didn't fit into any category; I was demoted from the soprano section to the altos, and from there, to the 'drones'. I had always enjoyed singing, but now I was too self-conscious to let any sound emerge. We had two girls with wonderful voices: an Irish girl called Marjorie, with black hair and bright blue eyes, who went on to sing at La Scala, Milan, and to join the Bach choir; a tall girl named Eileen rendered Ave Maria as I have never heard it before or since. Sadly she died very young. I can still 'hear' the three songs we practised endlessly: 'Linden Lea' (always performed at prize-givings), 'In Hans' old Mill' (his three black cats, searched the bins for the thieving rats – whisker and claw they crouched in the night, their five eyes shining green and bright . . .). My favourite was 'Old Meg she was a Gipsy' (and lived upon the moors, her bed it was the brown heath turf and her house was out of doors . . .). I wished I could be like Meg and stare 'full hard against the moon'.

Then I discovered Disraeli. FF rushed into the classroom as usual, catching us chattering away. 'Question number one', she cried imperiously, as she spread her books on the table. Desk lids flew up, paper and pencils located, but it wasn't until FF reached Question number three, that we managed to scribble an answer. No one ever received marks of ten out of ten for these quizzes on the previous lesson.

That day we were comparing nineteenth-century prime ministers. Gladstone seemed very dull to me – who wanted a bag named after them? Disraeli, pictured as a young man, with Sephardic ringlets, dressed like a dandy, well, Queen Victoria obviously had a soft spot for him and I could instantly understand why.

When FF asked us to write an essay on a person in history we admired, naturally, I wrote about my hero, Disraeli. I put aside the 'book' I was writing in bed, early in the mornings (still my favourite time for writing) in purple ink.

I looked up D for Disraeli in the encyclopaedia at home. We had a whole set of these hefty tomes, and until now David and I had only looked into a couple of them, mainly because it was a struggle to remove one from the shelf. We'd been fascinated by the diagrams of the human body, where you could 'lift' various organs to reveal further wonders beneath. So that's where the kidneys lurked, was it? And all those coils of 'sausages' were our intestines. These 'pop-ups' were in colour: Disraeli was portrayed in black and white.

I knelt by my chair, with the book opened up at his name. Despite the dry language, I was mesmerised by the life story and achievements of this man.

I wasn't so impressed by his distinguished parliamentary career as the fact that Disraeli was a writer, and much published. His novels were popular, sometimes satirical, but often romantic. Much later I discovered what the encyclopaedia didn't reveal: he was very attractive to women. However, his marriage to an older woman, the widow of a colleague, was known to be very happy. I also was touched by his devotion to his sister, whom he called Sarianna, and the fact that he visited her grave often.

There was just one thing missing in Disraeli's life, in my opinion: he had no children with his devoted wife. I thought he must have been very lonely after she died, even though he became Lord Beaconsfield, and held many distinguished positions, including Prime Minister. So, in my essay I gave him a large family . . .

Long after I left school, and met FF once more, she told me she asked AEC: 'Did you know Disraeli had seven sons?' 'No! Did he?' 'Well, according to the gospel of St Sheila, he did!'

* * *

Writing essays was the highlight of my school life. Looking back over all the years I can see that I didn't quite fit in – I was not sporty, I was 'odd' in lots of ways. I had friends, who were important to me, but I was not a leader. I was sensitive, afraid of being laughed at when I used my imagination. AEC would read a selection of essays aloud to the class, asking, 'Well, who do you think wrote this?' I actually wished she wouldn't read mine, but she always did. I would sit there, feeling miserable, because the moment would surely come, when all heads would turn in my direction and the entire class would cry: 'Sheila!' AEC beamed proudly, but I wished the ground would swallow me up.

CHAPTER 13

Glycerine, Greens and Gristle

I have to admit that after the first excitement wore off, I wasn't too happy that my mother was so absorbed in the baby who'd joined our family. Molly looked after Jenny all day, while her mother was at work. Lily took charge of Jenny in the evenings, bathing and putting her to bed: David's room, which had also been wrecked by the bomb, was freshly decorated, and another single bed, the family cot and chest of drawers installed for Lily and the baby. Which meant that David had to continue to share my room. We had endless arguments around that time about our lack of privacy. 'Shush! You'll wake the baby,' we were admonished by Molly.

I think Jim realised I was feeling as I was, and had a tactful word with Molly, because she encouraged me to join her in cooking at the weekends. Like all mums, she was determined to provide treats for the family, better than bread buns from the bakers.

Low on margarine and lard? Add a tablespoon of liquid paraffin, or glycerine to the cake mix! When chemists realised why there was such a demand for such items, it was decreed sternly that these could only be used for the medicinal purpose for which they were intended. I recall the puzzling wartime addition of Epsom salts to strawberry jam – 'for a moving effect!' joked a popular WI speaker reminiscing in the 60s about wartime economies.

Sweet treats? Pineapple chunks for a party? Dice swede and add pineapple essence. We had a gadget for making cream from the top of the milk but it needed a little precious butter and a spare hour or two to turn the handle. Jam tarts? Bake pastry cases 'blind', when cool, spoon in the jam. None wasted 'boiling over' in the oven. Best of all, when we had a tin of golden syrup, we made toffee, the way Molly had learned from her grandmother. We added peppermint flavouring to half the goo, looped rolls of almost set toffee round the door knob and pulled gently. When the toffee became paler, we pulled one roll for longer, so that we had two colours, the peppermint flavoured one almost white and the other golden brown. We twisted the strands together then snipped the long strips with scissors into humbugs. Much blissful sucking: Molly and Lily were as eager to eat the sweets as we were. There was 'an extra ingredient', a hint of brass from the knob . . . Honeycomb was another favourite, which involved the use of bicarb to make it 'bubble'. Mint 'lumps' were made with powdered milk and a little icing sugar. These were rather sickly if you ate more than one.

We loved Molly's eggless fruit cake. Dried fruit was precious, but we used what we could get, like blocks of pre-war dates, adding flavour with ground ginger and mixed spice. This cake took very little margarine, brought to the boil with a cupful of sugar, flour and water in a saucepan, then a spoonful of bicarb, to enable the cake to rise, and in the oven. 'Weevils!' Molly exclaimed once in dismay over the flour. Possibly some the grocer had produced from under the counter.

Puddings, savoury and sweet – semolina was used for milk puddings, in the absence of rice, likewise tapioca, known as frogs' spawn. The butcher sold kidneys encased in suet. This was removed and grated to add to the flour to make the topping for steak and kidney pud. This 'free' suet was saved for the Christmas pudding, too, along with dried apricots. I am ashamed to admit I once raided the apricot jar and the pudding was not quite so fruity that year . . . When lemons were unavailable, we drizzled baby's orange juice on our pancakes, courtesy of America and Jenny!

Maggie and I were allotted a plot in the school garden for growing vegetables. She was more knowledgeable than me, and I was far too squeamish about worms in her opinion. We had the most success with a packet of red cabbage seeds. In triumph, in due course, I bore home an enormous cabbage. On Saturday, Molly and I pickled the shredded cabbage in vinegar. For supper that evening, we had our usual salad and we couldn't resist it, we opened the first jar and had a liberal helping of red cabbage! Molly wrote to tell Jim of our success and he answered wryly: 'This must be a record, pickling cabbage in the morning and eating it the same day!'

A girl named Mavis with a Welsh accent following evacuation to Wales, grew tender rhubarb. She picked it one lunchtime and put it in her desk and forgot to take it home. It was the day we broke up . . . Over the summer holiday the juice ran all over her books, and the acid almost destroyed them. This was a catastrophe for we often shared text books then. The same girl, I seem to think, put a parcel of fish, intended for the family supper, in her desk, and forgot that too. Following a warm weekend, the fish smelled to high heaven. Mavis was obviously a day-dreamer, too.

Desks were obviously vulnerable. A group of us decided to scrub our desks clean and re-polish them. The varnish disappeared, and so did we, when we heard a teacher approaching . . . I think she was alerted by the smell of lavender polish.

David grew tomatoes in our flower beds, and was very upset when a toddling Jenny picked 'the lovely little green apples'. They didn't even ripen on the windowsill.

We had an unusual plant in our school plot one day. We couldn't pull it up. It had quite a lot to do with school dinners, I'm afraid. . .

* * *

I feared lunchtimes almost as much as double Maths. (On typing this, I noticed that I hit the i key instead of the u in 'lunch' – maybe I should have left it uncorrected for 'linch' (lynch) might be more apt!) I sat with a different set of friends in the dining hall – Marjorie, the singer, Jean, who surely became an artist, Mavis, the rhubarb grower, and me. I had a new role now, encouraged by these girls, who all excelled in games, as a joker – they laughed at my prattle, bless 'em all. However, at the end of the table were the two who completed the six in our group. These were twins, identical, not small and appealing but large and determined. I shall just refer to them as the twins! They actually had cherubic faces and wide, disarming grins. They were favourites of course with Miss GT, as they were athletic. They were also brilliant at maths. Anne liked them; later, she told me that the twins came from a strict religious family. I can think of them more charitably now, knowing that, maybe they were just letting off steam in picking on weaker brethren . . . They were bossy, exuberant teases rather than violent. (They actually went into caring professions when they left school.)

The twins appointed themselves in charge of our group, telling us when we could go up to the hatch and collect our dinner plates. There was a teacher in charge, usually Mademoiselle, who became tetchy when deprived of her cigarettes. 'Zut!' she cried in exasperation. Was that a swear word in French? We gasped in pretended shock. The rest of the staff wisely shunned the school lunches.

We were provided with a pre-lunch nibble – rusks, baked from stale bread. Whether these were to fill us up, or to preserve our teeth, I know not. The twins loved these rusks – they made good missiles, too, if one of the group wasn't paying attention. At first we were provided with jugs of water, but after several spills, these were banned. We also were deprived of the nice white table-cloths, which we had fun with after the meals, taking it in turn to pair up and shake out the crumbs, chanting 'Shadrak, Meshak, Abednego' as we folded the long linen neatly. So we ate on long trestle tables with plates on the bare wood.

The lack of linen revealed the horror beneath. On the trestle supports were bags of gristle, grease spotted. Like escaping prisoners-of-war, we concealed these on our persons when we rushed to freedom in the field, after lunch. Maggie didn't stay to lunch, she had permission (the gates were locked unless you had this) to go home to make sure her mother was all right. Despite the wheezing, little Maggie ran valiantly the short cut through the wooded area of the local park, scared stiff of who might jump out on her, to make a sandwich and a cup of tea for her mother and herself. Her mother, a sweet woman, had her two children late in her thirties, and I suppose she was suffering from depression, perhaps from the menopause. Maggie arrived back all out of puff just before the afternoon bell, to find me waiting one day, with a gristle bag. We buried it hastily in our Victory plot, and thought no more of it, until that giant, tough weed appeared. Maybe it was Jack's beanstalk!

Maggie wasn't the only one who had chores to perform for her mother during the lunch-break. Others, like Mavis, on occasion, had shopping to do, hence the fish in her desk. Chrissie had smaller siblings to collect from the nursery while her mother was at work, to take them to her grandmother to look after. She was a clever girl, but these responsibilities (she was one of eighteen children) meant she couldn't keep up with school work, and like several other nice girls, she left when she was fourteen, just before the school leaving age went up to fifteen. Another girl I really liked, Barbara, left then too, after her father was killed in action. Her mother later remarried a G.I. and Barbara and her sister had two small half-sisters.

Molly told me, 'You're one of the lucky ones having a good meal at midday. Maybe you won't be so fussy when I serve up something you don't like in future!'

The twins didn't worry about whether the food was edible or not. They had enormous appetites. Where all that extra energy came from, I suppose. I had trouble with the tough, dark greens served with nearly every meal. The horrible smell of them boiling on the stove wafted down the corridor to our classroom and made me gag; I found it a real problem trying to force them down. We had to present empty plates for inspection at the end of the meal. We were often served with stringy mutton with lots of fat. Cooked beetroot was another problem for me: diced, purple and tasteless, not a bit like slices of beetroot in vinegar. We were given large mounds of lumpy mashed swede, too, which most of us disliked. When potatoes were in short supply, the creamy looking potato mash, we discovered, was *Pom*, 'instant potato'. A favourite meal was corned-beef pie, until one day we had corned-mutton instead. The cooks did their best with unpromising ingredients. They tried hard with the puddings, although mostly it was semolina in various guises, sometimes coloured pink with cochineal. The best was chocolate pudding and white sauce. One day I was looking forward to this, while trying to munch the greens. A twin offered me a solution. 'Pass your greens to me, I'll eat 'em.' We watched in admiration as she forked them up, chewed and swallowed. 'Now, you've got to give me your pud – I've done you a favour, haven't I?' No disputing that.

Molly was right, I never complained about home cooking again.

* * *

We had bitterly cold winters during the forties. Heating was rationed, too. With a couple of like-minded friends I came in from the cold outside, creeping into the empty classroom to the bliss of sitting on a radiator, warming the atmosphere for the afternoon's lessons. We sat there quietly, absorbed in our reading books. FF patrolling the corridors startled us one day: 'What are you girls doing indoors – you should be outside getting lungfuls of fresh air!'

'My mum thinks I could get pneumonia . . .' one of us said.

'Rubbish! Don't be a ninny – move around, chase a ball, you'll soon warm up, and get off that radiator at once, you'll get piles!'

I was nudged, being urged to speak up. '*You* sit on it during lessons,' I dared to say.

She had an answer for that. 'I speak from painful experience – *I've* got them!' She couldn't resist a grin. Nor could we.

On another occasion, FF came into the classroom one day, and we almost didn't recognise her. She'd had a disastrous perm – a shame, because she had such pretty wavy hair framing her attractive face. She was in a mood, not surprising, as she obviously couldn't get a comb through such an explosion of hair.

'What are you girls staring at? Go on, don't stop – I know I look a fright . . .' She paused, seeing our shocked faces. Suddenly she was laughing and we joined in with relief. What a sport she was. We made up romantic stories about her – surely she must have had a young man at one time, had he been killed in the war? She was politically minded – she'd told us about the Commonwealth party of which she was a member. Jim joked, 'Are you sure it isn't the Communist party?' 'Of course not, dad,' I said indignantly. Now I know that her mother was widowed, and left with two little girls to bring up on her own. Our FF had a fine intellect, she was given her chance to go to college. I imagine she looked after her mother after her sister married, once she became a teacher. Long after I left school I received letters from her: she was active in retirement, one message asked me to write to my local MP and demand the release of Nelson Mandela. She admired Frank Field – 'I don't always agree with his politics, but he is a good, fair man.'

Our secret huddles in the classroom on cold days were abruptly curtailed. The Bookworms were ambushed by the twins – my protests were muffled by parcel tape, but suddenly we became aware that the Head was in our midst. She demanded, 'Who did this to you?' I couldn't split on them. She hauled me off to her study for a lecture and dished out a hundred lines – 'hand them to me before you go home this evening.'

There was barely ten minutes to go before the bell. Miserably, I began to write. Tears welled in my eyes, it wasn't fair. A hand touched my shoulder, the twins stood there, looking at me. 'We'll help you,' they offered. We crowded on to my desk seat. They were experts in writing lines and had even tried tying two pens together to write two lines at a time. This time they just copied my handwriting and even though the Head's keen eye probably spotted the difference, she didn't comment, except for 'I hope you have learned your lesson.'

I certainly had, but best of all, the twins, if not my best friends, didn't bother me anymore. I had earned their respect.

CHAPTER 14

Sealing Wax and Other Crafts

The Motts next door had been home for some time now. They had two children, too. Paula was a year older than me and attending the school I had not chosen. Perhaps this was just as well, for although Paula and I played together from an early age, we didn't have a lot in common. She had her school friends, I had mine. Her brother was much younger and still at primary school. In black and white snaps of the pre-war years, she wears the bridal veil (a net curtain) and carries the bunch of flowers, David is the bashful 'bridegroom', I am the bridesmaid, wearing wellington boots, and Paula's little brother is escaping the line-up in the Mott's garden in his pedal car. Paula was ever the one in charge of our little group.

Paula was considered to be more responsible than me, it was actually because she was capable of catching the bus somewhere and alighting at the right stop. I retained a short-sighted view on most things unless they were close-up, despite the new glasses. Paula and I went to the Applegarth dancing classes together, and she, being taller, was my partner in the polka, which was our set piece. I got to wear the ballet dress which would have fitted her better, and she had to bow while I made a wobbly curtsey. I expect she felt she was saddled with me, but she was always polite and we never argued.

Our family always attended the local church both at home and in the country, but now we had no vicar in charge, just a succession of young curates, all awaiting call-up papers. David was in the choir, which made up most of the congregation. We had Children's Church with the Rev. Wilmshurst, who heard that I had been a regular reader in church since I was seven, and encouraged me to climb into the pulpit to read the lesson to the children. Then he asked me if I would be responsible for the CC log book. I tackled this with great enthusiasm, and wrote a glowing account of the Rev.'s wise words. I'm afraid I also described him as 'very handsome'. I should have heeded my dad's opinion: 'Sheila, you let your pen run away with you!' I guess. The Rev. grinned when he read my piece, but I was the one who blushed when asked to read it aloud to the other youngsters the next Sunday. When Rev. W departed, the CC folded, the choir continued, but that was all.

Paula, like Anne, went to the Methodist church. There was always a packed congregation, lots of happy singing and music. 'Why don't you come to chapel with me,' Anne suggested, 'All the young people sit in the gallery – no one tells you to be quiet, and we can sing as loud as we like.'

Anne had been going to chapel on her own, whereas Paula went with her family. I decided to give it a try and Molly agreed, 'So long as you go to church, I don't mind which one.' David stuck with the choir, they had a short service at the old church when they met up. 'We sent toffees to each other in the collection plate.' That sounded tempting, but the choir was boys only.

I loved the atmosphere in the chapel gallery and the lusty hymn singing. They also had serious musical events, like Handel's *Messiah* to which folk flocked.

It was Paula who introduced me to the Guild, the Methodist youth club. There were so many activities on offer, it was hard to choose, but I decided to take up a new handicraft which involved sealing wax . . . I also joined the drama, which I thoroughly enjoyed. Our coach had been a professional actress and she taught us how to project our voices without a microphone (I've been able to do this ever since) and, in particular, I learned how to do a stage 'fall' without breaking any bones! She also encouraged me to sing and I regained my confidence in that respect.

Molly wasn't too sure about the sealing wax – this involved filling a little lamp with methylated spirit (which Paula said tasted quite nice!), lighting a wick, and holding the end of a stick of sealing wax in the flame . . . Highly dangerous, if hot wax dripped on your person. We cut out shapes from cardboard and made patterns from blobs of coloured wax. Then we pressed a little sharp tool (some of us used a manicure file) on the soft blob to mark petals or leaves – the design was often a rose, or other flower. A safety pin glued on the back of the cardboard, and you had a brooch. Molly wouldn't let me practise at home, with little Jenny around, because of the unguarded flame from the lamp, but when I went round to Paula's, her mother had no qualms, because it was a quiet, sitting at the table activity, even though Mrs Mott was very house-proud and her children had to play with their toys in a pair of sheds, built by kindly Mr Mott, which were linked together by a roof over the entrance from the alleyway behind, so known as 'Peking'. I had a peek inside one of the sheds once: there was a huge Georgian dolls' house, fitted out with tiny furniture and figures. I wasn't allowed to touch, but was invited to watch while Paula changed a room around.

Paula had inherited two French dolls from her grandmother, exquisitely dressed, with real hair wigs. The dolls had porcelain faces with eyes which opened and shut, and rubber bodies, which surprised me. They smelled faintly of hot-water bottles. Again, I longed to handle one of these but had to wait while Paula brushed their hair into a new style. All I had was my old cherished teddy, Timothy Tapps, and he was almost bald after David shaved him with Jim's razor when he was about eight, assuring me, 'TT's fur will grow again . . .' Secretly, I thought I was luckier than Paula because we had a dog which could do tricks, like walking on her hind legs.

Mrs Mott's bedroom, in which we poked around when Mrs Mott thought we were playing in Paula's room, was full of 1920s fashions kept from when Mrs M was a 'bright young thing'. Once Paula squirted some ancient perfume at me from a cut-glass bottle with a perished rubber ball: Mrs Mott sniffed the air suspiciously and gave me a look. She and Molly were not on Christian name terms until they were over seventy, and both widows.

* * *

I soon had a stockpile of brooches for Christmas presents. It made a change from the doyley holders (two doyleys in a parchment pocket: as we painted the doyleys, I shouldn't think the aunts fancied them under their cakes). I had made too many writing cases from parchment, too, punching holes to hold the sides together, with a figure in a poke bonnet (no face needed) on the front. We split a pad of Basildon Bond paper, and added four envelopes. The Christmas before the sealing wax I asked Molly, 'Can I have some pieces of the firewood?' She agreed, but then wished she hadn't, for I painted little scenes on the wood with my new oil paints, and these remained so tacky to the touch, they were never given away.

David, meanwhile, continued with the manufacture of plastic wire bracelets. 'Much safer than sealing wax,' Molly advised me, but

I couldn't pull the wire taut enough. The wire came in 'a tangle' from the electricity shop, in bright colours, and the bracelets were appreciated by our female relatives.

Maggie was a whizz at knitting and crochet, and she succeeded in teaching me not to do moss stitch instead of ribbing, and how to pick up dropped stitches, whereas my mother and aunt had given up on me.

Maggie invited me round to her house, which was very old and interesting – they had a gramophone with a horn, we put on records and danced about while clicking our needles and reciting 'Knit one, purl one, slip one, pass slipped stitch over . . .'

Her sweet mother made us cocoa, no milk and no sugar, 'good for you,' she said. Maggie's dad sang snatches of opera – he greeted me once at the door with a burst of 'Your tiny hand is frozen . . .' They were eccentric, and Maggie has inherited that charm. They made light of minor disasters – when rain came through their grandma's bedroom ceiling, the old lady called for an umbrella and sat up in bed to read the paper.

There was also a long garden, where you could pretend to be in the jungle, and rabbits in hutches. Maggie and her little sister Val cried when their pets ended up in the pot, and I felt for them. It was almost like being back in the country, making daisy chains and picking soft fruit from the currant bushes.

It was a strange time, the lull before the storm – getting back to more or less normality on the home front, at least as far as school was concerned, but listening on the wireless to news of the war raging in different parts of the world. We never missed *Children's Hour* and the classic serials. The *Daily Mirror*, Molly and Lily's choice, while Jim was away – when he was home he exclaimed: 'They've sent the wrong paper!' – of that time was very sparse, like all the papers, but the cartoons still kept going, though Jane became more saucy than she was pre-war. We saw newsreels in the Pav, but they were quite upbeat, even when showing weary soldiers in tin hats, smoking as they marched. We knew all the rousing songs and errand boys on bikes still whistled.

I went with Paula to a Knitting Squares meeting. We were the only young ones there. We were given small balls of wool, needles, told to cast on twenty stitches, and to knit squares for blankets – these were for use in air-raid shelters. We missed out on an Anderson shelter in the garden at the beginning of the war, when we were away in Suffolk, but now we had an indoor shelter, a Morrison, which took up most of our front room. It was steel, as I recall, and it made a good den for children.

Anne was busy with other sorts of craft at home, unknown to her mother, who was known as Jem, short for Jemima. She was an only child, like so many of our generation, and her parents were ambitious for their clever daughter. Anne came to school one day with little bags containing delicious, fizzy sherbet. She soon sold out at three pence a bag. We dipped into our bags, blissfully sucking our fingers. Like David's trade in white mice, the powers that be found out and stopped the selling of these in the classroom. I begged for the secret of how to make it. 'Well,' she said, 'it all depends if your mum takes Andrews Liver Salts. No other kind will do. Mix with sugar . . . Simple, eh?' (Or were there other ingredients, if so, she didn't let on to me.) Jem wondered why the Andrews tin was empty, that was another snag. Anne went on, 'I shall have to think of something else . . .' I shouldn't be surprised if this made her determined to be a scientist. She eventually became a university don, which didn't surprise her friends.

Wartime children were encouraged to keep busy. We were always making something – mostly recycling things, as we do today once more. One day, we were told that a supply of new wool could be bought at school, no coupons, but only to dedicated knitters. Molly was all for it. 'You can make a school jumper,' she suggested. I made a face, I didn't want to knit in navy-blue wool.

AEC unpacked a large box in front of us. It was full of skeins of soft, brightly coloured wool, with evocative names – Spindleberry Pink, Coronation Gold, Sapphire Blue were my favourites. We were given simple patterns to knit jerseys with raglan sleeves. It was stipulated that these garments were for our own use.

I rushed home that night with my bag of wool, and before we had tea, Molly and I wound the first skein into a nice, fat ball. Well, she wound, and I held my arms wide with the skein looped over my wrists. She checked the pattern. 'Number twelve needles for the ribbing, then number nines. Bone or steel needles?' I chose the bone, though there was always the danger of them snapping mid-row when the knitting grew longer and heavier, but they were nicer, more pliable, to knit with than the rigid steel. I finished the rib before I went to bed that first knitting night. It stopped me from playing with the spills which we poked into the fire when Molly wasn't looking and whirled in our hands like sparklers.

I heard Molly say to Lily, 'Well, that was six shillings well spent . . .' I was proud that I was now an accomplished knitter. Thank you,

Maggie, for all your encouragement! My only regret is I never followed suit with sewing, but then I married John, who was quite capable of sewing on his buttons (and mine), and despite my ineptitude in that respect, our daughters (and sons) are all handy with a needle and thread (and sewing machine).

The sealing wax brooches were becoming more sophisticated, too. We discovered glitter wax. This sparkled, as the name suggested. At Christmas our designs were holly and berries, mistletoe sprigs, the little blobs of red and white were very effective. We made all our Christmas cards and calendars. We made dress-dollies, small cardboard figures, and designed tiny clothes for them. I also knitted a woolly hat and mitts in red with white bobbles so that Jenny would look like a mini-Santa on Christmas Day.

Of course, I never stopped reading and writing my stories – or dreaming . . . I also moved up to third place, next to Paula, in the tap-dancing troupe. We were booked for concerts in church halls, and even, though Molly would have disapproved had she been present, the local working men's club. Our turns didn't stop the throwing of darts or the swilling of beer. I didn't mind we weren't paid, like David was for singing in the choir at weddings and funerals, because I got to wear a saucy pill-box hat and a red plastic costume, which you had to peel off at the end of the performance.

CHAPTER 15

Dodging the Doodlebugs

The war was not over yet, even though we were now enjoying uninterrupted schooling. In the freezing January of 1944, Maggie, Anne and I queued outside a local sweet shop after school. The kindly, enterprising proprietors had hit on a winner: hot blackcurrant drinks. At 3d. a beaker, we were warmed up for the trudge home. The drink was fruity and delicious.

Although the evidence of the Battle of Britain was still all around us, we were not apprehensive like the adults, for we were confident the Allies would win the war. We listened to Vera Lynn singing 'When the Lights Go On Again All Over the World', on the wireless, to Churchill's inspiring speeches, to *Workers' Playtime*, when we were having a day off school, and pups and kittens were named Monty after the General, who wore a beret, not unlike the majority of the juniors, which included me, in our school. Pudding basin velour was, thankfully, out of favour, with wartime shortages.

The Mini-Blitz which began on 3rd February, took the general public by surprise. There were a number of night bombing raids on London. The ominous sound of the siren sent us scurrying to our shelter in the front room. Molly and Lily lugged the double mattress downstairs and manoeuvred it inside the steel cage.

Our shelter was intended for a family of four. There were now six of us, when Jim was with us. He was about to transfer from Bath to Harrow 'for the duration of the war', which meant he would be able to live at home, although now he had given up the car he faced a lot of travelling each day to work. He was backwards and forwards at the moment, but as usual he didn't discuss his work. Once or twice a friend came with him, a nice chap in his forties, a bachelor, who obviously took a shine to Lily and Jenny. I guess Molly and Jim were doing a spot of matchmaking.

When we were all in the Morrison at the same time, we had to lie in a line across the width, rather than down the length of the structure. This was all right for the children, but the three adults wiggled their protruding feet ruefully, and hoped they'd have time to draw their knees up if disaster struck. Lily and I had Jenny between us, Molly was in the middle and David slept at the end, next to his dad. The only advantage of being squeezed together like this was the shared warmth.

I said 'sleep' but this was very difficult. The boom of the guns, the relentless roar of the enemy planes – our torches flickered feebly as we attempted to read. It was reassuring to hear Jim talking to Molly, we didn't feel so fearful when he was with us. Lily didn't say much, she was a quiet girl and we were all fond of her. She cuddled her baby close and if Jenny cried, we sang nursery rhymes to lull her back to sleep.

After the *All Clear* we slept for a while, then returned to the daily routine. The bombing appeared to be confined to night-time. David picked up shrapnel on his way to catch the school bus. Eventually he had a suitcase full. We imagined it would be worth a fortune one day . . . I walked to school as usual. The shelter there was opened and aired, and ready for emergencies, but I only recall a couple of false alarms. We carried our gas masks as well as our bulging satchels, but our Iron Rations had been consumed in 1940.

Paula and I had what we thought was a good idea. We collected cigarette butts out of the gutter and painstakingly, and covertly, of course, removed the tobacco. When we had quite a wad, we left it to soak (and hopefully lose any germs) in the Motts water butt. Her father discovered it, and our parents gravely pointed out our foolishness. 'What did you intend to do with it?' asked Mrs Mott. We responded truthfully: 'Send it to the forces!' I think they were so relieved we hadn't intended to re-roll and smoke it, no more was said. I shudder still when I think how Paula and I trailed behind a filthy old man and snatched up his smouldering cigarette end! I hope we washed our hands well.

The climax of the Mini Blitz came on 23rd February, although the terror didn't end until 24th March, 1944: thirty-two boroughs reported incidents, including seventy-two people killed in a block of flats in the King's Road, Chelsea, when a direct hit was recorded.

In all there were one hundred and sixty fatalities and serious injuries that night. More than one thousand Londoners lost their lives during the Mini Blitz. Was this the final sting in the enemy 'tail'?

* * *

There was euphoria when D-day came at last on 6th June. The head-lines in the *Mirror* took up the whole front page. The entire school cheered in Assembly. 'Wonderful news!' beamed the Head. We sang 'He Who Would Valiant Be – Let Him Come Hither!' Our pianist almost fell off her stool in her excitement at our fervour.

We were not aware then, of course, of the background to this his-toric event. We, and that probably includes most of the adult popula-tion who were not directly involved, only knew what we heard from the wireless, read in the carefully edited newspaper articles or viewed in the newsreels in the cinema. We knew nothing of code-breaking, or secret intelligence, or the massive preparations taking place for the Normandy landings. We were unaware of the gathering and special training of Allied troops in remote places in our island. We didn't know that the enemy had been fed false information and believed that the landings would be around the Pas de Calais where they had most reserves, while their troops were massed near Paris.

We did know that the Russians were fighting back and that the German Army was in retreat, and we were told that the Allies had gained air superiority over western Europe. We learned that General Eisenhower, soon known to us all as 'Ike', was now the Supreme Allied Commander.

I can only relate how it seemed to me, as a twelve-year-old, at the time. John, who is two years older than me, realised what was hap-pening more than I did. The boys at his school talked of spies and col-laborators – of becoming old enough to join up, if the war lasted long enough . . . There was actually a reason for the rumours. The headmas-ter of the school, who had been evacuated with many of his pupils at the outbreak of war, was a compiler of crosswords in the *Telegraph*. Just before D-Day he incorporated several of the code names used in the battle, like *Omaha* and *Utah*. Some of the boys at the school, it was said later, had 'fraternised' with G.I.s who were based nearby. The headmaster must have listened to their prattle and subconsciously remembered those names.

John, who'd joined the old-established school in Streatham, on his family's return from Scotland, where his father was involved with managing building runways for Lancaster bombers, was unaware of this at the time, or that the headmaster, whom he hadn't met then, was under suspicion. (John's and his sisters' memories of Scotland during the forties, are woven into my novel *The Spirit of Millie Mae*, later retitled *The Girl by the Sea*. The character of Barney is based on John.)

The summer of 1944 was an indifferent one – cold, wet and windy, but the events in June commenced when there was a sudden break in the stormy conditions. British and American airborne divisions landed behind the beaches before dawn, and at first light, British, Canadian and American troops moved on to the beach code-named *Utah*, where the opposition were unable to stop their advance to contact the airborne divisions. The Americans were not so fortunate on *Omaha*, the other landing area, where they met a fierce barrage.

It was an exciting, if anxious time for those 'back home'. However, a new period of terror was about to begin for Londoners, who had already suffered and survived so much.

* * *

Before dawn on 13th June, 1944, the first V1, a small unmanned robot plane, a flying bomb, launched from Belgium, plummeted down and exploded in the capital. The railway bridge across Grove Road in Hackney was breached. This was a vital connection with Liverpool Street Station to East Anglia for the Great Eastern Railway.

From June until September, 1944, more than 10,000 doodlebugs (sometimes called 'buzz bombs', because of the noise they made) landed in Britain overall, but the main target was London. Our suburb was in the 'pathway' from the coast. Croydon became known as 'Bomb Alley'.

Londoners carried on despite spending sleepless nights 'under the stairs'. Milkmen and postmen climbed over rubble as they had during the Blitz, to deliver milk and letters.

In our shelter in the front room, a little voice piped up: 'Them damn doodle-buggers!' For a moment there was a shocked silence: where on earth had young Jenny heard those words? Swearing was taboo in our house. Then, if the shelter hadn't been of such rigid construction, it would have rocked with our laughter.

Lily went to the factory in the morning, and Molly poked the sheets in the steaming copper in the kitchen. Jenny 'read' to Dinkie the dog. David and I went our separate ways to school. I'm sure Molly was fearful for our safety, for the doodlebugs arrived 'out of the blue' at any time, day or night, but we were expected to attend classes, if possible.

The R.A.F. didn't let us down. When the doodlebugs arrived our side of the Channel, the pilots of Spitfire, Mosquito and Mustang planes were waiting to tip the glider wings and to turn them back, while those which got through were bombarded by anti-aircraft guns.

I was wending my way along the high street, unaccompanied, when I became aware of the now-familiar buzz. The doodlebugs flew low at around 350 miles per hour and were clearly visible, if you looked up. I quickened my pace, but it appeared to be following me – in mounting panic I looked vainly for shelter. The shops were still shuttered, no one was about. Then the buzz abruptly 'cut out' – the doodlebug was diving. I flung myself down on the pavement, hands over my ears. If I hear the explosion, I told myself, it hasn't landed here. A few moments later came the great blast. Fearfully, I got up on my knees and opened my eyes. Way up the road I saw a crater, with smoke and flames. I heard the fire engine bell, and people were already gathered with stirrup pumps.

Shaking all over, I stumbled on to school. 'Why didn't you come home?' Molly asked me that evening.

'I don't know,' I said.

I can't remember if the teachers questioned me about my dishevelled appearance. The rest of that day, until I somehow managed to get home, is a blank.

* * *

I'm not sure if school broke up early for the summer holidays because of the doodlebug menace, or if our parents decided to send David and I back to Suffolk to our ever-welcoming family there for a break.

Molly decided not to join us there for a time, because Jim was now working in Harrow full-time. She also felt responsible for Lily and Jenny. Lily couldn't leave the factory and she was needed to look after Jenny all day.

David and I took Dinkie with us, and were old enough now to help with carrying our luggage. We stood on Liverpool Street Station, the train came alongside, and even as doors opened, the siren wailed. Porters ran up and down the platform slamming doors and making sure windows were closed. We didn't have time to say goodbye properly to Jim. Distressed, we waved frantically at him from the corridor of the train, not having yet found seats.

Even through all the station cacophony we heard the ominous sound of the doodlebug, right overhead.

'Dad!' we shouted, even though we realised he couldn't hear us. We spotted him hurrying away among a crowd of people, then they all disappeared into a waiting room. The buzz stopped abruptly. We heard the explosion, as the train gathered steam.

David held onto my arm, and I clutched the dog's lead. 'It's all right,' he tried to convince me, 'come on, they've made room for us in the carriage.' He paused then added unsteadily, 'It went over the station, I'm sure . . .'

Our uncle met us at the other end. We climbed aboard his lorry and were soon back at the cottage to a warm welcome from Dolly, Auntie Rum, Jassy, now six years old, and her baby brother, red-haired like his mother and sister.

Telegrams were sent between Suffolk and Surrey. Ours said simply, '*Arrived safely, love to you all*' and Molly's read, '*Dad all right, love from us. Mum.*'

* * *

Come September, we travelled back home. The VI threat had dwindled, but shortly there was another horror to contend with, the V2. This was a ballistic missile, aimed mainly at London during the autumn and winter of 1944. The first V2 fell in Greenwich, the second in Epping. They travelled faster than the speed of sound, so there was no warning: survivors were only aware of a sonic boom after the crash. Half the V2s failed to reach the capital, but caused havoc in the suburbs. South and East London took the brunt of the new wave of bombing.

We went to school, we went to work, we spent our days at school often in the shelter, and at night we slept in the Morrison. Life had to go on, you see. We stoutly believed that the end of the war was in sight.

CHAPTER 16

All Those Begats and Shakespeare Too

When our school had an influx of pupils, due to the return of the evacuees, for a term or two our class moved temporarily to the science lab. This was designated our form room; we met there for registration with AEC and had the first lesson of the day with her there after Assembly, then moved around the school to vacant classrooms, when the usual occupants were elsewhere, like the art room, domestic science block or gym. I usually just followed on the end of the crocodile, confident I would then arrive at the right place at the right time.

The mention of *Pilgrim's Progress* evokes the smell of the lab, of substances used in experiments. We moved aside the Bunsen burners and test tubes, on slab like tables which bore the marks of spills and burns, and opened our books.

I needed to pay attention, not to turn the pages too far ahead while AEC read aloud to us, because it was very likely that she would pause, then ask: 'Who would like to read the next chapter to us?' When no immediate response was forthcoming, she would say brightly: 'Sheila?'

Later, there was an unexpected reprieve for those who were keener on sport than religious instruction. For some time in the gym we had been learning to swim – no water in sight: it was called Land Drill. I actually enjoyed this and lying on my front on a form, I performed a credible breast stroke. Miss GT was so impressed she called the rest of the gymnasts over to watch me in action.

Molly gave me the written permission needed to join a weekly swimming class at the Municipal Baths. These had recently reopened, and local schools were keen to take advantage of this out-of-school activity.

The water was chilly, the smell of chlorine was powerful, there was much jostling in the changing rooms. The noise was horrific, the tiles slippery and we were told we would never make swimmers if we couldn't duck our heads underwater, as we shivered in the shallow end. Miss GT pounded up and down calling encouragement, 'Hold your noses, you duffers!' but I failed dismally to go underwater even for a few seconds. I never got a chance to show off my breast stroke; anyway, I daren't take my feet off the bottom of the bath, and I couldn't believe the assurance, 'You'll float!'

How I wished I was back among the Bunsen burners and reading aloud.

In the end I was unexpectedly released from purgatory and shame when the swimmers (and one non-swimmer) were lined up ready to leave the baths one morning. We were waiting for Miss GT to join us and blow her whistle for the 'Off'.

'Look!' pointed one of the twins (who were of course already powerful swimmers). We crowded to the edge of the baths to watch a diver on the springboard. A solitary male among all the adolescent girls present! He was, we learned later, a soldier on leave, a keen swimmer.

I was so entranced by this performance, I failed to notice that the rest of our team had melted away at the sound of the whistle ... A hand gripped my shoulder. I was summarily banned from the swimming lessons, but I can't say I was sorry. AEC was sympathetic and listened to my version of events. I was back with the *Pilgrim's Progress* and although I have always regretted not being able to swim, I was much happier. Even though I had to put up with a painful verruca on the ball of my foot, which I 'caught' at the swimming baths!

We were back in a regular classroom when we read the bible from beginning to end. I was apparently the only one interested in reading aloud in R.E. I projected my voice to good effect: All those 'begats' – I soon learned that if you could make dull phrases sound interesting, the class would listen. I wasn't really aware of it then, but I had a captive audience, and have been a performer, ever since.

I expect some of my classmates considered I was becoming a show-off, but looking back, I was only hoping to be liked, while masking the fact I actually felt inadequate beside confident, popular Big Girls who excelled at sport and whom the rest of us admired. I'm sure I was not alone in this.

There were some very nice, upright girls in our class. Marion and Marian, they spelled their name slightly differently, were admired by their fellows and teachers alike. They were 'girls to be trusted', and Marion with an 'o' was my house captain. I tried hard not to let Marion and the green team down. When I was feeling poorly one day and was too bilious to eat my lunch, Marion found me in the cloakroom, and helped me clean myself up. Then she washed her comb under the tap, and gently tidied my hair. I felt much better after her ministrations. Marian was extremely artistic; she still produces beautiful paintings of plants and flowers. These days, she sets up her easel on her balcony overlooking the sea.

*   *   *

Years after we left school, I met them both, along with other school friends, at an Old Girls' reunion organised by Di, who like me became a writer; by then, she was President of the Romantic Novelists Association, a post she still admirably fills. Anne was there too, recently retired from an illustrious career, and now working tirelessly in her local community. It was good to see Eileen and Vivien after so many years: Eileen had possessed a lovely evening dress, given to her by a glamorous aunt, and I had not been the only one to borrow it for a formal dinner and dance when we were seventeen or eighteen! Vivien had a very special place in AEC's affections, having survived a serious accident when we were still juniors at the school. It was great to see her, tall and beautiful, fit and well. I wished Maggie had been there, but like some others she felt too much time had elapsed.

Di produced our final-year school photograph. She was now sophisticated and glamorous, a top editor with a prominent publisher, but there we both were, sixteen, going on seventeen, like the song, side by side in the front row, looking bashful. I wear my (old) school tie. As I failed to knot it correctly when I was eleven, Molly inserted elastic at the back, so I could slip it easily over my head after gym. She could always find a solution to problems, my mum. She'd done the same with my Brownie scarf when I couldn't tie a reef knot, though I was only seven then.

I recognised Marion and Marian right away. They had lived up to their early promise and it was good to see them again. All of us who met that day had experienced adversity in one way or another, but come through, the stronger for it. FF joined us at several of these meetings, and she remarked that we must have been a 'good vintage year' because so many of us had succeeded in life. We wondered what had happened to some of the less conventional girls – Rosemary, for instance, who had the exotic (then) middle name of Scarlett, and who sent AEC a card from Egypt, a year after she left our class . . .

I was never monitor material – though I was made responsible for a girl who was prescribed a daily dose of cod liver oil and malt following our first Medical. She tried hard but she just couldn't swallow the required tablespoonful. I was supposed to encourage her to open her mouth and see that it all went down her throat. She cried so much at her first attempt, 'I can't do it! I just can't! I'll bring it all up again!', that I offered nobly (because I disliked it, too) to take the dose for her. We were alone in the Domestic Science kitchen, where the large jar was kept in a cupboard. I took a deep breath and did the deed. I was literally stuck with this thereafter, and the girl who needed the supplement was duly pronounced, 'Much improved.' I don't think she felt guilty, but I certainly did.

I was once called a monitor – by the Head, no less. I'd been spotted whispering to Maggie during a lesson, and was told to stand outside in the corridor 'until you can control yourself.' This was a mild punishment, but the chatterer, of course, felt conspicuous, and apprehensive of who might pass by . . .

That particular afternoon, I heard footsteps and voices in the corridor which led off the one where I stood. I recognised the Head's bell-like tones. In a panic, because I could tell they were headed my way, I nipped into the adjacent store. Would I be spotted? I bent over a pile of text books, as if I had just put them down.

The Head stood in the doorway, after flicking on the switch. I hadn't thought to turn the light on. She spoke to the accompanying school inspectors: 'And this is one of our young monitors . . .' I looked up and saw the glint in her eye. She knew, and I knew, I was nothing of the sort. She was human, after all!

Miss C was a handsome woman, with auburn hair wound round her head, not plaited, but twisted. She was the niece of the original head mistress, and was proud to be carrying on the family tradition. She would point out the names on the impressive Honours board, in the Assembly hall. She knew what these special girls had achieved in later life. Among them was 'dear Peggy Ashcroft, who is a famous actress.' I wished Peggy was still my age and at the school, for I would have loved to know her.

Whenever I came face to face with Miss C, my knees turned to jelly. She knew the name of every girl in the school. She always managed to temper praise with a rebuke in my experience. Many years later I received a letter from her, after she read of a writing achievement. 'You have a gift, I do hope you use it, Sheila.' Oh, I try, Miss C, I do. Thank you for remembering me. I shall never forget you.

* * *

Only once did we perform Shakespeare on stage – Anne was producer, and she cast me as Henry V's Queen. I had to tell her I didn't feel I looked the part. I could project my voice yes, but I didn't well, have the figure for it. In a couple of years that would change, but then I felt I would be underdeveloped forever . . . Rosemary, she who went off to Egypt and was never heard of again (by us anyway), stepped into my shoes. I took on several roles that others spurned as too small. I was in my element, playing old and young, male and female, and employing different voices. Unfortunately, the play, which was performed after school hours, was far too long, and some of the audience sneaked out before we reached the final act. Anne had put her all into the production, and the cast felt for her, and her disappointment.

Palgrave's Golden Treasury: those wonderful poems have remained in my memory always. Like most of my friends, and my husband, I often quote much-loved lines. Keats and Shelley were my favourite poets.

Some of the books we studied – we began with *The Water Babies* – and learned the message behind it, the exploitation of child labour. *Jane Eyre, Pride and Prejudice*, and *The Thirty-nine Steps*, all the classics were enjoyed in turn, due to AEC's presentation and skilful interpretation. I found Sir Walter Scott somewhat indigestible – the plots were good, the scenery marvellous, but they were too wordy. I admit to skipping some of this author's pages, not compulsively turning them . . . *Lorna Doone* caught my imagination *Travels with a Donkey*, Robert Louis Stevenson, now there was a story-spinner after my own heart. I didn't really relate to Dickens during my school days, but when I saw the cinema versions (often with John Mills) and later enjoyed the serialisations on TV, I went back to the books, which pleased my father, for Dickens was his favourite author.

As for William Shakespeare – we read aloud one of his plays in class each term – I was in my element, thanks to AEC casting me, as Bottom, Shylock (much rubbing of hands and oily tones) and Lady Macbeth! Ditto the wringing of hands but with a Scottish accent. In the latter, when we reached the more eloquent speeches, AEC would invariably say: 'We'll leave out the next two pages, I think . . .' But I did get in 'Out damned spot' and gave it my all. Naturally, the forbidden pages were read with much interest by the rest of the class!

A few years later I went with John to Theatre in the Round and saw the great Bernard Miles in the title role. We discovered that we had both been taken by our schools to see the film *Henry V* with Laurence Olivier – we may even have been in the audience at the same time, but we didn't meet then . . .

A highlight of those middle school years was the Elizabethan Week – in which every single pupil was involved. Our class chose to do the art work. Maggie made tiny boots and shoes with scraps of leather – I do hope these are preserved somewhere. Others made costumes. Doublet and hose, paper ruffs. Who made the lovely miniature four-poster bed? With linen and bedspread, too. Wisely, I opted to illustrate the Globe Theatre. Well, it was a pen and ink drawing, but I gave it a 'wash' of pale green. Visitors were invited at the end of the week to view the displays – all subjects were covered, like maths, science and sport. This event was a great success and much reported in the local press.

I like to think that William Shakespeare would have approved. I'm not so sure about Queen Elizabeth the First. She had an aloof expression in her portrait, whereas Sir Walter Raleigh had a twinkle in his eye . . . Our bright young art teacher was leaving us, for pastures new – an art college. Some of us, including me, were asked if we would like to transfer there with her. I rushed home to tell Molly the exciting news. 'Certainly not!' she cried. 'You can do all the drawing you like at home – you've got exams to pass, my girl!'

I consoled myself with the thought that I would illustrate my books myself, in the future. Alas, no one has ever suggested that I should. However, two of our daughters are artists – and teachers – though I think their talent in that respect comes from their father, rather than me. Some of the grandchildren have inherited this gene too, in fact all our children are creative in one way or another. As for writing, I have hopes!

CHAPTER 17

Dancing in the Street

How can I describe the relief and sheer exuberance of VE Day, which was celebrated on 8th May, 1945? The *Mirror* proclaimed: 'It's Over in the West!' followed by: 'London has Joy Night.' Winston Churchill broadcast to the nation from No. 10. Huge crowds gathered outside Buckingham Palace and cheered the Royal Family when they appeared on the balcony. The King's speech was relayed to the crowd.

We heard that effigies of Hitler burned on bonfires, that long-hoarded fireworks exploded all over the country, maybe there were a few damp squibs, but who cared? In our own high street, there was dancing ... the trams were at a standstill. Singing, too – some of it sentimental but some ribald. '*Show me the way to go home*,' was traditional, but '*Roll Me Over in the Clover*,' I knew was rude. The church bells pealed and we found standing room only when we went along to the special thanksgiving service at midnight. Lights blazed everywhere, in homes and shopping parades.

I wrote about this time in *The Family from Number Five*, which was later retitled *A Winter Hope*. It was based on personal experience – but because of my own mixed emotions at the time, I was thirteen, remember, and easily embarrassed by adults when they behaved like adolescents themselves. It is better, I think, to quote from my story:

> *Glory and Don walked along together. She was well aware of his sidelong glances. She was pleased she was wearing the new blue skirt Mirry (her mum) had finished this morning, a dirndl, like Miss Fizzbang's, a style her mum agreed was economical with*

material. It went well with the Hungarian blouse Grandma had brought home in triumph from a jumble sale – fine muslin, brightly embroidered yoke, drawstring neck and short, puffed sleeves. A bit see-through her mum said doubtfully, so she must hitch up the straps of her petticoat to conceal her cleavage. She was proudest of her Clarks sandals: with cross over straps in brown leather leaving her toes bare: another sixpenny jumble prize. She still wore her hair short, the bubble cut was becoming popular now, so she was ahead of fashion.

The Spa gardens were crowded with people: children played hide-and-seek around the rose bushes and the men queued patiently for drinks. Junie eyed the local boys, dripping with Brylcreem, seemingly unaware of her proximity. Mirry and Laura (Junie and Don's mum) were still talking animatedly, only Bar (Mirry's sister) sat quietly with the older ladies. Glory and Don ostensibly kept watch on Boo and Robin, while sitting on the grass, making daisy chains to amuse their charges.

'You've got a cherryade moustache,' Don told her.

'Better than pickled onion breath,' she retorted.

'They went down well, with that spam roll,' he said, 'disguised the taste of marge – I hate marge! When I get married, I shall order only butter in my house!'

'If we ever get rid of rationing, Don.'

He looked at her in surprise. 'The war's over, isn't it? Surely rationing will end soon?'

'How can it? The countries we used to import from are struggling to survive – people are starving – it will take years for the world to recover from this war.'

'You're very knowledgeable, Glory! I didn't think girls were interested in politics. Oh, I know my mum says you're too clever by half—'

'Oh, does she! That drop of cider has loosened your tongue, I see, Donald Sims. What a cheek!' But she smiled at him, because it was nice to be thought clever, even by half.

Maybe it was the illicit glass of cider, which he hadn't expected to get, although he'd grandly requested it, mainly to impress Glory, when his dad asked for their orders, but Don suddenly saw her in a fresh light. She was a pretty girl, the sort boys would fight over, and he'd known her all his life, so he was in with a good chance . . .

'Like to come to the Pictures this weekend?' he asked casually. 'There's an Edward G. Robinson film.'

*Glory didn't like gangster films, she took after Mirry for musi-
cals and love stories, with spunky heroines, of course. But – she'd
actually been asked out on a date! Her very first. 'Don't see why
not,' she agreed casually, then, 'where have those two terrors got
to, Don? We'd better go and look.' As she jumped to her feet, he
noticed that she had painted her toenails with pink varnish, and
that her long legs were shapely and golden from the sun.*

* * *

*Down the hill they rolled the pickled onions, gathering dust, with
the smaller children shrieking their delight as Mirry and Laura
continued to let their hair down. The older children, in an agony
of embarrassment, kept well to the rear this time, stony-faced.
The rest of the party displayed tolerance. Actually, Fred (Glory's
dad) could hardly believe his eyes, there was Mirry, retrieving her
battered onion from the gutter, and Laura singing out: 'I've won!
Loser gets to eat the champion onion!'*

Boo and Robin were doing a jig of excitement.

*'No fear!' Mirry replied, 'Anyway, we haven't quite reached
the bottom of the hill . . .' and she bowled her onion past Laura's,
where it hit the lamp post and smashed to pieces.*

*'Draw!' Jim said hastily. 'Now sober up you two, those three at
the back think you've gone quite mad!'*

This was the first and last time I ever saw my mum tipsy – after two
glasses of gin and lime! Alcohol was rationed too . . . And I shall never
forget the Great Pickled Onion Race – ever!

* * *

There was one last hurdle to overcome, and it was on a visit to the
cinema that Maggie and I saw the terrible effects of the atomic bomb
in full colour. I can still conjure up in my mind's eye that great mush-
room cloud and how disturbing it was. VJ day followed: we were staying with Dolly and family in Suffolk for the summer holiday. Beacons
were lit along the coastline and there was a celebration fete in the village and country dancing on the grass.

It was the summer our little dog wriggled through the garden
hedge into the field beyond and met up with the school caretaker's
ancient wire-haired terrier – my cousin Laura, who was engaged to

an American airman then serving in the Pacific, and visiting for the weekend, jumped the hedge and brought Dinkie back, but it was too late: a couple of months later, little Dinkie gave birth to six big pups. It was exciting at the time, but she was too small to cope. I was heart-broken, when the vet told us she had hysteria, and must be put down. Molly took on the pups, who had to be weaned, of course, at three weeks old – they all survived, but we decided not to keep any of them. I declared: 'There will *never* be another dog I will love like Dinkie' but, thankfully, in time, there was . . .

There were other changes: Lily married Bob, Jim's friend, in Bath, where they settled with Jenny. This was a happy outcome for them, but I know Molly missed the baby. We were getting back to normal as a family unit at last. I had my bedroom to myself, so did David, and he helped Molly plan a lovely surprise for me for my birthday. Molly was always a dab hand with a distemper brush and at hanging wallpaper. The latter wasn't readily available, so my bedroom walls were painted pink and butterflies, cut from a pattern book, fluttered in each corner. The ceiling was painted blue and David cut silver stars from milk bottle tops and stuck these on. So I got my wish, I was like Old Meg in the song, looking up at the heavens above, but comfortable on my feather mattress! My friends were most impressed.

This was a new chapter in school life, too. There were outings to London, to exhibitions like *Britain Can Make It*, to museums and art galleries, a trip down the Thames on a boat with AEC and FF – enlivened by the fact that some girls (the twins and friends?) had got aboard the wrong Tube train, and we all had to wait on the platform for their return. Later, there were holidays in Walmer, with the school. Maggie went on one of these but her report put me off joining them the following year! I enjoyed her descriptions of teachers in steel curlers at breakfast, but not lights out and no talking, at 8 o'clock!

FF planned a historical walk for the third form. One Saturday Maggie and I and several others caught the bus to Croydon, and followed a route to Westerham, to see General Wolfe's statue, and Winston Churchill's country home. We went in pairs, in a straggly crocodile (the twins I expect, were in the lead), looking at our instructions and wondering when we could open our gas mask cases and take out our packed lunch. But this was not permissible until we reached our destination, and met up with FF (who hadn't come on foot!).

Maggie and I were in a group of six, including another Marion, whose father had just been demobbed. As we sat on a patch of grass opposite General Wolfe, who naturally ignored us, to eat our spam sandwiches, Marion casually produced a banana. She proceeded to slice it into six portions and generously shared this treat, brought home by her dad, with us. Just a mouthful each, but we felt the luckiest girls on the walk! We wrote the essays expected of us, later, and I think the banana was the most memorable part of the exercise.

* * *

The yearly examinations were very serious affairs. Because we sat in double desks, classes were intermingled, so there could be no chance of cribbing. This meant that a third former could be sitting next to a first former. The sixth form, being lofty individuals, were by themselves in the hall. The only sounds you could hear during exams were the rustling of paper and the scratching of pens. Later, would come the suspense of results. I always kept my head down during the maths call. I knew it wasn't worth raising my gaze until the forties were reached, and that was being hopeful. Thank goodness for English Lit., English Language, History and Art – I could breathe again then.

Once, the whole school sat a special examination. It was one I really enjoyed, because we were only told: 'It is General Knowledge.' We heard no more for ages, and forgot about it.

The Head came unexpectedly into our classroom one day. We rose obediently and wished her Good Morning, then resumed our seats. Her piercing gaze swept across our faces. Then I realised she was looking at me. There was an audible sigh of relief from my classmates. AEC smiled encouragingly at me, from the front of the class, but I was blushing, all over it seems. What had I done wrong? I frantically went through any very minor misdemeanours in my mind. I swallowed convulsively.

Miss C continued to regard me thoughtfully. 'Sheila?'

'Yes . . .' I managed at last.

She tapped a sheet of paper she held. 'You will recall the unusual test you all performed some time ago?'

'Yes,' chorused the rest of the class.

'We didn't enlighten you at the time, but this test was given in all schools in the country. Each school has received an individual report. The Education Department wanted to know if pupils were reaching their full potential. This is an I.Q. test – of intelligence.'

We were all trying to take this in. I was also wondering, 'Why me?'

'You, Sheila Langley – stand up, so we can all see you – have scored top marks in this school. I am pleased to report that the Head Girl came second . . .'

The Head Girl – how on earth could I have gained more marks than that brilliant girl, of whom we were all in awe? Or even Anne, who was always top of the class, sometimes tying with Myra, another mathematical and scientific minded girl. (Anne admitted later that she found the paper 'boring'.)

While I stood there, scarlet and silent, Miss C added the expected 'put you down'. 'Now we know what you are capable of, Sheila, we shall expect *much* more of you.' Then she swept out.

The class clapped, I sat down and AEC said kindly, 'Well done, Sheila. Your parents will be proud of you.' But I had already decided I couldn't tell them because they might well agree with Miss C! After all, they had queried a remark on my last report which stated, 'Sheila is not steady enough'. Later I enlightened them sheepishly about that: 'The teacher was Miss Barker, she'd long been retired, but she helped out in an emergency. We thought of Eric Barker, and his catch phrase, on the wireless. 'Steady Barker!' When she shouted, 'Steady, girls, steady!' we murmured that in return. She couldn't hear us, fortunately.'

Jim told me: 'That wasn't very kind.' And it wasn't, was it? I'd felt ashamed when she stopped me in the corridor, the day she left, and told me, 'I shall miss your lovely smile.'

Looking back, others had their problems, like me. Maggie struggled gamely with her asthma, but never complained, our friend Pat stammered badly. The amazing thing in her case was that when asked to read aloud, she was transformed – she had a lovely voice. Pat emigrated to Australia soon after we left school – I wonder if she became an actress? For my part, I became increasingly myopic, prescriptions were not changed often enough: at times I was squinting at the board, even from the front row. I also suffered bilious attacks, as Molly termed them, which meant time off school – I then had to attempt 'catch-up'. This developed into migraine. I was on a long waiting list for a tonsillectomy. Molly always suspected I had a weak heart, because I often turned 'blue' as a baby, but the leaking valve was not discovered until I was in my fifties!

* * *

I come from a fair-skinned, often combined with red or fair hair, family, and all the females blushed: I was sometimes thought guilty of something which I knew nothing about – but when a teacher demanded: 'Who did this?' I flushed from head to toe – or that's what it felt like. Molly couldn't understand why I spent so much time in my room, reading and writing, instead of wanting to go out with my friends. I was nothing like my extrovert mother at my age. From what she said, I gathered that teenage tantrums and hormones then were ignored!

David, on the other hand, was certainly out and about – very involved with a new youth club and sport, including long-distance running; he loved playing table tennis and in later in life became a national coach. He persuaded me to join the club, which was for teenagers upwards, unlike the Guild, and although reluctant at first, I shortly found myself editress (as it was termed then) of the club magazine. Here I was in my element, although not so keen on typing the stencils on an antiquated typewriter where the keys flew up and stuck firmly in mid-air, or applying sticky red correction fluid to my many mistakes. Contributions from the club representatives were often scribbled scrawls, and one from I.K. had Jim exclaim: 'What does the I stand for – illiterate?!' I'm afraid I was soon writing the whole magazine under different guises, which I didn't mind at all . . . In fact, the local paper congratulated one of these fake correspondents for an excellent report – I got to meet the cub reporter, one Gerald Williams (you may have heard of him!), who took me out for coffee. As he reported on Crystal Palace football club my brother was keen to meet him, being a fan, and asked me if I would let him go in my place! I refused, naturally!

Anyway, I was about to embark on a social life, much to Molly's relief, But that's another chapter.

CHAPTER 18

Donkeys, John Bull and Tangos

Our first seaside holiday for seven years was taken the year after the war ended. We shared a bungalow with Dolly, Russ, Jassy and young Nick. Jaywick, near Clacton was the choice, being roughly halfway between our two homes. There was still barbed wire to be seen on beaches, and some places were signposted out of bounds due to danger from unexploded mines or because the beaches had been used by the army on manoeuvres.

David joined us both weekends, for he had not long been in his first job in a London stockbroker's. He said running came in useful there! Whit week, at the end of May, was chosen, and we were lucky, for there was a heatwave.

My cousin Laura, a GI bride, now in the States, sent me a parcel of clothes, most as good as new. I had worn hand-me-downs and make-overs for so long, I could hardly believe my luck! Laura was a tiny girl, and later her offerings, alas, were too tight (she must have been a size 8), but I made the most of my new wardrobe while it fitted! Among the items was a super swimsuit. Having worn an old, ruched costume of Molly's at the swimming baths, I was disappointed that this one was rather tight round the middle. Molly had an inspiration – she cut it at the waist, and I had a two-piece! 'You look like a film star,' she told me. Poor Jassy had to make do with a bathing suit knitted in stripes by me, which sagged when it got wet. I don't think she minded, as she was only eight, but she was good company for me, as I was a rather immature fourteen-year-old, like most of my friends. We were the first generation not to go out to work at an early age – our parents seemed determined to keep us innocent and to enjoy a belated childhood which up to now had been restricted by the war.

The 'bungalow town' was a great sprawl, and some of the holiday lets were quite a way from the beach. It was nothing like the places we had stayed in pre-war Norfolk, with countryside all round and cliff paths to descend to soft, clean sand and sparkling sea – but we soon overcame our initial disappointment, for now I was considered the responsible one, and Jassy and I were allowed to go off on our own sometimes, like first thing in the morning, to collect newspapers and milk.

The bungalow was very basic, with three bedrooms, and a sofa bed in the living room for David, but Molly and Dolly were impressed with the pull-down ironing board – I recall them ironing their cotton dresses while clad in their petticoats because it was so hot. Jim and Russ riled them by snatches of 'Marta (Martyr!), Rambling Rose of the Wild Woods', but they never joined us on the beach until lunchtime. Actually, I think they enjoyed time on their own together.

We didn't have a dog then, but we had a tabby cat, called Tikki. We took him on holiday with us, and he didn't mind being on a puppy lead and collar, and was agreeable to being transported in a basket on the train. He was really Jim's pet, and known to him as 'The Old Gentleman'. 'Oh,' he said, when the cat was curled up on his lap on winter evenings, and Molly looked meaningfully at the empty coal bucket at home, 'I'm afraid I can't disturb The Old Gentleman.' She retorted: 'I can!' and she did.

Jassy and I were in charge of Brandy, a golden cocker spaniel, but not so keen on her little brother tagging along with us.

We discarded our shoes on the first day of the holiday, and didn't put them on again until we went home at the end of the week. It was fine on the beach, but we hobbled sometimes up the road, particularly if we trod in something nasty.

Ice-cream was still a real treat. Back home, Paula and I had recently left the Applegarth dancing school, and now we went to Croydon to spend our pocket money on Saturday mornings. Our favourite shop was Kennards store, which always seemed like a covered market place, bustling, with many departments and an overriding smell from Pets Corner, down in the basement area, which led out to Surrey Street Market. There were sweet puppies in runs, which I lingered over, and parrots and other exotic birds on perches, calling out 'Hello!' or squawking loudly. The pups were of indeterminate breeds, and I'd be warned not to buy one by my mother. As they were five shillings, this was unlikely, for I had other things to spend my money on. This included ice-cream, which was made in the corridor immediately outside the Pets' Corner. The first time it was on sale after so long, we _ queued for a couple of hours, and the queue had to part now and then to let the pony rides through on their route. Paula and I bought two ice-creams each, and licked them blissfully in turn. One small boy had his cone snaffled by a large dog, and wouldn't stop screaming.

Here, in Jaywick, there was a rather tacky general store, where we bought an ice-cream in the morning, and were treated by our dads to another in the afternoon.

I bought lots of saucy postcards to send back to my pals: these often had the slogan: 'Meet you at your convenience.' We knew all about conveniences, for didn't our mums always find a spot on the sands immediately in front of the Ladies? This convenience appeared on most of our holiday snaps ... Perhaps I should have collected these postcards, rather than send them out, as they might be worth a bit after all these years! I also couldn't resist slotting a sixpence in the newly installed juke box – always the same tune: 'Temptation' or was it 'Jealousy'? We listened to this as we danced our way down onto the sands.

We were always among the first on the beach. We'd had an early awakening because, amazingly, we could hear the rallying call from Butlin's Holiday Camp in Clacton – 'Wakey, wakey campers – rise and shine!' Jim groaned and said, 'Now you know why we won't take you *there* on holiday! Anyway, you couldn't have stood up to the Physical Jerks!' I had a cheeky reply: 'But *you* might have won the knobbly knees contest!' Jassy whispered to me, 'And you could've been Miss Bathing Beauty in your new costume!' Flattery that worked, as I treated her to a sno-fruit, the forerunner of the ice lolly.

On our second day on the beach, we were making a sandcastle for Nick, while the two dads read their papers in deckchairs, with the legs of their trousers rolled up in case the tide came in unexpectedly, and in Jim's case, a clean white handkerchief knotted at the corners to protect his bald head from the brilliant sun, when we spotted the donkeys plodding along the sand nearby. The owner was touting for custom: 'You youngsters want a ride?'

Jassy and Nick were lifted up on to the smaller donkeys, and I was allotted a larger animal. We had our ride, and as we returned saw a waiting crowd of children, mostly toddlers. The donkey man turned to Jassy and me. 'How'd you like to lead the donkeys with the little 'uns aboard?'

The dads agreed, while our mums probably would have not. For an hour at a time, with a rest between, we trudged tirelessly up and down. Our reward came at the end of the afternoon. 'Would you like to ride in the middle of the pack, home to Clacton?'

'Oh please,' we pleaded to Molly and Dolly, who had joined us with a packed lunch to be eaten in the open.

'Well . . .' Then Russ and Jim rose to the occasion. 'We'll walk the dog along the beach to meet you coming back, eh?'

'They'll be about an hour,' said the donkey man hopefully.

I was glad I was wearing shorts, like Jassy. Mine were borrowed from a Girl Guide friend, and were more a divided skirt, with box pleats. It was actually rather hair-raising, for the donkeys didn't plod as they did during the rides, but moved en masse very fast indeed, anxious to get back to the stables and their feed. That first time, we clung on, but as we were hemmed in by grey, hairy bodies, there was no chance of being thrown off our steeds.

At the end of the week we were unexpectedly paid a few shillings,, and then came the highlight of the holiday: we went to a Butlin's open evening with the rest of the family and the entrance fee entitled us to some free rides! We went on the Big Wheel, the Carousel, and the swing boats. *Steel Stella*, the roller coaster would have to wait for another year, our parents said.

The following year, we went there again, but I was too old to ride the donkeys by then. I spent most of my days glumly in the bungalow, writing cards to all my friends, saying I was having 'a wonderful time'. I don't think I even had a paddle in the sea. Typical teenager, I suppose.

* * *

Saturday evenings were spent, after the donkey summer, with Paula next door, while she listened out for her young brother, who was so good, we never heard a peep out of him, for our mothers were enjoying a night out in the church hall, at a whist drive! Paula's dad went too, but Jim wasn't one for cards, and he said Molly deserved a break. David was usually out and about too: the club was in the table tennis league.

Paula's dad was what Molly and Dolly called 'A fine figure of a man.' He had joined the newly formed Flying Corps in the First World War as a P.T. instructor. Paula told me that he'd been injured and had a steel plate in his crown. She didn't tell me exactly where this was located but it was an intriguing subject. The war wound meant that he was in a reserved occupation during the recent conflict. He was a very pleasant man, and he had an interesting job, in publicity for Odhams Press in London. Every weekend he brought home a pile of magazines and newspapers.

I'm afraid I wasn't very scintillating company for Paula. This reading matter was largely untouched by the young Motts, but I fell upon it with glee. We were supposed to be listening to the wireless, Max Jaffa and the Palm Court Orchestra, *In Town Tonight!* and *Saturday Night Theatre*, with Cicely Courtneidge and Jack Hulbert. I did listen to the play, but otherwise I was reading all the magazines. I flicked through *Picture Goer* with interest, My favourite was *John Bull*. The politics passed me by, but I found the serials absorbing. In the pages of *John Bull* I became acquainted with H.E. Bates – and have loved his writing ever since.

Paula sighed and looked fed up. She went out into the kitchen to make us supper. She wasn't allowed to cook, but she had her speciality: triple decker sandwiches, one layer marmite, the other sandwich spread.

Not surprisingly, she rebelled against staying in on Saturday evenings. Being a year ahead of me, she wanted to dress up, to go dancing, and to meet boys.

So, Paula went out with her friends and left me behind. That turned out to be the parting of ways for us, we had outgrown each other, I suppose.

'*You'll* have to learn to dance,' Molly said, when I moaned. David had been to the same ballroom dancing school as Paula, but I'd never had the inclination to join him. Molly decided, unbeknown to me, to call on Maggie's mum and to ask her if Maggie would be allowed to accompany me to Taylor's Academy. She said yes.

I never really mastered the tango, although Maggie and I practised often, or reached the heights of my brother, who achieved gold medal standard, but Maggie and I blossomed to the strains of Victor Sylvester. 'Everyone gets a partner!' was little Miss T's rallying call. She was partnered by her niece, Joyce. They were super teachers and full of enthusiasm. God bless them both!

The studio was the top floor of the house. There was a sprung dance floor, which had to be chalked before each lesson. We had to wear proper dancing shoes with leather soles. I was really upset when Jim, as he always did, applied a rubber sole (you could buy these at Woolworths) to my new special shoes. 'How can I wear them now?' I cried. He was upset too.

'Stop grumbling!' Molly said, but she bought me another pair.

There were separate cloakrooms for boys and girls. Ours was like a boudoir, with face-powder in cut-glass bowls, clean powder puffs, to deal with shiny noses; long mirrors and flowers. Maggie and I always looked to see if anyone was wearing the same dress as us – it only happened once, thank goodness, to me. The girl concerned said cheerfully, 'Snap!' and I hid away in the alcove in the studio, instead of sitting on one of the chairs round the dance-floor, waiting for a partner.

Miss T wasn't having any wallflowers. She despatched Big Tel to ask me to partner him in a waltz. He was a lofty chap, but very kind, and when we turned a corner, he lifted me effortlessly off my feet and twirled me round, which made me feel very special.

The boys, in turn, rushed to turn the handle of the gramophone, when the music began to slow down. We had all the latest tunes, but they were always recorded by Victor Silvester, so you could mutter quick, quick, slow, one, two, three, etc. When it came to the last waltz, the lights were dimmed, and so no one noticed that Maggie and I were dancing together ... 'Hear the music of the waters,' we sang, 'softly come and softly go ... come back to Sorrento ...'

We loved Taylor's Academy, and we were soon attending local dances and feeling confident. We also met boys! They were all very well-mannered and in the interval they treated us to tea and buns. No alcohol – and the evening always ended at 11 p.m.

That Christmas, the teachers planned a lovely surprise. The Upper School were joined by hand-picked (I suspect) boys from another local school for a joint Christmas dance. I had a pink crepe dress, and a trace of Tangee Natural lipstick. In the cloakroom, I removed the hated bows from my bunched hair, and combed it loose. All evening, girls complimented me on my 'lovely hair'. I refused to tie it back ever again, and like the rest of my class, I felt liberated and grown up.

Pride comes before a fall they say, as you will see ...

CHAPTER 19

Life Itself is a Roller-Coaster

The year 1947 was a year of ups and downs, not unlike *Steel Stella*. There was the exciting news of a Royal Wedding, but we had to wait until November for that. John and I still hadn't met yet, but he was off to do his national service that month in the R.A.F., and on 20th November, recalls being on a train to his first camp, looking out on flags flying in gardens. It was a foggy, sleety day in the north. He did get a slice of cake, on his arrival, but it wasn't wedding cake and like the other young men he was about to grow up quickly.

It began with the Christmas holidays before and after the New Year. Our beloved grandfather had died in 1946, and how we missed his joyful exuberance. We didn't converge on the old Swan as usual, but stayed with Dolly and family in the cottage in Suffolk. Our grandmother was naturally sad, and despite all our efforts, we felt the same. It was the end of an era. Tilly, our youngest aunt, reunited with her husband after six years apart while he was in the army, was overjoyed though, to be pregnant at last.

In freezing weather in February, there was a new little girl cousin to join Laura, me and Jassy. Dolly, who helped with the confinement at Tilly and her husband's home near Southwold, recalled 'nappies like stiff boards had to be wrenched from the line, and we were all, oh, so very cold . . .' I knitted baby Susie some pea-green booties, and Molly made a matinee outfit.

At school, there was some serious revision to be done, with Mock Matric examinations looming. It was 'heads down, no talking' time. Outings at this time for Maggie and me were a Saturday afternoon at the Pavilion, when we forgot our worries about the exams by viewing all the romantic pictures of the time; we were great fans of Joan Crawford, Bette Davis and

Cary Grant – I also liked Van Johnson, and sent off for his picture and autograph. We weren't so keen on Abbott and Costello, or even Laurel and Hardy, but I've appreciated the latter for many years since their films appeared on TV. We enjoyed the musicals in colour, too. Who remembers Carmen Miranda with her sky-scraper hats piled with tropical fruit?

The Pav was known as the Flea-Pit, so we were careful not to lean back in our seats. I can still conjure up instantly the mixed aromas from the Pav, some of them not too pleasant, despite the cheap disinfectant lavished in the Gents. Once, a woman in our row was joined by her husband, just back from work. She had his dinner, hot and steaming in a wrapped casserole dish, on her lap. He spooned up stew and we were overwhelmed by the smell of onions. Oranges were another favourite, and the crunching of boiled sweets disturbed our concentration.

We still had our weekly dancing lessons, but Saturday-night dancing was restricted for a while due to our studies.

One day we had pork for school lunch. Mine was pink and obviously tough and undercooked. I wasn't sick at the time, and I didn't hear that anyone else was affected by this dinner. Next morning, I woke feeling extremely ill. I staggered out of bed, and on passing the wardrobe mirror, noticed that my face had swelled, and that I had a rash too. I don't remember much of the ensuing days, except the doctor coming (a very rare occurrence) and that he thought it was either acute food poisoning, or perhaps glandular fever. I lay in bed, burning up, and the doctor's perplexity continued. I had some puzzling symptoms. Blood tests were not routine then.

I was actually away from school for a couple of months, but then it was the summer holiday, which thankfully meant no more time off, while I was slowly convalescing. In photographs of that time I am wearing a green and white cotton frock which Molly bought me from Marks and Sparks to cheer me up. It was from their first rail of clothes on sale after the war. I loved that dress because I was the first to wear it. It was very simple, with cap sleeves and horizontal stripes. We still had clothes coupons, but they would be one of the first things to go, and the New Look and longer hemlines was just around the corner . . .

In September, I returned to school, very lethargic and not really up to doing so. Then disaster struck. First, my skin began to peel all over, just as it had done after scarlet fever, but there was worse to come. My hair fell out in handfuls. The Head took me aside after Morning Assembly and then I learned how kind she could be, under her tough facade. I wept about my growing bald patches, and she comforted me. I was about to appear in a school production of *She Stoops to Conquer*, and the staff decided to hire me a wig to wear. It was just the boost I needed. I got a rousing reception for my part.

I no longer had long, blonde wavy hair – I had a thin, miserable straggle, which my school friends tactfully didn't mention. However, the hair loss ceased, and new hair began to grow in tight curls which was such a relief, apart from the fact that it was a different shade, more chestnut, like my brother's colour. Molly took me to the hairdresser. She helped me to come to terms with my changed appearance; my hair was cut very short and I looked very different with my bubble-cut.

Fortunately, I couldn't know that the mystery illness would have repercussions many years later. I went on to have a large family, as I'd hoped, and ignorance is indeed bliss!

Molly, who had been shopping one afternoon, followed Maggie and me down the high street after school. She said later that it had been a real tonic to her to hear us giggling all the way, as girls together tend to do. Dear Maggie kept my spirits up at that time, and when I went back to the dancing school, I never lacked a partner and nor did she – we were growing up fast.

David had been in the cadets at school, which was good experience for him, with his national service days coming up the following spring. He even had a girlfriend who took him out on the back of her motor-bike: he was saving up for a bike of his own. When he achieved his ambition, he monopolised the small kitchen with motorcycle parts on newspaper, and even, on occasion, the monster itself, propped against the table. We had a lot of arguments at that time: I couldn't bear the grease and the smell of some gunk he cleaned his hands with, or even the sight of him polishing his boots, or winding his puttees round his legs. He retaliated by telling Molly that I hadn't cleaned my shoes for weeks. (True.) I do regret having greeted one of his many mates at the door when I called out to my brother: 'One of your funny friends!' I met this particular chap much later and he confided: 'I was terrified of you!' What me? I was no doubt thinking, why do I always have to blush? JD didn't bear me a grudge; I'm told that he reads all my books!

* * *

I was eager to go up to London and to camp out on the pavement along the route of the Royal Wedding coach. Jim had a more prac-tical idea. 'You'd have a better view of the passing parade from my office, and at least you'd be dry; rain is forecast for the 20th.' So Jim, Molly and I travelled up very early and I took a notebook to record my impressions. We were given seats by the window. It was an upstairs room, which was lucky as you could look down on the scene. As we ascended the grand staircase in the Admiralty, Jim observed: 'I can remember a young Jimmy Hogg sliding down the banisters here!'

The last time I had been in my dad's office, I was six years old, and the 'young ladies' kept me busy with paper and pencils, drawing them at work. I intended to do plenty of sketching this day, and writing too.

The newspapers' special editions, published throughout the day, reported that Princess Elizabeth was also up early, looking out of her window in her dressing gown, and I imagined, perhaps with rollers in her hair, before the long preparations to transform her into a bride, began. She was just twenty-one, and her prince five years older, so it seemed to us the stuff of fairy tales, a real romance. We toasted their happiness in Admiralty tea.

I was glad that I wasn't shivering on the wet, cold pavement and drinking lukewarm tea. The rain had thankfully ceased just after dawn, so the crowd in Whitehall was stretching cramped limbs, yawning, and then rolling up soggy blankets and bedding, to make room for more arrivals. Soon they were standing in a solid mass, excited and cracking jokes. Sober ministerial cars were cheered. We were eager for the music to begin: I could glimpse children, pushed to the front, so that they could see the processions, sitting on the kerb, munching breakfast rolls. An old lady, perhaps suffering from hypothermia, was lifted onto a stretcher and carried away by the first aiders. Bobbies moved the crowd back, with courtesy and encouraging banter.

First the Royal Marines, then the R.A.F. marched along, then grouped to play the National Anthem in honour of Princess Elizabeth's grandmother, Queen Mary, widow of King George V, who was in the first carriage, which was followed by Royal guests from other countries. In the office, we all scrambled to our feet, and stood to attention, just as we did when the anthem was played in cinemas. The loudspeakers relayed the band music loud and clear.

The cheering from the crowd alerted the window watchers: the bridegroom in his car, smiling, and seemingly relaxed, resplendent in his naval dress uniform. The glass coach with Queen Elizabeth and the chief bridesmaid, Princess Margaret Rose, followed, escorted by the Household Cavalry on their black horses. The bells pealed in the Abbey. The wedding ceremony was due to begin at eleven o'clock.

Windsor Greys drew the state coaches and at last, the crowd had their reward, the first sight of the bride in her golden coach, but not her magnificent wedding dress, for this was covered by a fur coat, draped round her shoulders to keep her warm. Her father, the King, sat beside her and a voice behind me said softly, 'Oh, he looks so proud . . .'

The service was broadcast round the world, and we too crowded round the wireless. We would later relive the occasion at the cinema, and the newspapers were no doubt kept as souvenirs – they certainly were in our house. We had a change in government, rationing was still in place, Britain was struggling back to normal, the big cities which had taken the brunt of the bombing, would never look the same, but the Royal Wedding made us optimistic for a better future.

* * *

We shivered constantly in the bitter winter which followed. Coal was like gold dust. John and I could well have met, but it was not time for that yet, when we both queued outside a local depot, when the rumour went round that they had a supply. We trudged through snow with our precious sacks in old prams or boxes on wheels.

Molly queued endlessly too – we had some bright pink sausages for supper one night, she didn't reveal that they came from the horse-meat shop. We may hear now that we had the perfect diet, but I would disagree: we were always hungry. Even bread, which had never been rationed in the war, was, for a while, available only with BUs (bread units.)

I returned, initially reluctantly, to the fold – we had a new vicar at the parish church, and attendance was back to pre-war levels. My parents wanted me to be confirmed in the Anglican church. The vicar had been brought up a Methodist, so the two churches often had joint services which Maggie began attending with me. Now we were considered young women, not children, we bought our first hats: *beanies*! We were inseparable at that time, and are still close, although we live too far apart – and both have family commitments – to meet up. She supported me enormously through that roller-coaster year. Thank you, Maggie.

CHAPTER 20

Moments of Glory

Collecting wastepaper during and after the war years was something I tackled with enthusiasm. I met some interesting people when I knocked on their doors, something children were not usually encouraged to do, for obvious reasons. I suppose Molly didn't mind, because my 'regulars' were usually middle-aged women who enjoyed a chat with my friends and me, or elderly couples, shuffling to the door in slippers. They not only parted with ancient newspapers, they sometimes had a treat in store for compulsive readers, like bulky pre-war comics, which they presented with: 'You might like to read 'em, before they go in the sack . . .' I didn't feel guilty then, at smuggling these up to my bedroom.

'Who are you writing to?' Molly enquired one evening, as I dipped my pen in green ink – I tried all the colours before I settled on blue-black.

'A girl on this page –' I indicated a colourful comic – 'is asking for a pen friend . . .' I must have been about eleven, and loved writing letters.

'Look at the date on the front page,' Molly advised. 'She is probably about thirty years old by now!'

A school story is a school story, and it didn't occur to me that the illustrations were all of girls with shingled hair wearing gymslips with lots of pleats and belted low on the hips. The comic had been published before I was born!

I actually loved books from this era and earlier too. When Lily came to us, she brought a case with all her worldly goods. She'd been orphaned at an early age, and the only thing she seemed to have from her old home was a couple of books. *Little Women* and *Good Wives*.

She lent me these books soon after she arrived. When she left us to marry Bob, she said: 'I would like you to keep my books, Sheila.' In turn, I passed them on to our elder daughter, Sara, who shared them with her sisters. It's only recently, that I realised how precious these dog-eared volumes must have been to Lily.

Maggie was with me at a later date, when we were invited into a large house and taken into a drawing room, dusty and rather oppressive, with heavy Victorian furniture and rather grim paintings on the walls. There was a stack of boxes on the window seat. 'I am packing up the ornaments – this place is too much for me to keep up, now – I can't afford to heat it properly, for one thing,' the old lady told us. She indicated what I thought was a piano. 'Have you heard one of these play?'

We shook our heads, not sure what she meant.

'Come closer, and watch what happens,' she invited us, lifting the lid.

She inserted a roll of what looked like parchment, pierced with holes. 'This, girls, is a pianola – listen – this is probably the last time I will play it . . .'

We saw the keys rise and fall, unstruck by human hand. The music was beautiful, as if played by a classical pianist. We were spell-bound.

A great sheaf of the musical sheets was thrust in our hands. 'Take it. It's just wastepaper now.' The lid was closed on the pianola. 'It will probably make good firewood.'

A moment of glory, over.

* * *

This is more a gory moment: I was suddenly summoned to hospital to have my tonsils removed. I actually had to have the operation twice, due to bleeding excessively on the first occasion, and didn't arrive home the next day as planned. Molly visited me to cheer me up – I was in the children's ward, but my feet stuck out of the end of the small bed – and she gave me a large bunch of grapes. In my dopey state, I ate all these after she left. Consternation from the nursing staff: 'Were there pips? You didn't have permission to eat anything yet!' I had to admit, I had no idea if they had pips or not, but I'd swallowed the lot.

I was brought home eventually by ambulance, which had to stop twice so that the nurse could deal with me being very sick. I had to be carried indoors on a stretcher. Molly put me straight to bed. However, after a week I was much better and able to return to school.

A few weeks later, came my second 'op'. This was just a matter of removing 'tags'. I was told: 'Your tonsils may grow again.'

'I'm not going back in hospital, even if they do!' I said firmly.

I was five feet two inches tall when I had the tonsillectomy, and suddenly I grew two more inches, much to the family's surprise. At last I was among the Big Girls in my class!

* * *

AEC had an announcement to make after registration one day. 'All schools in the area are invited to submit pupils' essays in a competition, sponsored by the local newspaper. There are several categories, according to age, and I hope that you will all write something. The best essays will be entered. The subject is "Wastepaper".'

There were a few groans: 'What can we write about *that*?' To me, those words were a spur. I would find out what happened to the wastepaper after it was collected. I was already an avid researcher, and the encyclopaedias would help!

I wrote my essay in pencil, because I could keep up better with my thoughts, than dipping pen into ink – blots were always a drawback. Dialogue has always been part of my writing, and I didn't plan the essay, just let it flow. Maggie was part of the story, of course, and our forays in collecting the wastepaper over the years. I found out about papier mâché, which resulted in more craft work for us, and how the paper was pulped and recycled. Once written, I stuffed the untidily written papers in a dressing table drawer.

The deadline drew nearer, and AEC requested that all essays be handed in. I forgot to bring mine and only remembered to hand it in on the last day. At lunchtime, I was summoned to the Head's office. Miss C brandished my pencil-scrawled papers: 'Disgraceful! You must write this out again in ink – now!'

It took me all lunchtime and an hour after school, to copy the essay onto fresh paper in my best handwriting. With a sigh of relief, I passed it to AEC, patiently standing by. 'Just in time,' she observed in relief. She had stayed to check my writing and would deliver our essays to the paper personally first thing next day.

Relieved, I promptly put this experience behind me, or so I thought.

We didn't have the local news delivered with the daily paper, Molly always bought it from the newsagent's later in the day. That way, she got to read it before I crumpled it up! At least she didn't sit on it as Jim's father had done, to prevent the family opening the paper first!

I was mystified when I was greeted one morning at school by whispered 'Congratulations!' during registration. I was reprimanded for hissing: 'What for?' I didn't find out until later.

Then came my own moment of glory.

Into the classroom swept Miss C, carrying a folded newspaper in one hand, and we all stood to attention, chanting 'Good Morning!' I became aware that all eyes were on me again, that everyone was smiling, even Miss C. Then there was much clapping of hands, before the Head indicated that she wished to speak to us.

'I see you already know that congratulations are due to Sheila, who is the overall winner of the essay competition. There were over 3,000 entries. You look surprised, Sheila—'

'I am.' I said truthfully.

'You didn't see the paper earlier?' she queried.

'No . . .'

I expect you can guess who came second – the Head Girl! Miss C was pleased that several of 'our girls' had done well. We would be presented with our prizes at the Town Hall by the Mayor, we were told.

However, nothing could surpass this moment of glory for me, except maybe, the publication of my first book, *Tilly's Family*.

I have been zealous regarding wastepaper ever since.

Revising for the coming important examinations was now a most serious business. We were allowed to pair up and to study quietly unsupervised in the library or in certain areas where we would not be interrupted. Maggie and I chose the Sick Room. We took turns to lounge on the bed to answer questions from the other, sitting on the chair. We concentrated on absorbing facts; there was no giggling or messing around. This dedication paid off when we took our French oral examination before the written papers. We had to describe a painting. I'm not sure if it was a happy coincidence, or whether it was suggested to us, but we had visited the National Gallery shortly before, and conversed in French all day. We did get the giggles then when we were approached by a couple of French tourists, who spoke so rapidly we couldn't understand what they were saying! I expect our version of their language was very laborious!

One day, a careers adviser came into our classroom. We were all asked in turn if we had any idea what we wanted to do when we left school. Some girls were staying on to take the Higher School Certificate and hoped to go on to college. (University wasn't mentioned.) They wished to become teachers. The most popular choice was a career in nursing. As a squeamish person, that was not for me, although, nursing turned out to be a large part of my maternal duties later, with all the childhood ailments still rife, like measles, mumps and chicken pox . . . Some girls had still to make up their minds, but I knew exactly what I wanted to do. When it came to my turn, I said simply: 'I want to be a writer.' The adviser regarded me thoughtfully for a moment. Then she said kindly, 'But Sheila, are you aware there is still a shortage of paper?' Those words have been on my conscience ever since.

As for becoming a cub reporter on a newspaper, I gathered you had to be able to ride a bike! I felt very deflated, as no helpful suggestions were made.

Later, I would find that the biggest drawback was not being able to type or take shorthand. Nowadays, with computers in schools, students learn how to use a keyboard when they are very young. Our school was academically excellent, but most of us continued our studies after we left, in order to secure employment, for jobs were like gold dust then. I went to evening classes for several years.

* * *

The examinations were not as fearsome as I expected. I remember the joy when I looked at the history paper and saw that I had revised all the right information! I did my best with the mathematics, but I knew I would never work in a bank. When it was all over, we awaited our results, and happily for me, like the rest of the class, I had done well, in particular in English Literature, English Language, Art, History and French. I failed Domestic Science by a single point – I wasn't surprised at that, because when washing a cabbage under the tap, I inadvertently sprayed the invigilator with cold water. My heart sank when I saw her grim face and the way she stabbed her comments on my inefficiency with her pencil in the notebook. My brandy snaps unrolled in the cooking, too.

The only things I really remember about Domestic Science were, like the rest of the group, eating an illicit 'pinch' of 'raspings' from the big jar in the pantry (these were stale breadcrumbs baked in the oven, and tasted as if they were very ancient), and being caught standing in the bath in the flat to clean the taps. On that occasion, the teacher ignored the paddling, and ran her finger along the top of the bathroom door, then held the digit under my nose accusingly. 'You didn't clean up there!' Perhaps this is the moment to reveal that my family consider me a good cook! This is thanks to my mother, mother-in-law, husband – and grandmother's cook book. All our children are excellent at the culinary art, too.

We then looked forward to our final prize giving. For the last time, our voices were raised in 'Linden Lea', and we had our moment of glory, when our results were announced. In turn, we went up to receive our certificates. Autograph books were signed, promises were made to keep in touch, to meet up. Our class photograph was taken. We all appear so fresh faced, and happy.

I didn't want to leave school, and asked Molly if I might stay on. 'It's not too late, other girls have changed their mind,' I pleaded.

'You say you don't want to go to college,' she reminded me.

'No, but . . .'

'It's time you grew up,' she told me, 'went out into the world. You can't be a schoolgirl forever.'

It seemed to me she was unfeeling then, but she was right. David was already 'off hand' and Molly wanted more freedom too. She was only forty years old.

It was my last day at school. Dear AEC told me, 'I shall have to buy a new bookcase to hold all your books.' I never saw her again, though we kept in touch, and she remembered me on my wedding day. FF said, 'I knew you could do it!' I was fortunate to meet up with her from time to time, and have a bundle of her letters.

I had already attended one job interview, at the BBC, with Maggie. Several other girls from our class were selected to apply. This was quite exciting, but there were only clerical positions available. However, we soon discovered that the first two girls interviewed secured the jobs. Mr Mott kindly offered to see if there were any openings in the publishing business. However, Molly took this the wrong way and told me, 'We don't want to be beholden to them.' I think the real drawback was that Mrs Mott was sometimes patronising to my mum. I don't think she meant to be, in fact they worked tirelessly together as volunteer helpers for the local Darby and Joan Club, even when they were older than many of the members!

Maggie and I were now seriously seeking employment. We were both sad we would no longer see each other every day, but we would meet up to go to the Pictures one evening in the week, there were the Saturday-night dances – we might even go to the new dance hall, we decided. We would continue with our Saturday shopping in Croydon or Streatham, and church on Sunday mornings.

During that final school summer holiday, we walked often down the Green Lane to the Grove, where we practised our serves with two elderly tennis racquets and a tired, rather bald ball. We were great Wimbledon fans. There was also a day trip to Brighton, when I was invited to go there with Maggie and her family. It was a lovely day, we travelled by train, and ate our picnic lunch on the pebbled beach, enjoying the spray as the sea rushed in and foam tickled our bare feet. We girls were keen to have a paddle (neither of us could swim). We were waist deep and crying, 'Ooh!' as the cold water lapped round us, when Maggie suddenly disappeared – the beach shelved sharply at that point. She came up spluttering, but thankfully laughing, and we beat a hasty retreat to the shore. We were walking back along the beach as it would soon be time to catch the excursion train home, when we heard a voice booming through a megaphone. 'Last trip of the day!' We went out in a motor boat as the sun set and the colours were reflected in the water. A magic moment.

* * *

There was a former teacher who lived locally who was on the lookout for recruits to join the company in London where she was personnel officer. She had left teaching before I started school, but I knew her by sight, as she rode her bicycle to the shops. When I was trusted to go to the corner shop as a child, I was also trusted to 'look right, look left, look right again' by Molly. This I did in a most perfunctory manner, I'm afraid. Once I stepped out to cross the road, and this same lady almost ran over my foot and could have fallen off her bike. She seized my arm in a vice-like grip and told me off in teacher-tones. I didn't tell Molly about this incident, but she did, so I was told off again. For some time I had a recurring nightmare about – what shall I call her? – Miss P, will do . . . In my dreams she more resembled the Wicked Witch from *The Wizard of Oz*.

I digress: Miss P had obviously forgotten that I was once hopeless at road-drill. She was impressed by my examination results, and arranged an interview. She didn't discuss this with me, but with Molly.

'*Insurance!*' I cried, when I heard. 'I don't want to go – didn't Dad say I wasn't cut out for the Civil Service?'

'It's not the Civil Service—'.

'I don't care! It sounds like figure work, anyway, and you know—'

'And I know, you have to start your working life somewhere!'

So I sat another examination, presided over by Miss P, and despite my misgivings I was offered a clerical position. Molly was pleased because it was a North American company and three-course lunches were provided free of charge. There was also the lure of a food parcel at Christmas.

You will find out how I got on in the next chapter! Maggie, meanwhile, went to work in a local bank. We were lucky to find jobs at all, we were told.

CHAPTER 21

Down Among the Dead Men

Molly insisted that we have the usual family holiday before I commenced commuting to London each day. The insurance company wanted me to start work at the beginning of September, but that was the only time we could book the bungalow on the cliff at California, Norfolk. It was agreed I could join the company in the middle of the month. In retrospect, this was unfortunate, for several other girls had already been through the initial training, before I arrived, and I would have to 'catch up'.

California has always been one of my favourite places. It has featured in two of my books, and in a short story, 'Californy Here We Come', published in *Woman's Realm*. This was the song we sang as we motored there, having met up in Suffolk, to travel the rest of the way in our uncle's car.

In this further excerpt from *The Family at Number Five*, later retitled *A Winter Hope*, I describe a visit to California just before the outbreak of WW2.

> *The little car was bursting at the seams with all the baby paraphernalia. 'We'll have to make do with one pair of shorts and a couple of tops each, and hope to goodness it doesn't rain,' as Mirry told Fred and Glory. They were off on a summer holiday, the third week in August.*
>
> *The chalet bungalow was almost teetering on the cliff edge, which caused Mirry to twitter anxiously, until Fred pointed out there would be four of them to keep an eye on Glory, when Bar and Clive arrived later in the day. They were travelling here on the motorbike. Anyway, Glory could be a sensible child when she chose, and*

there were steps carved out to the sandy beach below and a handrail which was, well, adequate. As for baby Beaulah, at six weeks old the only demands she would make were the middle-of-the-night 'Hurry up and feed me, Mum!' cries and a long line of nappies blowing like white flags against a perfect blue sky, for the swooping seagulls to target and splatter.

They were on the east coast, in a windswept place with far-reaching views, and the red flag flying more often than not. But it was just the place for shrimping, with plenty of rock pools for Glory to paddle safely in, with water warmed by the sun. In the lanes around, the scarlet poppies waved among the long grass at the edge of the fields, the sails of the tall white windmill turned and the church spire gleamed gold like the corn. Clusters of cottages with neat gardens with pea sticks and sweet peas intermingled with cabbages and cabbage roses. Wooden shacks, which were dark and cool within, with fish laid out on marble slabs, still bright-eyed and shiny. The post office sold stamps and sweets and opened and closed at the owner's whim. They were in Poppy Land, Mirry fancied. She didn't know that was what the locals already called the place . . .

Young Cora, just released from hospital after being very ill with diphtheria, in *The Gingerbread Girl*, is taken by her mother, Biddy's friend Eliza, to California to convalesce. They travel by train . . . This part of the story is also set just pre-war.

Steam billowed, doors opened, folk disembarked. Porters appeared with trolleys to transport luggage. Cora and Eliza stood back until the chaos cleared, then Eliza helped her young friend aboard . . .

'Where are we going?' Cora ventured.

'Californy, here we come!' Eliza sang out sweetly with a smile.

'California, d'you mean? That's in America!*' Biddy had a sister there . . .*

'This one's in Norfolk. Not far from Great Yarmouth, where I sent them bloaters from, last year . . .'

* * *

The final stage of their journey was in the early evening.
They bowled along the winding lanes by pony and trap,
driven by Ginny Brooks; small and round like her sister,
with a man's flat cap on a bundle of hair which was faded
but still streaked with red.

'Look!' Eliza pointed out to Cora 'Californian poppies!'
It was June, a bright, golden evening, and they caught
glimpses of the sea below the cliffs before they veered
inland.

'They're yellow,' Cora observed, 'not like the ones on
'memberance Day . . .'

California, the village, was much like that still in 1948. There was one important change, however: the erosion of the cliffs. There were DANGER! signs – including by our steps down to the beach, which were crumbling. We descended carefully, and when on the soft, fine sand it all seemed as before. It was to be our last family holiday there, unfortunately. Poppies, both red and yellow, still captivate the tourists. However, the bungalow we stayed in then, where Tikki the tabby pounced on lizards which wriggled away, leaving their tails behind, long ago toppled into the sea.

* * *

Jim took me as far as the impressive doors of the insurance company on my first morning. The bus stop was conveniently near the building. He kissed me 'good luck' and I waved him goodbye.

I could hardly complain of being on my own, for I was given a desk in a large room, open plan except for a glassed-in office at one end. The girls who were already established in the routine eyed me superciliously. I recognised one from school, but she had been part of a different group of friends. She looked very grown-up in a smart new outfit with plenty of make-up on her face. She wore sheer stockings and court shoes. I had a new coat, serviceable tweed, worn over a skirt and blouse; rayon stockings, which I kept up with elastic 'garters', disdaining a suspender belt, and school shoes. Molly had dabbed powder on my nose.

The supervisor obviously regarded me as a nuisance, for she had to repeat all her instructions to me, having finished training the first girls. They were already a team, and not keen to show me the ropes. I was given all the filing to do, while they went on to better things. I kept my head down to disguise the tears in my eyes and shuffled the great mound of papers. I had the feeling the supervisor wanted to punish me for taking a holiday before I even started work . . .

I didn't realise how fortunate I was to start work in surroundings which were much better than I might have experienced in other offices in post-war London. Desks, chairs and filing cabinets all appeared new. The latter were ranged along one wall, and during my first week when I pulled out one of the long drawers to file away the endless papers, the drawer slammed shut on my right hand. The pain was excruciating, but I didn't cry out, and not a head was raised to see my predicament.

I managed to free my hand, but the nail on my forefinger was badly crushed. I felt as if I was going to pass out. I steadied myself and asked the supervisor if I might be excused. In the cloakroom I ran cold water over my bruised hand and then tied a clean hanky over the finger. I went back to my desk and wondered how I would get through the rest of the day. The supervisor, noting the improvised bandage, obviously guessed what had happened and commented: 'You must be more careful.' Vera, a middle-aged clerk who sat at the next desk, fetched me a glass of water and an aspirin. The damaged nail turned black and eventually came off; it was ages before I grew a new nail.

Vera was rather eccentric but after that kept a motherly eye on me. I valued her quiet advice. 'We all started with filing, dear. Things will get better.' She invited me to join the 'sugar club'. We were provided with cups of tea mid-morning, and again during the afternoon. These were delivered on a trolley by the tea lady, who allowed us two sugar lumps each. I took sugar in my tea then, so this was bliss. Vera opened a drawer and showed me a box almost full of sugar lumps. 'We save them until we have a couple of pounds then I take them to a shop where you can exchange the sugar for chocolates! We all put something in the kitty, because you have to pay for them, of course, new girls like you usually contribute sixpence a week. Would you like to join?' I couldn't say 'no', could I? Though I only received two chocolates from the first box, because there were so many members of the sugar club, it was worth all those cups of sugarless tea.

I knew that the glass box office was occupied by the Manager, but I never actually saw him arrive or leave. Various privileged members of staff, male, mostly, entered his sanctum occasionally. They were usually from Accounts, upstairs.

I met the Manager after I had another mishap. I broke my glasses. As I was fairly helpless without them, I was summoned to his office. He was of short stature, and not intimidating at all, a kindly man. He said: 'I have arranged for my optician to see you today, to supply you with new frames as your lenses are intact. Here is his card. You may leave work after lunch as you will have to travel to the West End, and then you are free to go home afterwards. How are you getting on with your work? I understand you are an artistic young lady.'

Who on earth had told him that? It surely wasn't relevant to insurance, I thought. Naturally, I fibbed, 'Very well thank you.'

He regarded me thoughtfully. 'We are short of staff in Accounts – would you be interested in moving up there temporarily? It is good to have a fresh challenge, a change of scene now and then . . .'

Even though I knew Accounts equalled mathematics, I had a lunchtime friend Audrey, who worked upstairs, so I was indeed interested.

I still shudder at the thought of my journey into the unknown, i.e. the West End of London. It took me ages to find the superior opticians, not surprising if you can't see the number on the bus or decipher the destination. It was a consulting room, not fronted by a window full of spectacle frames as I expected.

Another little man with a nice smile, wearing a bow tie, treated me like royalty. I didn't like to tell him I wasn't too keen on horn-rimmed specs, because he said, with satisfaction: 'Ah, this is the pair for you. Very intellectual.' I just wanted to look attractive, that's all. I decided immediately I wouldn't wear the specs to dances.

It was late afternoon when I emerged from the shop, it would soon be dusk and I panicked. Even with the glasses, I had no idea where I could find the right bus stop home. I walked in one direction, then another: It was November, and there was the acrid smell of fog in the air. I found a phone and two pennies and rang the office. Would anyone still be there? The supervisor answered. 'Stay where you are,' she commanded 'and we'll come and get you.' She arrived after half-an-hour with Kay, the girl I'd known at school, in tow. 'Kay will escort you home by train,' she said.

We had to stand in the corridor and weren't able to converse, but I was too embarrassed to talk anyway. We parted at the Clock Tower. I thanked her for her company and hurried home.

'Oh dear,' Molly exclaimed, 'I expect you'll get a big bill for those frames – why on earth didn't you ask to go home then we could have gone to our usual opticians?'

The bill eventually arrived, written by hand on thick, watermarked paper. £2–10 shillings. More than half one week's wages! I had to buy a postal order in order to pay it.

We were paid monthly, which meant I had to budget carefully for fares and house-keeping, but I was proud to be able to buy my mother a big bunch of mimosa to mark my launching into the business world.

* * *

Thankfully, I actually enjoyed my time in Accounts. I met other jolly girls about my age, but Aud, as we called her, was the general favourite. She was a thin girl, with black hair, green eyes and a very pale, freckled skin. She came from Golders Green. I was invited to her next birthday party there. We rolled back the carpet in the living room and placed her one and only record on the gramophone turntable. 'Put another record on, On the Nickelodeon,' we sang along with Teresa Brewer. Aud was a live wire, full of fun. She showed us how to jive to the beat of the music.

However, she suffered from terrible boils, and sometimes I stood by her in the cloakroom at work as she sobbed with the pain of these monsters, one inside a nostril, as I recall, and another under her arm. She would dry her eyes, and smile, squeeze my hand, and say, 'Don't tell anyone, will you?' Her mother took her to the doctors but they couldn't offer much relief. Penicillin must have been available then, but it was the early days of the National Health Service. We lost touch when I moved on, but I do hope she had better health in later life. Where are you now, little Audrey Maynard?

Fortunately, we had calculators in Accounts, but mostly what we did, was to stick stamps on receipts for instalments on policies received. Accounts wasn't dry and stuffy, it was a busy hive of chatter and laughter.

Another summons by the Manager. I had done well, he said, but would I be able to help out in the Vaults? This was known as Down Among the Dead Men.

I was to assist Anna, who was half-French, and, I was delighted to discover, a story-weaver like myself. It was rather alarming, on my first morning, to be escorted down steep stairs, with doors unlocked en route, to what seemed like a dungeon. When the last doors clanged shut behind us, we were in another world. The many boxes and files in here were not exactly covered in cobwebs, but were battered and often bursting at the seams. They were the dead claims, and some were labelled with famous names. Anna had a long list of instructions. Sometimes she climbed a library ladder and handed down untidy parcels to me.

'These are deeds, wanted by a solicitor, when a will is read, or if there is a dispute over inheritance,' she informed me.

I was intrigued by crackling, yellowing pages and red wax seals. We placed our finds in boxes which would be collected at the end of the morning. We were escorted up the stairs at lunchtime and back again after an hour.

'It's secret, I'm not allowed to talk about it,' I informed my friends as I sat blinking in the daylight. 'You're all dusty.' Aud brushed my hair with her hand.

My parents were not too happy about me working Down Among the Dead Men. 'It sounds unhealthy down there to me,' Molly worried.

The novelty was beginning to wear off, when Anna told me she was leaving at the end of the month. She was going to train as a house-mother in a children's home.

When I first started work, Jim suggested that I buy an evening paper after work: 'Something to read on the bus,' he said. He brought home the *Evening Standard*, and when David was at home, before he went off to the R.A.F., he chose *The Star*. The familiar cry of the corner news vendors was: 'Star, News and Stannard!' So I was left with the *Evening News*, which was rather difficult to handle when opened out on the confines of the bus.

The *Standard* had classified ads, like job vacancies: I preferred my paper because of the daily story. Now, Jim drew my attention to an advertisement. 'Trainee Proof Reader wanted for Publisher.'

I'd achieved my first year with the insurance company, as I'd promised, Molly had been delighted with the Christmas parcel. I was fit and well due to all the nourishing meals. Time for a change. It sounded good to me.

CHAPTER 22

Twelfth Street Rag

Meanwhile, Maggie was settling in at the bank. Despite her misgivings, she found the staff friendly, although they were older than her. A couple of the men had returned there after the war, as their positions had been kept open. The main drawback, she confided to me, was having to balance the books at the end of each working day. 'You're not allowed to go home until you've accounted for the very last halfpenny,' she sighed. Then she brightened up: 'If I don't get married for about ten years, I'll get a bonus when I do.'

'How can they expect you to wait *that* long?' I marvelled.

Maggie had to work Saturday mornings; I was luckier in that respect in my first job. However, the publishers worked longer hours, including some Saturdays, and there were no free meals, or cups of tea and sugar lumps . . .

We fitted in our shopping sprees when we could. Clothes were now coupon-free, the New Look was here, and C & A had arrived in Croydon with up-to-the minute fashions! The pretty dresses were affordable, cotton and easy to launder; the skirts were full enough for twirling when dancing; we wore lace-trimmed petticoats from Dorothy Perkins and graduated to roll-on girdles. We cinched our small waists with wide belts with fancy buckles, which was a hazard if you were dancing with someone in uniform and your belts became 'attached'. We bought sandals from Bata (which didn't last long if you went out in wet weather) and in the winter, crepe-soled fur-lined boots from Stead & Simpson. I later had a nasty accident in icy weather due to squidgy crepe soles. But that's a later story . . . Colour, it seemed to us, was coming back into our world.

Best of all, we had Saturday evenings at the Grandison Ballroom, just a tram ride away, with live music, including regular visits from Kenny Ball and his Jazzmen.

It took me some time after Saturday high tea to prepare for the evening out. First, a bath, though I could never have a good soak as five inches of water was the rule – was that a government decree, or family economy? Then, draped in a towel, it was time for the Drene shampoo. This liquid in the bottle, which smelled similar to washing-up liquid of today, had replaced the old Amami sachets of gritty, grey powder, and resulted in a lovely shine on your hair. The way we dried our hair was certainly rather dangerous. Molly lit the gas oven on low, and I poked my head inside and 'flapped' my hair until damp-dry. She then encouraged the wave in my hair with her fingertips. It was a relaxing experience and the results were pleasing.

Make-up was applied before slipping my dress carefully over my head. I used Ponds cream as a foundation, face powder on nose and chin, Vaseline on eyelids and lashes, to make them glisten, and finally, lipstick. Maggie and I had graduated from Tangee Natural, an orange stick which changed colour on your lips and was indelible, to brighter shades: we both used the new lip 'pencils' and blotted our lips carefully with good old Bronco toilet tissue. Neither of us used mascara or eye shadow, after a disastrous evening when it rained and we had 'panda eyes' when the black ran. The final touch was perfume: my favourite was Muguet des Bois (Lily of the Valley to you!). I would tuck my glasses in my handbag after I left the house.

We sat side by side at the back of the hall, but we weren't wistful wallflowers – we chatted to each other in an animated fashion, and partners would appear. It seemed to us that they arrived in pairs, a tall chap and a shorter one. Very often, little Maggie was invited to dance by the taller boy, and I would be asked by the short one. I expect they wondered what on earth we were giggling about. Then, one evening Maggie met her match in Leslie, and it's strange but true, that she did indeed wait ten years – and gained the bank dowry! – before she married him. He was older than us, and generously included me at refreshment time. He even took me along with them to the Pictures on occasion! The small box of chocs was passed to me, too, and I overheard him whisper to Maggie: 'She's had the caramel!'

I had my share of 'dates' too, but nothing serious. I didn't have the time, because I was attending night school twice a week, and still studying as well as working. When I met a date one evening at the cinema, he complained that I slept through most of the film! I'm afraid I did the same thing in the gallery at the Last Night of the Proms in the Albert Hall . . . My escort thought that was beyond the pale. I *almost* went out with a Wimbledon prospect – David, who was a keen tennis player, was envious of my good luck. But 'almost' doesn't mean I took up the offer of playing mixed singles at a prestigious local tennis club – after all, Maggie and I had only practised serving, not perfected any other strokes. I had the white shorts, but I knew that was not enough . . . I made some feeble excuse and this handsome individual immediately lost interest in me. David said, 'I would have gone! Why didn't you tell him I'd like to play him?'

'Because you're not a girl,' I told him. He had no answer to that.

Dancing was a different matter – I loved it. The jive was becoming popular, but was frowned upon at that time. Eventually, the couples who couldn't resist this kind of dancing were permitted to perform their sometimes amazing contortions on one side of the dance floor. We often paused to watch, when in the middle of a waltz or foxtrot.

There was always a feeling of excitement, of anticipation near the end of the evening when the jazzmen were playing. A roll of drums, and the call: 'On your feet – "Twelfth Street Rag", everyone!'

We surged on the floor, with or without partners, the music swept us up, we improvised the steps and sang along – it was a wonderful climax to our dancing.

If there was an encore, we sometimes missed the last tram home, but we trudged home under a starry sky and even if it was cold, or drizzly, we didn't care.

* * *

My new job was not far from Fleet Street, which I liked to walk along and dream of working in the hub of the writing world. However, this was a dingy office in a building which had suffered war damage, and faced demolition in the future. It was a large room, with rows of tables and unfriendly faces. The copy typists, all old hands, didn't welcome newcomers, particularly trainee proof readers, I gathered, because they were disgruntled that one of their number had not been offered this position. I certainly wasn't aware, until I was told much later, that I was paid more than them, from the start, which was unfair after all their years of service. I was assigned to a grim senior proof reader who wore an overall to keep her office clothes clean. She told me right away that she hadn't asked for an assistant but she supposed she'd have to put up with me, and I'd better learn quickly. She handed me a huge catalogue and told me to cut out every single advertisement and paste on to separate sheets of paper. 'These are often changed, and you will then make the relevant corrections,' she told me. The first thing I learned was 'stet', meaning same, or no change.

After a week of cutting-out, I had red ridges on my thumb and forefinger, but I battled on. Corrections were marked with a mapping pen. This was a business dictionary – the interesting part was designing new advertisements to the customer's directions. But it wasn't the sort of publishing I had hoped for – magazines or books. Nevertheless, I was learning the jargon, proofs and galleys, the symbols. My typing expertise came in handy, but I hadn't found a use for shorthand yet.

We ate our sandwiches in the rest room – which had a sagging sofa, a few hard chairs, no kettle, but a Burco boiler to heat the water for tea. We were provided with a pint of milk, and a quarter of tea, and that was it. The typists ignored me, and so did the more elevated staff, who all seemed to be related to the two men in charge, who had a cubbyhole office off the main room. I was not accepted as part of either group. The lavatories were awful. There was one on the end of the block, which was kept locked. Only the more privileged members of the staff had the use of the key. I got a glimpse in there, one day. This cubicle had a flowered pedestal and tiles on the wall – and toilet paper! We had to wash at the restroom sink and queue to look in the cracked mirror on the wall.

I did finally find a friend there. A young girl called Joy. We shared chocolate biscuits, with a delicious jammy centre, from her father's grocery shop. We began going out at lunchtime, buying a milk shake at a milk bar, and eating our sandwiches, on a seat with pigeons hovering around. Joy didn't like it there any more than I did. We decided to try the Stella Fisher Employment Bureau. We both had interviews lined up. The one I went to, was on a newspaper. The man who saw me might have had the green shade over his eyes, but he also had his feet up on his desk, and he had big holes with his toes poking out of his socks. He also badly needed a shave, and he smoked cigars. 'Can you handle a switchboard?' he asked. When I said, 'No,' he lost interest and I beat my retreat. Joy was luckier, she was offered a position as a trainee photographer.

I began studying the Sits Vacant in Jim's paper. I spotted one for a comptometer on a women's magazine. I had no idea what a comptometer was, but I had visions of writing articles and short stories – when I was established, of course! For the first and last time in my working life I took an illicit sick day off. I caught the bus in good time for the interview, but things went wrong thereafter. The bus was stopped halfway, because a man refused, or couldn't pay his fare. The argument with the conductor seemed to go on for ages. In desperation, I tapped the shabby man on his shoulder and offered to pay his fare. The conductor advised against it, but I handed over four-pence, and to my relief the bus moved on. It had been a sunny start to the day, but when I alighted at my stop, there was a cloudburst and torrential rain. I was soaked to the skin, hair in rat-tails, shoes squeaking, and I was running late for my appointment. Needless, to say, I wasn't offered the job, I must have looked like a drowned rat, and by then the sun was shining again . . . I was also told there were no prospects of anything other than operating the machine, and they needed someone with experience. I didn't want to make another mistake, I decided. I knew it would upset my parents if I did. I kept quiet about how unhappy I was with such unsociable fellow workers, after Joy had left. We still met up at lunchtimes and that made it bearable. Then something happened which made life good again – *I met John*!

* * *

Maggie and Les had tickets for the United Dairies annual dance, to be held at Streatham Baths. (The pool was covered in the winter, for such a purpose, and it was November, 1950.) They invited me to join them. I was to make my own way there, as Maggie was never sure what time she could leave the bank.

It was raining, and I wore my new mack, red with white spots, with dinky white rubber boots. I had a red umbrella to protect my head and newly set hair. I shivered, because the mack wasn't as warm as an overcoat, and I was wearing a pretty, sleeveless blue crepe dress with cross-over bodice, fastened discreetly with a favourite Woolworths brooch, a little mermaid. People arrived, but hurried inside and there was no sign of my friends. I didn't want to go in on my own, and was considering catching the next bus home, when I was joined by a tall young man in a stylish white mack with the collar turned up. After a few minutes, I ventured to ask: 'Do you have the time on you?' Then I had the embarrassing thought that he might think I was 'picking him up' – something no well-brought-up girl would do. However, he looked at his watch and replied politely, 'Almost eight o'clock. Are you waiting for someone?'

'My friends,' I said. 'They're late.'

'I'm waiting for friends, too.'

Then both sets of friends arrived together, so we smiled at each other, and went inside.

'He looked nice,' Maggie said, excited for me. I'd been down in the dumps lately over my job. 'I bet he'll come over and ask you to dance!'

But he didn't – not until the interval waltz, that is. Not that I lacked partners. I danced with a Scotsman, an Irishman and a Welshman in turn – so it was time for an Englishman to ask: 'Would you like to dance?'

We sat up on the balcony and talked over our tea and biscuits. We danced every dance together after that. However, we parted at the cloakrooms at the end of the evening, to collect our coats.

'Didn't he ask to see you again?' Maggie asked.

I shook my head, disappointed. But when we emerged to leave, he was waiting to ask me: 'Can I see you home?'

Maggie gave me a nudge, whispered. 'Go on – he's genuine, I can tell. And we'll be on the bus, too . . .'

John escorted me to my front gate. 'Can I see you again? Would you like to come to the pictures?' I said that I would. Then I told him to hurry or he'd miss the last bus back to Streatham.

I looked in on Molly and Jim, reading in bed. 'Did you have a good time?' she asked.

'Oh, I did! I met such a nice boy—'

'That's funny,' she said, 'I was just looking at wedding pictures in my magazine. . . '

'Oh, *Mum*!' I said.

CHAPTER 23

Black-Eyed Susie

My fur-lined boots were great for keeping my feet warm when trekking through snow to work, after leaving the morning bus. The crepe soles were, however, an accident waiting to happen . . . In the freezing conditions of January, soon after I met John, I came a cropper. One moment I was treading cautiously along, the next I was sliding helplessly at speed and smacked into an imposing edifice – the solid front wall of a bank, no less.

I came to, lying in a heap with a concerned crowd round me. I looked up, trying to focus, and saw a man, bending over me to check my injuries.

In my confused state, I thought: I've died and gone to Heaven . . .

The doors to the bank were opened and I was carried inside. There were more puzzling images. The bank staff attempting to help me, were all small people, and speaking in a language I couldn't understand. Much later I would learn that this was the Malaysian bank, that they had opened up before the usual time, and were doing their best to help. I was laid gently on a padded bench and questioned in English: 'What is your name, please? Who shall we contact? Do you need a doctor?' I opened my mouth, but couldn't answer.

A doctor was called, and said I was concussed. I came to sufficiently to tell them my father worked at the Admiralty, but I couldn't remember his number. 'You must not worry,' they said, 'We will contact him.'

Eventually, Jim arrived. He had caught a later bus than me, but fortunately was in his office when the telephone rang. He decided to take me home, because by then I was sitting up, though very groggy and he could see that I was going to have a black eye. The bank staff made us hot, sweet tea to fortify us for the journey.

There were no taxis to be hailed, it had to be the bus. I leaned against my dad and closed my eyes. 'What's wrong with your right arm?' he asked me, alarmed. It hung limply at my side, but didn't hurt then. 'Bruised,' I murmured.

Molly put me to bed, and my arm in a sling. I could move my fingers, so they thought it wasn't broken. The doctor said he would come first thing in the morning if needed. He was rushed off his feet with minor accidents that day. 'A couple of aspirin and a hot water bottle,' was his advice.

The doctor sent me to the hospital the following morning for X-rays. Molly and I spent most of the day there. I had broken my collar bone and dislocated my shoulder. Eventually I returned home with the injured arm immobilised across my chest with a giant strip of Elastoplast. Only my hand was free, but unusable from that position. I would have to struggle left-handed. Ruefully, I thought of the ambidextrous twins at school. Because of the concussion, I was told I must rest for several weeks and would be signed unfit for work.

The firm was unsympathetic. After a couple of weeks I was asked to show myself in the office so that they could see I was really incapacitated! They were also reluctant to pay me the sick benefit to which I was entitled.

This clinched matters for me. I would return to work, in due course, but I would definitely leave there as soon as I could.

John was a great support, and when Maggie's little mum asked me: 'Is he the One?' I beamed, and said simply, 'Yes!'

From then on, once I was working again, John left his home, some miles away, very early, turned up at our house just after breakfast, and escorted me to the door of that dismal building. He did this in reverse in the evening. It was wonderful to be young and in love. We've been together ever since.

I met his family – and we all got on splendidly. Still do. John and I have a lot in common, our ever-increasing family of course, and art, books, love of country living. We have had an adventurous life together. We differ in some things – he is keen on most sport, and when he was younger participated in it, too. He is more practical than me, but we mix and match, as it were . . .

* * *

Stella Fisher came up trumps. She passed me a card. 'These are well-respected publishers, lovely people, they intend to move to premises in Holborn soon, so don't be put off by the present building.'

147

She was right. Butterworths were a super firm to work for. It wasn't quite what I hoped for, as they published medical and law books, but it was civilisation.

Hooray! I joined an office of five other girls, as a junior secretary.

Breams Buildings – is it still in existence? – was in Fetter Lane, and the exterior was unpromising. There was an old-fashioned lift (which 'appears' now and again in my stories, plus the liftman, Fred Head – both affectionately recalled, I have to say). Fred had a powerful pull on the rope which swung the cage upwards, despite having lost an arm in the war. He was the most cheerful chap, and what we now refer to as a 'people person'. There was a notice in Fred's lift, which intrigued me the first time I read it. SHOULD YOU LOSE YOUR RIGHT GLOVE, I SHOULD BE GRATEFUL FOR THE OTHER. He wore out a lot of gloves on that rope.

The large room where I joined my new colleagues was freshly painted and the desks were all by the windows, except for the office boy, who sat with his back to the girls and ear-wigged on our conversations. He was a nice lad, and told me cheerfully one day, 'When I'm manager, you shall be my secretary!'

Part of my duties was to act as assistant to the manager's secretary, Nita, a beautiful girl of Italian origin. She was a great fan of Arsenal football club, living in Little Italy. I took dictation mostly from the Major, who, like the Manager, had his own office adjacent to ours.

There was Lilian, who was married to a regular in the air force, Valerie, Ann and Joan, who worked with Phyllis (who also had her own small office), and at break times we linked up with more friends from the other side of the corridor. There was another office where the editors and copywriters worked and later I would join them. Most of these were older than us, but lively and interesting women.

The first day when everyone disappeared for lunch, I suddenly wondered what I should do. We were given luncheon vouchers, only 1/6d. but welcome all the same. Then Joan, who had been busy all morning, but smiled at me now and then from her desk opposite, spoke. 'Would you like to come out to lunch with me?'

So I found a kindred spirit – a girl like me, always reading, who apologised for propping her current book against the salt pot on the ABC cafe table, but who walked with me after our tomato soup, bread roll, plain yoghurt and cup of tea (which used up all the voucher!) and took me down all the little streets full of history which she had already discovered. We are friends to this day.

Terry, the office boy, tailed John and me in the mornings, when he walked me up to the office as usual, until we moved to Holborn, and said later: 'Cor, he looks like Dick Barton, Special Agent in that white mac!'

*   *   *

This is a short chapter, but a happy ending. I became engaged while I was at Butterworths, and well, you can read on to *Knee Deep in Plums*, to find out what happened next . . .

PART 3

KNEE DEEP IN PLUMS

1962–1970

CHAPTER 24

Knee Deep in Plums

One last cough from the overheated engine of the Morris 8 and the bulging doors appeared to burst at the seams, with children tumbling eagerly out and dispersing in all directions – rushing past the shabby old weather boarded cottage into the tangled orchard and, with joyous whoops, discovering the gnarled plum trees groaning under the weight of huge, glistening purple-red Victorias. Bombarded by drunken wasps was much overripe bounty, split and oozing golden juice, nestling in the long, lush grass.

'Mummy, Daddy, oh *look*!' called six-year-old Sara, soft, rounded cheeks aglow, fair hair glinting red in the sun and feathering in a faint breeze, 'We're knee deep in plums!'

'J.P.', Jonathan, skinny, knobbly-kneed, overflowing with seven-year-old energy, was already shinning up an enormous apple tree, revealing a jagged tear on the seat of his new drill shorts. Jo and Ginge, four and three, gathered plums in their folded-up cotton skirts.

'Mind Chris – see he keeps away from the wasps – don't bat them like that or they *will* sting you – and don't eat too many!' I shouted back, clutching at Michael, the baby, who was wriggling at not being permitted to crawl rapidly away to join two-year-old Chris, big, blonde, smiling and sturdy.

We stood by the car in the sultry heat of that August afternoon in 1962, gazing apprehensively at the cottage with the jumble of furniture, mostly elderly and 'inherited', stacked outside to be sorted out: we observed, for the first time it seemed, the peeling shiplap boards, the rotting windowsills, the wormy Colonial style porch (as described so enthusiastically by the agent), the tumbledown chicken sheds, the antiquated stable, the rampaging back garden dominated by a row of stern, sentinel pines set far too close together, keeping out the light, but, no doubt, originally planted as a windbreak.

'Let's go inside,' my husband said, squeezing my slumped shoulders. We smiled ruefully at each other.

'It smells like *home*,' I murmured. The mingling of earthy, fruity even decaying aromas which assailed our nostrils reminded me overwhelmingly of my wartime childhood in Suffolk, evoking that tiny cottage and long garden with its well-turned black earth, the pungent privy, and the mealy smell of the chickens.

Mum, understandably shocked at her first sight of our dream home, decided on first things first. 'I'll keep an eye on the children from the kitchen window and boil the kettle for the tea,' she offered briskly. She was a youthful grandma, with curly fair hair. She was perpetually surprised that her dreamy little bookworm daughter had grown up to marry and to produce six children in as many years. (Did she also attribute that fact to too much dreaming, I wondered?) Mum *had* approved of the semi on the prim new estate and considered this move to be out in the sticks. Now, she took Michael from me and strapped him firmly into his pram, where he sat without a murmur, knowing who was boss. She parked him under the shade of an apple tree where he could see the others playing and she shooed Seamus, our determined little Scottie (whom we had acquired in a pause 'twixt babies four and five) into the orchard, where he proceeded to christen each tree in his path.

Somehow, when Mrs Decker was in residence, the cottage had not seemed so down at heel. Now, the real horrors of the narrow dark kitchen were revealed. An ancient cupboard when cautiously opened, emitted clouds of dust and smelled strongly of *mice*.

'We'll get rid of this right away,' John said firmly. We tugged – the cupboard literally fell off the wall, we struggled outside with it and dumped it on the lawn. Now I had a rip in *my* trousers.

John lit the primus stove for Mum's kettle: 'All the wiring will have to be sorted out before we can use the electricity.'

There was merely a stained Belfast sink with a greenish brass cold water tap; a partition concealed a bulbous bath on splayed claw feet, but no water connected. 'Never been used!' Mrs D had told John cheerfully while he stared in fascination at the saucer of unidentifiable meat reposing within its cavernous depths. 'Just a little "parg" for my dinner,' Mrs D explained – and she invited him to share it as a reward for mowing the front and back lawns for her! The mower had practically seized up, it was a veritable steam roller, and afterwards he had an agonising backache and blistered palms. 'Worth it,' he grimaced as I rubbed him later with Elliman's.

'How can we put the beds up, until we've swept right through?' I was suddenly near to tears. It had been exhausting earlier getting the excited children organised and tidying up the little house, which we had left behind without a backward glance. Now I thought wistfully of hot water 'on tap', of small, square rooms with everything in place.

* * *

We had first seen Crabapple Cottage in March of that year, we drove up Carters Lane admiring the raised, cobbled footpath, not realising that this indicated the probability of flooding. We discovered the cottage hiding behind massive hedges, with a creaking front gate between two great oaks. There were masses of daffodils in delicate shades from white to orange-gold to one side, and sheep grazing in the orchard. We had visited hopefully all spring, when the trees, some fifty years old and unpruned, were heavy and heady with blossom.

Mrs D, that wiry old lady, with her skin weathered from many years spent sheep farming in New Zealand, had retired seven years previously to this Kentish smallholding with her late husband. She wore faded print dresses and had flat, grey plimsolled feet. She pointed out the exact spot where Mr D had passed away in a chair (which she bequeathed to us) in front of the French windows in the living room. (All of us, in turn, fancied we 'saw' Mr D – well, perhaps not John, he's artistic but not fanciful like me! – in that chair, during the years we lived there.)

Anyway, Mrs D took a fancy to us and wanted us to have the cottage, despite the tempting offers made by other eager, prospective purchasers, hence John obliging with the mowing. Our problem lay in selling our house and raising more money, for the cottage was not mortgageable. From the deeds when it was finally ours, we discovered that the holding had been the first, and last, of a proposed co-operative involving a group of ex-servicemen after the First World War. The scheme had been abandoned during the Depression (when the current owner sold the topsoil of the holding, such was his desperation) and Crabapple Cottage had obviously known other impoverished owners of its three acres. Even so, it was always a happy, enchanted place to us: and to those who remembered it from idyllic childhood holidays between the wars. They would call and ask tentatively if they might look around; one or two wistfully hoped we would sell!

Many old varieties of roses rioted in June. Tiny, tight Paul Scarlett twined round the secretive garden at the back. There were winding little paths going inconsequently between the trees, a patch of wild, white violets, a huge mock-orange bush to make a perfect play under and hiding place for the children; fragrant lemon verbena crowding the back door and a japonica in the front garden.

'A Wendy house,' we mused, when the children called us to inspect the little creosoted shed which had housed Mrs D's ailing chicks. 'A *Windy* house!' they cried, jostling in, excitedly. With its gaping roof and floorboards, that really was the more fitting name, we thought.

Each time we came, there was some new wonder to exclaim over, to make us more determined to live here. Now we had arrived. Crabapple Cottage was, less rather than more, ours.

* * *

We ate a picnic supper on the lawn, carelessly crushing the daisies. There was homemade pork pie, plums for a sweet finish. We drank tea, fishing out the flies, and what Sara called 'fizzled out' lemonade, warm and flat. I lay back with the baby sprawled asleep across my stomach, giving his fuzz of red-gold hair an affectionate rub, idly watching the little trickle of milk from the corner of his mouth. Chris sat impatiently on his potty, with Seamus standing guard.

'Come on, J.P.,' John said to Jonathan, 'Let's get those beds up, cots first, those little ones are flaked out.'

Mum appeared with a bowl of warm water, a flannel and towel. 'Who's first?' she asked cheerfully, balancing the basin on a tree stump.

There were four bedrooms, two of which had obviously been added on to the original single-storey cottage. The inside walls, once covered with brown hessian to keep the draughts at bay, now bore cracked, discoloured wallpaper. All the paintwork was a depressing mud brown. Only the living room had a reasonable floor – the front-room boards were rotting and would need replacing before we could put that to use.

Our bedroom was vast and we felt lost in it, that first night. We were overtired, aware of every creak and sigh. We didn't need to tell each other that the scratchings, scuttlings and squeaks were mice. Once, we woke, alarmed, to find moonlight flooding the room and heavy breathing outside the uncurtained window. John investigated. 'Courting hedgehogs!' he reported.

Birdsong at dawn, rambling roses tapping on the window. We looked out at the older children already in the orchard, still in their pyjamas, bare feet soaked with dew, shrieking joyfully with no one near enough to care, or complain. That was to us both, a wonderfully warm feeling. We collected the damp and chirpy little boys from their cots, boiled eggs for breakfast, while Mum rounded up the rest and cajoled them into washing and dressing too – into laying the table and buttering the mounds of bread.

J.P., posted to the front gate to watch out for and to waylay the milkman, rushed in with news: 'There's lots of bikes in the front garden!'

There was indeed a tangle of ancient, rusty steeds which had obviously been thrown over the hedge. But when – and why? Was our garden a repository for the rag and bone man? Had someone made us a gift?

'Can we ride them round the orchard?' J.P. and Sara pleaded. Better not, we decided, perhaps the mystery would be solved later. Instead the bicycles disappeared during the afternoon, and we were none the wiser.

'Where's Seamus?' was the next question. Someone (who?) had let him out first thing, he had obviously found the gaps in the hedge and wandered off, as was his wont.

Jo's round green eyes brimmed with tears. 'Jo-Jo's crying crocs!' Ginge said, hugging her protectively. 'Snow white and rose red,' we called them, one being so fair, the other with a cap of dark hair and even darker eyes.

John and J.P. went searching for the dog, while Mum and I tried to make some headway indoors. 'I'll have to go home tomorrow,' she reminded me. I couldn't help thinking she sounded relieved. Back to normality, eh?

Our first caller, and it wasn't yet 9 a.m., was a tall, stooped old man, who presented us with a giant cabbage, teeming with fat, wiggly caterpillars. I placed it gingerly in the sink. Mr Jackson had an engaging smile, bright, inquisitive eyes behind wonky glasses, and a perpetual drip on the end of his nose, which unfortunately fascinated the children, of course.

We learned that he was a retired tailor who lived next door to the little shop, a hundred yards along the lane. 'My place was in a similar state to yours when I moved in,' he said: 'I dredged up hundreds of old, yellow bricks and made an impressive drive.' He liked children. 'They can come and feed my ducks any old time,' he said kindly, 'and my old tree has the finest conkers around here, so I shall expect to see them then, my brother and I still have rare old conker fights when he comes to stay.'

Our second visitor was also long and lanky, but much younger. He lived next door. We learned later that he had been a surprise (and shock) arrival for his parents in middle age: he appeared disappointed when he saw our small fry, hoping no doubt for a companion of his own age, early teens, despite his height.

'I hear you've lost a dog,' he began, having spoken to the departing Mr Jackson. 'Well, I found a little black, hairy dog earlier this morning and took it along to the police station in the village – I didn't know anyone had moved in here yet.'

Unobservant, we thought, but still, we must be grateful that Seamus was 'in custody'.

'I expect you're busy, I'll cycle down and fetch him back,' Chas offered. 'For five bob,' he added, after we accepted gratefully. I mentally changed my first impression: not 'poor lad', more 'shrewd lad'. However, he was even cannier than we thought. Mrs Gee at the shop informed us later that Chas had 'discovered' Seamus sitting by our front gate!

Mrs Gee's house was wooden, like ours: the shop was a little room tacked on to the front, with a rusting tin roof. 'Players Navy Cut', 'Brooke Bond Tea', proclaimed disintegrating signs outside. The shelves were practically empty, there were just a few packets, a tray of soft, sticky penny sweets and some tired-looking tins.

'Ten years ago, this was a little goldmine,' Mrs Gee said. 'Then everyone got cars and went shopping in town. I just get in what folk ask for, from Mr Brick, the village grocer, he drops me off a box when he delivers round here on Fridays.'

I took to Mrs Gee immediately. She had a cheerful, round face, no-nonsense grey hair cropped short by the local barber, and she made the most of a hard life. She was grateful that her husband had achieved his lifetime's ambition, when they moved here from London, to grow pot plants under glass. This too brought in little money.

Now she produced some flour from under the counter. 'I'm sure you do lots of baking with your little crowd, how about these, at half-price? I had a bit of trouble with the mickeys.'

I must have looked blank, for she enlightened me with a grin: 'Mickeys? Mice, dear. They only nibbled the corners.' Little trails of flour on the counter endorsed this.

The children took time over choosing their sweets and then Mrs Gee escorted us outside to inspect the sleeping baby in the pram.

'Six, oh my dear! And you know what they say? New house, new baby!'

Relating this to John later, we both laughed, but of course, Mrs Gee was shortly proved right!

CHAPTER 25

Everyone Calls, Dawn to Dusk

We needn't have worried about being so far from the shops, all the local tradesmen vied with each other to secure our custom. As Mrs Gee said, 'Everyone calls,' and they did – dawn to dusk.

Mr Brick had a complexion to match his name and I felt quite concerned the first time he staggered up our long path, clutching at a giant cardboard box with a dangerously bulging bottom, containing amongst other weekly necessities, 8lb sugar, 3lb butter, 1lb tea, several toilet rolls and tins of dog food to last us, and Seamus, until his next visit. The total, carefully budgeted for by me before I ordered, seldom came to more than £2.10s.0d.

Mr Brick's shop was a larger version of Mrs Gees, but well-stocked. I enjoyed making the occasional long trek to buy hand-sliced bacon, cheaper from the fatty end, currants and demerara sugar weighed out into dark blue bags, broken biscuits (Mr Brick was always generous with the chocolate ones), and sweets for the children in deftly turned pokes. The first supermarkets were appearing in the villages alongside the new estates and Mr Brick was, in his turn, experiencing the desertion of long-established customers, except for the elderly and infirm, or the young wives who came in, now and again, at the end of the week, and requested boldly: 'Please chalk it up.' He didn't refuse, because he had known most of them as little girls who spent their pocket money in his shop. So Mr Brick relied more and more on those of us who lived further out, with no transport, young children or gammy legs.

He called on Thursday afternoons for our order, providing a little book with stiff red covers for me to write my requirements in. When he was paid, after the Friday-morning delivery, he penned with a flourish: WITH THANKS, FB. Then he staggered back down the path.

Mrs Gee told me that Mr Brick suffered from anaemia, which his hectic colour belied, but he knew better than the doctors who advised him: 'Sell up and retire, take things easy.' Mr Brick, you see, had his own well-tried remedy: 'Guinness – finest thing for enriching the blood.' He drank a bottle of this medicine several times a day, and it certainly seemed efficacious and kept him going, as he remarked.

However, Mr Brick was not the first caller in the day. This was the fishman. I never actually met him, because he called one day before it was light and left a note, redolent of kippers and shiny with fish scales: FRESH FISH DELIVERED TO YOUR DOOR EVERY THURS. EARLY. PLEASE PUT OUT PLATE AND MONEY. No price list. So I duly left two tin plates and half-a-crown and ordered smoked haddock or cod, which always appeared without fail, until we acquired Tiger our wild ginger tom, who slept in the coalhole. Two weeks running the fish disappeared, only a penny or two in change remained on the plate with the fishy odour.

So, reluctantly, I wrote a farewell note. 'No more fish, thank you, we did enjoy it, but so does our cat.' With a scaly pencil the fishman thanked me for my valued custom. We felt as if we had lost a real friend.

The next caller, around 6 a.m., was the milkman. The only time we saw him was on a Saturday morning, when he called for his money at breakfast time. True, we were often up and about in the kitchen when we heard the rattling of the eight pints being deposited in the crate, but we were usually still yawning as we boiled up some of the previous day's milk to satisfy the hungry babes.

In hot weather, the milkman moved the crate to where he considered the first rays of the sun would not curdle the milk, so we often played hide-and-seek among the bushes and trees, desperate for a cuppa.

Cecil, the cesspool man, always chose to call at lunchtime, reducing our appetite, connecting up giant pipes which oozed pungent black slime along the path, across the lawn to the cavern near the finest apple tree of all.

'Quick, close all the windows!' I called to J.P. and Sara.

But J.P. often dodged out to report back: 'He's eating his sandwiches, and he's still got his gloves on!'

'You'd think he'd catch something *awful*,' Sara said. 'Those gloves are absolutely—'

'You don't need to go any further. We *know*,' I told her firmly.

Sometimes Cecil was parked outside our place for a couple of hours, pouring black tea from an enormous flask, placidly enjoying the hum, and breathing it in, too, for his cab window was always wound down, while our excesses were drained from the pit.

Finally the pipes were uncoupled, and then would come the polite tapping on the door. 'Could you oblige with a bucket of water, please, Ma'am, and a stiff broom?' The children crowded behind me as I opened the door a mere crack because of the terrible smell, to marvel at Cecil's enormous, grimy red rubber gloves, his squelching thigh-high boots, the checked cap tilted back on his bald head and his disarming, toothless smile. I usually failed to prevent J.P. from following him down the path as he poured water (which I had liberally laced with disinfectant) on the slimy dribbles, brushing them briskly into murky puddles.

'Good day to you, Ma'am,' he called, once outside the gate.

Despite eating his lunch with his gloves on, Cecil always looked in the best of health. We missed him when we achieved main drainage at last, but it was also a relief financially; we had three emptyings a year, but needed several more at twenty-five shillings a time. We didn't manage to fill the cesspit until we moved, when we presented it with defunct television sets and other rubbish.

The coalman called after dark. Even we could afford coal by the ton (with a month to pay) then. It was our busiest time, with babies to bath, bedtime stories, John's supper to cook – time to clear the toys from underfoot and to chivvy the youngest bunk-bedwards.

The coalman was almost as invisible as the fishman, only his teeth gleamed white in his sooty face as he enquired: 'Usual place, Mum?'

The coalhole was then way up the orchard, and approached via a gap in the front hedge. As the coalman went to fetch the first sack, I alerted J.P. 'Quick, find your torch, count the sacks in!' Whether he lost count before he reached twenty, or whether his torch battery was low from reading under the covers in bed, we never knew, but always the coalman came to ask: 'How would you like a sack or two extra, I managed to squeeze on some spares – cash for 'em though, as the bill's made up.' As coal was in short supply, and deliveries erratic, I always agreed, and we anxiously rifled money boxes for the necessary. We've wondered since, of course, if we were paying twice for our own coal! Even when John made a large coal bunker adjacent to the outhouse, the coalman continued his after-dark calls, and J.P. his excited counting with his flickering torch.

The butcher seemed to call whenever we were out. More wise to the waiting cat than the mysterious fishman, he made neat newspaper parcels of liver and sausages and dangled them from a loop of string tied to a beam under the covered way. One day, the cat made a flying leap, caught at the package with his claws, chewed through the string and fell with a thump to the ground with his prize. All *we* found, on our return, was shredded, gory paper and a bill for 6/9d. So, we left the back door unlocked, and the butcher placed his parcels on the draining board, and his bill on the windowsill. No one ever took advantage of that unlocked door.

The breadman changed frequently, and so did the quality of bread. The green van breadman staggered like Mr Brick, but his breath reeked of something stronger. He loathed dogs and usually aimed kicks at friendly Seamus if he encountered him up the path. Seamus was a sucker for car rides, and on one occasion, stowed away in the back of the battered green van, among the racks of loaves and cakes, to be discovered further up the lane at the next stop.

'Your so-and-so dog!' roared the puffy little breadman, coming unsteadily to complain, lifting a miniature black boot at the cowed little dog in front of him. Fortunately, he missed, so I thought it prudent to say: 'Sorry about that!' After all, we *needed* our daily bread, and hopefully there would soon be a new breadman as old hot-breath had lasted a record three months. But I couldn't help saying to John later, knowing Seamus's proclivities only too well: 'Thank goodness we had *our* bread first!'

A real friend was the postman, who not only delivered letters, but took our outgoing mail, and posted off parcels, too. He came twice a day and I soon knew that when I was housebound with sick children, I could ask: 'Please can you take this prescription to the village chemist?' and that he would cheerfully oblige.

'A letter from your mum, today,' he would remark, 'a postcard from the Channel Islands – now, who do you know there?' And always, 'Anything to post?' The highlight of my day, being a prolific letter writer and receiver, was his rattle on the letterbox and the friendly call: 'Postman!'

Before John installed the central heating, our only warmth was provided by a small fireplace in the living room, so from autumn onwards we had to rely upon various oil-filled heaters. So the oilman became a regular caller. Most of our 'deliverers' were small in stature, and Norm was no exception. He worked long hours in his ironmonger's shop as well as driving out to remote parts with his oil, and this despite having only one sound arm and leg. He may have been disabled, but he certainly was not handicapped, and he could be relied upon to arrive even in the hardest weather. Fog and ice did not deter him. He never spilled a drop of oil and always insisted on carrying the heavy can up the path for me.

The dustcart man called out, rather than in, as he cleared our verges of their crumpled paper and bottles thrown carelessly from car windows. He pulled a handcart, and his back was permanently bent, but he had the most brilliant blue eyes with clear whites and a cheery, piercing whistle. He liked to stop for a chat about the state of the world, he was a gentle, unassuming philosopher. We once observed him tenderly lifting the body of a poor, stiff stray dog which had been run over and pushed to the side of the road. Freddie took off his tattered overcoat and covered the sad remains so that folk like us, glancing into the cart, would not be distressed. When he retired, he was replaced with a noisy motor and an anonymous driver.

These were our regular dawn-to-dusk callers, but others came knocking on our door.

A loud thump on the back door, and uncharacteristic growling from the dog, usually heralded the rag-and-bone men. As they asked, unsmiling: 'Any old iron? Old batteries?' their sharp gaze was directed here and there, penetrating the gloom of the outhouse, far seeing up the orchard, staring over my shoulder into the kitchen.

To begin with, we were not unpleased to see them, as Mrs D had not cleared the outbuildings; most of the relics pre-dated her time anyway. John warned me to be wary, what appeared to be rubbish at first sight might just have a use. But we were glad to see the back of some ancient mattresses, which were accepted with alacrity, with 'I'll be back with the money in a moment, my dear – two bob all right?' and that, naturally, was the last we saw of *him*.

One of John's first tasks had been to remove the hallowed bath and to dismantle the sagging partition, thus enlarging the kitchen. The bath he dumped by the chicken shed, intending to make a sunken garden of it, at some future date.

One of the rag-and-bone men spotted the bath and asked: 'How much?' jiggling coins promisingly in his pocket.

'Not for sale,' John said briefly.

'Ten bob?' the man persisted.

'No thank you.'

The same evening the bath vanished. We could guess who had 'called back' for it. 'Why didn't you take that ten bob, while we had the chance?' I chided John.

Then we were actually given some money – for nothing.

A polite middle-aged man tapped diffidently on our open door one summer's evening. Seamus welcomed him in, so we knew him to be an acceptable guest. He was slim and dark skinned, blue chinned, with a Cecil-style checked cap which appeared to be part of his head.

He asked John, in a quiet, country voice: 'Might you have a spare shed to rent, sir? I breed rabbits – for showing – not table, you understand, and my neighbours have complained to the council and I've been told I can't keep them in my garden. I promise you, there'd be no smell, and you wouldn't know they were there.'

We liked him immediately, so we said, 'Yes, why not?' and he inspected gravely the shed which leaned against the coalhole for support, and thought it to be ideal for his purpose.

'I'll make a gap in the hedge and put in a stout gate,' he offered. 'Then I can come and go without disturbing you. I'll patch the roof of the shed and fit a padlock.'

On his next visit, he presented us with a small rent book and six months' rent in advance, six new pound notes.

We awaited the arrival of the rabbits – and the rabbit man. But we never saw him again, we couldn't trace him, no one knew him, it seemed. For three years we preserved his money. Then, finally, baffled, we bought school shoes with the windfall our benefactor had given us.

If you ever call again, Mr Rabbit Man, at dawn or dusk, or any time between, we will of course, pay you back. The six pounds, I mean.

CHAPTER 26

Frozen Apples, Frozen Pipes and Festive Fires

We just didn't know what to do with all the fruit which ripened after the plums; long before the windfalls were used up the fruit on the trees needed picking. Sorting through the relics we discovered a holey, fraying picking sack which John patiently darned (all my family have learned to sew in self-defence as I'm known for my hot needle and burning thread – and subsequent disasters . . .). John wore this on his back. He seemed to climb effortlessly up those stout trees, being tall, strong and athletic: we couldn't afford to buy a ladder that first autumn.

We brushed the encrusted chicken messes from some sturdy bushel boxes, gathered piles of newspapers, and proceeded to wrap meticulously our keeping apples and pears. Bowls brimmed with Worcesters and Annie Elizabeths, a scarlet-cheeked apple, crisp and juicy, and later we tasted our first mouth-watering Charles Ross and Newton Pippin (who grows them nowadays, with their distinctive 'Newton knob'?). We enjoyed these delicious apples round to the following May. Despite what dentists now decree about the sugary effect of apples, none of our children needed fillings in their teeth for years, and they ate, at a guess, around four apples each every day – and that's not counting the ones they nibbled at, as they wandered round the orchard.

The pears were round and nutty flavoured, no longer commercially grown. There were just a few giant golden Williams's, but these were invariably pecked, or bored, or sampled, before we could pick them and they splashed and sploshed to nestle in the grass only to be trodden with a squish! underfoot.

Visitors came frequently to our orchard paradise and all we asked was: 'Please, can you bring your own boxes?' J.P. became his dad's assistant and nimble Ginge soon joined him.

'See me, Mum?' came the cry the first time.

'I daren't look!' was my reply as she fearlessly leaned out on an out-stretched bough and grabbed an apple to throw down to Jo, an expert at the awkward catch – an accomplishment which stood her in good stead in family cricket.

Michael was toddling now, and he and Chris spent hours with a short pair of steps, climbing up and leaping off with glee into a pile of fragrant grass clippings.

When picking sessions were in full swing at weekends, Sara and I busied ourselves with food for the troops, after gathering in our abundant harvest. We couldn't do much housework anyway, I told myself, until the house renovations commenced, so beds were hastily made first thing, we washed up en masse, I strung out lines of washing to flutter like flags between the trees, and blew the dust from the mantelpiece to make the most of our freedom and fresh air.

Then it was time for school once more. The first morning I accompanied J.P. and Sara to settle them in, and to meet the teachers. It was an early Victorian school with lofty ceilings, battle-scarred desks with a patina of chalk dust. The staff matched their surroundings, being all near retirement. Miss O'Grady, J.P.'s teacher looked him sternly up and down and quoted from A.A. Milne. 'Jonathan Jo, with a mouth like an "o" – move up boy, yes, *you*, make room for him.' So J.P. sat down next to a boy who might have been his twin, with a similar shock of fair hair and horn-rimmed glasses. They grinned sheepishly at each other.

Miss O'Grady showed us firmly out, and Sara and I walked hand-in-hand to her classroom. Miss Sharp fortunately did not resemble her name, being cheerful and welcoming. I was allowed to linger whilst she listened to Sara's fluent reading.

'What a confident little girl, and how nice – she should go far in life,' she predicted.

As I walked away from the school, I knew I would worry until they arrived back safely on the school taxi. I had promised to meet them at the crossroads, a fair way up the lane. Mum was here for a couple of days to help with the rest of the family. I'd guessed right: during my absence she had emptied the mending basket. And the kettle was whistling a welcome, too.

The taxi was a capacious, square, ancient black motor with extra pull-down seats in the back. Eight children were carried to and fro, and J.P. and Sara were taken as a concession. After all, if you don't mind going as the crow flies across ploughed fields and along the busy main road (no paths) it *is* less than the statutory three miles – just. The regulars naturally bagged the best seats. Among these were two little traveller children, fair of skin and hair, whose large family rivalled ours. We discovered that it was their older siblings who left their bikes under our hedge, whenever they went to catch the bus at the end of the lane to town.

The afternoon walks to meet the taxi became an enjoyable ritual. There was so much to see. Each cottage on our route had its place in the pattern and the occupants and livestock were the object of our friendly curiosity and imagination. The children gathered blackberries and rosehips, acorns and cobnuts; ate 'bread'n'cheese' and 'popped granny out of bed', collected the turning leaves, made fishbones from the green chestnut ones, and jumped in and out the ditches. In October, Jo was five, then there were three of them to meet.

Suddenly it was much colder and we were about to endure our first winter in an inadequately heated, draughty home: the honeymoon was over. The trees, almost leafless, still had apples, the outhouse was packed with stacked boxes, we had given to all and sundry, what to do with the rest?

'Cider apples wanted,' John pointed out the advertisement in the local paper. A man came out to look at our Bramleys and provided a pile of sacks. 'Just shake 'em down,' he said tersely, 'Ten pound a ton.'

As always, at weekends we all pulled together. Monday to Friday, the under-fives and I were on our own. We achieved most when Mike was having a nap.

Battling with morning sickness, with dressing up squirming children, who wanted to run straight outside, I pulled on a woolly hat and old gloves and gulped a few lungfuls of misty, chill air to ease my queasiness before I bent my back to my task. John was anxious: 'You don't *have* to do it!' But I was determined.

First thing, he and J.P. went out to give the trees a good shake. Each day, the apples seemed colder and harder to pick up, eventually they froze to the ground and needed prising up. Our gloves soon became hard and soaked through, the fingers holey. For three weeks we raced against time. Each night, John sewed up the tops of the full sacks and put them ready for collection. I was told sternly that on no account must I hump the sacks around. It takes an awful lot of apples to make one ton – forty sackfuls, in fact – and we eventually reached our target of three tons. Only the odd wizened apple clung precariously to the topmost branches, swaying in the bitter wind. *Thirty pounds!* We were rich. New wellies all round and the prospect of a good Christmas.

* * *

I had been collecting presents from August onwards, but the big-buying session was reserved for the church bazaar in December. Our favourite stall was the UNWANTED HOLIDAY GIFTS – these rejected items, still boxed and wrapped, were our bargains, and often became our treasures. From October, I bought extras each week from Mr Brick, like dried fruit and almonds, jellies and icing sugar. This way, expense was spread. John made splendid wooden toys; his masterpiece was a super rocking horse, with a blond mane and tail fashioned from teased-out string, a leather saddle with studs and a bridle. The children loved it. This Christmas there was a train big enough for the small boys, incorporating parts from an old vacuum cleaner (he's very ingenious) and dolly-buggies for the girls, with their names embellished on the sides. J.P. and the girls made their presents, too, like little boxes mostly filled with cotton wool with a few (sucked?) fruit gums adhering. We all looked smart at Christmas, for our mums had been busy sewing and knitting.

The day came at last, and it was *oh, so* cold. Mum and Dad were with us, and we all shivered in our beds, despite the layers of blankets and our bedsocks.

On Boxing Day, the first snow began to blow ominously in the biting wind, and much to our disappointment my parents thought they should go home while the trains were still running. When they had gone, seeing all the forlorn faces, John suggested: 'Why don't I take them for a walk? It's not snowing much and they ought to make the most of it, it might have all disappeared by the morning.'

It was bright, light and exhilarating outside and the children were eager to go. Seamus was not so sure, he picked his way daintily down the path as Mike and I waved them off. 'You stay by the fire – we'll be about an hour – back by three,' John called.

I laid the table ready for tea, plenty of goodies. Christmas cake. I opened a gift tin of biscuits and placed a cracker by each plate. Then I cuddled Mike and we turned the pages of a book. Within ten minutes we must have fallen asleep.

Awaking with a start, I discovered the room in darkness, with just a flickering from the fire. Mike began to whimper, and slid off my lap. We were alone, and it was half past six. I snapped the lights on and peered outside. Flurries of thick snow were dashing against the window and as far as I could see all was white, and there was an eerie quiet. I strapped the little lad into his chair, gave him milk and biscuits, then, with panic rising, I ventured outside the back door with a torch. I immediately sank in piled-up snow; like a fool I wore slippers. I shouted – no answer. I trod fearfully down to the drive, flashed my light each way along the lane. All I could see was blinding white covering trees, rooftops, everything. Then a glimmer of light from the nearest house reassured me that we were not quite bereft. I yelled again, but no response.

Back indoors, I stoked the fire, and Mike and I played with building bricks on the rug. He was happy, but I was taut and fearful.

It was past seven before I heard the excited chattering and J.P. burst in, treading icy globules all over the carpet, closely followed by Sara, still gripping her little sisters by the hand. The small girls were crying miserably, their faces blotched with cold. They had obviously tripped on occasion as their trousers were soaked.

'Poor Mummy, were you worried? We got lost and Chris was grizzling, and Daddy had to carry him – they're just coming,' Sara said bravely, choking back her own tears.

'Oh, it was exciting, like exploring the North Pole!' J.P. exulted, already cramming a mince pie into his mouth. I gathered up my lambs and stripped off their saturated clothing, filled the baby's bath with the hot water intended for the tea – their father could jolly well wait for that! The younger ones soaked their feet, while J.P. draped blankets round them.

A weary John came in and unbuttoned his coat. Chris, warm, pink and sleepy, uncurled like a puppy and rushed at the tea table. My wrath evaporated and I cried with relief, clinging to John as he explained: 'They wanted to call on Mrs D in her caravan on the farm. We completely lost our bearings. Don't cry! We're all in one piece. Where's the tea? Mind you make it nice and strong and spoon in *lots* of sugar!'

* * *

We saw the New Year in and woke late the following morning, snow still falling. John was the only victim of the walk, he had a painful throat and high temperature. He couldn't get to work anyway, because the trains weren't running. But the tradesmen still got through to us, somehow.

Confined indoors the children became fractious, but Seamus began to enjoy bouncing in the snow. We cleared some grass for the chickens. We all watched *Huckleberry Hound* on TV, and we had supper plates piled high with scrambled eggs – a neighbour had slipped on icy ground and broken 180 eggs! The least broken were sold off at 9d. per dozen. This was fortuitous, our own fowl were on strike.

Time to return to school: the children all bathed in the little tub before a roaring fire, and then enjoyed a special tea while viewing *The Old Curiosity Shop*, with Michelle Dotrice as Little Nell. 'Wish I could get in the bath and have a soak, too,' I said wistfully.

'Go on, then,' John laughed huskily. So I did, when the children had gone to bed. Had to hunch my knees but it was blissful, even if the misplaced water did slop over and soak the hearthrug!

John was still unwell, so I took the children to meet the morning taxi, and on my return found he had rescued a little robin from the cat.

On 8th January I wrote in my diary: 'This was the day – that was!' Returning from the doctors, as I came up the lane, I became aware that a small crowd was gathered outside Crabapple Cottage, where smoke and flames billowed from the chimney. Rushing indoors I found John battling furiously with wet sacks while red hot lava roared and poured down into the hearth.

'The children are in the bedroom – go and ring for the fire brigade!'

The crowd parted to let me through and watched as I hared down the lane and hammered on Chas's door. His mum looked at me cautiously through a crack in the door. We hadn't been introduced, after all. 'Please let me in,' I shouted desperately. 'We-ell . . .' 'Oh, *please!* I must ring the fire brigade!' So I dialled 999 and within minutes the firemen were dousing the fire, within and out, and reprimanding John for burning the Christmas evergreens. 'That chimney hadn't been swept in years – the old girl must have burned green wood and the resin caught light,' they added.

After school, Chas arrived. 'I see your chimney pot is broken – we've got a spare one – only five bob!'

* * *

The big freeze went on, but the children managed to get to school most days. There were power cuts galore and our primus was put to good use. At the end of January, school was closed due to frozen pipes. Then our own pipes seized up, John was back at work, and I had no idea where the stopcock was located. Again, I tore along the lane for help. Bert was slow and ponderous and took his time, but discovered the stopcock in the middle of the front lawn. He took ages to turn it off. In the middle of the mopping-up operation the Public Health Inspector arrived! The children and I ferried buckets of water from the plant nursery opposite and John made temporary repairs when he came home.

My diary for February was full of sickness and setbacks, but suddenly, on the 23rd, I was able to write: 'First sign of spring! Sunshine and snow disappearing fast.' We'd come through our first winter, 'out in the sticks'.

CHAPTER 27

Who Lives Down the Lane

'Made any friends yet?' asked Mrs Gee.

'Well, *you*, of course, and Mr Jackson next-door-to-you—'

'Oh, *him!*' she winked. 'He's all right, I suppose, but when you see him and his brother together – *well!* Right old set-to they have sometimes, like a couple of kids.'

In her garden, Tish and Tosh, her pet geese (better than any old dog for guarding your property, Mrs Gee assured me, with a sly look at Seamus) had a set-to of their own, hissing and rushing at each other with elongated, snaky necks. I suddenly recalled the 'rare old conker fights' and grinned.

'The nursery people seem nice, she always smiles and waves, but I haven't spoken to her yet.'

'Busy people, my dear. He's a milkman, finishes his round at nine each morning and then joins her in the greenhouses. Their ground's no good for growing, like yours; their topsoil got sold too, it takes years to get it right again.'

As we meandered, as usual, to meet the taxi, I wondered about the people who lived down the lane. We had made up some weird and wonderful stories about most of them, but really we only knew them to say 'hello' to. There always seemed to be somebody out in each garden we passed, too busy with cutting hedges, mowing lawns or sawing logs to stop to get to know us. We were disappointed that there were no other under-fives around. Weren't they as curious about us, these shapeless people, clad in old coats, however clement the weather, and outsize rubber boots, as we were about them? Before long we would find out.

Next to our cottage was another orchard, owned by a local, wealthy farmer, with orderly rows of sturdy young apple trees. These perfect

Worcesters were picked carefully in just one day by a team of chattering women. Not an apple remained either on the trees or on the ground when they departed at teatime. However, their coat pockets bulged.

'J.P. and Sara got us some of those apples,' Jo remarked innocently later. 'They were very juicy.'

'The man was counting his boxes and he saw them, and he chased them away!' added Ginge. I wasn't surprised!

'And we have all these apples of our own,' I mused. Yet I couldn't help recalling the childish delight (and fearful anticipation) in scrumping. However, I now dutifully pointed out the error of their ways.

Beyond this orchard was a field where the woodcutters had set up camp in a corrugated iron shelter, flapping with rotting sacking. Here we paused to watch the elderly man and young girl, whom we guessed to be his granddaughter, stripping the chestnut spiles and pointing the ends for fencing. When the weather was colder, the woodcutters made a snapping, sparking fire with the wood shavings before their primitive headquarters. They set a black, dented kettle to boil, or sometimes had a fry-up. They never spoke to or acknowledged us, but once, as we stared curiously, the girl, thin and stooped, threw down her knife and came up to the fire and slowly rubbed her cold, calloused hands together as if praying for strength as well as warmth.

'Mrs Nosey's in.' Jo tugged at my arm and pointed.

'Shush . . .' I cautioned. 'You mustn't call her that.' But, sure enough, the snowy curtains fell back into place, as we hurried on, past a drab little house with scarcely any garden to speak of. This was a farm cottage: 'They don't let 'em have any ground round here – not even enough to grown a cabbage or two,' as Mrs Gee said.

* * *

There were two of these cottages, neither had electricity or running water for years. When they were eventually linked to the farm generator, the farmer and his good lady 'rationed' the points, one to each room, and switched off the current when they retired for the night at 9 p.m. One family bought a small TV but were unable to watch much, being cut off at vital moments in a play or film. Also, they had to keep the old oil lamps primed ready in case they were suddenly plunged into darkness and forced to grope their way to bed.

Then there was the Colonel's house – we called it that because the sign on the gate proclaimed grandly COLONADA. The military title suited the present occupant, with his bristling moustache, ramrod straight back and booming parade-ground voice.

'*Put that dog on a lead!*' he yelled at us, going puce as he yanked at his huge hound's collar. '*He eats little dogs like yours for breakfast!*' Seamus was wise enough to keep a low profile and to slink beside the pram until we were safely past. The Colonel ran a dog kennels and his diminutive wife, Fluff, bred Pekingese. She looked not unlike her favourite breed, with her snub nose and prominent 'bolting' blue eyes. We dubbed her 'Fluff' because she had bottle blonde curls in soft wisps, like those little Easter chicks fashioned from bright yellow cotton wool. She was much nicer than the Colonel, and if he were not about, she sometimes came to the gate to proudly display one or two of her latest pups to the children. Her aged mother lived with them, mumbling and grumbling, mainly about her son-in-law. We could understand why. We once heard the Colonel bawling at her: 'Pick up your feet, woman!' as the poor old lady creaked to the kennels in down-at-heel checked slippers with insecurely sewn pompoms on the fronts, slopping a bucket of water. She was obviously expected to work for her keep.

On the opposite side of the lane was Mrs Gee's shop, with Mr Jackson's cottage behind, as if hiding behind her skirts. The yellow brick path was indeed impressive and the conker tree magnificent. Mr Jackson's lawns were close-clipped and straight edged, as befitted his calling, and the pond looked as if it had been buttonholed around with little clumps of flowers at exact intervals, in harmonious shades of course.

Carter's Farm was no longer functional but was the grandest house down our lane, luxuriously renovated into a pseudo-Tudor mansion. Here lived a wealthy stockbroker and his wife. The only dealings we had with them originally was when we were forced to share a telephone party line. The Ayres informed the post office that this was most inconvenient for *them*, as Mr Ayres' work was of National Importance, so we suddenly found ourselves sharing a line with Chas's parents. Whenever we wished to make a call, it appeared that Chas's mum was already ensconced, telling us, as we lifted the receiver, 'Go away! This conversation is private!'

Later, we came to know the Ayres quite well, and they were genial, in a 'lofty' way – keen to employ our bigger children to clean their limousines and to mow their lawns. J.P. earned his half-crown in a swift blitz on the Rolls, taking perhaps half an hour – Sara patiently laboured for two hours over the Daimler.

J.P. was full of stories about Carter's Farm. We particularly enjoyed this anecdote: 'I looked through the French windows and they were still having their breakfast. You know I told you about the aviary in the conservatory? Well, all the birds were flying loose about the room and swooping on their plates, and Mr and Mrs Ayres just carried on eating their sausages, and didn't notice what the parrot had deposited in the mustard!'

Chas's home was large, opulent and newly built and there were cats all over the garden – his mum was mad about them. Seamus usually nipped up their path before we could restrain him and caught us up further along the lane, licking his whiskers. 'D'you know,' Chas's mum told her cleaning lady, who passed it on to us, 'a dear little black dog visits me every day, and I always have a little treat ready for him. Goodness knows where he comes from.' Unobservant, like her son, we thought.

Looking at Mr Ruggles's pigs was one of the highlights of our walk. They were gigantic and usually smothered in mud. While they wallowed in their bath, a hollow which Mr Ruggles had obligingly dug out for them, he, it was rumoured, wallowed indoors – in gin. Once, we scattered in alarm, as the pigs charged towards us, having escaped from their almost-bald-of-grass field. Behind them lumbered Mr Ruggles, bleary eyed and ruddy of complexion, mumbling incoherently, wildly waving a crooked walking stick. After him lolloped his evil-eyed collie, Mordecai, snarling at us, and at Seamus, as he shot past his master to snap at the rear porker's hind legs. The little boys began to cry, and we cowered against the hedge and watched with half-fearful, half-delighted anticipation as the pig, infuriated, suddenly turned and pursued Mr Ruggles – and his dog – back to the farm.

When we eventually judged it to be safe to continue our walk, we saw the pigs back in their field, rolling energetically in the mud and making a terrible noise. Mr Ruggles wallowed with them, having obviously slipped up in the mud. Mordecai was adding to the din – howling with his head high, ears back, cowardly watching from the safety of the farmhouse porch.

'D'you think we—?' I wondered aloud. Mr R struggled to his knees, there was a rude, loud sucking sound as he parted company with the slime, then he stood up. He looked like a bog-man. We stared at each other. He raised his stick and we all flinched involuntarily.

'Good afternoon,' he remarked mildly. Then he and his dog retreated into the house, for fortification, no doubt. The pigs rolled on.

'Hello, my dears,' called Ben's gently dotty junior aunt as she picked daisies on her front lawn. Ben came round the corner of the house, humping a sack of cement to load into his little grey van. He was a bricklayer, could slap up a wall in an hour, so Mrs Gee told us. Ben's home was a battered old wooden house, rather like a doll's house, we thought, and the octogenarian aunties, whom he cared for with tolerant bachelor affection, were usually about when we were. They loved to see the children and chattered away artlessly to them.

'Don't delay the lady, now,' Ben said. 'She've her children to meet from the school taxi up the crossroads.' He added, seeing Seamus sniffing eagerly through the slats of the gate at his collie, a sweet natured one, this time: 'That dog'd need a ladder.' (Throughout his long life, Seamus was to remain devoted to Daisy.)

Ben was resigned to having his tea 'cooked' on top of the electric fire and to being woken in the middle of the night to be informed: 'We tried to turn the wireless on, but can't hear a thing, dear.'

'No wonder,' Ben related to us ruefully, 'not even a small-hours' hum or crackle – they were twiddling the controls of the Rayburn!'

One evening, John arrived home to find Ben's senior aunt sitting on an upturned bucket in our garage. J.P. had opened the doors as usual a little earlier.

'This is my new home,' she informed him, folding her arms firmly. Her untethered stockings concertinaed round her ankles and her feet were set in a pool of oil. John had to park the car outside and, in turn, we tried to persuade Auntie to go home. 'What about Ben's tea?' we asked her.

'Oh *him*,' she replied offhandedly. '*She* can look after him for once. She told me to stop interfering so I said, "Right, I'm off – I know when I'm not wanted."'

'J.P. – run and see if Ben is home, if he is, ask him to come down here and fetch his aunt – tell him, we can't budge her,' John told him.

'Come on now, old Auntie,' Ben said firmly. He tugged at her thin arm. He saw that I had spotted a nasty burn on the back of one frail hand. 'Don't worry, the doc's seen that. It's not really safe to leave 'em, but what can I do? I'm not a nursemaid. I said I'd never put them away, but I never realised, when I took them in, what it'd mean.'

'Who are you?' Auntie glared at him. We all gathered round anxiously.

'Auntie, it's me, Ben, I'm hungry, you've got to see to my tea—'

'Who are you calling Auntie?'

'You! Come on, it's getting cold, these good people want to go back indoors.'

At last she allowed him to shepherd her out and to shoo her up the lane.

Beyond Ben's house was the chicken farm. The family here also had an aged parent to care for. She was almost blind and would call out to us, 'Who's there?' from her chair in the front garden, where she sat in the afternoons to 'feel the sun on my face'. We would always pause to chat for a few minutes. The old lady's mind was still sharp. She would draw the children to her and gently stroke their heads; they looked at me apprehensively, but stood there quietly to be petted.

'Might just as well sell-up and run an old folks' home,' sighed her daughter, tucking a blanket round her mother's bony knees. It was her husband who had broken all the eggs, when we'd enjoyed a surfeit of scrambled egg. He commuted to London like John, while his wife, who had four quarrelsome teenagers to contend with too, collected the eggs from a thousand battery hens and looked weary and much older than she really was. So they did sell up, and did buy a nursing home, and the new owners planted three acres of strawberries which grew amazingly, due to all that chicken manure.

Mr Turner was a great favourite of ours. His home was another decaying, neglected place, but he had a secret in his woodshed. J.P. found out about it first.

'He's got a railway in there!' he reported breathlessly, having pelted home full tilt to tell us. 'He said – come up and have a cup of tea this afternoon, then we can all see it.'

'Come whenever you like, I love youngsters around,' Mr Tucker told me as we drank our tea in his faded front room. The children were occupied watching J.P. proudly operating the trains in their complex set-up, obviously the result of years of patient work.

On the mantelpiece was a row of photographs in gilded, ornate frames. Centre, was a lovely young woman, smiling faintly, with shingled, shining hair and round, expressive eyes. These eyes were repeated in the other photographs of babies and young children.

'Your family!' I exclaimed. Mr T smiled. 'They are,' he said softly.

Mrs Gee enlightened me later. 'His wife died in her thirties of consumption, they had seven children, and five of them died before they were ten, of the same complaint. He raised one boy and one girl, but lost her when she was seventeen, like I did my daughter' – her voice trembled, but she did not enlarge on this – 'and, of course, that boy was everything to him then. He, the boy, was married young, not even twenty, and had a little baby son of his own. Mr T built that railway for him. Then something really terrible happened: his son was killed in a road accident. Mr T goes on, and on, all on his own, but all he's got left are those photos and the railway.'

'What happened to his daughter-in-law and his grandson?'

'She got married again, the boy took to his new dad, and Mr T thought it best to fade out of the picture and allow them to be happy again. But everything is for that boy, when he goes . . .'

I was choked as I repeated this sad tale to John. Yet Mr T was always cheerful and pleased to share his wonderful railway with his new young friends. He also gave J.P. a ponderous old bike, with heavy tyres: 'You have some fun on that, young Jonny, make a track among your trees, don't you go out on to the road mind, 'til you can ride it proper.'

Past Mr T's place were fields and woody areas, and then, at last, we reached the crossroads. A winding lane unfurled to the right, where lived a traveller community. To the left, a broader lane curved round to the railway crossroads and eventually met up with the main road to the village. Ahead of us rose a hill, and a solitary house marked the beginnings of another community along our lane.

CHAPTER 28

Dear Sister Susie

The travellers, and the ghosts, were part of the pattern of our life at Crabapple Cottage. The former were certainly real enough and as far as the ghosts were concerned – who knows? There was nothing to be afraid of, in either case, which is all that matters, surely.

Hanging out the washing one morning, I became aware that someone was approaching me across the grass. John had fixed a plank across a tree stump, hammered on hand grips, and now Ginge sat at one end, and Chris the other, of the seesaw. As they were unevenly balanced, I paused occasionally to lean on Chris's end to enable Ginge to rise triumphantly into the air, clinging tightly to her handle.

'Them pegs won't last you long,' observed the newcomer. She was tiny, less than five feet tall, shrouded in a long, black dress with a capacious pinafore over. Her long hair was strained back from her dark face and hung in a heavy, oiled plait right down her back. Her eyes were almost black, almond shaped, and knowing. In her arms she bore a sheaf of artificial flowers fashioned from wood shavings, with curling petals crudely dyed in shades of brown and orange. 'You'd like some flowers, my love?'

It was late summer and we were still surrounded by real blooms, both cultivated and wild. I hesitated. Her gaze was intense. Who was she? I wondered apprehensively.

'You can't afford them, I know,' she stated, putting the bright bouquet down on the grass, then feeling in her apron pocket. She brought forth a bunch of stout dolly-pegs and a bundle of lace.

'How much – the pegs?' I enquired awkwardly. How much had I left in my purse? Probably about a shilling, I thought.

She knew that, too. 'One shilling for six, look my dear, all hand-made, will last you forever. You like the pretty lace?'

'I, er, don't sew much—'

'You can have the lace, and one flower from me. Next time you can buy more,' she stated.

She followed me to the house and stood on the kitchen step, looking in, as I located my purse.

'This place is good for you,' she told me, holding out the pegs and her gifts for me to take. Then she pocketed the shilling. Chris, who had sidled past her, was now peeping curiously at the visitor from behind me. I heard the creak of the pram as Ginge rocked it under the fir trees. The woman's thin, worn hand stretched out and touched Chris's golden head. 'You have many fair babies, but' – Ginge had now arrived under the covered way with the baby in the pram – 'that one, the dark one, is a special child, kind and clever.'

'She made me feel a little funny inside, I had a sort of eerie feeling,' I confided to John at bedtime.

'You weren't frightened of her, were you?' He sounded concerned.

'I don't *think* so – *no*! But she seems to know all about us and I didn't tell her a thing.'

A few weeks later, I was pushing the pram along the main village street when I was hailed from the pavement on the other side.

'Hello, my love – I see you is expecting again!' Mrs Lee, dressed as before, this time carrying a basket brimming with her wares. She was obviously out and about, selling.

I felt my face burning red. Blushing is a bane to our fair-skinned family. There were too many people about, looking curiously and smiling at me. I waved at Mrs Lee, called, 'Hello!' in return, and hurried on my way. Mrs Lee knew something I didn't realise myself, just then.

* * *

I had an uncomfortable pregnancy with high blood pressure and swollen, aching legs. Following that traumatic winter the children were often ill, and Sara was finally diagnosed with glandular fever. John's mother, concerned, took her home to cosset her while I went into hospital early to have the baby induced. 'Better make this the last one,' advised the doctor.

Another big, flaxen-haired baby boy. J.P. whooped with delight: 'I was praying for another boy!' Four boys and three girls, quite a family, yes, but wonderful, we agreed.

I was most surprised to learn that Mrs Lee had also produced a new baby, at the same time as our Roger. Her little son was as dark as ours was fair. She hadn't predicted her own pregnancy and had shown no visible signs of it; being in her late forties, as she told me wryly, when we met up in the village a week or two later, 'I thought I was too old, but this is it.'

'Me, too!' I laughed. Her baby was Joshua, a traditional name like Reuben, Susanna and Janie, who shared their taxi to school with our children.

'*My* last baby,' repeated Mrs Lee, tucking Josh into her shawl, despite the heat of the July day, 'not *yours*, my dear.'

In the 'picking season' the young Lees were often away from home, and absent from school. The taxi journeyed as usual to collect them, returned without them – the school was never advised officially about their 'holidays'. Our children were envious: wouldn't it be fun to be taken in a lorry to live in a little hut on a farm, to pick hops, cherries, plums, pears and apples all day long.

Once, innocently picking bunches of primroses along the lane, they were confronted by the younger Lees, with their lurcher dog in tow.

'Them's our primroses!' shouted Susanna, hands on narrow hips, eyes flashing. 'Our mum sells 'em in the market!'

Our lot beat a hasty retreat! I tried to explain that the Lees felt that they had a traditional right to the flowers and that perhaps they needed the money.

'So do we!' Sara cried vehemently. 'But wild flowers are *free* – for everyone!'

Around this time the girls began their 'gypsy' books: each had a family, the Peckbrights, the Brambles and the Ragshawes. They spent many happy hours absorbed in inventing their large jolly families and illustrated their books with fascinating pictures of their characters. Josiah, Beck, Joycee, Rosey, Marley, Jelli (short for gelignite!) and Bumeroy, the shaggy dog, became very real to us all. The rumbustious wives (alias our trio) wrote to each other wonderful letters about their offsprings' progress, or their husbands lack of it, and the great bargains, for which they had many ingenious uses, they had gleaned at jumble sales. (First-hand experience here: our girls were rummage enthusiasts, too!) The fictional families exchanged recipes, propped up their caravans with soap boxes and were generally endearing characters. We all loved them. They weren't a bit like the travellers we knew, who lived in houses, but an idealised fantasy.

Naturally, the Ragshawes, Peckbrights and Brambles didn't need to go to school – they led a wonderful, free existence.

I wrote letters for the travellers, too. One morning, Mrs Lee arrived just as I was feeding the baby. She waited politely until I was through, then asked me: 'Please my love, could you write me a letter?' So I fetched paper and pen and wrote as directed:

> Dear Sister Susie,
>   I do hope it wasn't you who had that fright on the Common. We has been worrying it was you. All of us is well. We shall meet you for the cherrying.
>   Your loving sister,
>   Emmeline

I felt rather uneasy. I, too, had heard on the radio, of an unpleasant occurrence on a Common in Sussex, but I did not feel I should comment.

'How shall I address it?' I asked, slotting the folded paper into the envelope.

Mrs Lee pondered, then: 'Sister Susie Lee, The Caravan, The Common, Sussex.'

'But where – which village?'

'It'll get there,' Mrs Lee said with confidence.

So I posted Sister Susie's letter – I bought a stamp for it, of course.

Now I was a Confidential Scribe, I was trusted to read the infrequent letters, mostly official, which the Lees received, and to answer them. I never expected to be reimbursed for the stationery or stamps, and, really, it was a privilege to be a friend of the travelling community.

* * *

The Wandering House Painters knocked on our door one bright morning. They were tall, broad and swarthy and had driven up our drive in their battered, rusty old vehicle.

'Your ol' house could do with a lick o' paint, my lovey,' they informed me jovially, tickling the baby under the chin and letting Seamus sniff impudently at their odorous trouser legs. 'Nice little baby – nice little ol' dog,' they added winningly. They quoted a reasonable price, John had enough to do with all the inside jobs, so we decided to hire them – all we had to provide, they said, was the paint and the brushes. And the money!

On the appointed morning, our painters arrived early – so early, that I had to dodge about the house to feed the baby, as they appeared at various windows, whistling cheerfully and tapping with their brushes, leaving blobs of paint on the glass, to let me know they were there. The small-fry followed them everywhere and were much speckled with white, then blue paint. The brushes were plied with abandon but the results were really not too bad.

Halfway through the week, they asked: 'May we have half our money in advance, my lovey?' They then disappeared for a couple of days.

'They won't be back,' John said pessimistically, 'and just look at all the paint on the windows, it'll take ages to scrape off.'

I felt guilty. I had spoken on their behalf, but I was only wanting to ease John's workload.

One morning, Chris came rushing in, out of breath, to tell me: 'The men's back!' The paint was sloshing again and soon Crabapple Cottage was dazzling white with blue doors and windowsills – quite a transformation.

In a year or so, the paint began to peel off. 'Waste of money,' as John had predicted. However, we hadn't seen the last of our Wandering Painters. They called back from time to time to admire their handiwork, to suggest that it needed doing all over again, or to ask: 'Any old clothes?' I didn't like to say, 'We're wearing 'em!' So I gave the big, burly leader of the gang an old suit of John's, and ever after he was wearing it when he called. The sleeves were too short, but otherwise it fitted – in places. I always felt as if I should say an extra 'hello' to that suit! After all, I'd been to the cinema often enough with it, in our courting days!

Once the painters suggested: 'We might park our caravan in your orchard for a while? We'd be no trouble, we'd run a cable to your electricity supply!' I had to think of a good excuse double quick, and I won't tell you what John thought about that idea!

Some other travellers settled on a site not far from us and the womenfolk were often led on shopping expeditions by a stately giantess. As she strode ahead of her band, we marvelled. In our very first supermarket, to which I sometimes ventured, feeling disloyal to Mr Brick, the followers filled their wire baskets and the Queen brought forth a roll of notes and solemnly paid for everything.

My fortune was told by another caller at the door. I received an urgent phone call from a neighbour: 'A man with a case of things to sell is on his way! He won't take no for an answer!' Sure enough, as I put down the phone, a man with gimlet eyes regarded me through the open kitchen door, while already snapping open his attaché case.

'I can't afford, I'm sorry . . .' I began apologetically as usual, and of course, I was telling the truth. The caller took my hand, pressed something into my palm, closed my fingers on it and told me, smiling: 'You are a very lucky lady. You have many babies and you will have still more. You have a gift with writing words. This is a lucky bean, and it costs you only threepence.' I pushed the bean back into his hand and said hastily: 'I'm sorry, I don't want it.'

His expression changed. Now I was really afraid. 'I take away your luck,' he scowled, and clicked his case shut. Then he turned on his heel and went away.

My neighbour rang again: 'Did he come?'

'Yes, and he wished me bad luck because I didn't buy anything – I was actually trembling.'

'Well, he's *given* me bad luck! I bought a shirt and it's only got one sleeve!'

* * *

John's sister parked a caravan on our land and used it for a couple of holidays. Then she decided to sell it. I offered to show it to prospective purchasers as she lived some distance away.

A gruff voice asked for details of the caravan, over the phone, and later a traveller couple arrived. I was paid with ten- and twenty-pound notes – I hadn't handled that much money ever before. The wife, tiny compared to her huge husband, pushed the caravan out on to the road, while he directed. She shook her head at my tentative offer of help.

That night, John and I slept on the money, tucked for safety under our pillows, fearful of having so much cash in the house. Four hundred pounds! We were really relieved to hand it over the next day.

The ghosts were all around us.

We all treated the late Mr Decker with respect. After all, he sort-of lived with us! So, we apologised if we 'trod on his toes' or if we had to move 'his' chair to open the French windows. Visitors, unaware, sometimes sat in his hallowed seat.

One day, we discovered his family Biblio mouldering with some rubbish in the outhouse. (We have it to this day.) We cleaned it up and turned the pages carefully. Here was a fragile palm cross marking a page – here a fragment of a letter, written during the war, which war, we wondered. The letter had obviously been treasured, much read and refolded. Turning it over, we read a message in a different handwriting, signed *George*. I read aloud: 'Fear not, for I have redeemed thee. When thou passeth through the deep waters, I will be with thee.'

'I wonder if he kept it because the person who wrote it died in the war?' John mused. 'Look at this,' he continued, referring to the back cover of the bible. The writing was faded and blotched, some of it indecipherable, but here were all the names of Mr D's family, dates of birth and demise. Sometimes these were but a short time apart. The names were often repeated: George, Henry, Eliza, Sarah, Mary, Nelson, Alfred, Albert, John and Thomas, and finally the names of Mr D's parents, Alec and Edith. She was born in 1865 and died in 1933. Here the list ended. No mention of Mr D, and he and his wife had been childless, but now we knew that Mr D was at home.

Other presences were familiar to the children, and to Seamus. When we first arrived here we had seen a blind and deaf old golden Labrador walking slowly along the lane, oblivious to traffic. Then the dog died, but sometimes the children thought they 'saw' it, ambling still, stiff-legged and unaware.

Seamus was wary of a cold spot along the lane. He had to be tugged past there. Ben told us: 'Oh, yes, a dog was run-over just about there. My Daisy hates going over that part, too.'

'When did that happen?' the children asked him.

'Oh, more'n thirty years ago, I reckon . . .'

We were all nervous of another cold spot, the place where a Spitfire crew were said to be entombed. We always trod carefully and quietly by unspoken consent to show our respect for those young lives so suddenly ended.

To us, our ghosts, if indeed they did exist, were gentle and undemanding.

CHAPTER 29

Piano, Pets and Pests

'John!' I urgently poked him awake. He groaned. We had spent too many sleepless nights of late soaking sickly sheets in the bath, cold flannelling fevered foreheads and dabbing chicken pox blisters with soothing pink calamine.

'Who is it this time?' he mumbled.

'Someone's playing the piano . . .'

He sat up with a jerk, tossing the bedclothes aside, bleary-eyed, listening.

'They're not playing it in tune, then.' He subsided again, humping up his pillows defensively.

The ghostly tinkling was spasmodic as if the perpetrator was prodding keys at random – a one-finger player, perhaps? I jabbed John in the back again. Why should he sleep, when I couldn't?

'The birds are making a racket!'

Seamus was our solitary pet when we arrived in Stonebrook, but now we had added considerably to our furred and feathered friends; after all, we had plenty of space and it was good for the children to grow up caring for pets, wasn't it? J.P. had become an avid reader of cards in shop windows. Now, two budgies, plus cage, FREE to good home, *must* mean us, he thought. The cage was no ordinary affair. It proved to be very solid, extremely heavy, being home-made from oak. Where could we put it? It was a perfect fit for the piano top – another bargain buy for £3. J.P. was confident that they would all learn to play by ear; meanwhile their experiments were somewhat excruciating. I had to agree that performances by the birds, preening and pecking, beat the stuffed birds in glass cases which had menaced me on visits to my grandparents as a child. The problem was seed –

they were messy birds and some of the husks were infiltrating the piano works . . .

'I suppose you want *me* to investigate,' John groaned reluctantly at last. 'D'you realise what the time is?'

As usual, it was around 2 a.m., a time which always seems unearthly, and most unfair to be awakened at.

Resigned, he rolled out of bed, felt his way into his slippers and sighed heavily and reproachfully as he went through into the living room.

The music ceased abruptly and I heard the crash of the piano lid. Simultaneously, there was a wail from the baby and Michael called out fretfully: 'Mummy – I want Mummy!'

I collided with my husband in the corridor.

'*Mice!*' he fumed. 'A whole *colony* of 'em mucking about inside the works. You'll have to get rid of those birds!'

I shuddered. I'm terrified of mice. I've passed that on to my daughters. Irrational, I know. As John often pointed out, when the girls and I shrieked at the sight of one: 'Look how big you are compared to them. Poor little devils must be petrified at the sight of *you!*' However, tonight, he was obviously immune to their doubtful charms.

Pests, we discovered, come as a package deal with pets. And I'm not talking about fleas!

'We've got a chicken shed just waiting to be filled with hens – we can sell our surplus eggs!' we imagined, after our arrival at the smallholding. First, we bought half a dozen Rhode Island Reds at point of lay. (They didn't get the point for some time, not until they had consumed several sacks of expensive feed.) Then we reared the tiny Maran chicks that first, awful winter. These were now big, black hens (and unfortunately cocks) and condescended to lay an occasional dark brown egg. Delicious bright yellow yolks, but, 'cost us about a shilling per egg to produce,' we moaned.

All the hens were fiercely ruled by a giant cockerel, known to us as 'that Lionel'. He was particularly vicious and attacked humans at every opportunity. One day, he leapt at John's wellington boot, fell down in a frenzy, and snuffed it. We couldn't bring ourselves to eat him, or to be sorry. We presented him to the family at the nursery, who had no such qualms.

One morning, Jo and Ginge, chief egg collectors, came rushing in to report an interesting fact: 'One of the hens has turned into a cock – she's grown spurs!' From then onwards we examined our breakfast eggs suspiciously. 'I don't want that cock's egg!'

J.P. and John developed a fowl enthusiasm. The hens were joined by an odd trio of guinea fowl, being two males to one (militant) female. A clutch of pointed eggs was laid and discovered belatedly. I cracked one, it exploded and the contents fired upwards and smacked on the ceiling. The pong was so powerful I almost expired. The male guineas, splendid lavender-coloured specimens, fought furious battles and John decided to settle the issue by despatching one for Sunday lunch (after all, we hadn't named *them*) as a special treat for his mum, who was with us for the weekend.

We all kept well away from the shed whilst mayhem was being committed. Sometime later, when my conscience pricked me, I ventured in that direction just as John emerged, battle scarred, to tell me ruefully: 'I thought I'd wrung its neck, but it just shook itself indignantly and came right back at me. You'll have to buy a joint instead!' John's mum confessed that she was very relieved.

A day or two later I went to feed the hens and the sparring guineas flew out and tangled in my long hair. I screamed blue murder! *That* did the trick, the trio flew away and were never seen again!

J.P. soon replaced them with Muscovy ducks. They trod arrogantly around the orchard, eventually raised a crowd of fluffy ducklings, most of which turned out to be drakes, and proceeded to lose them, one by one, on their hourly perambulations. Eventually, there were just two surviving youngsters.

The drakes were belligerent, splatted nasty messes outside the back door and demanded bread – with menaces. They, too, abruptly departed. We spotted them swimming happily on a neighbour's pond, so left them to it. After all, we had the neighbour's geese in exchange: ours was *their* stamping ground.

Bantams, now, are great little characters. We enjoyed keeping them. But we were all fond of Henrietta, the ex-battery hen. We took her in, when she turned up after the egg folk had moved. She was puny, almost bald and comb-less. Too frail to put with the other hens, she lived in the outhouse and regarded herself as one of us. For nine years she joined the family picnics, snatching at the sandwiches and making off on speedy, skinny legs. She pecked buns from babies' hands and she left trademarks all over the place, often on visitors' skirts or trousers. Resourceful Ginge always climbed a tree to eat her tea! One day, dear Henrietta disappeared. We never found her, but we mourned her.

'I 'spect a fox took her,' Chris said woefully. She had often nestled on his lap, fluffing up her brown feathers and giving contented chirrups. Much later he found Henrietta's last offering, a solitary egg, and I didn't try to crack that.

The chickens brought with them a nasty problem – rats. Only once, though, did one of these venture near the house. We had carefully wrapped in newspaper some giant and glossy Newtons and stored them in a big box in the outhouse.

'Just look at this!' John cried in horror. The apples had been bitten and disgusting deposits littered the box.

Rats! We dreaded we might see one indoors. However, at last our unwelcome visitor was captured and we could relax – but we had to discard all those beautiful apples.

Seamus, naturally, being the first, was the best loved of all our pets. He was stubborn, as Scotties invariably are: if we whistled him when he was intent on escaping, his ears would twitch, but he just kept on going. Yet he was faithful and sweet natured, polite too. He never liked sweet things, so remained fit and lean into old age.

One visiting aunt always brought a pound of sticky boiled sweets to dole out to the children, but Seamus was always presented with the first sweet. He retained it in his cheek, and dropped it discreetly in a dark corner, so as not to hurt her feelings – he wasn't aware that it would gum up the Hoover later.

He enjoyed being dressed up for the family plays and joined in all the games, he was a great fielder in cricket, though he didn't always choose to relinquish the ball. If he approved of you, he lay across your feet when you sat down; he was never a lap dog.

'Now where's that dog off to?' I remarked when I first noticed him rising from his afternoon snooze and almost glancing at the clock. I let him outside: off he went purposefully, short legs gathering speed, along the lane to meet his master from the evening train. They usually coincided at the crossroads. One evening, as John scooped up the little ones, two at a time, for an 'It's good to be home' hug, he told us: 'As we walked along together in the dusk, suddenly the hedge seemed to twinkle with fairy lights, illuminating our way ahead. Quite magical! Must have been hundreds of glow worms. Just Seamus and I to witness it.'

After Seamus had eloped with a spaniel twice his size – 'I expect the other owners'll leave a basket of puppies on our step for us to adopt,' Sara said hopefully – we acquired for him a lady companion.

Like J.P., I was always on the lookout for bargains in the paper. So John brought home plump little Hattie in a bag. She was the runt of the litter, but she was a fellow Scot, and they were soon a team. Never as certain-tempered as he, she was a better house-dog, and didn't welcome undesirable callers.

Seamus waited patiently for Hat to scoff her food first, and allowed her to bag the best spot by the fire. He was faithful to her in his way; maybe she was unaware of his permanent liaison with Daisy up the lane.

'Mrs Gee says we need a cat round the place – that'll deal with the mickeys,' Sara told us. 'She knows where there's kittens – please can J.P. and I go and get one?' 'Now!' added J.P. quickly. Dad not being around, Mum's a sucker, was unsaid.

They brought the kitten home in a heaving sack. 'It was the only way we could manage him – he's *wild!*' J.P. displayed the weals on his hands.

The furious, spitting, ruffled ginger scrap was released by John, and promptly bit his thumb. Needle teeth pierced deeply and with an anguished yelp, John put him down. The kitten shot out of the back door and disappeared under the outhouse where he remained for almost three weeks.

The minute the children arrived home from school, they knelt down, peering under the rotting floorboards, making coaxing noises to entice him out. During the day, I wasted much time with saucers of milk and tempting scraps. I talked to him constantly and the little boys echoed me: 'Nice puss, c'mon puss!' Well, I had the first rewarding glimpse of him. A tiny head poked out, and he lapped at the milk, green eyes glaring. Each day he became a little bolder, until one afternoon we found him sitting on the mat outside the door. We took no liberties, but he allowed us to stroke him gently.

He refused to step over the mat indoors. Tiger was an outside cat. He lived in the outhouse and on sunny days, when the grass was newly mown, he made little nests in it and purred, watching the children at play. He brought us gifts, like tiny voles and shrews, which he deposited on his mat. 'Too bitter for him to eat,' John thought. Fortunately, he was no bird-catcher, his golden coat betrayed his presence.

Birds were a delight. We had a regular robin and a one-legged blackbird. Maybe it was born that way, because it had adapted beautifully. There was an albino blackbird which was persecuted by its fellows. We made sure to feed it.

In the little greenhouse John planted asparagus. 'It'll take three years before we can pick it, but once established we can sell it,' he enthused. 'We'll make our fortune, eh?' I asked wryly, recalling a similar venture with mushrooms in our loft. 'Well, they made jolly good compost!' he returned.

'Dad's got a pet toad in his greenhouse,' Chris reported.

'That's very lucky,' Ginge decreed.

'You'll never be without water if you have a toad,' added Jo.

That figures, I thought, with flooding in mind . . .

J.P. weeded the greenhouse as a surprise for his dad, and that, I'm afraid, was the end of our cultural crop. But the toad stayed on. I believe he really was lucky.

It took the children a long time to discover every nook and corner of their orchard play paradise. One day they reported: 'We found a little grave, with a cross, saying PAT, 1925–39.' Eventually, our pets joined Pat in this sanctuary.

* * *

'He's a birdman!' J.P. informed us. He had a new friend at the far end of the lane. For a school project on wartime in our area, he'd bought a threepenny notebook and called on the retired Home Guard major. He was almost ninety and was cared for by a formidable nurse/companion. 'She rides a 500cc motor bike!' J.P. said in awe. The major had a vast aviary of birds ranging from the exotic to plain old pigeons. Nurse bred guinea pigs. She brought us a baby one in her saddlebag, saying that J.P. had requested it be delivered on Sara's birthday, and then spent a good half-hour giving us complicated instructions for feeding and housing. I had to promise that John would make it a home before he ate his supper that evening: 'Animals come before self,' she intoned sternly. I waited until she kicked her bike into throbbing action before I remonstrated with J.P. Still, Sara was pleased with her gift!

'We need a bigger animal to keep the grass down,' John thought. Goats? But they'd eat the flowers too. We decided on a donkey.

John went to view one in a rectory paddock some ten miles distant. They walked home together and it took a long time – a very long time – as Ted was a typical donkey. 'A car stopped – a man leapt out and shouted: "Hold it!" He pulled out a cine camera and he filmed me leading the donkey along,' John laughed.

Jo was so excited: 'Oh, Daddy – you might be on television!'

'I don't think so, he was obviously an American tourist, filming donkey taking man for walk.'

Maybe John and Ted stroll on into the sunset at flickering family film shows in the States. We like to think so.

Ted, I'm sorry to relate, was another mistake. For two days the children, and all their friends, rode him bareback round the orchard trails and I wasted much time when I could have been doing the chores (only this was much more fun) leading Ted like a seaside donkey patrolling the sands.

Then he turned nasty. A huge boil erupted almost obscuring his left eye. Ted was in pain – and enraged as a result. He kicked out viciously, bared his teeth and ripped the washing off the line, to trample furiously on it. Trembling and afraid, we cowered indoors awaiting John's return from work. The vet came out and told us: 'Someone's tried to put one over on you, this is a chronic condition and the owner must have known about it. I suggest you contact him immediately and ask him to take the animal back.'

Reluctantly, we did so. Ted was taken away in a horse box – our money was refunded, but we were out of pocket, with the vet's bill to pay.

It was some time before we could think of buying another four-hooved friend. Our second Christmas, in fact. We had a small, unexpected legacy and decided to buy a Shetland pony as a surprise present for all the children.

Bumble arrived late on Christmas Eve, which meant that we could keep him a secret until Christmas morning.

At 6 a.m. we all trooped behind the swinging lantern to view the wonder in our stable. Bumble was just a baby himself, eighteen months old, a tiny black pony. We lifted our little ones to stroke his neck and the girls laid their cheeks along his flank, loving him. 'It'll be some time before you can ride him,' we told them. 'You see, he has to be broken-in first.'

We went back indoors to our Christmas grapefruits, pink, sweet ones, rarely seen then, a gift from Trinidad, to our shilling-an-egg (soft boiled) and to the Grand Opening Up of parcels.

There was a knock-knocking on the kitchen door. There stood our pony, nose twitching, tail swishing, waiting for *his* breakfast.

CHAPTER 30

The House that Ben Built

'Look at this!' cried Ginge triumphantly, pulling up a long, mouldy bacon rind. I was just in time to prevent Seamus from receiving a tidbit.

'You *all* encourage mice,' John told us sternly. 'Now just you keep that box tidy this time – and eat those crusts up!'

We had decided to open up the living room and to integrate it with a little room at present occupied by the babies. We had to walk through this room anyway to reach the bedrooms in the newer section of the cottage. The dividing wall was easy to remove, it was merely a tongued and grooved wooden partition. From this wood John had fashioned several useful things, not least a long toy box the length of one wall which doubled as seating at mealtimes. Every few months the children had an enthusiastic treasure hunt: toys piled up on the floor, stale odours were released, and rock-hard crusts of bread were revealed.

'Here's One-Leg Ted's other leg!' Ginge cried.

'Sew it back on, then.'

'I like him better without it – I'd have to change his name.'

Sara emerged with a handful of chewed-up paper – 'My *Girl* comics – I was saving them!'

'Who for? The mice?' J.P. grinned.

Sara didn't deign to answer. She dived into the box again and came up triumphant: There you are,' she told her sisters, 'I knew we had lots more Sindy clothes – J.P. just chucked them in here, last time *he* tidied up.'

I thought fondly that our eldest daughter was a most satisfactory mix of practicality and creativity. She took after both her grandmothers for sewing beautifully; her sisters were more into designing the tiny garments and cobbling 'em up à la Mum at this stage, though later we were to marvel at Ginge's mending skills when she went to college – her colourful jeans were more patch than trousers. And Sara, who always said she'd be a nurse, took a degree in fine arts . . .

The small boys played gleefully among the debris and protested when the girls tidied it all back inside the box. J.P., of course, had helped to get everything out, but was now absorbed in finishing his jigsaw with missing pieces which had surfaced.

More of the wall wood had provided a splendid settle with its high back embellished with cut-out diamond and club shapes. Jo and Ginge dived on to this and peeked out through these peepholes whenever the theme music of *Doctor Who* began on TV. 'Dang-der-dang-der-dang's coming on!' they cried to each other, emulating the sinister music. They enjoyed the programme, nevertheless.

Until we received our little windfall, we were unable to make drastic changes except where we were entitled to a grant.

'Now, if you had thrown that bath outside,' the Council man informed us, 'you would have qualified for a new bathroom.'

'But, nothing's connected – *it's never been used!*' (Echoes of Mrs D.)

'Sorry – I can *see* a bath, so you have a bathroom.'

Wise, after the event, we trundled the bath up the orchard, only, as already related, to have it promptly pinched.

So, we tightened our belts even more, believing in a decent bathroom, with our brood a necessity, and eventually we had our wish, but first, we needed a source of hot water. We *could* get a grant for this.

John was determined to do every job himself, so there was much talk of copper piping, airlocks and where to site the stove. Pipes had to be tapped, joints fused: I always associate central heating with the smell of meths, the scorching flame of a blow lamp and knockings-in-the-night in the system.

Eventually, we had a Rayburn in the kitchen and a stove in the living room: oh, the joy of turning on the hot taps! John worked on the kitchen at the same time. In came a nice big window so that as I washed up in my primrose enamelled sink, I could watch the children at play outside. I was particularly pleased with the new flooring and enjoyed scrubbing the quarry tiles.

Being still pregnant with Roger while the dust was flying indoors, my main contribution was to be the paintwork. The paint made me feel nauseous, but I resolutely brushed on. For years now we have preferred white paint, perhaps as a reaction against all those cheerful pinks, mauves, blues and greens which livened up old Crabapple Cottage.

The week the baby was born, I painted everything rose pink in the girls' bedroom. Furniture, bed heads, windowsills – the floorboards retained forever the speckles bestowed by my dripping brush. The paint seeped through the slats of the built-in cupboard and Sara had a nattily spotted dress as a result. The door of this cupboard was 'sticky' ever after, but it proved a blessing in disguise.

Ginge had a hang-up in that cupboard. The children were playing hide-and-seek and she dashed indoors and concealed herself in the closet. She wasn't discovered for some time because she had become hooked-up among the clothes, so that it was fortunate my painting prevented the door from closing properly or she might have been asphyxiated. I pointed this out to John when he complained mildly that my hard work made more work – for him, cleaning up after me.

'You're lucky to have a wife who doesn't banish you to a cold shed to do your woodwork!' I retorted. He had to agree that I was very forbearing (and still am) about the shavings on the carpet and the sawdust in the settee. But he always tidied his tools away after he had finished planing, sawing and hammering. You see much more of your husband, I thought, if you allow him to use the living room for his projects and the dining table as a bench. I quite like the smell of linseed oil and its soporific watching French polishing. J.P. was kept busy too,, in sorting out the boxes of nails and screws on spread-out newspaper and hammering them straight for reuse later. He was learning how you could make something worthwhile from unpromising material, too.

One day J.P. was helping out a neighbour. He bunched the flowers she had picked to sell at the gate, tied them, renewed the water in the pails. Then he waited hopefully for the customers, but it was a slack time.

Our friend took the opportunity to go shopping, and J.P. became tired of hovering by the old kitchen table, re-arranging the produce. Stacked by the house wall were planks of dark wood and a box containing saw, hammer and nails. He'd make something out of nothing, he thought, on impulse. A good strong trestle to replace the old table. Being a fast worker like his mum, he had the trestle in place an hour later to greet his employer on her return.

She blanched. 'Oh, what *have* you done?' J.P.'s face lost its wide smile. It took him the rest of the afternoon to dismantle his work of art. She was very nice about it, but she urged him to hurry. You see, her husband had taken a wardrobe to pieces, to sand, paint and reassemble, and she'd placed it prominently to remind him of his promise to do so, when he arrived home that evening . . .

* * *

Our renovations had coincided with promotion at work for John; now he travelled the UK and Ireland each spring and autumn, liaising with clients.

I never thought I'd survive the first night he was away. There had been torrential rain and the end of the lane was flooded; we now saw the raised path in use. The children were all keen to go wading in their wellies; I was worried that we might all float away on top of our big wardrobe and would be all at sea, before John's return.

'It hasn't come this far for years,' Marjorie, from the nursery, comforted me. 'Don't worry, you'll have to come over to us if the river rises further, after all *we* can go upstairs.' And their house was more substantial, being built of brick.

So I went to bed at the same time as the children, eight o'clock, and kept the light on 'til dawn.

'The water's going down.' J.P. was disappointed, next morning. The fire had gone out. He obligingly chopped me a big box of wood as a surprise. I winced when I thought of that sharp blade; it wasn't a job he'd yet graduated to. Oh horror! 'We'll have to burn it all, before Dad comes home,' I told him. He'd passed over all the rubbish for a piece of mahogany which John had prized for years.

I was 'all hot under the collar' when I viewed Jo's school notebook. WE ALL WAVED OUR DADDY GOODBYE ON HIS HOLIDAYS, she'd printed under her picture. There was the train, in orange crayon, and there was Daddy leaning out of a window with a broad grin on his face, and all of us, with our matchstick legs and raised arms, left behind, ah! *Deprived*.

'Um – can't you tell your teacher that Daddy has gone on a business trip?' I suggested, wondering what opinion she had formed of the heartless father who went off to enjoy himself whilst his family languished at home.

* * *

John was always on the lookout for bargain lots while in London, but never remembered, until too late, that not only did he have to negotiate cumbersome packages on and off the crowded commuter train, but also that the walk from the station could seem an awfully long way when he had a heavy load to carry.

One 'half-price' prize had to be fetched home over four evenings.

'Sound-proofing tiles!' we were informed. They were solid, large and weighty, sold off cheaply due to damage from flooding in a warehouse; some were marred by watermarks, but all were useable.

It took John ages – *hours* of work – to nail these hefty tiles into place on the ceiling of our enlarged living room.

'Not quite the right place for soundproofing, I suppose?' He moved along his steps and pressed the next tile neatly into position. 'No one being above us to be muffled.'

'What about the mice, Daddy?' Sara kept a straight face.

J.P. was eager to demonstrate the efficiency of the soundproofing by going up into the loft and dancing around. We dissuaded him.

'Insulate your walls inside,' we were advised. 'That's what that old hessian was for.' John tried this in the kitchen with a special lining paper which attracted all the daddy longlegs who made horrible zzzing sounds as they tried to leg their way up or down the walls. It was useless.

We bought plasterboard to cover our tongue-and-groove in the living room; a shame I know to cover the wooden walls, which soon became very fashionable, but ours were only a few inches thick! Then I discovered the delights of emulsioning, with a nice big brush. You can change your colour scheme in a few hours, great stuff. We always had a quick sweep over the walls whenever a family celebration was in the offing, like a christening or a birthday party.

Another bedroom was now our priority. We decided to utilise the roomy hall, which was wasted space. Cut in two, it provided a little room for J.P., which he proudly occupied. The three little boys now shared the room in which he and Chris had slept since our arrival. John built in bunk beds, leaving plenty of floor space.

'Needs a new floor, it'll cost a lot,' John told me. I had remarked wistfully that it seemed a pity to have a large unused room at the front – the sitting room. We had wet rot, a reminder of that last flooding before our time, to contend with here, but at last we were rewarded with a super, polished wooden floor.

It was spring again before we could put the finishing touches to the room. A great stone fireplace with glowing copper canopy was much admired by our visitors, but because of all the trees around we were too often smoked out of our lovely room, if the wind was in the wrong direction. We tried various remedies, including a chimney cowl, but still we sat stoically enduring smarting eyes and choking in a haze of blue smoke. It was most disappointing.

Our home improvements took us years. Ben rebuilt his house in a single day!

'You'll never guess—' J.P. was out of puff, he and Seamus had raced back from their early-morning Saturday walk. 'Ben's taken the whole front of his house off!'

'*What?*'

'Honest, Mum, he has – come and see!'

I struggled with my conscience. Childish curiosity is excusable. The adult equivalent can only be classed as nosey!

'Can *we* go and look?' pleaded the girls.

'We-ell, I suppose so. But please be discreet, you can have a quick look when you go to Mrs Gee's – here's a penny each. Don't forget to take Chris and Mike.'

They set off eagerly, breaking into a trot, as soon as they thought I couldn't see them, but they held on to the little boys.

Reports came back at intervals via despatch runners, i.e. J.P. and Ginge.

'It looks just like a real doll's house, Mum; you can see *everything* – they haven't made the beds even, and you can see a potty under one of them!'

'Whatever are the poor old aunties doing?'

'Oh, you can see them pottering around in the kitchen, 'cos the living room door's wide open.'

'They keep bringing out cups of tea to the men.'

Did the wooden front of the house just fall down? I conjectured. 'I'll bring Roger in the pram after his bath,' I said, giving in to temptation. 'Then we'll all go for a walk, we can't just stand there and gawp, that's very rude.'

'Bye Mum!' and they were gone again.

By the time Roger and I reached Ben's house a few courses of bricks had already been laid. A cement mixer churned noisily, being fed continually from mountains of sand and cement while the aunties ferried out slopping buckets of water. The front garden was littered with the discarded ship-boarding and Ben and his mates dunked their bricks and applied their laden trowels with lightning precision. The children stared, fascinated, from the other side of the lane.

Ben waved his trowel in a cheery salute. Bachelor-like, he really hadn't thought to tidy his doll's house interior. I couldn't resist looking up to see if my informants had exaggerated about the receptacle under the bed – they hadn't!

The aunties waved too. They seemed rather bemused, but pointed to the growing wall with happy smiles. I nodded back my approval. The roaring of the mixer precluded any conversation.

The children were happily occupied all day.

'Ben doesn't mind us watching – honest!'

As it was summer, and the evenings long and light, J.P. and Sara stayed there until nearly seven, then sauntered home reluctantly to supper, and to bed.

'Ben reckons he'll get all the bricks up, but the windows and front door will have to wait until tomorrow,' Sara told us. They bolted their food.

'Can we go back?' they dared to ask.

'What d'you think?'

'I wonder if those poor old dears will feel the draught tonight,' mused John. Evening jobs over, we sat close together on the settee, Seamus stretched across both our feet. We shared our Saturday treat, a Mars bar.

'It's mild enough, I suppose.'

The next day the glazing was completed by Ben and his pals and a new door fitted. We were there unashamedly to view it.

Ben stood back, admiring all his hard work.

'Like it?' he asked us.

'Looks just like a new house, Ben!'

So now we had a new nursery rhyme to add to our repertoire. We often slotted in our own names to the old familiar chants, like Roger – or Chris – or Michael who lived down Carter's Lane, as in 'Baa Baa Black Sheep'. Now, we could recite: 'This is the house that Ben built!'

'Just the same inside,' as Ben murmured laconically.

Even to what lurks 'neath the bed? we wondered.

'Pity you can't lay bricks that fast,' I dared to remark to John as he laboured away at the new coalhouse near the back door.

'You're not so good at providing cups of tea for the workers like the aunties, well, worker, in this case,' he countered. 'I'm as dry as a bone!'

CHAPTER 31

Mumps, Mopes and Moggies

Mum often reminded me: 'You always said *you'd* never have a child with a runny nose!' I still give an involuntary shiver at the memory of Clive who shared my desk when I was five, with those 'snail trails' on the sleeves of his holey, green jersey. Poor child, he had his hair cropped short because of ringworm, too. Mum provided my brother and me with a clean hanky each morning. Mine was invariably chewed round the edges, which made her cross, but we did know how to 'blow'.

When I became a mother myself, I soon realised that the runny infant nose is a *fact*. Before we arrived at the cottage we had already survived the trauma of measles, when Jo was seriously ill, and the milder German variety. The moment J.P. started school, he set the ball rolling, spot-wise. Fortunately, we didn't envisage going through all those childhood ailments twice, sometimes three times, with our large family.

However, much to our surprise, apart from a broken collarbone – J.P. was pushed over at school in his first term when I was about to produce Chris. 'Well, I'm in the right place if anything happens,' I attempted to joke as my five-year-old was strapped up: 'No, you're not!' Sister replied indignantly. 'We don't *allow* babies to be born in the Cottage Hospital!' – the only other broken limb during their collective childhood was a greenstick fracture of the wrist sustained by Jo, whilst roller skating. They climbed all those trees with no mishaps at all, despite my fears.

Hospitals and operations were minor events – babies for me, tonsils mainly for the children, and Michael with a hernia. He was home after two days and a stout nurse arrived to take his stitches out. The children were all playing outside, I called to him, and he answered cheerfully from his perch near the top of a tree. Nurse was cross, I was chastened – and Mike was fine!

The chicken pox struck them during our third summer and kept us quarantined for the long holiday. Sara hated being ill and refused to entertain the thought that she might succumb. On the last day of term, when she was going with her class on a much looked forward to trip to Canterbury Cathedral, I looked suspiciously at her face.

'Isn't that—' I began, as I handed over her packed lunch.

'No, it isn't!' She was out of the door like a flash. 'Bye Mum – see you tonight!'

On her return she was covered in the now all-too-familiar blisters. 'You see,' she said triumphantly, unaware that proof was all too evident: 'I told you I was quite all right!'

I felt somewhat guilty at making the current invalid comfortable on the living room settee so that he/she was in sight of muted family life – the others were always co-operative at keeping the noise down – and I was happier myself to be able to keep an eye on developments, whether soaring temperatures or urgent needs like: 'Please Mum, can I have another jigsaw?' However, our doctor told me that my instinct was sound, he didn't believe either that children should be isolated when ill, unless, of course, there was a medical reason for this; he felt it was reassuring for them, and their parents, to be in the hub of things. Ours certainly recovered quickly.

We had a wonderful new doctor when Roger was a baby. John and I still quote his maxims to this day. He was young, black-bearded, gentle and kind. If I rang him at dawn, after we had endured a sleepless, anxious night, he would be with us within fifteen minutes. 'I know if you ring me, you need me,' he replied quietly, when I apologised for calling him out. Our doctor was patient, always ready to just listen, and he was in favour of homely remedies; he didn't laugh at our bread poultices to 'draw' a splinter from a finger, or hot lemon and honey for a sore throat.

A few battle scars were unavoidable and gained by the majority. One evening, feeling very unwell myself, I was persuaded to bed by John. I was wakened from a feverish doze to hear raised voices.

'Don't tell Mum – she's asleep – straight into the bathroom now.' (John.)

Sara: 'I'll get the cotton wool, Dad.'

Wailing from injured party – obviously J.P., backed up with sympathetic sobs from his small brothers.

Jo burst excitedly into our room. 'J.P.'s cut his finger off!' she shouted.

'*What!*' I was out of bed and hammering on the bathroom door.

'Now, just you go straight back to bed,' came my husband's calm voice. 'Everything's under control.'

J.P. spurting blood under the cold tap, agreed. 'It's all right, Mum, you know you can't stand the sight of blood—'

'Your finger . . .' I murmured faintly, leaning against the door jamb.

'Just a deep cut, I can cope!' John pushed me out and closed the door firmly.

Years later, J.P. admitted that he had sustained this injury when sliding from the roof of the chicken shed – clinging to the edges of the corrugated iron sheets before dropping to the ground. I shuddered all over again.

Sara's knees were much abused – once she needed a row of stitches after stumbling over a metal toy fire engine – I've been in favour of cheap and cheerful polythene toys ever since, even if you do tend to crush them underfoot.

Despite the hazards of our mainly outdoors life, most injuries were not homegrown.

As our fourth Christmas drew near we were becoming used to John's absences and awaited his return with eager anticipation. He arrived back with small surprises for us all and our eyes were always focused on his case. In November, when he made his last trip of the year, to Scotland, it was already bitterly cold and we waved him off in the first snowfall of the winter.

'Keep the fire going, mind,' his words blew back at us as he trudged along the lane on the Sunday afternoon en route to the train.

By the time he returned on the Friday the girls were sickening for mumps. This time I did turn their bedroom into a sanatorium as they felt so poorly; they could barely eat as their jaws were so swollen. Ginge cried with terrible earache and her bout was prolonged as the two 'mumps' came up separately, three weeks apart. The girls were still languishing in bed when the three small boys succumbed, one by one, in swift succession. School broke up, and J.P. was the only one still lively and unmumpy. He was a great help to me, offering sympathy, cheering up with jokes, delivering sustenance and reading stories.

'Mumps equals grumps!' I told John disconsolately. 'I just can't get around to thinking about Christmas this year. The girls can't manage to eat anything but fish and the boys can't even eat that.'

'I don't feel so good, either,' John said in a tired, listless voice. He was hunched in his chair and had hardly touched his supper.

'Have *you* had mumps?' I asked in trepidation. I was nursing fretful Roger in a blanket cocoon, in my arms.

'Mmm. I know I have; I can even remember the agonising pain when you try to chew, swallow or worse, yawn ... I'll get an early night, sleep it off, whatever it is.'

He struggled into work for the last two days before the break, arriving home at lunchtime on Christmas Eve, bearing the Christmas turkey from Leadenhall Market and tree.

'I guess it's flu, two or three of the others at the office have gone down with it, already. Can't face any food, sorry. A hot drink, and a couple of aspirin – my head's pounding,' he groaned woefully.

So, it was J.P. and I who trimmed the tree with a decided lack of enthusiasm. We all usually had a hand in delving into the battered cardboard boxes and bringing out a frond of tarnished tinsel, a coloured glass ball, a homemade tiny cracker – mementoes of John's and my own childhood as well as our own growing collection of baubles. There were lights which did not work but were beautiful, being Snow White and the Seven Dwarfs, and twinkly lights which did work; a hefty fairy, almost bald, in a tawdry dress – when spotlighted at the top of the tree she seemed transformed, almost an angel.

I went out to fetch a little wood to ginger-up the fire and stamped on an old fruit box to split it. I was only wearing slippers. The stabbing pain in my right foot and the fact that the box remained firmly attached to it, made me sit down suddenly on the back doorstep. J.P. came running and helped me to pull the box free. A long, rusty nail parted company with me; it had pierced through my slipper sole and thick sock and driven deep into the ball of my foot.

'It's not bleeding,' J.P. tried to console me.

'That's not good, it's a puncture wound, closes immediately and shuts in infection. Quick, fetch me a bowl of hot water and antiseptic and I'll try soaking it and squeezing the place.'

A knock on the door. 'Oh, no,' I moaned, suddenly remembering: 'We've got Chas's cats to look after all over Christmas, I'd completely forgotten!'

Chas bore a gift for the children, fifty sticks of liquorice in a big bag! He gave J.P. a pile of Just William and Jennings books and to me he presented the back-door key of his house and a sheet of instructions from his mother. They were just off to his grandparents. He looked curiously at the sight of me soaking my injured foot in the washing-up bowl. 'You should go to the doctor,' he said, in his old-fashioned way.

'No, I can't bother him on Christmas Eve – I expect I'll survive! Have a nice holiday, and happy Christmas ...'

J.P. and I did the rounds with wrung-out flannels, potties and lemon drinks – I laced John's with whisky – sang songs and told stories to fretful little lads; peeped in at their dad, snoring away in bed, his hair dark with sweat, and we refilled hot-water bottles all round.

We stuffed the turkey both ends – a job I'd never tackled before. John always did (still does) the Christmas cooking to give me a break; anyway, he thoroughly enjoyed it. We pushed the big bird in the oven, turned the dial to the lowest setting and left it to slowly cook through overnight. I'd turn the oven up at around 7 a.m.

It was getting late, and I persuaded my faithful helper to go to bed so that I could fill the stockings and set out the presents. I didn't want to spoil the surprise and delight of Christmas morning for him. 'Thanks old boy – I couldn't have done all this without you.'

My foot was throbbing ominously by the time I had finished and stoked up the fire. I made a bread poultice and clumsily bandaged it into position. My bed sock should hold it in place, I hoped. I slid wearily into bed beside John, he was burning hot, so I heaved the hot-water bottle out – I obviously wouldn't need that!

It was a nightmare beginning to the festive season: Chris was violently sick all over his bedclothes, and required a quick bath, hair wash and complete change of bedding. Roger and Michael awoke several times demanding cool drinks, and the girls tossed restlessly, making frequent trips to the bathroom. John groaned, muttering incoherently as the lights snapped on and off and J.P. was distinctly unpopular when he presented us with slopping cups of tea at 2.35 a.m. 'I thought it was ten past seven – honest, Mum!' Judging by the chocolate smears on his pyjama jacket he'd already sampled the goodies in his stocking.

'Don't you dare wake your brothers up! Straight back to bed – now! – and turn that light off!' I warned in a wrathful whisper. Belatedly I remembered: 'Happy Christmas,' I added weakly. J.P. grinned forgivingly.

'Happy Christmas, Mum – how's your foot?'

'Ouch!' I said, touching it gingerly.

The invalids rallied a little as they tore open their packages, then they retreated to bed with their boxes and bags, and a stick of liquorice to suck, which I thought might well have a beneficial effect, leaving me with a pile of crumpled paper to clear and Christmas lunch to cook.

First, there were the animals and the outside jobs to tackle. My foot had swelled alarmingly, was really painful. John, I'm sorry to say, was distinctly unsympathetic. However, I made allowances as he was obviously feeling awful. 'Self-inflicted!' he snapped. I leaned on J.P.'s narrow shoulder and improvised a broomstick crutch. This could act as a deterrent if the Terrible Turk (That Lionel's successor) was on the offensive. He usually was.

We made several laborious trips across the iron-hard ground. Although it hadn't snowed for several days, the impacted residue was a chilling reminder and the atmosphere was threatening. We broke the ice on the chickens' water containers, filled feeding troughs, forked down hay for Bumble, raked his straw; carted coal, chopped wood, emptied ashes; indoors, we riddled and stoked fires, brewed tea, peeled potatoes, desalted a large jar of runner beans, basted the turkey and simmered the pud.

We'd better see to those cats before dinner, I thought. We slowly progressed to Chas's house.

J.P. opened the back door and reeled back in disgust. 'Ugh! Look out Mum, or you'll tread in it!'

There were odious piles of excrement all over the kitchen floor and we both 'heaved' at the appalling smell. The culprits were elsewhere, blissfully curled up on a bed – someone had left their door open.

We located disinfectant, a bucket, rubber gloves and set to. The dustbin was soon chock-a-block – choked – with nasty newspaper parcels by the time we finished, and there were still the cats to be fed. Our instructions were that the cats must be kept indoors; it was obvious that they had no intention of going outside, anyway. So, J.P. fetched wooden boxes from the shed, filled them with earth to serve as litter trays and I read the 'menu' and opened up the fridge. Liver to chop . . . Looked at least a couple of pounds of it, and not too fresh. My unfavourite task, dealing with offal (next to cleaning up messes), particularly with the blunt knife provided.

'They don't deserve it!' I groaned, with much feeling.

'Probably what gives 'em the runs anyway.' Well, J.P. said it.

Those felines sniffed daintily, rejected our offerings and retired to scratch and yawn on their eiderdown.

'I hope Chas and Co all catch fleas!' was my bitter comment. 'I'd rather have our old tomcat any day.'

The turkey was served. Three of us sat at the table, and John was in his pyjamas and dressing gown. Shaving had only accentuated his pale gills. He carved a slice or two, blenched and made a run for it. 'Sorry!' he cried.

Tears coursed down my cheeks and salted the turkey. J.P.'s arm went round my shoulders in a comforting squeeze. 'Please don't cry, Mum – can I have my dinner? I'm starving!'

That turkey lasted an awfully long time, but in a few days the family were reviving and enjoying it. The bread poultices cured my foot; I ceased hopping, and the thaw set in outdoors. Chas's cats ate little but performed regularly, not often in the litter boxes. J.P. and I gave Chas's kitchen floor a good going over the day his family were due to return.

A knock at the door. Chas bearing a gift and thanking us for all our kindness. The messes were not mentioned.

'Well, at least they showed their appreciation,' John said. 'Come on, open up!' The family crowded around, while I peeled off the cellophane wrapping from the pound box of Dairy Milk.

That box must have lurked in their cupboard for many a moon. Every chocolate bore a white bloom and tasted stale, but we scoffed the lot.

CHAPTER 32

In and Out the Orchard

Gingerbread, hot and moist; pressed with the palm of the hand it bounced up again in the approved manner. I prodded the jacket potatoes already steaming in the Rayburn. Almost ready, I thought. The pea soup, thick and glutinous, simmered on the hot plate; you'd need a knife to cut it. From a long, crusty loaf, I sliced my usual reckless doorstops and piled them on a plate. Brown pottery soup bowls were warming, the table laid ready; it was quiet in the kitchen, just me and young Roger, already wearing his warm blue duffel coat with hood, who was nearly asleep in the sturdy little Victorian chair with tray which John's dad had discovered years ago in their loft, and which John had refurbished originally for his niece, Penny. There had been seven sitting tenants since, and I wondered how many more had used it since it was made, towards the end of the last century.

'Hurry up, Mum!' Sara urged me from the back doorstep. I was holding up proceedings as usual; the fun couldn't commence until we joined the gang, Roger and me. The darkness of the orchard was illuminated by the huge bonfire, which blazed and crackled, sending showers of sparks into the air; it had taken the children weeks to build it from fallen branches and rubbish to its splendid height. Our nostrils were assailed by the pungent scent, the children already reeked of smoke and their breath curled like a gaggle of dragons. They were wound around with scarves, woolly hats pulled down over their ears, grey flakes already clinging to their clothes and boots.

Once the bonfire was really blazing, only John was allowed near it. We sat on a plank suspended from the forks of two apple trees a safe distance from the firework display. There would be no big bangs, we didn't take chances. A fine mizzle of rain dampened our upturned faces and outer apparel, but not our spirits.

We sat within that gentle, golden circle of flickering firelight, encompassed by mysterious, looming tree trunks, just a glance away.

Poor old Guy hung limply on top of the pile, smouldering and doomed to become ashes. I noted with a wry grin, that he wore my old slippers. I'd have to do without until Christmas.

This year we had a special visitor, who had come to celebrate both his seventy-fifth birthday and Guy Fawkes night: John's uncle. He had arrived this afternoon, carrying an old brown cardboard case, battered at the corners. Maybe the one he had gone off to the Great War with, I fancied. Like a conjuror, he snapped it open and revealed a mass of fireworks. Uncle loved visiting us and telling us stories of when he was a lad, the eldest, like J.P., of a large family.

Fizzes of candyfloss pink and flares of lime green; sudden pops and cracks, flurries of silver stars, showers of golden rain; a rocket soared high – we watched its flight with awe and secret trepidation – where would it fall? The glimmering end of the lighting stick, John's steady gloved hand, the anticipation as the glowing tip touched the next firework and the eerie pause before it suddenly burst into life, held us all spellbound.

Uncle, I believe, was watching the children's faces rather than the display. Michael peeped out from the security of his arms. Roger pointed excitedly, and I cuddled him close, the cold was becoming apparent as the fire diminished.

J.P. darted out unexpectedly, threw on some twigs and there was an instant flare-up and a tantalising smell – baked apples! A spark had ignited a low-hanging branch and roasted the large apple which had somehow escaped the picking sack, before John could douse it. It added to the excitement.

We trooped into the cosy kitchen, lined up our wellies to dry out, hung our damp clothing on the airer above the stove and tucked hungrily into our bonfire beanfeast. Always the same supper, every 5th of November.

'We all smell like *kippers!*' Sara wrinkled her nose. The others were too busy spooning up the soup, dunking bread and eating to care.

That was our biggest bonfire celebration, but we always looked forward to that special conflagration.

* * *

Sundays were quiet days for us, beginning with Sunday school in the morning. John and I are both Anglicans, but I like to worship where I feel 'it's right' at the time. We were delighted to send our young ones to the local chapel, where there was a warm-hearted lady preacher. She had been a missionary teacher in an inhospitable climate, returned to marry and to become ordained. The children went most willingly to her Sunday school, joined in all the youth activities, gained their Bible reading certificates; Ginge's fluent expressive reading brought her full marks on one occasion. In time, Sara taught the younger ones too.

The chapel, a modern building, had honey-coloured plain pews, lovingly polished. It was always fragrant with flowers and the sunshine seemed to stream perpetually through the windows to gild and en-circle the smiling faces of the tightly packed congregation.

Mothering Sunday was wonderful – embarrassing for me: each class from the Sunday school wended its way down the aisle and came back with posies of flowers for their mothers. I, of course, was the recipient of *seven* such sweet-smelling bunches; my arms were full, and 'my cup ran over'. I hit upon a solution. There were several maiden ladies who worked cheerfully and unselfishly for the community and helped others – including us – in many unobtrusive ways. In particular, there was Miss Jeeves, almost ninety, who chauffeured our lot to and fro each Sunday in her old-fashioned, gleaming motor. So, I shared my flowers with these lovely ladies, who were proxy 'mums and aunties' to so many. The pleasure this obviously gave them, was reflected by my own warm glow of satisfaction within.

We trusted Peggy, our preacher, with our children, and once J.P. and Sara went on a holiday to a seaside village with a group from the chapel; there were more girls than boys, so they were segregated at nights. While Sara and her friends enjoyed the larks in the main part of the village hall, J.P. and his single companion occupied a dusty space behind the stage! We still have the card Sara dutifully sent us:

ARRIVED EARLY – IT'S LOVELY HERE. HAVING A SUPER TIME. LOVE SARA. P.S. J.P. HAS FORGOTTEN HIS KNIFE, FORK AND SPOON – I DON'T KNOW WHAT HE'S GOING TO DO!

There was another missive towards the end of the week.

AUNTIE MET US IN TOWN AND TREATED US TO KNICK-ERBOKER GLORIES – J.P. HAD TWO! THEN WE HAD SARDINES FOR TEA.

What a mixture, we thought.

There were plenty of activities connected with the chapel: youth club, a drama section – the children wrote their own plays for Easter and Christmas. I suspect it was J.P. who penned those unforgettable (to us!) lines: PILATE'S DONE A BUNK! There was also an organisation run on similar lines to scouting, open to both sexes, with badges to be earned. Chris was the only one to jib against joining this; he was proving to be a strong-minded little individual. 'Soppy!' he said scornfully. 'You have to pretend you're in a boat, the girls always get chosen to be Captain or Bo'sun – *I'm* only an able seaman and have to do all the work!'

J.P. belonged to the Cubs too and eventually became a patrol leader. He thoroughly enjoyed his first cub camp, back came the report: '*I'm in charge of the lats* ...' 'Hope he doesn't catch something nasty,' I fretted. The girls pounced on his toilet bag on his return, triumphantly revealing his soap with the legend LUX still imprinted on it: 'Ooh, look, Mum, he hasn't washed all week!'

'Some days I did, Mum,' J.P. said defensively. I certainly hoped so, particularly after he'd told us the ins-and-outs of 'lat duty' ...

He'd obviously worn his wellies day and night, too, well it had rained unceasingly.

'I don't believe it!' cried John, as J.P.'s feet emerged at last from their rubber encasing. 'He's got *foot-rot!*' His feet were white and soggy looking, but a hot bath helped matters.

The four eldest were growing up fast. J.P. lit sneaky, smoking bonfires of his own now and then, in remote corners of the orchard, well out of sight of my kitchen window. I'm not too sure where he got the matches, maybe from his friend Greg, who showed J.P. and Sara how to roll the contents of old teabags in a dock leaf, making a passable cigarette, but which, fortunately tasted foul. I never suspected a thing! Just as well, I suppose. On their little fires, J.P. and the girls made 'jam'. They suspended, from crossed sticks, rusty old cans. Blackberries, apples and water were the ingredients hopefully stirred. The black toffee-like substance glued up their teeth. Chris even said it tasted nice.

* * *

Greg and his brother certainly encouraged J.P. to venture further afield. They had been firm friends from that first day they met. A definite track ran across the fields between our houses.

In a forlorn patch down the lane was the ruin of a cottage. The children had been warned to keep away from this crumbling structure.

But there was access through the gap where a gate had stood, into the remains of what had once been a garden. Flowers bloomed leggily among the weeds.

The chimney of the cottage was visible from hearth to pot. One day, J.P., who had been reading *The Water Babies*, decided to find out how it felt to be a boy chimney sweep. Also, as he told Greg: 'In the olden days people used to hide treasure – bags of gold and stuff – up the chimney . . .'

So, his friends didn't try to dissuade him. Being J.P., he didn't go *up* the chimney, he shinned up the stack and went *down*. He slithered and slid, clutching desperately at ledges, dislodging much soot, nearly choking himself. 'I couldn't see a thing, it was terrifying,' he confessed on his return home. 'I called out to Greg and Barry, but they didn't answer – then, suddenly, I was stuck – by the corbelling, I think that's what you call it? I couldn't move an inch, up or down. I thought I'd be in there forever. I thought the others had run off.' He hardly ever cried, but he was sobbing then, in great gulping gasps, still trembling from his ordeal.

'But did they help you out?' I asked. It was not a time for recriminations. He looked the part of a chimney sweep's apprentice all right. However, the other children must be made aware of just how serious this escapade could have been.

'Then I heard them calling, from the top of the chimney – "Shall we get help?" I gave a big heave and I somehow clawed my way up again, until the boys could get a grip on my shoulders and they pulled like blazes and I shot out of the chimney like a cork out of a bottle. They were just as scared as I was, they came with me as far as our gate, then they ran off. It wasn't their fault, Mum, don't blame them. They saved my life!' he ended dramatically.

I silently thanked his guardian angel who must have been watching over him, then made him solemnly promise never go near the ruin again. 'And that goes for the rest of you, too!'

* * *

We went to the cinema once a year, a treat provided by John's sisters. When Roger was three, I took all seven to see *Jungle Book* at the tiny cinema in the nearest market town. Even the bus journey was an adventure.

It doesn't matter what time of day it is, I *always* fall asleep in the cinema; whether it's the darkness, or the sitting down and relaxing, I don't know, but I just can't seem to help it (Jo has the same problem). This year, it didn't matter, the film broke down so many times I kept waking with a jerk at the very same point where I had shut my eyes. An extra half-hour was added to the film; I imagine it was the catcalls and whistles which jerked me back into wakefulness. The girls, I'm afraid, had to contend with those nuisances, small brothers, ferrying them to the loo (of course, none of them wanted to pay a visit at the same time) and trying to coax Roger out from under his seat. J.P. queued for ice-cream and drinks, and sat at one end of our row, while I (questionably) guarded the other.

'Don't put your heads back against the seats!' warned Sara in a fair imitation of me. We all immediately began to scratch. 'Have a look in my hair!' I always begged John on our return. He always reassured me: 'Nothing there!'

The second film was always the same, without fail, every year. *Old Yeller*, staring a golden Labrador. (Despite seeing it so many times I can't recall the story.) Michael was always affected by this sad tale, and is still very tender-hearted regarding animals, with an abundance of assorted pets.

Other outings might seem mundane to others, but we looked forward to our trips to the Ophthalmic hospital. This meant a day off school for those who were short-sighted like me. The highlight was a fish-and-chip lunch and a stroll by the river to see the boats before we caught the bus home. Those who missed out were rewarded by Matchbox cars or Ladybird books for *not* going.

* * *

'What are you doing to those poor dogs?' I enquired one Saturday morning. J.P. and Jo had slipped past me furtively, I imagined: rummaged in the toy box and rushed outside again with bulging jumpers. After a decent interval I went to investigate.

Seamus was bounding about in a felted-up red pullover – what, no trousers? And Hattie looked coy in a baby bonnet, with booties on her hind feet and mitts on her front paws. Sara was just fastening a piece of lace curtain round her ample middle – Hattie's that is. The girls at that stage had the exact same measurements – 26/26/26! The young ones crowded round.

'Oh, Mum, please go away!' they beseeched. 'It's a surprise!'

'I must hang the washing out,' I retorted mildly, relieved really at the innocent proceedings.

'Don't look then!' Jo implored. Ginge captured Seamus and he suffered the indignity of having his rear covered with a pair of terry training pants, obviously filched from Roger's drawer. There was a convenient gap for his tail to poke through. Released, he rushed off and raised his leg. 'He would!' Ginge grinned.

Whisperings and nudgings over lunch, the usual steak and kidney pud, a concerted assault on the washing-up, then John departed to his endless mowing and merry-tilling, and the children – out of sight.

I came out of the bedroom, with Roger, red-cheeked and drowsy from his nap, balanced on my hip, to discover a large notice stuck on the kitchen door. I recognised the printing – and the spelling – J.P., and the illustrations were obviously the work of the three girls.

THE CIRCUS IS IN TOWN (OUR ORCHERD)
YOU ARE INVITED TO ATEND A GALA
PERFOMENCE THIS AFT. AT 3.
ADMISION FREE!
P.S. REFRESHMENTS.

Ten minutes to go. I went in search of John with our invitation.

There was a circle of kitchen stools, deckchairs: the Ringmaster, J.P. (who else?) wore Grandad's old bowler and a natty red cummer-bund. He cracked his whip, well, hockey stick plus string. 'Roll up! Roll up! First the amazing Black Panther will demonstrate his ag-il-ity by jumping through a paper hoop.' He flourished a circle of paper, the trainer, Miss Ginge, guided Seamus through the hoop to much applause.

The Intrepid Bareback Rider, in gym shorts and shirt, big bow in hair, was Sara. Bumble ambled forward, nosing for apples to crunch up in the grass. He flicked his tail at the flies and then refused to budge. Quick-thinking Sara demonstrated a few perilous exercises, then dismounted, abashed.

Now came the Unicyclists, though they were actually on three wheels. Chris's short legs worked furiously as he rode round the ring at speed with Mike perched on the carrier. 'Look, no hands!' They tumbled off, but were unhurt.

The cyclists obviously doubled-up as the Clowns – with the addition of the Ringmaster – there was squirting of water – the audience was sprayed, too, and I wondered if my lipstick was a write-off – judging by the make-up, it was.

'Now the amazing Midget with his strange baby.' Roger had been coaxed away from the stalls to disappear into the Windy house with Sara. Now he reappeared, beaming, pushing the doll's pram in which reposed Hattie, a fatuous grin on her face, spread-eagled on her back, her head on a pillow. She had obviously been tummy-tickled into blissful submission. The Black Panther, untrained, unrestrained, leapt about excitedly at the Midget's heels. Suddenly, Hattie, coming to her senses, jumped out of the pram, shot between Roger's legs and streaked indoors to sulk in her bed.

'Miss Jo-Jo will walk the tightrope.' Unable to contain himself, J.P. sprang into a handstand, walked on his hands, and fell in a heap at our feet.

A length of clothesline was stretched tautly between two trees, about a foot from the ground. Jo, grimly determined, frilly frocked, bare-footed, clutching a paper parasol, managed four quick steps before she, too, subsided. We clapped and cheered.

Henrietta performed without prompting as she pursued Michael, carrying refreshments (biscuits) on a plate, round and round the ring.

The Grand Finale consisted of acrobatics all round and the Circus was voted a great success. John and I – and visitors when they came – really looked forward to these shows.

CHAPTER 33

Bramleys by the Bushel

Every now and then, when family are visiting en masse, someone requests: 'Come on Dad, let's see the slides!' Crabapple Cottage, the orchard, the energetic children are suspended in time, in colour.

'*Ah, the Family Tree . . .*' there they are, on and up the branches of an enormous Bramley: J.P. and adventurous Ginge near the top; Sara and Jo a little lower, mindful of their pretty dresses; Chris, Mike and Roger, three flaxen heads bobbing between the boughs with bashful grins on their faces.

'*D'you like butter?*' 'Can you spot them?' is perhaps more apt. John's vegetable patch is a golden haze of buttercups and the children are there – somewhere.

'*Ginge, the winner!*' Chin up, long dark hair flowing behind her, she charges at the 'tape', well, the holey (with an e) tennis net. John's wartime experience in a Scottish school learning how to mend fishing nets, came in very useful there – when he could get around to it. The buttercups in this slide have given way to lumpy grass, the veggies having moved to more fertile ground by the hens – and we have a tennis court of sorts. Here we played with more enthusiasm than talent: even I, who am hopeless at games, was transformed into 'Big Margaret' (Court) and the uneven surface helped me no end. Ginge was naturally Virginia (Wade) and Jo, Billie Jean (King). The boys – well, ball boys, what else? They had their own assault course and cycle track and were trained by their big brother!

'*Blossom time . . .*' If you squint very hard you can just discern John amid a froth of pink, gazing out over his domain. 'It was like sitting on a cloud,' he now mused.

Liz was a great friend of ours back then. She was a local girl, who had been to Australia and back when she was first married, but could not settle so far from home. We learned a lot from her. She had an animated, smiling face, long brown hair and bright blue eyes. Green-fingered, she cut huge bunches of asters and gladioli and sold them at the gate. With the money she saved, she and her husband bought a second-hand greenhouse and soon we, too, were enjoying sweet tomatoes, still warm from the vine. 'Too small to sell,' Liz pretended, for she helped us in any way she could. In return, because she worked so hard, I often looked after her baby girls, Laura and Milly.

It was Liz who took us down to the river and showed us where it was safe to swim. One scorching day, we were entranced by the sight of a traveller family diving into the deep pool at the other side of the bridge; fully-clothed, boots and all, surfacing and diving again and again with shrieks of pure joy, shaking themselves like puppies. We waited respectfully until they departed.

J.P. was joined by Sara at the new comprehensive school that September, Jo and Ginge would soon follow. Chris and Michael were at the village school and it seemed strange to have just Roger, and he was rising five, at home with me. However, in October, during half term, I had good news to impart to Liz: 'I'm having a baby!'

She hugged me. 'How *wonderful!*' We sat on the steps below the arch of the bridge, watching the children exuberantly kicking the football in the adjoining meadow, while we dangled our feet in the sparkling fresh water. I thought: *I hope it's a girl . . .*

Liz had inspired us to sell at the gate. We painted a board black, chalked up BRAMLEYS BY THE BUSHEL, filled some forty-pound boxes and waited for the ten bobs to roll in. They didn't for some time: we were off the beaten track; Liz, who was along the main road, caught the eye and the pockets of those hot, hungry and thirsty Londoners in their motors, heading for the sea.

We were inundated with windfalls that summer and autumn, so I penned cards for the local shops: JUICY APPLES, FREE TO OAP'S!' The pensioners were too proud to accept our largesse it seemed, so we bagged up those apples and delivered to the Old Folk's Home, where they were obviously appreciated.

Then, one day an elderly gentleman arrived on a vintage bicycle. He dismounted carefully at our gate, padlocked his steed, removed his cycle clips and proceeded arthritically along the drive. In his hand he clutched a rolled-up oilcloth bag. Hopeful, I waited his arrival: I had been emptying tea leaves on the compost heap.

'Good morning.' He sounded diffident. 'I understand that you have some windfalls to dispose of?' He smiled at Roger, who at this time had temporarily decided to change his name to Brian Snail (a favourite on *The Magic Roundabout*), was in a shy phase, and so ducked behind me.

I filled the visitor's bag to the brim and we escorted him back to his bike, where he spent some time fastening the bag to his carrier.

'Thank you so much,' he said, 'my wife and I enjoy apple pie.' We waved him goodbye. Next day, he was back with a gift, a hydrangea.

Once a week, our new friend called back to refill his bag, always with something to give in return. Comics (several years old) for the children, a lettuce from his own garden, a bunch of perfect sweet peas or a bar of chocolate. We looked forward to his visits and the only problem was the hydrangea. Mr Hubble always inspected it – fortunately, his eyesight was not spot-on, because we replaced that plant twice; either our soil was unsuitable or Seamus watered it more than John and I had. Mr Hubble was over eighty, with an invalid wife we learned, and we respected his dignity in not taking something for nothing, although this meant we were thwarted in our original purpose.

* * *

Mrs Gee's little shop had closed at last, but I was so glad that she was still there, and invariably popped out for a chat, whenever she saw me going past. She had some sad news to impart one day: 'Mr Jackson has died my dear. Poor old soul, his brother went three weeks ago . . .' Well, who could he spar with then? I thought, with tears in my eyes. 'His niece has asked me to "pick a piece or two, anything you fancy, as I know how kind you've been to Uncle". I think he'd like you to have a little something, too,' Mrs Gee added. I still treasure the little pink-and-white striped pot she selected for me, which is perfect for spring flowers, but alas the willow-patterned vegetable dish went the way of all broken crocks: it brightens up the rockery. We never got to know the people who bought Mr Jackson's house. They soon chopped down the conker tree.

Marjorie and her family also departed, having failed to make a go of the nursery there: they were not giving up their dream, however, but buying a smallholding elsewhere. *She* bequeathed us their large enamel bread bin, already thirty years old then, and still going strong to this day! Ben's aunties popped-off too; Mr Turner had gone quietly into a home and a local family were in the process of rebuilding his old house. (We wondered about the wonderful railway.) Even Mr Brick talked of retirement, then finally sold his shop which was 'transformed' into a mini-supermarket. I never went in there again, but for a time Mr B continued with the deliveries for the new owners.

Liz had her first little car. 'We'll go once a week to town,' she offered. But I still made my weekly trek with Roger to see how the village fared.

John had been one of only half-a-dozen commuters in 1962; now there were new estates springing up all over the village and there was an army of dark-suited men marching to and from the station. We were thankful that our lane remained inviolate. A rural pocket in the mainstream.

Still, we now had many customers for our produce. The newcomers sought us out, and we were in business. John fashioned us a stall in the front garden, and at weekends the children picked and displayed the fruit. We had our regulars and they came back time after time. Our jam-jar till brimmed, then it was new shoes all round, and still a little left in the kitty.

My favourite meal remained a modest one, however, spaghetti bolognaise, with John on a Saturday night, after the children were all in bed. The butcher provided meaty bones for the dogs for 6d. a week; John removed the meat, I produced the spaghetti, he did the cooking, we apologised to the dogs for removing the juicy bits, and we thoroughly enjoyed our steaming platesful. We didn't know that often we were spied on, through the keyhole!

None of our fruit, plums, pears, apples, or our vegetables, runner beans mostly, cost our customers more than 6d. per pound – but Bramleys, at ten shillings a bushel, were our best sellers.

'These should keep right round to May,' I told a customer as we carefully placed each perfect Newton in a large box, after weighing them.

In March, the following year, that customer returned, with two apples, slightly marked. 'Can you replace these? There's still two months to go!' We kept smiling, and did!

* * *

Roger and I paid regular visits to the antenatal clinic in the spring of 1968. He was such good company for me – a happy child, a real Anglo-Saxon with his fair skin and almost white hair. He was now almost the same age as Chris had been when he won an art competition at school: his drawing depicted John up a ladder, sack on back, and a tree of round, perfect red apples. Mike was very nippy, one of the dark-eyed ones. He was our general knowledge expert, he had a quick intelligence and continually wanted to know '*Why?*'

I was again not too well and was whisked into hospital two weeks before my due date. John and Roger visited us daily, but I was so sedated I can only recall Roger telling me proudly, after a morning as builder's mate: 'I helped Dad knock down the old toilet!' which revived a vague memory of J.P. and the lats. And a bowl of rice pudding sliding away across the polished floor as I closed my eyes in my starched white bed.

That evening, I awoke just in time, or our darling little Katy might have been born in a bedpan! Times had changed: John was present at the birth, not relegated to the waiting room, or boiling water and stoking fires as he had been at the home confinements. Katy was a tiny baby, but compact and beautiful: she weighed three pounds less than Chris at birth – he had been our bumper baby.

My dear mum was holding the fort while I was away. I seemed to sleep away my time in hospital; once I awoke towards the end of visiting time to discover John's mum and auntie patiently sitting beside me: 'You looked so serene, we just couldn't disturb you . . .'

I was full of energy on my return home and despite John saying 'Don't you think—?' I went with Roger and Katy to pick strawberries up the lane. She dozed in her canopied pram in the fresh air, wearing a little cotton 'angel top' and matching sun bonnet; Roger fitted the punnets on the trays for me, and I picked and picked, and of course, we ate quite a few, the ones we plugged that is. It was like a holiday, out there in the sun, creeping along on straw-flattened knees, feeling among the cool, green leaves for the luscious scarlet berries. We ate our picnic lunch stretched on the grass verge in the shade of the hedge, gave Katy her bottle and changed her. And there were strawberries and cream for us all for tea, of course.

Then Roger was off to school, and the house and orchard were very quiet. John struggled home with another heavy load, a cumbersome old typewriter with a lengthy carriage – oh, how I enjoyed sending that back and forth with that satisfying loud, ping! 'Now, at last,' he told me, 'you've got time to concentrate on your writing . . .'

Katy was such a contented baby, I could sit down and type away each morning during her nap. I wrote short stories for children, some were published in the States, bedtime stories for Hull telephone exchange, tales for playgroup tapes, and *King Fred's Dragon* (his fortieth birthday present from Queen Sophie!) was read on local radio. (This later became a play for the local school children to perform.)

I wrote many articles, too, about the family: later I would turn to short stories and eventually to writing novels. Then, as I spooned puréed food into Katy's mouth at lunchtime, I would read aloud to her the morning's effort and she would blow approving bubbles.

* * *

The river was now out of bounds for swimming, since I had learned, well after the event, that the children had gone there with their dad while I was in hospital, that they had entered the water further along where they were unaware there was a strong current, and that Ginge had been caught up in some reeds, and John had to rescue her. It was not as safe there as we had imagined, it seemed. Now they enjoyed their splashing in the school pools: following much fund-raising by parents, Mr Pastry (Richard Hearne) declared them 'open.' Then, much to the children's delight, we invested in a portable pool of our own. The younger children learned to swim in this, Mike alarmed me by dog-paddling under water, and the girls devised a Busby Berkeley routine to amuse the constant streams of children coming in and out for frequent, cooling dips in the summer holiday. I seemed to spend all my time mopping up puddles on the kitchen floor, hanging out dripping swimsuits and providing dry towels. When no one else was around, I sometimes ventured in the pool myself, floating about on an old tyre, with Katy on my lap, swishing her toes in ecstasy.

J.P. had taken up fishing in the local ponds. He hid a tinful of maggots in the outhouse. Turning out, one summer day, I discovered this tin and opened it. Out buzzed a cloud of beastly bluebottles! Despite our best efforts, these loathsome flies kept turning up indoors. J.P. was most unpopular, as you might guess. John remembered something old Mrs D, our predecessor had told him. 'She said, in New Zealand she used to hang a ball of mutton fat in the kitchen window, to attract all the flies – when they were all bloated . . .'

'Don't tell us!' the girls and I squealed. Undeterred, he finished: '. . . she disposed of them.'

'For a start we haven't got any mutton, let alone fat – and it sounds too disgusting for words!'

'I agree,' John said mildly. After all, there were four of us females. We encouraged J.P. with his fishing though – with dough balls.

* * *

The school taxi was pensioned-off. The children were accommo-
dated on the bus which took the comprehensive lot to school. Even
our daily stroll along the lane was no longer necessary, but Katy and I
still wended our way along the familiar route for old times' sake: like
the others before her she liked to linger at the pigs, to clasp a wilting
bunch of short-stemmed dandelions, and to grin engagingly at her
admirers, remarking on her soft, golden hair and round green eyes.

J.P. invited the Scouts around for a barbeque and sing-song around
the camp-fire one Saturday evening – the rest of the family watched
wistfully from a distance. 'We ought to buy a tent and take them all
camping,' John mused.

'Can you fit ten in a tent?' I wondered.

We bought a Commer minibus – installed a small stove and a table
for eating on and playing games, on long journeys – John came home
with a super tent, sleeping bags and camping gear. We couldn't wait
to try it all out. Though he warned us that the 'thunder box' (Portaloo)
was only for emergencies! The world was bigger than Carter's Lane,
Crabapple Cottage and the orchard – wasn't it?

There was much practising with tent erecting (the boys) and poring over maps.

I was now four months pregnant. 'Katy would be like an only one
being so much younger than the rest,' we had reasoned, but I was game
for the big adventure. One day in August, we packed all day and when
John arrived home from work, all was ready for the 'off' next morning.

'Let's go now!' he decided, seeing our expectant faces. We needed
no second urging! We piled in, each to his/her allotted seat – I sat in
the back with the smaller ones, Ginge in the front because she was
prone to travel sickness and – shush! – better at navigating than J.P.,
and we drove off into the late-evening sunshine. Liz had promised to
look after things for us at home.

How *do* you fit ten in a tent? Well, it's quite an art! So, John and
J.P. slept in the van with the dogs, and the rest of us curled up on the
hard, hard ground, head to toe, because there wasn't room for camp
beds, and fervently hoped that no one would need the bucket in the
night!

We were washed-out by a violent thunderstorm on our second
night en route for Cornwall, but we survived to have a wonderful
holiday, the first of many, under canvas. There was plenty of copy
here for articles – like 'Wake Up Dad, We Can't Find The Tent
Pegs!' recalling the time an exhausted John, who had been driving
his slumbering family all night, pitched the tent at the first site we

came to, crawled inside and was soon wide to the world around him, i.e. all the other tents where the occupants lay doggo. As we shivered in the cold, cold dawn and started the sausages sizzling, a great wind got up and sent the insecurely fastened tent billowing upwards like a parachute – and as we hung on grimly to the corners, we let rip our plaintive appeal!

* * *

The orchard, and the cottage, welcomed us back – the fruit swelled and needed picking, we put the board out, the stall was erected and we sold our first bushel of not-quite-ripe Bramleys. (Customers were persistent.)

We had ventured far from our 'nest' and although we were bliss-fully unaware of it, this was just the start of spreading our wings.

CHAPTER 34

Come In, Number Nine

'Could you oblige with a bucket of water, Mum?' Familiar words but not from our old friend Cecil. We were in the throes of having main drainage installed, along with the rest of the lane. Naturally, this coincided with the summer holidays and with me being very pregnant, ponderous and over-tired.

The lined, weather-beaten face creased into a sympathetic smile. 'You've got your hands full, my dear – *I know* – I've got six little divils of me own, we'll be as little trouble as is possible, don't you fret about the little boyses, they can watch . . .'

'Can I have a bun for Paddy, please?' Chris requested, plonking his grubby fingers on some cooling cakes.

'Paddy says, "I wonder if your Mum is thinkin' of puttin' the kettle on, now",' added Michael, in a passable Irish brogue.

'He only had a cup half an hour ago,' I sighed.

'But he says it's hot work, Mum, he'd finished his flask by ten o'clock. Strong and sweet, so the spoon stands up in it, that's what Paddy likes. He says you make really good tea!' Chris pleaded.

'It's hot work for me keeping Paddy's inner-wheels oiled, too,' I stated, with feeling. 'At least Cecil brings his own refreshments.' I thought nostalgically of the oversized rubber gloves, even the pungent pong: we'd miss our emptyings.

Sara collected up a box of fallen fruit: 'They haven't got any gardens and their children don't get any fresh fruit . . .'

Roger: 'Jack says, have we any new-laid eggs to sell?'

'You know we don't have enough from our lazy hens; tell him, you can buy 'em, shilling a dozen – cracked – up the lane.'

'Jack's wife says cracked eggs are full of germs.'

I gave in, passed over half-a-dozen dark brown eggs.

Seamus seemed to have aged since the holiday – feeling the heat, he lay about, lethargic, harsh-coated, dry-nosed. He'd hardly been to the vet's in his life, now we knew he must. John scooped up the frail little body – 'He's just a bag of bones' – wrapped him tenderly in a blanket and we all said a tearful 'goodbye', just in case.

We were jubilant when he returned. 'The vet gave him an injection, he'll need a course of four, one a week – I'd better not tell you how much! We've also got to get a sample of his, er, water. Any offers?'

This was easier said than done. Ginge finally managed to catch a few drips on an old saucer after she and the boys had followed Seamus patiently most of the morning. 'Poor old boy could hardly lift his leg – he nearly fell over.' We transferred this to an empty aspirin bottle and John relayed it to the vets.

For a few days there was an improvement: Seamus even tottered along to Daisy's – the vet, in passing, spotted him and called in to mildly reprove us for allowing him out, but also added with a grin: 'That's the last thing to go!' It was our old reprobate's last fling. He faded quietly away over the next month or two, despite the injections. He began to smell so badly we had to move his and Hattie's baskets into the outhouse, and we looked in on him frequently, holding his head while he lapped a little milk and wiping his lips as if he were a baby.

The house was quiet; the children and John having departed school- and work-wards. Katy lay asleep, arms flung up, in her cot. When she awoke each morning, Sara, Jo or Ginge rushed in, picked her up, changed her, fetched a drink and carried her back into their room to 'help Mum get some rest.' I was under strict instructions from the doctor to do as little as possible.

So I was still in bed when I heard the unearthly howling. Hattie, head up, baying in distress. I rushed out to the outhouse. Seamus was curled in his box. I stroked his head tentatively, then his fur; he was already cold. My sobs were added to Hattie's howling. I felt as if I had lost a member of my family.

Our doctor – I had not heard his arrival – bent over me, lifted me to my feet, guided me indoors to a chair and proceeded to take my blood pressure. He calmed me down, advising me to merely cover our old friend and to leave well alone until John's return. 'I'll be in first thing tomorrow morning to check you again when you are less upset. Meanwhile, you are not to do a thing – I'll call your friend, and ask her to come to look after you . . . Put your feet up!'

It was Saturday, the next day. 'Are you ready?' John's face was grey and drawn. The doctor had been, and gone, with firm instructions to get to the hospital as soon as possible. It wasn't as easy as that, of course.

'I'm not going until after lunch,' I stated stubbornly, rolling out pastry for meat pie. I had packed my case reluctantly; the baby was not due for two months. Mum couldn't hold the fort this time as my father was ill – he was nearly twenty years her senior. (He wrote to me every day while I was in hospital, and I treasure his letters.)

We all piled into the minibus, the children refused to stay behind with Liz, who had come to say 'Good luck', and to promise us that she would look after Katy, eighteen months, in the daytime, and that she would give Chris, Mike and Roger their tea after school and keep them with her, until J.P. and the girls arrived later, to collect them.

Just one brief stop – to buy a toothbrush!

Sister was very cross: 'We had a Caesar lined up for you this morning! Too late now, the surgeon has gone home!'

I was to regret that meat pie, as I languished for another month, flat in bed, under sedation.

'Please don't ring anymore at 8 a.m.,' pleaded poor John. (That was the only time I seemed to be fully awake.) This was after I became agitated to learn that Ginge, who had answered the phone, was tackling last night's washing-up. 'And Michael's still in his pyjamas!' I must have been a pain in the neck.

'Dad's a great cook!' the children enthused, when they visited. 'He invented floral art cakes – remember that name from the Chapel Flower Festival? – when we ran out of bread. Dad mixed up flour and milk and dropped spoonfuls in the bacon fat . . .' After they had departed, I put away their offerings – jam puffs, fruit cakes – in my locker and then presented them later to the grateful, ever-hungry probationary nurses. I had lost all interest in food, myself.

'I see you're expecting twins,' the hospital padre remarked, admiring my bedside cabinet decoration, a cardboard rocking boat with a 'baby' each end, to cover all eventualities – well, a boy and a girl.

The girls busied themselves with making cards ready to despatch the moment the baby arrived. My favourite was: COME IN, NUMBER NINE! by Ginge, depicting a racing car zooming past the finishing post.

I was unaware that Liz's two were sick with mumps – Katy, of course, had been in close contact with them, but fortunately did not catch it – or that John was having to drive her over to his mum's each morning, some twenty miles away, before going on to the office. The boys having had the mumps (as with *Mopes and Moggies*), Liz kindly took them in after school as promised.

Then it snowed, it was late November – I wasn't told about the two narrow misses in the minibus en route to visit me, either. The roads were really treacherous, but they would come, to keep my spirits up.

Early in December, the baby arrived. The incubator was whisked away, unused, for Matthew was almost 7lb, although probably five weeks early. He was very red and sleepy, but extremely *all right*.

'Start with a boy, finish with a boy,' as Mum had predicted.

WELLCOME HOME MUM! sang out the colourful banner. (J.P.'s spelling was still erratic, but who cared? *He* did, for me – to paint it so boldly!)

John's sister had been down for a few days, and so everywhere was spanking clean. Sara cooked a tasty dinner, liver and onions; I fussed about putting everything back where I wanted it to be, however illogical; the children produced all their bed linen and pyjamas: 'We didn't want to make more work for Dad, or Auntie, so we waited until *you* came home to change them!' John had looked after them so well, he was worn out, so I said quickly, 'That's all right!'

Young Katy, unperturbed by all the fuss, wriggled free from my enveloping hug and peeped in at the baby in the Moses basket. 'Nice,' she approved.

There wasn't much time for writing for a while, Maff, as Katy called him, was a very lively lad indeed. I just about managed to squeeze in my post-natal exercises: 'I gave the boys a fright today,' I related later to John. 'I suddenly became aware that I had an audience outside the French windows! The boys were goggle-eyed in amazement at the sight of my blue tights bicycling furiously in mid-air!'

'I'd have been alarmed, too,' John remarked unkindly.

It was one of the familiar family evenings. 'Just off to Boys' Club, Mum,' announced Chris. A father at the primary school, an ex-professional footballer, had gathered together the soccer enthusiasts and coached them twice a week. Chris was in his element and the younger boys were envious. 'You can't join 'til you're in the top class,' he told them. One day, Chris would say to me about his childhood that he was grateful for 'such a wonderful start in life, it was such a great place to grow up . . .'

Sara bent her pretty head over her school books. Thirteen and a half now, she was petite and slim, very conscientious regarding her homework. She was still a great mix of capability and creativity: she drew, painted, embroidered, sewed her own clothes to her own designs; she adored cooking and cleaning, too, and was a second – sterner! – Mum to her younger siblings. It really was no surprise that early on in her career, she would opt to work in local television, or that later she would be involved with disadvantaged children, and teaching them art.

Jo and Ginge were of a height, almost as tall as their sister (in a year or two they would surpass her). Jo was writing fluently, swiftly in a fat exercise book, she was busy on her latest novelette. Her English teacher would later tell her proud parents that this was outstanding! She still had her great sense of humour, of the ridiculous; her characters were sharply drawn and her imaginative story brought tears of laughter to our eyes. But I don't think then we could have envisaged her travelling the world and working in Israel and America. (All our girls are very determined young ladies who have amazed us! But that's another story, isn't it? One for Jo to tell, perhaps?)

Ginge, as usual, was drawing; wings of dark hair brushing the paper. She was undoubtedly very talented, her art would always be a major part of her life. She, like Sara, would pass on her knowledge and teach special needs children. She also wrote with panache, and her children have inherited her athletic prowess. Her elder daughter runs, and rides horses, as Ginge did. And Ginge still has her shining hair hanging down her back.

J.P. seemed to spend hours in the bathroom in those days, agonising over a spot or two, re-combing his *Beatle* fringe over his eyebrows and cutting his upper lip with his dad's razor. He was so bright and happy-go-lucky (still is), the most loving of boys. His genial disposition has since stood him in good stead – he works like the blazes – a real family man, who nowadays lives on a smallholding with his family and a regular Noah's Ark, just as we did in those days.

Michael and Roger were building a space station on the rug, and Hattie, fatter than ever, snored beside them. Mike knew all the correct procedures and Roger applied himself obediently. Michael was our mathematical wizard – at that time he was the only one of our boys John would trust with anything mechanical. It was no surprise when he went into engineering, and later, almost re-built his own house, just like Ben did!

Roger was as sunny as his hair, kind and thoughtful. Full buckets of coal appeared without the asking. Later on, Roger too would acquire a country cottage and maybe, one day, he and Chris (who both trained at agricultural college) will revert to their first love of farming – though all the older boys are now in business on their own account.

John was enjoying his evening cuddle with his little girl, and I sat nursing Maff; his dark eyes 'snapped' open whenever I ceased jiggling. He never napped in the day, was happy leaping energetically up and down in his baby bouncer watching me at work, or attempting to crawl with Katy's encouragement. At four months old he still had two feeds in the night and slept but fitfully.

'If I were a blackbird, I'd whistle and sing . . .' I droned to those boot-button eyes. He grinned so disarmingly. He still does – at 6 foot 3! You could see he'd be an athletic type even then – but I didn't guess that he'd become an accomplished craftsman, and creative like his sisters. He is a great favourite with all the family.

'Actually . . .' remarked Katy, this being her usual conversational opening. She had an acute ear for music, could hum or sing any tune after a brief hearing. Her favourite song then, was 'Raindrops Keep Falling on My Head'. It was often said to us that we should put our little daughter on the stage. (Much later, we were to read on her school report: 'Katy is the Goldie Hawn of the Third Form!') Like Jo, she had a ticklish sense of humour.

* * *

Katy was almost two when she appeared a little drowsy one morning, just a fraction off-colour.

'Cutting a tooth,' I believed, settling her on the settee for a mid-morning snooze. Even Maff was quiet and dreamy, so into his cot he went and was soon fast asleep. I took advantage of the lull, whizzed through the chores for once, not suspecting what was to come.

Katy awoke with a strange cry, shuddering violently. I lifted her up immediately, thoroughly alarmed. She was burning hot, her limbs began to jerk uncontrollably and the horrible truth hit me – she was having a convulsion. Clutching her to me, I managed to lift the receiver off the phone, to dial our doctor's number. 'Please come . . .' was all I could manage. I doubt if I even said who was calling. He left a surgery packed with patients and drove straight over. Meanwhile, I dialled Liz with the same request. She arrived literally seconds before the doctor. Together, we stripped Katy, sponged her down, threw the windows wide: at last the terrible jerking lessened, her eyes focused and she gave a thin wail, and relaxed.

There was an answering shriek from the bedroom and Liz went to bring out Matthew. She rushed back, face white and shocked. 'He's having one, too!'

We repeated the stripping, cooling, swabbing, until Maff too came round. By then, Katy was sleeping tranquilly.

It seemed to be the longest hour of my life; the doctor diagnosed an acute throat infection (the source remained a mystery – the rest of us were well) but he thought the danger was past. He left antibiotics and promised to call back later.

Home from school, the older children fussed around the babies, lovingly concerned. Katy was wan, but perky once more. Ginge nursed her and told her a story while I made tea, and the others watched over Maff.

'Mum, quick!' Ginge yelled. Katy over-warmed by her embrace, had gone into another seizure. Sara sped to phone the doctor, Ginge held on while we began the battle once more.

This time the doctor was ready with an injection, which calmed Katy down. 'Any more, and it's the hospital,' he told us gravely.

It was a long drawn-out night for us all, but the babies came through and slept peacefully toward dawn.

'The children were wonderful, we couldn't have managed without them,' I said to John as I slipped a weary arm around his waist when we finally dared to lay down in our own bed.

'That's what being a family is all about,' he whispered.

'Oh, John, if anything had happened to them – I just can't bear to think about it . . .' I cried.

'Shush,' he said tenderly. Then we slept too.

* * *

I didn't know I would end my story here, but somehow I feel this is the right place. It was not quite the end of our time at Crabapple Cottage, but we were once again knee deep in plums.

'Katy – watch out for the wasps!' I called, as I had to Chris that first day.

Maff wriggled, like Michael before him, eager to crawl away into the long, lush grass.

I smelled the good odours. Crabapple Cottage was – more than less – ours.

PART 4

SEVEN POUNDS OF POTATOES, PLEASE

Mid-1970s

CHAPTER 35

Seven Pounds of Potatoes, Please

Christmas Day, the first in our new home. We sat in happy anticipation round our Victorian loo table, which rested on a pedestal embellished with lion claws. When we were first married, John and I purchased this for ten shillings from a local junk shop, and bowled it home upended, precariously, along the pavement, as we couldn't fit it into our motorcycle sidecar. The table was faded and scratched then, but John lovingly French-polished the rosewood top and it was now a treasured possession.

The girls had laid the table with our wedding silver and the frosted pink glass water set. The turkey, basted to perfection, sat on a huge dish in the centre. The splendid home-cooked ham, coated in golden breadcrumbs, was adorned with a paper frill. Steam wafted lazily from the vegetable dishes. We'd been cutting a cross in the stem of the sprouts while awash with Christmas wrapping paper. John was about to carve the first succulent slices on to the top plate of the pile, when we became aware of a strange noise – our dining room opened directly onto the courtyard outside the shop, and something was being pushed stealthily through the front-door letterbox. Could this be a belated Christmas parcel? We stared, mesmerised as a long, dun-coloured, folded object appeared, then plopped on to the mat. I recognised it immediately – I encountered that old oilskin bag daily on the counter!

Cautiously, I opened the door and glanced up and down the street. It was deserted. Probably the whole village was sitting down to Christmas dinner, I thought. I closed the door, bag in hand, wondering why whoever brought it had disappeared in haste.

'Oh, no!' I exclaimed. 'Surely Mrs Dean doesn't want a delivery today . . .' There was a pencilled note inside, written on an old envelope: It read, 'Seven Pounds of Potatoes Please (my daughter's had a baby).'

'We're closed,' John said firmly. 'We stayed open until almost seven last night – remember? She had plenty of time to do her shopping then.'

'But – her daughter's had a baby . . .' I said. 'She was probably up most of the night.'

'So were we,' he reminded me. 'We had all our own Christmas preparations still to do . . . Eat your dinner first. Surely they can wait?'

'They're obviously out of potatoes,' I insisted. 'It won't take me long to weigh them, then one of the boys can run round to the Dean's house with the bag.'

'Aw, Mum!' the boys sighed reproachfully. 'We're hungry!'

My dinner plate went in the Rayburn, while I hurried up the hill with the heavy bag, still wearing my golden paper crown, to the row of old farm cottages on the edge of the council estate, where the Dean family lived. Mrs Dean, a tiny woman with a permanently worried expression, appeared at the door with an apron over her nightgown, and brand-new Christmas slippers. A couple of her smaller girls clutched her apron strings. Somewhere a baby gave a plaintive cry. A strapping girl clad in just a brief top, revealing long, bare legs, came out from the back room, pushed past her mother and pounded up the steep stairs, to answer the call. There was no sign of the reclusive Mr Dean. I wondered if he actually existed. We'd heard he was retired – he was certainly retiring – had we almost met him today? As the rest of the family were not yet dressed, it seemed likely that he had left the bag.

'Thanks, love – we wasn't aware my daughter was even expecting – quite a night, I tell you . . . Get peeling them spuds you lot! Merry Christmas!' The door closed in my face.

'Bet she didn't pay for the potatoes,' John said.

'Think of it as a special delivery!' I replied.

* * *

We left our old home on a perfect summer's day the previous June. Our goods and chattels had been packed and removed the day before. I had supervised this as best I could, as John was summoned to the last day stock-taking at the shop, and wasn't due back until the early hours. We slept for the last time in Crabapple Cottage, lying on the floor in our sleeping bags. The kindly removal men had been super-efficient and packed everything in sight, including my shoes and the Swan Vestas. When John came wearily in, we tried to strike a solitary match on the wooden boards to brew tea on the camping stove, to no avail.

At first light, we were thankful to rise and flex aching joints. We ate a picnic lunch in the orchard, as we had the day we arrived there. The chickens, including dear Henrietta, the bun-snatcher, and other livestock had not been replaced, the old dogs had gone, and now we had a lively, tiny Jack Russell pup named Florence. Tiger, the ancient ginger tom cat was around – but where? We searched in all his favourite places, but he was not to be found.

A kind neighbour told us not to worry, she would look out for him, feed him, and despatch him to us by train. We learned later that another neighbour (remember long, lanky Chas, another unexpected child, whose standard charge for services rendered, was five bob? Well, this was his mother who much preferred cats to children) had enticed him into her shed, and hidden him until after we departed.

John's family joined us in the orchard for the picnic and we looked around us at the trees and back at the old house with its now blank, reproachful windows. One thing we were sure of, we would never forget this place – although we didn't realise then, that it would always mean 'home' to all of us . . .

'Don't look back,' we said to one and another as we drove away in our Commer minibus. But I know I was crying, and I couldn't understand why.

CHAPTER 36

From the Crossroads

It was like stepping back in time – the village appeared to be just as it had been for generations. From the shop, the road wound down lazily over a hump-backed bridge. There was another big house attached to ours, where nice middle-aged Martha lived alone, now her parents were gone. She played the organ in the church and was the school cook. She also practised on a harmonium in her bedroom, the other side of the wall from the girls, and snatches of rousing hymns entertained them, amplified by the joint chimney breast. The girls sang loudly to let her know she was disturbing their slumbers, but then she pulled all the stops out, obviously appreciating their involvement.

Next, there was a row of two-up, two-down cotts, where most of our regular customers lived, conveniently opposite the pub, which we gathered was also the working men's club.

On the same side as the cotts was the primary school, which until about five years ago, we learned, had a handful of pupils, an ageing head teacher who plied the cane, and the furnishings of the 1880s, when it was founded. Then, on the plateau of the steep hill along which the bus ran morning and evening, to the village, turning at the crossroads, a large, posh estate of houses was built, which attracted affluent strangers with cars who commuted to town to work. These newcomers didn't deign to shop at the stores, but the school was a different matter; they saw its potential. By the time we arrived, there was a young, enthusiastic headmaster, modern equipment and, amazingly, a swimming pool. The money had been raised by the parents of the new intake of pupils. Katy would shortly be in her element as a new pupil and enthusiastic water baby with floats.

Turn the corner across the road at this point and you were going uphill again, past a little front-room post office run by a brother and sister who viewed us with suspicion, and there was the church, seemingly in the middle of nowhere, silhouetted against the horizon, where the crows nested. Most of the villagers were chapel, and the parson, known as Bouncy 'Ball', his surname, and yes, it described his shape, met most of his flock in the pub, rather than in the pews. He was well-liked, but his congregation was, on occasion, just the church warden and grave digger. Once, it was only John, me, and a stranger. The parson disappeared mid-service, we sat on in apprehensive silence, but eventually, we went home. We heard later that he had totally forgotten we were there . . .

He did indeed bounce home to the vast, chilly rectory . . . His cassock was fastened with safety pins, and we treasure a letter from my dad to the big girls, which suggests, 'Why don't you sew him up with your needle and thread?'

Little Moor Road was more a lane, branching off from the crossroads in the opposite direction to the snooty new estate and downhill all the way. You had to watch out for the cattle grids. Here were all the big houses behind high walls with iron gates. Retired colonels and their like lived here, and did not mix with the hoi polloi. The moor tumbled green and verdant down to a bubbling stream and beyond that was a lovely old farmhouse. Miss Dingle was in charge of the dairy and the Jersey cows – her clotted cream was much coveted. We were privileged to receive a carton of it each week, which we paid for, of course, but it built up in the fridge. You can't eat this luxury food every day.

The view from our shop window was as idyllic. Another stream splashed clear water where children paddled, and rising above this low point was a meadow with two or three gentle cows with following calves. These were the pets of the neighbours across the road, a kindly couple, the Trews, who made us welcome. Mrs T had only one son, whom we never met, and she shared her home with her daughter-in-law Dee, an attractive young woman, and also an adopted daughter, Anne, who had cerebral palsy. Anne communicated with us in her own way, a delightful, happy girl. She worked in a sheltered workshop and liked to come into the shop after she received her modest wage packet to choose a small gift for her foster mother and a mixed bag of her favourite sweets.

Anne, we learned, was one of twins, born prematurely. Her young mother couldn't cope with two babies, one of whom was handicapped.

When her grandmother, who remained in touch with Anne, heard that she was to be placed in an institution, she brought the tiny baby wrapped in a shawl, to her friend Mrs Trew, who had always wanted a daughter. Although Anne was in and out of hospital most of her young life, undergoing operations, Mrs Trew didn't falter in her devotion to the girl, and it was obviously reciprocated.

Mrs Trew was tall and slender, with striking auburn hair, blue eyes and pale skin; her husband was obviously of village stock, being short, with black hair, swarthy skin and brown eyes. Talking of eyes, it was rather disconcerting to notice how many of the older male locals had one good eye and one 'wonky one', so we assumed they were all related ... 'Everyone shopped here 'til a few years ago,' Mrs Trew observed. 'The old owners sold everything from corsets to corn plasters. Not much money passed hands – people paid in kind, like the odd poached salmon or half a pig. Then when the folk afore you come along, they only lasted a year, they altered everything. They don't take to change round here, m'dear. Most went up the hill to the Co-op. Mind you,' she added to soften the bombshell, for we'd thought we were taking on a thriving business, 'the shop is cleaner and brighter, with much more variety. It's good to have a family here again. If they take to you they'll be back ...'

CHAPTER 37

We'll Fill the Shelves

(whether you want it, or not)

To our eyes, the shop was attractively laid out, with labelled shelving, cold cabinets and a huge modern freezer, with frozen peas and fish fingers alongside much-requested bright pink sausages and yellow dairy ice-cream.

We had a splendid bacon and ham slicer. One of our most urgent tasks was to clean this, after our arrival, for the previous owners' Persian cats had obviously groomed themselves in close proximity to the slicer and it was gummed up with fur. The thought crossed our minds that the cats had enjoyed licking the blades . . . It was unfortunate that the preparation area was in the kitchen beyond the shop, and when we had to leave that unattended, we worried, with reason, what was happening during our brief absence . . . On our return, it was to cast an eye over the packets of tea, or cans of baked beans, to check if pyramids were in danger of toppling.

The shop was supposed to be self-service but most, like Mrs Dean, ignored the wire baskets and filled their own bags. There was the odd 'forgetful' customer who disappeared out of the door, bypassing the up-to-date electric till, which necessitated a breathless dash outside by whoever was serving and a polite 'reminder' to pay up, please – however, we soon discovered that most of our customers while very poor, were honest. It was a minority, mostly incomers, as Mrs Trew told us firmly, to whom getting one over new shopkeepers was a way of life. We had to show them we knew what they were up to. A strategically placed mirror helped somewhat, alongside the five bottles of expensive His'n'Hers perfume – six had been counted on the stock list, but over the night before our arrival, one had mysteriously vanished. (We never sold any at all, but two bottles were missing after the final stocktaking. The same culprit, was our rueful guess.)

The counter guarded the tobacco and cigarettes on the wall unit behind – no self-service allowed in that respect. Also out of reach was a card of sachets of saffron. Despite its luxury price, no celebration cake was made in these parts without a few strands, and the taste made rich fruit cakes even more special.

There was a newspaper stand, and we whittled down the contents after we noticed that most of the wonky-eyed brigade were more interested in stealthily riffling the pages of top-shelf lurid magazines than buying fresh Cornish pasties (giant-sized) and stale chocolate sponges with a tinge of green 'decoration', which we'd inherited, piled high on the cake and biscuits shelf. We shortly disposed of the services of the Cadbury Cake man and purchased fresh cakes from the wholesalers.

We were supplied with local produce by those who assured us that they had been doing this for so many years, they could judge exactly the amounts needed. We were grateful for their expertise in the beginning, but very soon twigged that most were pulling a fast one.

Tinkerbelle, we dubbed the thin man with oiled back black hair and pencil moustache, who supplied the stocking stand with his Belle tights, pop socks and sheer nylons. He came every month and counted up how many we had sold – we could never prove that his sums added up, because he always slid sideways into the shop at a busy time, assuring us in a stage whisper: 'Don't worry, I can manage – I'll give you the total when you're free . . .' Tinkerbelle was obsequious, I thought. He asked me, the first time he called, 'May I speak to your mother, dear?' When I told him that I was the co-owner of the shop, emphasising 'with my husband', he was unabashed. 'You look so young,' he gushed.

Tinkerbelle's tights often laddered after one wearing, and we were resigned to replacing them for customers. As Mrs Dean said, 'Can't you get the lisle ones anymore? They lasted forever.' (She pronounced lisle as 'lissel'.) This was true, I thought, seeing wrinkled tan stockings on a very ancient customer, who commented, regarding the Belle stand, 'Them flimsy things show all your varicosities.'

The pasties and a weekly batch of farmhouse crusty bread were made by a farmer's wife with a heavy hand and rolling pin. The filling in the pasties was tasty and well-seasoned, but there was the traditional wide, crimped edging to enable a hungry worker with grubby hands to grasp the solid pastry, bite into the middle, then discard the crust. Our worry was that those who placed a regular order, sometimes omitted to collect on the day and then refused to pay for 'stale goods'. We ended up having to eat the surplus, because *we* certainly were expected to stump up, in advance. I'd never had a weight problem until then, but eating the leftovers set me on the road to Weight Watchers.

The sausage man, beaming and red-cheeked, also delivered great tubs of ice-cream, I suspect some of the same ingredients were involved. The sausages as I said were a lurid pink, fat and slippery in great ropes, which the sausage man festooned in loops taking up half the freezer. You could request chipolatas, but they were all jumbo size. They were obviously a village staple food and we often sold out.

The fruit and veg man proudly presented items grown on his own allotment. Everything he grew was enormous and we knew he had won prizes at flower shows, but big is not always tender, is it? When customers asked for a pound of anything, like leeks or swedes (always called turnips, while cauliflowers were known as 'broccola') they usually received a single vegetable – the range also included an onion like a beach ball, or a carrot that no bunny could manage to nibble. There was good earth caked under Les's fingernails, proving things were fresh-dug. You had to watch out for caterpillars in the cabbages, and wrigglers in the pea pods, and you needed a cleaver to dice the carrots. We sold more of the latter than any other vegetable, a good many to a neighbour of Mrs Dean's, whose complexion turned bright orange, so we gathered she was addicted to them. We learned to have only a couple on display at a time. We were forced to tell this poor woman that carrots were in short supply due to – er – carrot fly . . .

What else did we sell in the shop? Plastic buckets and bowls, torches, bandages and, yes, corn plasters, milk and yoghurts, toys, sweets in jars, chocolate bars, plus trays of penny candy on the counter, for the little ones to choose from. Occasionally, these were dribbled on, when a mother held her toddler over the dolly-mixtures while she picked out the jelly ones.

Other commodities were bought regularly by John from the wholesalers on the outskirts of town. We priced it all carefully according to the 'Grocer's bible', but our customers could always sniff out a bargain. When we sold a month's supply of loo rolls in a day, it was time to re-check the price, too late. We also learned to our cost that when we obliged by getting in a special item, the customer who wanted this so urgently, no longer required it, and probably nobody else did, either.

My unfavourite task was to fill the various containers presented daily for a 'pint of paraffin'. It appeared most folk cooked on an oil stove. Toddy, a big lad, with a blond cowlick of hair, aged fourteen, well mannered, who caught the school bus with our boys each morning, often scarpered home, after registration, and usually turned up when there was a lull in the shop and John was collecting goods in town or out delivering to a farm. I asked, 'Couldn't you wait until my husband gets back?' but he said quickly, 'Mum says she needs it *now!* I'll mind the shop, Missis . . .'

That darn tank produced a thin trickle, and I agonised over what pilfering could be going on while I tried to fill a lemonade bottle, with a fervent little prayer.

When I returned, Toddy was always leaning innocently against the door, and nothing appeared to have been disturbed.

'I didn't let nobody in,' he said virtuously. 'They all went away.'

Thanks Toddy, I thought. 'Here you are,' I said feebly, handing over the bottle. I couldn't help having a soft spot for Toddy despite my suspicions. I also knew he'd be back when the bottle was empty to claim the refund. The Corona man would not be pleased at the whiff of paraffin, but he'd continue to fill *his* allotted shelf with Dandelion and Burdock.

CHAPTER 38

Early Doors

The newspapers arrived with a thud before dawn – thrown at the front door by a passing van. At 5.30 a.m. John stood, yawning, marking them with his pencil, and folding them ready for delivery. We had our own family paper boys, of course, who pedalled cheerfully up and down hill, hoping the guard dogs kennelled outside the big houses were still asleep, but we shortly heard a crescendo of barking, in Little Moor Road.

Still, that was preferable to the irate retired naval commander, who only came in the shop to complain that if the staff of a certain broadsheet were on strike, thus no paper, what were *we* going to do about it? We also discovered early on that some people don't like to pay for newspapers *after* they've read 'em. Bills were often queried.

From 6 to 7, I was busy with breakfast, and the girls kindly encouraged the young ones to wash and get dressed. I cooked on the Rayburn in the kitchen, and family soon appeared at the appetising smell of frying bacon. As always, we 'all pulled together'.

We officially opened the shop at 8 a.m. Unofficially, I listened out for the hacking coughs of farm workers out there in the still dark, misty morning, plus the damp and cold from late September until spring. The amount of wet weather in the west during these months, came as quite a shock to us, although it was certainly not as chilly as it was in the south-east.

As I laid the first rashers of bacon in our huge frying pan, there would come a tapping on the shop door. Sighing, I went through to unbolt the door, but left the sign at CLOSED.

More coughing, a wheeze or two, then the early workers, wound round with scarves, wearing fingerless gloves and woolly caps – I never knew their names – requested, 'A packet of green papers, Missus, please, and half an ounce of the strongest . . .' They rolled the first fag of the day as they stood outside for a moment, and the lovely smell of bacon was eclipsed by that of rank tobacco. Although, as a non-smoker, I wished we didn't have to stock this commodity, I appreciated that these, often elderly, men needed their smokes to cope with all the hard graft ahead.

We had a potent remedy for coughs by the till: lozenges which had been formulated for deep sea fishermen and these proved a best seller, too. John tried one for a sore throat one night in bed, went to sleep, and woke in the morning to find the lozenge glued to the roof of his mouth. He complained about the taste for several days, but it did the trick.

The before-hours customers kept arriving, all through breakfast. It was a tradition we couldn't break. I'd be flipping the eggs in the pan, and there would be yet another knock, more timorous this time. I could guess who. 'Mrs Diddley – can someone finish the eggs off?' I asked.

I was right – it was Elsie Diddley from the cotts. She was shrouded in an old overcoat, but her faded fair hair was combed into a snood in the style of the forties when she had been a pretty young girl, doing her bit for the war effort in a factory. Mrs D certainly didn't smell of His'n'Hers perfume – she absolutely reeked of bleach. She was the school cleaner. She got through about three large bottles of the stuff each week, which her poor red hands bore testament to. I tried tactfully to suggest rubber gloves might help, but Mrs D shook her head. 'You got to get the feel of what you're doing,' she said, in her soft, almost inaudible voice. I could picture those hands scrubbing away in the toilet block, and winced to think how much they must pain her. She was one of several small, frail looking women locally who had produced large idle offspring on whom they appeared to wait hand and foot. Cuckoos in the nest, I thought compassionately.

At 7.30 a.m., the first bus was due at the crossroads. A minute or two before this, several women, including Mrs Trew's Dee, some with hair in curlers under turbans, arrived to buy their daily cigarettes, a newspaper and a bag of Everton mints. They had the best paid jobs, making wireless components in a factory. They would return that evening at 6 p.m. to knock on the shop door if we had actually closed on time, for 'sausages, m'dear, for tea. Quick to do: it's Bingo night in the village hall.' The Rev. Bouncy Ball had introduced this attraction, and was the caller. He also organised monthly discos in the hall, and the most requested record, which caused us to pull the covers over our heads in bed on a Saturday night, was 'Viva Espana!'

The High School bus came at 8.15. The shop was now officially open at last, and John and I joined forces to control the influx of teenagers. Our lot escaped the back way, to be first in the queue at the bus stop, with a modest choc bar apiece for break time.

Katy and Maff sat on stools behind the counter, and were made a fuss of by Toddy's younger sister, a boisterous nine-year-old named Loretta, with freckles and a loud voice, who sometimes yelled out to John, 'You want to watch my brother, mister!'

The till rang incessantly, and we hoped the bus would arrive early so that the shop would empty in double-quick time.

Just time for a reviving cup of tea, before it was time to walk Katy to school. Loretta would be sitting on our front wall, swinging her legs, waiting to accompany us, and to impart Toddy's latest misdemeanours.

'Mum said you just wait 'til Dad comes home, but Toddy knew he was safe, 'cos Dad was down the pub with his mates, and *he* was going to get it from Mum first, I reckon!' she said, adding, 'She forgot to give me 10p for the swimming today – could I borrow it from you, Katy's mum?' Of course, I obliged. Her mum was a large lady with a fierce expression, and always hard-up, but she made sure her family were well fed. Ten-pence pieces were in short supply in her house, I guessed.

At the school gate, Loretta took Katy's little hand in hers. 'Don't worry, I'll look after you, and help you in the pool this afternoon. I'll mangle all the water out of your costume, when I do mine, eh?' She was the youngest in her family, but was a real little mother.

'I'm on poolside duty,' I told her. I wanted to be sure Katy was confident in the water, it wasn't the same as paddling in the sea, which she loved. I'd added my name to the parents' rota, for Wednesday afternoons, when we were open only half the day. I'd had plenty of experience with the portable pool in the orchard when the others were growing up. This was also an open-air pool, and two supervisors were required, facing each other on either side, one a parent and the other a qualified teacher/instructor, who was in charge.

I needn't have worried: there was Katy, already in the shallow end, when I hurried round to the school at 2.30. She looked so tiny, in her blue costume with a yellow sunflower on the front and her bathing cap. She took to swimming like a duck to water, with inflated armbands, and her chubby limbs flailing – within a week she could do a width, and float on her back. Maff watched from the side but shook his head when invited to join his sister in the water. He liked to weigh up things before he joined in, he still does. He was the responsible one of the two, even though he was younger. They balanced each other nicely.

'Watch me, Katy's mum! Watch me!' called Loretta, attempting to swim a length under water. I obliged, but I thought, her own mum is missing out – Loretta is sometimes a pain in the neck, but she's a real character! Not only did she later put Katy's costume through the wringer which had been presented to the school by Mrs Trew, and kept on the step outside the boys' and girls' changing rooms, but she cheerfully stood there in her own dripping costume, a baggy navy blue one, obviously passed down by an older sibling, seeing to all the other children's swimming togs first, as they emerged in their dry clothing. Oh, we did like Loretta!

CHAPTER 39

Old Cat, Young Dog and Roaming Tortoise

A month elapsed before Tiger was located and sent by rail to be collected. John and the children met two trains before he finally turned up. He stepped, stiff-legged, out of the carrying basket on to the kitchen floor. He ignored the saucer of milk, the bowl of food, but he began his rumbling purr. He was lifted up, which he wouldn't have tolerated in his prime, and it was as if he weighed hardly anything at all. We stroked his faded ginger-striped coat, and carried him to inspect the barn. This was more like it, we could tell, and he chose a cosy corner to sit and watch comings and goings. Unwisely, we decided to keep him safe indoors overnight. I even buttered his paws. The store room seemed a good place, with all the goods well off the floor. He was too arthritic to climb. However, he marked every corner of what we'd dubbed the dungeon, so like Mrs Diddley, we had cause to resort to bleach and a scrubbing brush. Tiger had always been an outside cat and was now too old to change his ways, we realised. He soon settled down to his mouse-patrol in the barn, and continued to regard little Florence, the Jack Russell pup, with his unblinking gaze. She was eager to be his buddy, but Tiger the once-feral cat certainly wasn't about to permit to any familiarity.

The family persuaded us that we needed a canine pal for Florence. A bigger dog, perhaps. One or two dark-jowled men, observing her over the five-barred gate which closed off the back garden, had enquired slyly if they could buy Florence to use for hunting purposes – poaching, we thought was more it. When we declined, they went off, but we worried they might come back and take her anyway. Florence needed a protector!

We scoured the local ads and were struck by one which read:

OLD ENGLISH X
BORDER COLLIE PUPS – £20

We rang the number given, and were told there were just two left – a bitch which took after the mother, a collie, and a dog pup which was, like its father, an old English sheepdog.

John recalled a dog from his childhood which had belonged to an elderly lady, Miss Moses, whom he had helped with hay-making during the war. 'He was a beautiful Old English – he was called Blue Billow,' he said.

'Dad – can we go and buy him today?' the family chorused. 'We want a Blue Billow, too!'

It was a Saturday – I said I could manage the shop – so they all piled into the minibus, plus Florence, and drove off to Bodmin Moor.

I wish I had seen it myself, but I could picture the setting from their vivid description: dogs were everywhere, mostly collies, on moorland grazed by sheep. The dogs were atop grassy hillocks barking furiously. Chickens were flapping and scratching around. The farmhouse sat in a hollow below, near the road, where the minibus was parked. It had been quite a climb up the hill.

The pups were huddled together in a chicken coop, noses poking through the wire mesh. They were thin and shivering, and the dog pup was not the beautiful animal we had envisaged. He was still black and white, as Old English pups are until they grow a top grey coat. He had a whippy tail, but soulful eyes which seemed to plead: You're going to take me home, aren't you? His sister was already booked; just as well, as the family wouldn't have liked to leave her on her own.

Our third daughter, sixteen-year-old Ginge, now a tall girl with long chestnut hair and dark eyes, was great with animals. Florence, we accepted, was her special charge, although we all enjoyed our pet. Billow loved us indiscriminately. When he was out with the lads, he was 'one of the boys' – he joined in all the games, puncturing the foot-ball, but scoring many a goal. He swam with them in streams and in the sea, he was a real water dog, and he enjoyed shaking droplets all over anyone nearby. He grew into a very handsome dog, resembling a bearded collie, with grey fur and a splendid, plumed tail. He had kind brown eyes under his fringe, and an amiable nature. However! He was quite an escape artist. He could clear a five-barred gate in a graceful leap, and he was a would-be Romeo – he was drenched with the occasional pail of water, I'm afraid. But when he shook hands with you and put his nose on your feet when he sat snoozing beside you, well, you could forgive him anything. We were fortunate to have him for sixteen years.

Sadly, we only had little Florence for two years. She was run over by a farm tractor, poor Ginge was inconsolable. We were all very sad.

* * *

Matthew wanted a tortoise, and got his wish. The tortoise had a shiny, patterned shell, and fascinated his small owner, who looked after him well and offered him succulent lettuce leaves. He laughed out loud when Torty's head popped out from the shell and he nibbled his food.

Unfortunately, it appeared that Torty, like Billow, enjoyed going beyond the boundaries of the garden. Maff would run indoors to report: 'I can't find him, Mummy! He's disappeared.'

The first couple of times, I said, 'Well, he can't be far away – he's a tortoise and they are very slow, you know.'

We put up a notice in the shop window:

TORTOISE MISSING. SMALL REWARD
FOR HIS RETURN!

On each occasion, after a few hours, with the village children alerted, Torty was brought home. Toddy had found him, but was vague about exactly where. I indicated the chocolate section. 'Take your pick!'

'Cor, thanks Missus!' he beamed. 'Glad to help.'

Some rewards later our suspicions aroused, but unconfirmed, Loretta split on her brother.

'He nips in your garden, Katy's mum, and pinches 'im!' she said. 'That ain't right.'

'No – it – ain't – isn't,' I said, suppressing a wry smile.

I guess she told Toddy what she'd done, because the tortoise napping stopped. I didn't confront Toddy, because he knew that I knew, and that was enough. Anyway, as we had replaced the chocolate with a swizzle lolly of late, he probably reckoned it wasn't worth the bother.

However, this is not quite the end of this particular story . . .

'I found your tortoise – do you still give rewards?' another lad asked diffidently. This was Wim, short for William I suppose, a shy and silent type as a rule, who seemed rather a loner. Another big boy with a tiny, energetic mother. Wim held out a tortoise which was Torty sized, but with a crack on the shell.

Oh dear, I thought, Torty has had a mishap! The larger reward seemed to be fitting, and Wim departed with his Mars bar, and a bemused expression. I bet he shared it with his little sister.

John examined the crack. It was obviously an old wound, healed over. He took the tortoise into the garden, only to discover what I should have checked before, that Torty was ambling around out there.

So a notice duly went up in the shop window:

**TORTOISE FOUND (NOT OURS) IF YOU HAVE
LOST ONE, PLEASE ASK IN SHOP.**

So then there were two. Where Oisey came from remains a mystery.

CHAPTER 40

Concorde and Kites

We decided from our very first Sunday in the shop, that we would have to go out for the day if we were to avoid the taps on the door from the likes of Mrs Dean, requesting potatoes, or Toddy, with another Corona bottle for paraffin, which had probably been 'lifted' from the crate put out for the Corona man on Fridays. This doubled the refund on the bottle!

We had the moor on our doorstep, where we enjoyed summer-evening strolls before John settled to the shop accounts and the children to their homework, but on Wednesday afternoons, after they returned from school, we often drove a short distance to a magical place, which we fondly imagined was known to us exclusively. We had discovered by chance one day a crystal waterfall splashing into a rushing stream with stepping stones, and springy grass, nibbled by sheep, for ball games and picnic teas. We took our shoes off and cooled our toes in the spray.

On Sundays, we ventured further afield. Before our move we'd toured all round the lovely coast of Dorset, Devon and Cornwall during our camping holidays and were eager to re-visit two favourite places, one in Devon and the other in Cornwall.

The 70s were record summers for sunshine. We left home early in the morning, before the heat of the day, and returned when the temperature cooled, in the evening. Our minibus had a variety of seats: Sara sat in a single seat by the side door to control the entry and exit of her exuberant brothers – they sat together on a long seat facing a table, on which were spread comics, board games and their young brother's toy cars. I was on the opposite bench, with Maff, ostensibly minding the boys, while, J.P. and Ginge (the only one to suffer travel sickness) were in the front with John.

Jo and Katy shared a seat behind Sara, and the dog fitted in where he saw a space. Although we no longer used the van for camping, alongside our big tent we'd retained the stove at the rear, and the cupboard where we now stacked our bags and cold box full of food. We still liked to have a fresh brew of tea. The thunder box was also in its allotted spot, but as we were often reminded by John, who had to empty it, for 'emergency use only!'

It was an hour or so's drive to our chosen destination, along narrow lanes with fields either side protected by mossy dry-stone walls.

Curious cows, with long flirty eyelashes, regarded us over farm gates. A farm dog barked, and Billow pricked his ears. If we met a tractor, one or other of the vehicles would have to back up cautiously, sometimes for a mile or two, before a lay-by was reached. Like Gracie Fields, in an old film I had seen at the local fleapit as a child, we loved to 'Sing as We Go'. Katy performed her party piece, 'Raindrops Keep Falling on My Head', but it was, happily, that day, 'Blue Skies Smiling at Me'.

At last we came to the road which led down a steep incline to a field: private land, but limited parking permitted. We walked briskly across the grass – well Chris, Mike and Roger ran of course – inhaling the good sea air, carrying our towels, bathers and bags of items like sun cream, calamine lotion, plasters, dog biscuits, bowls and bottles of water, plus books and sunglasses. John carried the food! At least the box would be lighter, going back.

The boys disappeared down the cliff path to the soft sand of the tidal estuary beach. Across the stretch of shimmering water there rose a green meadow, on which cattle grazed. At low tide you could walk to the other side, but had to take care not to be stranded there when the tide came in again.

There were outcrops of rock to sit on, to spread our towels, and some flat enough for sun bathing. If the sun was too strong, we could retreat to where the cliff overhung and cast a welcome shade.

It really was a beautiful spot, and it was easy for me to relax and dream away the day, while the young ones napped on my lap, and the rest of the family dashed in and out of the water with Billow.

One afternoon, however, a coach load of trippers arrived to blast the air with music and loud voices, with binoculars which they trained not on the sea birds or the pastoral scene across the water, but on our three pretty daughters, innocently sunbathing on the rocks in their bikinis.

Not wishing them to be embarrassed, we decided to drape our towels round our shoulders, go back to the van to get dressed and go in search of a shaded garden where we could treat ourselves to a cream tea. The family thought this was a splendid idea.

As always, the boys led the cavalcade, with Billow dashing backwards and forwards, to make sure we were following. While the lads skirted the rowdy party, now unpacking their lunch, Billow had no such inhibitions: he bounded through the middle of them, scattering them with sand, and even as they shouted indignantly, he casually cocked his leg and peed over their sandwiches.

By unspoken, common consent, we thought it prudent to pretend he was a friendly dog who'd attached himself to us on the beach.

Vengeance was sweet.

* * *

We went by ferry from Plymouth to Cornwall, the young ones were as excited as if they were on a cruise! Then we drove on to a place with an Irish name – forgive me for not being specific! Maybe it has been 'discovered' in later years, but then it was not as well-known as the main resorts.

There we scrambled down a trail worn into the cliff-side – there was a 'drop' at the finish – I have no head for heights, so I closed my eyes, and leapt into John's outstretched embrace, cheered on by my fearless children, who would have been awaiting my arrival for some minutes. This route was a short-cut to the beach, or so they said. I would have preferred to take the long, official route down.

Mostly, we had the beach to ourselves until mid-morning. The sea rushed in round rocks, boys and dog were dripping wet most of the time, and once Billow swam out to sea after a beach ball, despite our cries of 'Come back!' When he was eclipsed by a roller, we thought he'd gone . . . The younger children were sobbing when the dog was spotted, staggering ashore, but wagging his sodden plume of a tail. He was soon wrapped in one of the family towels and I'm sure he was smiling in doggy fashion at all the cuddles and tidbits.

It was here that we had our first sight of Concorde. Amazing! Experimental flights were taking place around the coast. We shaded our eyes and craned our necks to watch this beautiful plane flying overhead.

At midday, more families came down to the beach. By then, the sun was beating down on us, and we had covered up bare limbs and retreated to the cool mouth of a cave at the foot of the cliffs. It worried me to see young parents carrying naked babies and toddlers without sun hats or T-shirts, running across sand which scorched bare feet. They believed their children were cooler without clothes, but they risked being terribly sunburnt.

We watched a wonderful display of kites one blowy day – the sky aerobatics were amazing. We acquired a box kite ourselves and had a great deal of fun. Sara, over the years, has made many unusual kites inspired by those days.

Another abiding memory is of the time Sara had a friend from Kent staying for a few days. We had been unable to park as usual by the cliff path down to the beach, and while we descended, John drove the minibus further up the road, and then joined us. When it was time to go home, he decided to scale the cliff beyond which the vehicle was parked. 'You go up the way we came down and I'll be there to pick you up, to save you the long hot trek up the road,' he promised.

We looked back as we made our way across the beach, to see him disappearing among a profusion of bushes higher up the cliff – he really would beat us to it, we thought!

We stood at the top, waiting, and waiting . . . Half-an-hour went by, then he had been gone more than an hour. We were becoming distinctly uneasy. Some people appeared at our level. I asked anxiously, 'Have you seen a tall man in shorts, walking along the beach?'

Heads were shaken. 'No. Most visitors went off the beach the other way . . . No one down there, now.'

'He . . . he went up the cliff, through the scrub – ages ago,' I said.

'Oh, it's like a jungle there – he'd never make it. Probably trying to get back.' Sympathetic smiles. 'He'll be back soon.'

But he wasn't. We could see the van in the distance, but we daren't leave where we were. Jonathan wasn't with us this day, he could have gone for help, I thought. The boys pleaded to go down on to the beach, promising no further, to see if they could spot their dad.

It was almost dusk before the shout went up, 'Here he is!' and John, scratched and bleeding, shirt ripped, came wearily along the beach.

I'm not sure how the poor chap managed to drive home – we caught the last ferry – but the outcome could have been so much worse . . .

CHAPTER 41

Good Old Bachelor Boys

Many families appeared to have an unmarried brother living with them. Some of these were solemn, quiet men who went to chapel and played bowls. They contrasted with their married brothers or brothers-in-law in that respect, who spent evenings in the pub with the parson. Often, it was the case that the bachelor brother, either the eldest or youngest of a big family, had looked after elderly parents before inheriting a rundown farm, or cottage, and then offered a married sister and her family accommodation in return for keeping house.

We rarely saw these bachelors except when they came in for pipe tobacco. They appeared content with their lot.

There were two good old bachelor boys who lived together in a tiny whitewashed house, one up, one down, with no kitchen, just a gas ring in the hearth and a kettle suspended over a fire; no indoor sanitation (though this was common to the cotts), a well in the back yard and a privy surrounded by nettles.

Fred, the elder brother, had been at sea most of his life – as a steward, not a sailor, he said. He was clean-shaven and his face had a ruddy glow. His brother Ted, with his stubbled chin and pale complexion, had been a bandsman in the army, been injured in the last war and not able to work since. Fred was always dressed in a dark, pinstriped suit, collar and tie, plus a well-brushed bowler hat, when the brothers went to the pub. Ted, in old trousers held up by sagging braces, a shirt with frayed collar and cuffs, his wispy bald head uncovered, shuffled behind Fred and smiled his sweet, vague, toothless smile. They spent most of Saturday in the pub and then wove their unsteady way home via the shop.

Fred did all the talking. People said he fancied himself as a gentleman. Well, that is how we found him. In his cups yes, but polite and caring for his frail brother as best he could.

Fred produced a neatly written list. It never varied.

Half a pound of best Cornish butter
A pint of milk
A crusty small loaf
Two tins of oxtail soup
Two tins of garden peas
Quarter of a pound of ham
Small piece of strong cheddar
Packet of Typhoo tea
Sugar lumps

Basket filled, he asked Ted if there was anything he wanted. Ted nodded. I handed him his weekly packet of cigarettes.

He spoke at last: 'Thank you, madam.' Then they went home and it was easy to guess what they had for supper.

* * *

Red Crump was a stonemason and Mrs Trew's brother. There was no sign of it now, but we presumed he'd once had auburn hair like his sister. We had been living in the village for some months before we met him. He usually worked on projects away from his home, a chalet built on the Trews' land.

In our sitting room was a splendid stone fireplace, with two round granite knobs protruding on either side of the grate. We imagined that if you pressed or turned these protrusions, the whole fireplace might swing open (like fake bookcases in many a mystery movie) and reveal a hidden chamber behind. We didn't try to find out because those of us over the age of ten were aware it would spoil the illusion ... The fascia was patterned with different shapes and colours – black, silver, white and even pink rocks.

One winter evening there was a knock on the front door. Mr Crump introduced himself, and a companion. 'May we come in? I wish to show him the fireplace I installed here, a few years ago.'

Why do visitors arrive when a room is untidy, I thought. I should have swept the hearth and polished the knobs ... The only thing I could do was to persuade Billow to remove his sprawling body from the mat in front of the fire. The family escaped stealthily one by one to the kitchen, though Katy returned briefly to ask, 'Would Mr *Crumpet* like a cup of tea?' She had been put up to this by a larger sibling, judging by smothered giggles in the background.

He was seemingly too busy extolling the wonders of his work to notice this interruption.

The two men sat down on the sofa to discuss a price. I hovered helplessly and suppressed a gasp, when a large sum was agreed.

At last they turned to me, and Mr Crump said: 'Now, I think we can have that cup of tea!'

'Mum, you should have asked for a commission!' the children said.

Well, at least we inherited the fireplace, not paid for it, I thought.

Always without prior notification, Mr Crump called in from time to time to show off his masterpiece and to deliver his sales talk. But I told the family not to offer him and his clients any more cups of tea!

* * *

A single man moved into the cotts next door to the 'refugees' – I believe they were Polish and had arrived during the war. Mrs Slooski – the name sounded like that, but I never knew for sure – spoke broken English and always wore a headscarf. They didn't patronise the shop. Their new neighbour, a small man with impeccable manners, was a good customer, right from his first day in the village. We supposed him to be newly retired, certainly a bachelor, who enjoyed cooking for himself, and chatting pleasantly with John and me. We learned that he came from East Anglia, like my family, and he still had the burr.

'Even though I haven't been back there in years!' he remarked, when I said it was nice to be reminded of my Suffolk roots.

He was obviously a well-educated man, and we discussed books we had chosen in the library. He liked ancient history and bird books, like John.

A year or two later, it came as a shock to us to be told that our elderly friend was on parole from prison. He had been placed in our community by social workers.

'Whatever was someone like him doing in prison?' we wondered. He was affable and unassuming, patently honest, we thought. We were enlightened: 'He killed his wife twenty years ago.'

A few days on from this revelation, Mrs Slooski actually came into the shop to say, 'That man next door, he's gone away.' We never saw him again. We worried if he was all right. Would he be forced to keep 'moving on' when his past was revealed?

CHAPTER 42

Platform Shoes and Lightning Strikes

Three daughters, two in their teens, accompanied their mother to help with weekend shopping. The older girls had jobs, and obviously enjoyed spending their wages on the latest fashions. They spoiled the youngest sister, Sharon, and she too tottered around on the highest platform shoes I have ever seen. On Saturdays they allowed her to delve into their make-up bags, and Sharon fluttered lashes thick with mascara and outlined her eyes with kohl. She was ten years old, with hefty limbs, not enhanced by brief emerald-green hot pants.

'I fell off me shoes,' she confided cheerfully to me one day.

'I'm not surprised!' I grinned back.

'Sprained me ankle,' Sharon added. She displayed a bandage.

'I see you know your right foot from your left, unlike Toddy!'

We'd spotted Toddy limping dramatically down the hill on a school day – by the time he reached the shop, John observed, 'He's limping on the other foot now!'

Toddy's explanation was that he had fallen down a rabbit hole. Not as original as falling off your shoe.

There was a distinct rumble of thunder. Then a flash of lightning. The three Cox daughters gasped, grabbed at their mother.

'Now, now girls,' she said firmly. 'If you've seen it, it ain't struck you. But let's get the shopping done before it rains ...' Despite these words, she was obviously in no hurry, for she had a story to tell me.

'My Sharon,' she said proudly, 'has been struck by lightning *three* times! She attracts it, you see.'

'Oh dear,' I said faintly, as the sky outside lit up once more. I added belatedly, 'Was she hurt?'

'*Scorched*,' Mrs Cox told me. 'Singed her hair, that's all.'

'Can't remember a thing about it.' Sharon was becoming bored.

It was raining by the time they left the shop. I worried whether Sharon would skid on the wet path and fall off her shoes again. And I crossed my fingers the lightning wouldn't find her attractive today.

Talking of shoes, there was a minor theft from the garage up the hill. A can of oil was missing and a few tools. The local bobby found a footprint in the mud. Later that day, Toddy visited the crime scene. To the garage owner's surprise, he removed his ancient trainer and fitted it to the impression.

His artless verdict was: 'Same pattern on the sole, same size as mine. Tell the bobby I reckon it's a size seven.'

I think he was actually disappointed not to be interviewed, following his detective work.

* * *

Our three boys were up on the moor and caught in a thunderstorm one day. They were discovered sheltering in a hollow by a gang of the village boys who ambushed them and chased them, intent on having a scrap. One or two of these boys they had regarded as friends at school, but these had led the gang to them.

'Run home!' Chris shouted to his brothers. He was captured, bowled over and engulfed in a ruck.

He told us later, when we anointed his grazes and bruises, 'They were so busy thumping each other, I crawled out from under them and guess who helped me get away?'

We couldn't guess, we were still shocked to think they'd been set upon like that, with no provocation. Later, we would realise this was a rite of passage for newcomers.

'Wim,' he said. 'He appeared suddenly, he was by himself, and he grabbed hold of me, because I was on the edge where the land drops away, and we rolled all the way down to the bottom, that's where I got all the bumps and scratches, and the gang looked over and shouted, but didn't follow.'

Wim, that gentle giant of a boy, was never involved in fights. We were glad our lads had a friend like him.

That first summer, storms were frequent. The sky would be blue, the sun blazed down, then the rumbles began. One Wednesday afternoon, I went with John to the wholesalers. The two dogs were in the barn, with access to the enclosed back garden, but unable, we believed, to get out to the road side of the garden because we had secured the other door. We took these precautions because although the five-barred gate was a stout barrier, Florence could slide under it while Billow could jump it with ease.

The storm broke on our way home. Somehow, Billow barged the barn door open and the dogs took flight. They were missing for hours. Florence returned first, shivering and scared. We waited up, but no Billow. Some time during a wakeful night, we heard a bark. He was back! Ever after, he was terrified whenever he heard thunder, and needed reassurance. We never knew where they'd been that day.

CHAPTER 43

What Can You Do With a Gallon of Ice-cream?

We learned along the village grapevine that the Hunt would be meeting outside the Crossroads Stores on Sunday morning.

'You'll be expected to open the shop,' we were told. 'The old owners reckoned it was well worth their while to do so.'

What could we tempt them with, we wondered. The sausage man came up with the answer. 'Ice-cream cornets!' He provided a gallon of his special recipe (family secret, of course), John got in the cornets and a scoop. I practised with mashed potato for a few days in advance.

Ginge painted a mouth-watering poster with a huge cornet overloaded with ice-cream and a chocolate flake bar for good measure.

The younger children sat on the front wall to await the arrival of the horses and the hunting fraternity. A crowd gathered opposite, by the stream. We turned the shop sign to OPEN. The girls peeked out through the front window.

Time went slowly until the allotted hour, nine o'clock. We had one customer before then, for a half-pound of sausages. I'd promised our lot a roast dinner later to celebrate selling all that ice-cream.

There was no chance now that any other of the locals could slip through. The forecourt was full of a moving mass of snorting horses and youngsters in smart jodhpurs, shiny boots and riding hats, using the mounting block to climb aboard a broad back. Most of them had riding crops which they used when their ponies fidgeted. Then suddenly the road was full of eager, panting hounds. The crowd moved back.

We'd become accustomed to soft clotted-cream voices with the expressions 'good as gold', 'all right, my lover?' of those who came in the shop – the loud cut-glass accents of the men in pink and their ladies was unattractive; their arrogance, the way they ignored the local children who wanted to pet the horses, was unkind. We were totally disregarded, too, hemmed in the shop, unable to open the door.

Before they cantered off, the hip flasks came out. We had not sold a single ice-cream. We consoled ourselves with a cornet apiece, then locked up, and decided ruefully to go out for the day as usual.

'Not to the moor,' the girls warned. 'Hope the fox gets away!'

In the middle of the night, John said aloud, 'What on earth can we do with a gallon of ice-cream?'

We thought we had the answer when there was news of a charity cycle ride. Our village was one of the stopping-off points. The poster went up again, bunting decorated the village. But alas, the organisers failed to advise the parish council of a diversion. No cheers, no waves, no ice-cream . . .

We did get the order for selling cornets at the Vicarage Garden Fete, but naturally, that was our contribution, so all the special-price ice-creams swelled the church roof fund.

There was still half a container of the stuff, yellower and stickier and harder to gouge out, but still edible, when the parson organised a community walk. John, Billow and the boys took part. It was eleven miles, and it was anticipated that the walk should take around three hours.

Katy, Maff and I were on ice-cream duty. The girls went off to the riding school. There weren't likely to be many other customers, after all.

The young ones were on look-out, perched as usual on the wall which separated shop from house. After about an hour, they came running in to report: 'Mummy, they're here!'

'They can't be,' I said, adding, 'Who?'

'Roger – and Wim!'

I could hardly believe my eyes, loping along came Wim in his worn plimsolls, with long dark hair flopping in his eyes, and just behind was our flaxen-haired eleven-year-old Roger, who only came up to the big boy's shoulder. They were all smiles, and hardly out of breath.

'Where's Dad, Mike and Chris?' was all I could think of to say.

'Oh, they're *walking*,' Rog said. 'But we wanted to get back first for the ice-cream!'

So that's how we discovered Roger had a talent for long-distance running, and both he and Wim had a double flake in their cornets.

I still use the ice-cream scoop – for mashed potato.

* * *

We had visitors of our own all summer, but there were also the tourists, called grockels by the locals, who enquired: 'D'you know where we can get a cup of tea and a snack?'

I'm not sure who had the bright idea of a couple of small tables and canvas chairs in the back garden. The girls and I baked scones and flapjacks (the boys' favourite, so we had to make extra for them) and fruit cake. All these went on the first Saturday afternoon, so then it had to be tea and biscuits, for 10p. The tourists lingered too long and we got hot and bothered, running to and fro from shop to garden. It was a short-lived experiment!

'We're a village shop and should stick to what people want,' John said. 'Not try all these other things.'

Well, we did know what they wanted. Jumbo pink sausages . . .

CHAPTER 44

Maff and the Big Bar of Chocolate

Maff was our junior assistant in the year before he joined his sister at school. He only 'worked' part-time of course, when he felt like it. He was a favourite with all our female customers, pointing out the day's bargains and locating other items for them. They patted his curly head and advised: 'Don't cut his hair yet, will you?' I was aware that John, who believed boys should look like boys, was hoping to wield the scissors one day when I wasn't looking . . . Anyway, I knew he couldn't go to school with that mop of ringlets. 'He'll tell us when he wants to be shorn,' I said feebly, and in my defence trotted out the old story of a mother we knew who worried her child wouldn't be parted from her dummy – this little girl went to the dustbin the evening before she started at school, lifted the lid, and dropped the mangled comforter inside. '*She* decided for herself,' I said.

(Maybe this is the time to confess that, like John's kipper tie, somewhere I have secreted away an envelope with guess-what inside . . .)

Once a week, a dear old chap came into the shop, half-an-hour before the bus to town was due. He was always dressed up with a Fair Isle pullover under a thick, hairy sports jacket, however hot the weather. Like Fred and Ted, he invariably bought the same goods as he had the previous week.

'I'm off to see my daughter,' he explained the first time we met. 'I like to contribute towards our lunch.'

John sliced three-quarters of a pound of best ham and I weighed out tomatoes, selected a curly lettuce, and popped four rolls in a bag.

If Maff was in the garden, he would twitch his nose, scenting the smell of Mr Brightling's Three Nuns tobacco, even though he always removed and tapped his pipe on the wall before entering the shop.

'Here comes the boy,' Mr B beamed. 'Now, while you tot that lot up my dear – don't forget the tobacco, will you? My allowance for the week! I'll let my young friend choose something *he* fancies, eh?'

He led his young friend by the hand to the chocolate display. Maff considered the Milky Ways. Mr B reached his long arm over the counter and selected a half-pound bar of fruit and nut. 'That's more like it, isn't it?'

By then I had rung up the till and packed Mr B's shopping in his bag. I had already passed over the tobacco and his change.

'Thank you kindly, goodbye.' And Mr B was gone. I could never bring myself to remind him that he hadn't paid for Maff's treat – I held out my hand to Maff and said: 'I don't think you'd enjoy that, darling. How about . . .' I indicated the threepenny candy. He was happy with six fruit chews and I was able to replace the expensive big choc bar. Phew! I thought. One of these days he'll open the wrapper before I can retrieve it . . . then I won't have the heart to take it away.

It's known as 'eating the profits', you see.

* * *

John's mother and two sisters arranged to stay not far from us our second summer, and over the Bank Holiday we had a lovely weekend with them, seeing the sights, and spending a day at our favourite estuary beach. Grandma Lottie, whom we all adored, seemed not quite herself, and a few months later was diagnosed with a serious illness. It was then that we realised how far away we were from our families. My father, eighteen years older than my mother, had recently celebrated his eightieth birthday, but now, he too was ill, after suffering a stroke.

'You must go and see them,' John said, concerned. 'As they can't come to visit us.' Both families had been so generous and encouraging in their support for our life-changing move. Now they needed us, we were not on hand to help.

'Oh, I can't leave you with the shop and the family – it's too much,' I replied.

'You could take Katy with you. Ginge and the boys are off school, Jo has a break from college, they'll keep an eye on Maff, so, of course you can!' John said firmly.

I capitulated gracefully. Best to go while most of the older children were still at home, I realised. Sara was working at the television studios and had recently appeared on local TV in an amazing patchwork dress she had designed and made herself. She was planning to study Fine

Art in Wimbledon, after a foundation year also away from home. J.P. had passed his driving test, he had decided to look further afield with regard to work . . . Anyway, I was only going away for a few days.

Katy and I travelled by train. We were met in London by John's sister, who kindly drove us home to my parents in Surrey.

I was kept entertained throughout the long journey by my lively little daughter. We sat in the buffet car, and she soon spread her comics out on the table and read and chattered at the same time.

In the seat opposite was a stern-looking woman who ignored us and turned the pages of a paperback.

It was a beautiful day, and the coastal route was breath-taking at times. Sparkling water, golden sands, under a cloudless sky. I felt myself relaxing. I must have dozed at one point, because I awoke with a start to hear Katy say, as she leaned on her elbows and regarded our fellow passenger, 'Can you take your teeth out, like my grandad?'

'Certainly not,' was the sharp reply, the first words the woman had spoken in more than two hours.

Even as I opened my mouth to apologise, Katy, not put off by our fellow passenger's abruptness, decided to enlarge on what she'd said before. 'My grandad can do tricks with his teeth. He can make them shoot out, and then go back, with his tongue. I can whistle, because my two front teeth dropped out. Can you whistle?'

'I . . . it's impolite to whistle.'

'We have to whistle our dog. Shall I show you how I do it?'

'No thank you.' But there was a little twitch at the corners of the woman's mouth. She glanced at me. 'You are very fortunate to have such a bright child,' she said unexpectedly.

'Thank you . . .'

While we had lunch, and Katy made a noise sucking lemonade through a straw, I thought, now I have a story to make dear Oz smile. When I was Katy's age, I had nicknamed my dad Oz, because his second name was Osmund. In return he called me Shelag, when I decided (for a week or two!) to change the spelling of my name to Sheelagh. I thought that was how it was pronounced!

It made my mum smile too, which was good, after all the worry she'd been through recently. 'We've missed you,' she said, hugging us.

*   *   *

John and Maff met us at the station when we returned. The first thing I saw was a little boy with cropped hair. No longer a baby. It's a fact of life, as my mum once pointed out to me, that babies grow up, just as puppies and kittens do . . . You have to accept it.

'He was so hot and sticky, with all that hair, it was the kindest thing,' John said in his defence. 'Ginge did it – I thought I might bodge it! We trimmed Billow first, for the same reason . . .'

There was a lump in my throat. I knew he was right. 'Did you use the same scissors?' I asked huskily.

CHAPTER 45

Sunken Sugar

After the glorious summer, down came the rain. It was an autumn of coughs and sneezes. In the shop, John and I were on the receiving end of all the germs and bugs going round the village. We sold a lot of patent remedies and sympathised with our customers. We listened patiently to the tales of woe and no one noticed that we also had watery eyes and red noses, or realised that we had sick, querulous children calling for our attention, too.

I suppose we should have seen disaster coming. After all, we had always had to keep an eye on river levels near our old home, although water never encroached our property in our time there, even if we were marooned because the road was flooded.

The babbling brook opposite the shop was lashed into a torrent by hours of relentless rain. Even the ducks flew away. Customers waded through puddles to buy tobacco, but not much else. Even the sausages stayed in the freezer. Sales of paraffin were up.

We went to bed with hot water bottles, a box of tissues and aspirin. Early next morning, around 4 a.m., we were woken by a thunderous knocking on the front door. Struggling into our dressing gowns, and wondering who on earth it could be, we went downstairs. Mr Trew and two other men, in oilskins and thigh-high fishing boots, stood there.

'The road's flooded. Came to see you were all right . . .' Water lapped at the step. 'Check the shop,' Mr Trew advised. 'The floor's lower that end. Close the door. I'll bring you some sandbags a bit later.' They went off to see what they could do for the folk in the cotts.

We stepped into ankle-deep water at the front of the shop. We hadn't thought to change our slippers for wellington boots. We spotted some submerged objects, the contents of the bottom shelf of the main unit – bags of sugar. No pea-green boat, as the rhyme goes, and we'd lost more than a five-pound note . . . We captured the bloated packets and placed them in a nearby bucket.

The sugar, fortunately, was the only casualty of the flood, but we were mopping up for hours, still in our night attire and, belatedly, rubber boots. Most of our neighbours were similarly occupied.

Later, John rescued the damp bundle of daily newspapers, and got on with the marking up. Fortunately, the family had slept on through the dramatic events.

'Porridge for breakfast,' I decided. Seemed the simplest thing.

The flood outside slowly drained away. Mrs Trew came over to commiserate with us. 'Didn't the folk before you say about the flood they had just after they moved in? The water ruined the carpet in the living rooms. They got enough back on the insurance to buy that lovely green carpet you've got in there now. Three hundred pounds it cost.'

I smiled wryly. 'They charged us an *extra five hundred* for that!'

Mind you, we took the carpet up when we left, and it lasted us a good twenty years. So I suppose we had our money's worth, eh?

* * *

The brook dried up during the drought of 1976. There was a hosepipe ban, a restriction on use of water generally. The reservoir a few miles away was empty, standpipes were installed in the villages. Life became very difficult for us all, especially the farming community.

The reality of living here was very different to the holidays we had enjoyed in the West Country in the past. Stories were related of other troubled times – folk here recalled the terrible winter of 1962–3, which was very like our own experience of being snowbound for months in rural Kent.

Mrs Diddley leaned over the counter to tell me in a confidential whisper: 'There was a coal lorry, got stuck in a drift on the hill. It stayed there until it thawed.'

'Oh, dear,' I murmured faintly, almost overcome by the reek of bleach from her person.

'Then,' she said, as if she still couldn't believe it, 'they discovered that all the sacks of coal had gone . . . No one knows who dug down through all that snow, to this day.'

When I repeated this tale to John later, he said simply: 'Didn't they check who had smoke coming out of their chimney?'

* * *

The local MP came into the shop one day, to enquire how we were coping. The locals crowded in behind him to air their grievances. He listened sympathetically, then apologised that he must go – other hamlets to call on.

'Shan't vote for him next time,' some said. 'Him in his grey suit and Tory blue tie.'

I don't imagine that most of them had the first time! Politicians were viewed with great suspicion. Only Lloyd George was mentioned with affection. 'He got us the old age pension,' they said. 'He's a good old boy.' I don't think they accepted he was no longer around.

The girls worried about the wild ponies on the moors. They were running short of food. There was an airlift of supplies to the ponies, and much publicity in the papers and on TV. They also complained about sharing bath water. They didn't want to hear my oft-repeated story about nine people taking turns in the old tin tub during the war, topped-up from a kettle of hot water and soap flakes to mask the scum. 'We know, Mum, you were number three, and you wondered what the baby had done in the water, before it was your turn,' they sighed.

'I didn't make a fuss like you are . . .'

'We had a bath that fitted under the kitchen table, when we lived in the country,' John put in. 'You lifted off the top and filled the tub from the copper where the sheets were boiled on Mondays . . .'

To the girls, that was beyond the pale.

We queued patiently at the standpipe, with a variety of containers. Toddy, of course, had Corona bottles. I hoped he would hang on to them because our supply of soft drinks was exhausted.

Every village received a consignment of bottled water. It didn't go far to solve the problem, but we were grateful.

The atmosphere was boiling, not simmering. When eventually it rained again, everyone rushed outside in great excitement and relief. There wasn't quite dancing in the street, but the crisis was coming to an end.

CHAPTER 46

Going Out

It came to us all of a sudden, the realisation that our daughters were no longer biddable small girls, but attractive young women. They were about to launch themselves on the world, and determined to make an impression. We were so proud of them and their achievements, but their new-found independence made us feel a little sad. Maybe, even, rather redundant . . .

Our small daughter and son helped to alleviate the sense of loss you inevitably feel when your grown-up children dismiss the old and familiar. You don't know then that when the grandchildren come along, they'll bring them up with the same values as you did them. That's a great feeling.

At the doctors one day, I was catching up on my reading in the waiting room, and settled Katy with a book too. She was in line for a booster injection. I was suddenly aware that the solemn people all around us were laughing. I looked up, and saw a smiling man with one foot, hopping across to the nearest available chair. How could they be insensitive enough to laugh at that, I thought. Then, to my embarrassment, I saw Katy, in her bright red jumper and kilt, hopping behind him.

'You won!' she told her new friend, as he sat down.

'Please don't apologise,' the man said to me. 'She made my day!'

* * *

Spring time, and a young man's fancy and all that: knocks on the front door in the evening meant the girls were going out, probably with one of the public-school types from the select estate up the hill . . . A dashing chap in a sports car called for Jo. (Some years later she married him!) Sara had a boyfriend at that time who wore a cape and a homburg hat, but it wouldn't be too long before she was picking gherkins in Sweden, with the young man she would eventually marry. There was also a love-lorn local boy who presented me with flowers on my birthday, hoping to win *her* approval. I had endless teasing about that! Ginge tried to convince us there was safety in numbers, going out with a group of excitable girls and boys for rambles on the moors. It would be a few years yet before she met her soul-mate at teacher-training college.

(In due course, all three of them were happily married, Jo and Ginge two weeks apart and Sara a while later . . . Jonathan beat them all to it, when he was just twenty-two! After two years, *we* were young grandparents!)

Ponies and riding on the moors might no longer be the girls' main interest, but the boys stuck to their football sessions, though they were developing a taste for pop bands. Maff was getting into football, but naturally he trailed behind them with regard to pop concerts! Though he did eventually inherit Roger's The Water Boys T-shirt! I miss that on the washing line nowadays!

We bought a radiogram, and now there were tussles over choice of records. It was no longer just the weekly discos which kept us awake: we had our own disco going on downstairs at night, clashing with Martha's more uplifting music upstairs . . . Gilbert O'Sullivan lingers on in our record collection, but the Beatles records, which belonged to John, disappeared one by one.

I don't wish to dwell on teenage angst, suffice it to say that running a shop, with all its restrictions, is not the ideal situation with adolescents. Waiting up anxiously at nights, listening out for noisy car exhausts, means bleary eyes the next day . . .

* * *

Christmas came round again, and now I didn't get hot round the collar when Mrs Deans' big girls, who appeared to share the care of the baby, now a toddler, who had arrived unexpectedly on our first Christmas Day in the shop, asked for 'crap paper'. I only twigged the first time when one added, 'You know, for decorations. Red and green crap paper . . .'

With relief, I bypassed the stack of Bronco rolls, and pointed out the crepe paper.

John strung coloured lights all round the shop and we enjoyed filling a few shelves with toys and items for the Christmas stockings.

The previous Christmas we had sold out of seasonal gifts, and the mince pies, Dundee and Tunis cakes, chocolate logs and boxes of luxury chocs sold like, well, hot cakes.

'I gave Toddy's mother a lift down the hill,' John said ruefully. 'She was loaded down with all her shopping. I couldn't drive past when she was struggling, could I?'

We really couldn't condemn them for buying things in the new supermarket near the new estate.

We had the old faithfuls, thank goodness, but how long could we last out? Funds were low. Expenses high. We had to keep the shop well-stocked.

* * *

One of our favourite customers was unwell. A friend of Fred and Ted called into the shop one Saturday.

'Would you be kind enough to deliver their usual order, later on?'

Of course we would. We enquired tactfully as to what was wrong with Ted.

'Oh, it's not him as is ill – it's poor old Fred. A stroke, I reckon. They've never registered with the doctor. Ted can't look after him – my missus is going to get in touch with their sister. Doris was a housekeeper in Somerset, but she's retired now. She's younger than them, and the cottage will be hers, when they go.'

I added a bunch of grapes, from us, to the order, and Ted's cigarettes.

Later, I rattled the letterbox; there was no knocker on the door.

There was the sound of shuffling feet, but it took Ted a while to open the door. He'd had difficulty in getting round the bed which took up most of the narrow passageway which led from the living room.

'Step inside,' he said. 'Say hello to Fred.' It was the most I'd ever heard him say.

In the gloom, I made out an inert form, covered with a grey army blanket. Fred's face was pale, his mouth a little awry. I saw then that, without the familiar bowler hat, he was as bald as Ted.

'Hello Fred,' I said, feeling that was inadequate. 'How are you?'

'He can't speak.' Ted leaned over his brother, extracted something from under his pillow. He held out Fred's purse to me, trusting me to take the right money for the groceries.

I could tell that Fred was struggling to say something, but he couldn't manage it. I touched the thin hands, motionless on the blanket.

'Thank you,' I managed. 'I hope you feel better soon . . .' I handed the carrier bags to Ted. 'Take care of him . . .' I thought, poor old Ted can't take care of himself . . .

As Ted saw me out he said, 'Don't worry. Our Doris is coming tomorrow.'

'That's good,' I said. 'I'll call again soon.'

I told John later, 'I don't think we'll see poor old Fred again.'

Sadly, Fred passed away the day after his sister arrived. Ted wasn't allowed out on his own. Doris came in the shop one day to tell us that she would be moving into the cottage permanently.

'I could have coped with dear Fred, but not Ted. He's never been all there, since he got wounded in the head in the war, you see. He was such a musical lad. Played the trombone. Anyway, there's only one bedroom, so he's going to a residential home up the hill. By the way, I was clearing out some of their rubbish, and I opened up a cupboard and a whole lot of tins fell out . . .' She looked at me suspiciously.

I could guess: oxtail soup, garden peas, I thought . . .

'I don't suppose you want to buy 'em all back? I'm a regular at the Co-op, always have been.'

I couldn't help hesitating, biting my lip.

'I suppose not,' Doris sighed. 'I know I wouldn't. Oh, if Ted should get down here and ask you for cigarettes, he's not to have them. Doctor's orders. *Don't forget!*' She departed.

We missed our good old bachelor boys.

CHAPTER 47

The Little Shop Can Save Your Bacon

Our neighbour, Martha rushed into the shop in a panic one morning. 'The butcher's let me down! We've no meat for the school dinners today!' she exclaimed dramatically, at full throttle, rather as she had been last night when the organ music had swelled and she had sung 'Lily of Laguna', not once but three times, obviously practising for an Olde Tyme concert, planned by Rev. Bouncy Ball.

'Ham?' John suggested helpfully.

'Hot meal today – what else can you suggest?'

'I've several big packs of bacon, Miss Dingle delivered the eggs yesterday – how about eggs, bacon, and sausages, of course!'

'Chips?' I said. I thought, half-a-dozen of Les's huge spuds would be enough to feed the children. I knew Martha had a machine to slice 'em.

'A fry-up! They'd love that,' Martha agreed. This was before school meals had to be low fat et al. – no doubt Martha would use slabs of lard in the cooking. 'Will you pack all that up please and deliver it to the school as soon as possible? I must get on!'

I volunteered to make the delivery. I'd never been in the school kitchen; indeed, it occurred to me, as I hurried along to the school, that I had not been invited into any of the village homes, apart from Miss Dingle's once, when she wanted to show us her new colour TV. It really was 'them and us', we were tolerated by most, made use of, as now, but we didn't belong here, and probably never would. Like Rev. Bouncy Ball, who tried so hard to get things going in the village, we were outsiders. It came to me then, that we had made no close friends in the area. We were fortunate that we had old friends, John and Joyce in Launceston whom we'd known since schooldays, but due to the long hours we worked, we were unable to meet up often. The other

John was kind enough to audit our accounts: he'd recently warned us that the recession was adversely affecting small businesses. We'd taken on the Crossroads Stores at the wrong time . . .

Six people sat round the table in the school kitchen. It was ten-thirty, the children were in the playground. Katy and Maff, who had just joined her at school, waved to me as I went inside. In the centre of the table was the largest treacle tart I had ever seen, glistening golden and obviously just out of the oven. Martha was cutting slices of this, and passing them to her two assistants, the two dinner ladies, and – I thought I could smell bleach! – Mrs Diddley. One of the helpers was pouring tea from a big teapot. My tummy rumbled.

Martha waved a sticky hand in greeting. 'Could you put the bacon etc., in the fridge, please? Send the bill into the school. You'll be paid at the end of the month. Thanks!' This was a blow. We'd hoped to be paid from the petty cash. John would need to buy more bacon now.

The treacle tart plate was empty. I wondered if the children would be as lucky. I wasn't offered a cup of tea. But I was glad for Elsie Diddley's sake that she was included in the gathering. I hoped her tart didn't taste of bleach!

As I returned to man the counter, tears pricked my eyes. I thought back to the days when I was 'just a mum' and made special things for the children's tea. I didn't get time for that now. I missed my dear friend Liz, who always put the kettle on when I called round at hers, just as I did, when she came to mine. I knew that John missed our old life, too. He missed going on sales trips, his colleagues at work.

All I said to John was, 'D'you know, I haven't written anything except letters since we've been here . . .'

The very next day he arrived back from the wholesalers with an advance birthday present for me – an Olivetti portable typewriter. I had it for years and most of the children's stories I wrote then were tapped out on the kitchen table. It was just as easy to use as a laptop.

* * *

The parson called one day to ask if we would help with the annual vic-arage garden fete as usual. In a lull between customers, we offered him refreshment. We opened up to him about some of our misgivings about how long we might last out here, and in turn he told us that he was the only child of a widowed mother, that he'd been brought up in a flat above the family confectioners and tobacconists, in a grim, industrial area in the north of England. He'd won scholarships and gone to university.

After being a curate in an inner-city slum area, he'd been offered the job of parish priest here. He'd jumped at the chance, brought his mother with him, and his new wife.

'Things didn't turn out as I expected,' he said slowly. His round, cherubic face was flushed. He didn't enlarge on that, but I don't think he was just referring to village life.

His simple advice was to sell up before we lost all we had worked so hard for over the years.

So, you could say, that a treacle tart led to an advertisement in the same national newspaper where we'd learned of the availability of the Crossroads Stores, in 'idyllic West Country village' . . .

* * *

It was almost a year before we sold up, and we thought initially, we should stay around the area, because of the boys' schooling, as they were all due to take O levels within the next few years, and Ginge, A levels. The employment prospects were not very encouraging. Our older children would likely all soon be working, or studying, elsewhere. However, property was still available for much less than in the south.

So in the interval between, we actually enjoyed looking over suitable – and often not so suitable! – places on our Sundays off. One that I recall was not far from the edge of a cliff. Some of the garden had gone over. The cellar that ran the length of the house was fitted up as a games room. The boys, naturally, were enthusiastic about that! Another property was built into a hillside, with a moss roof. This was a nature reserve (in miniature) where a local naturalist and his wife, with wild hair, had lived in a state of chaos for many years. They wore kaftans and beads and had filthy, hardened bare feet. We didn't get any further than the jungle of a garden – we weren't prepared to hack our way through the giant nettles. Katy and Maff couldn't stop giggling.

We didn't see many prospective buyers for the shop, either. We became resigned to the fact that we would be there a while yet . . .

CHAPTER 48

Then the Wall Fell Down

The growing recession was hitting us hard. Despite all our continuing efforts to make a go of things, it was a case of keeping our heads above water. To quote another metaphor, most of our customers were in the same boat – we were all struggling.

We had two farmers to whom we delivered weekly. The first was a wealthy gentleman farmer, the second was a tenant farmer. Both put in a large order on a Friday and John delivered a box full of groceries on Saturday afternoon. We were paid promptly, and this contribution to our income was vital.

I was away, visiting our families – we did this in turn – when the first farmer failed to put his order in as usual. John, extra busy, was actually relieved not to have to pack and deliver these goods. We fully expected to see this farmer the following week, but again, no list appeared. Then John, at the wholesalers one day, spotted our gentleman farmer wheeling a trolley. He had obtained a card, and he was not the only one. We just wished he could have told us, and not left us to find out. We couldn't blame him for getting his goods at cost price, now times were difficult.

Farmer no. 2 continued to buy from us, but he couldn't always pay on time. We received half a lamb in part-payment, then a small turkey, and finally, he too had a card and took his custom elsewhere.

Wim's mother, another of the small parents of large offspring, came in the shop every day. She could never make her mind up. She lingered by the freezer for about half-an-hour, trying to decide what to buy. I stood by patiently, making the occasional suggestion. The outcome was predictable. Her worried expression would clear, a decision had been made. It was always the same: 'Six sausages, please. You can't go wrong with sausages, can you?'

Six sausages among four people, I thought. Wim could probably eat that many by himself. I never knew whether she was a single parent on a very restricted income, or if she had a husband who was unemployed. She was one of a minority who did things the old way: she paid once a week, and her daily purchases were marked in a dog-eared little book, with a pencil attached by string. Recently, she had paid a week in arrears, and it was becoming obvious that she was unable to catch up. This was preferable to the less reliable customers who promised to pay 'in a day or two', but never came near the shop again. We were forced to take one of these unscrupulous people (not a local) to the small claims court, but never received a penny, because 'he had no assets'.

Mrs Diddley's sister called in regularly, but didn't actually purchase anything. 'Just looking,' she said. Unlike her sister, she was obviously a lady of leisure, well-dressed, with no children and a husband who worked. She had a perpetually mournful expression, though she enjoyed relating details of her latest operation – 'They opened me up to remove a *sponge* they left inside last time,' she said, awaiting my reaction. I rose to the challenge. 'How awful – how did that happen?' I shouldn't have asked. John always disappeared when he saw her coming, saying she was a time-waster. Ever hopeful, I thought she might buy a little something on our very last day – she didn't.

The strain was beginning to tell. I had suffered from psoriasis in my teens and now it returned with a vengeance. I was allergic to the ointments then prescribed – my only consolation was that the worst patches were on my legs, not my face – though I felt a pariah on the beach.

We learned from Mrs Trew that there were rumours going around that we were selling up.

'It doesn't seem likely,' I said truthfully, 'right now.'

She patted my shoulder. 'You're missing home, my dear. We'll be sorry if you go, but you must do what's best for you and the family.' I took that to mean I had her blessing.

When I repeated this conversation to John and the older children, Ginge said: 'She's right. We should go back to Kent. We fitted in there.'

'But ... what about your schooling – you, in particular?' we queried. In September she would be in her final A level year, and was doing exceptionally well.

'I'll cope,' she assured us. 'Sara will be in Wimbledon by then, and Jo will be glad to leave her job anyway – her boss is always going on about his double hernia!' Jo did a 'wicked' impression of this man, who made his female staff blanch when he opened a box delivered to the office and proudly displayed the contents – a formidable truss – to the startled young ladies.

'If a buyer turns up soon for the shop, we'll definitely think about it,' John and I agreed.

The boys were excited at the prospect of being again within reach of Chelsea and Arsenal football grounds, and Katy and Maff were, we felt, still young enough to adapt to a move. J.P. was also working temporarily in London with his uncle. We'd see more of him, which would be great.

If only we could return to Crabapple Cottage, we thought, but we knew that wasn't possible . . .

* * *

We advertised the shop one more time – we had to lower the price. The post office pair had already departed without selling: this might help us we thought, if a buyer for the stores bid for the post office franchise.

We knew we would have to start 'all over again', look for a property in need of modernising, as the cottage had been. It wouldn't be easy for John to find a job, either, now he was over forty, in the economic crisis.

A couple in their fifties, with a nest-egg, came to view. They drove a hard bargain, but they were cash buyers. We weren't in a position to turn them down, but we wanted a little time to consider their offer.

The deciding moment came when the garden wall fell down.

John and I were in the kitchen, rustling up our lunch. We were on our own as we always were Monday to Friday. It was a lovely day. I looked out of the window. Should we eat outside at the millstone table and soak up the sunshine, I wondered. Then, I couldn't believe my eyes – 'John!' I yelled. 'Look what's happening!'

The dry-stone wall which marked our property was tumbling, in slow motion, stone by stone, with a domino effect, in a cloud of dust. There was a faint rumble, like distant thunder. Billow, fortunately indoors enjoying his meat and biscuits, lifted his head and howled.

We were both speechless for a minute or two, trying to comprehend what was happening.

'Thank goodness,' John said at last, 'it didn't happen when the children were playing out there . . .'

There was now a big gap in the wall, and rubble strewn over the path. We were expecting the prospective buyers to return in three days for our answer – repairs were vital. We sought the advice of Mr Trew. The wall, he thought, had been built a century ago. Each stone would have to be painstakingly returned to its original place. It was like a jigsaw puzzle. No lunch for us – it took John two days to build back the wall.

We'd come to a decision though. We'd cut our losses and sell.

This was not the final disaster, but then, as the saying goes, things always happen in threes.

Our buyers were not ready to move by the time school began in September. The girls went to stay with relatives in Kent, after helping John decide on the location of our new home. Jo, with excellent secretarial skills, soon found temporary work – Ginge went to an all-girls (she didn't like that bit!) grammar school in Maidstone. The young ones continued at the village primary school, but I was advised it would cause less upheaval for the three boys if we tutored them at home for a couple of weeks. They were given set work. They had places lined up at a good school in Kent.

As I was busy in the shop, I had to trust they would concentrate on their studies . . .

One day when I wasn't able to supervise properly, they decided to be helpful and bring down some items from the loft. This they did, but they kept quiet about the fact that running along the rafters, one of them had slipped and his foot had gone through our bedroom ceiling . . . Knowing I wouldn't get a chance to go upstairs until that evening, they hatched a make-do-and-mend solution.

Gullible Mum allowed them out for a breath of fresh air that afternoon. I was unaware that they had pooled their pocket money and bought a can of white paint, lining paper and wallpaper paste. Michael, our mathematical wizard, worked out what they could afford. The ceiling was duly patched, hopefully by him as he had the most practical skills, while I was still occupied in the shop!

I am now going to quote from a composition which Katy later wrote at her new school, after the move – this incident obviously made a lasting impression on her after the consequence was discovered.

One day, my mum and dad were lying in bed, and my dad looked up at the ceiling. 'My God, Sheila,' he cried 'What's that?' Mum looked up. 'What do you mean?' she asked. Dad shouted, 'Can't you see it? That patch on the ceiling. It was not there when I went away, don't you ever look up?' 'I'm too busy looking down,' Mum said. Dad went to find out what it was and he nearly fell through too. He said 'how can we sell this place now?' But we did.

Katy's teacher had given this 8 out of 10, with the comment, 'What an interesting story.'

The third thing happened on moving day, after the contract was signed and the contents etc. agreed. The big kitchen fridge conked out, we had to call out an engineer and to pay the bill there and then.

CHAPTER 49

Goodbye

Our last weeks in the Crossroads Stores were surprisingly busy ones. Most of the village came in to say they were sorry we were going, and to wish us well. It was heart-warming. I was even invited on a Chapel outing to the beach, with Katy and Maff, and for the first time I felt among friends, but it was too late . . .

There were gifts from the regular customers, including tea towels from Mrs Diddley and chocolates from devotees of the Co-op.

Those who filled the shelves, whether they were due to call or not, came loaded with their specialities and hoped we would recommend them to the new owners. Tinkerbelle gave me a pair of sheer tights. Not the most tactful present with my bad leg. 'Lissel' would have been more of a cover-up.

During the final week, John had to travel up to Kent to tie up loose ends there. The girls were the only other members of the family to view our new abode; all I knew was that it was a 'partly converted Methodist chapel'. It was all we could afford with sufficient accommodation, though (as I was about to discover when we arrived there) no interior doors and a temporary staircase, more a ladder, leading to the gallery, unprotected by a rail . . .

While John was away, a familiar figure appeared in the shop. The bus had stopped at The Crossroads, and would wait there ten minutes or so, before turning back up the hill. It was midday, and a single passenger disembarked.

I wasn't too sure if I was seeing things. Ted, in pyjamas, dressing gown and slippers, smiled his sweet smile. He had obviously dodged the carers at the home, and slipped out.

Then I focused on the unfortunate fact that Ted had not 'adjusted his frontispiece', that his trousers were gaping – but how could I tell him that?

'It's good to see you, Ted,' I managed.

He pointed, with a trembling finger at the cigarette shelf. His breathing was laboured, and I remembered his sister Doris's strictures. I also recalled that Mrs Diddley had told me Doris was away.

'Oh, Ted, I'm so sorry,' I said, 'but you're not allowed to smoke, are you? Does anyone know you've come down here? I think you ought to catch the bus back . . .'

I came round the counter and took his arm. 'Come on, old boy.'

The bus driver hastily put out his cigarette, jumped down to help Ted aboard. 'He didn't have any money on him for the fare – but I couldn't turn him off, could I? I waited, guessed you'd suggest he make the return journey. I'll see him inside the home, don't worry.'

'Goodbye, Ted.' I was choked, because it really *was* goodbye.

(Remembering Ted (and Fred, of course) while writing this, I realise he must be long gone . . . I like to think he plays his trombone again in Heaven.)

* * *

On Thursday evening, John and I checked the stock for the last time. It was past 1 a.m. when we finally staggered to bed, exhausted. It was a comfort to know that Joyce and John were coming to help us load up the container lorry from Kent. We got that at a special rate because it had brought a load down here, and would have returned empty to base. It would even be possible to transport the small boat John had recently acquired, for 'a song', but never had time to use. (In fact, it was so decrepit, the cat took it over as his quarters!)

Before first light, I was roused by the sound of a heavy vehicle grinding to a halt, opposite the shop, beside the stream. There were voices, lights came on, then were switched off.

John looked at his watch. It was 4 a.m. The new owners, who had also hired a large lorry, were here. They had travelled by night, just as we had done three and a half years ago. But they weren't due to arrive until 10 a.m.

'They're obviously settling down for the rest of the night – so we should too,' John said wisely, guessing that I was about to get up, boil the kettle, and take them cups of tea.

We rose at 5.30 as usual, but stripped the bed and rolled the bedding – one job done, we thought. Fortunately, the three girls had packed their belongings before they left, after sorting out what they could take with them. Their beds were already dismantled.

There are always things you can't do until you are about to move out. John opened the front door cautiously to retrieve the papers, but there was no sign of anyone stirring over the road.

The boys started on their allotted jobs – their cases were already packed. At 8, kind Mrs Trew came over to take Katy and Matthew over to her house and to give them breakfast.

'Anne has planned some games to keep them occupied,' she said. We were very grateful.

The boys cooked a greasy plateful apiece of sausages, eggs and beans. John and I opted for boiled eggs and toast. Then I went into the shop to carry on until the new owners officially took over, while John mustered his troops and awaited the arrival of our helpers. They didn't let us down, arriving within half-an-hour.

Everything sold before 10 a.m. had to be jotted down in a notebook. The removal team had cleared the upstairs by then, but the dining room was chock-a-block with boxes awaiting their attention. Things were going according to plan it seemed, until the newcomers began moving their stuff inside ... This was an hour before we'd agreed they could, but they were obviously eager to take over.

At this point, a couple of unmarked boxes (which we didn't discover until they were opened up a few days later) made their way on to our vehicle. We gained a couple of blankets but the incomers did rather better with a chest of drawers!

Mrs Cooper was eager to take my place behind the counter. However, I couldn't do much to help the workers out back (where the container lorry was parked) as every few minutes I was called upon to explain something to her. She reported excitedly on her first customer – 'Well, he didn't actually buy anything, but he introduced himself, Toddy, I think he said his name was. He had six bottles to return, and he told me how much the deposit was, and when I paid him (lucky you'd put some cash in the till) he said thank you very politely. What a nice boy!'

I couldn't disillusion her so soon. 'I should bring the crate inside,' I said, 'for today, in case someone trips over it, with all the coming and going.' As I thought, the crate was empty, the six bottles it had contained were now lined up on the counter.

I don't know why, but my gaze was drawn to the perfume bottles by the mirror. I suppressed a groan. Two were missing! The stock list would have to be adjusted.

Then I made all the workers large mugs of strong, sugared tea, to keep their strength up.

It was well past lunchtime when the two Johns began their final task, rolling up the thick-piled green carpet and then the rubber underlay. Joyce and I followed them with a broom apiece to sweep the floor.

'We must go,' they said. They had boys of their own at home.

We said goodbye and thank you to our wonderful friends, and knew we would miss them, but thank goodness the bond between us has endured, and I know it always will be strong.

The lorry drove off. We hoped to be reunited with our goods and chattels the following morning in Kent.

Now, we had our personal possessions and the overflow (which included the pets!) to pack into the minibus – by late afternoon we were on our way, hoping to arrive in the wee small hours at our chapel.

CHAPTER 50

A Moving Experience

The mini-bus was packed to the gunwales. Due to that darn boat, we'd had to accommodate some pieces of furniture in the back. (I couldn't be a Jonah and tell John off, could I, when he'd been working flat out? Anyway, what about all my writing paraphernalia?) This meant the boys, dog, cat, tortoises and goldfish (Maff's) were hemmed in. We assured them we'd stop off for fish and chips and then they could snooze while Dad drove on as far as he could before the next break . . . We even optimistically thought we might arrive at the chapel by midnight. As none of the big girls or J.P. were with us, we felt incomplete after so many family outings. I had the little ones with me in the front. They had plenty to occupy them, as Mrs Trew and Anne had given them an I SPY book, a Ladybird book apiece and colouring magazines and crayons. We would miss the Trews and, I realised, the customers, despite their idiosyncrasies . . .

It was the beginning of October, not late September, when we'd intended to move, so we had to make the most of the daylight. However, we were still in Devon when the engine began spluttering. Overheating, was John's first reaction. He spotted a lay-by, and opposite – was it a mirage? – a *fish and chip shop*, lit up, in the middle of a row of other small shops which were obviously closed. We had come upon this little village (we never found out quite where it was) by chance.

We parked in the lay-by, and John went over to the shop to buy our supper and to enquire if they had a phone so that he could call the RAC.

'We'll stop a bit further up the road, to eat our food, where there are no houses,' I promised the boys. 'Then you can get out and stretch your legs and bob behind a bush . . .'

We managed to cruise along perhaps two hundred yards, then the vehicle lights failed and the engine seized up. By torchlight, for it was now dusk, we opened up our newspaper parcels and scoffed the contents with our fingers dipping in and out. Then I poured tea from the flask into paper cups and handed three back to the boys.

'We can't get out with all this stuff jamming us in,' said a worried voice, 'and we want to – *go* – now we've drunk the tea . . .'

John had the solution – 'You'll have to use the empty paper cups – then open the window.' He always deals with our dilemmas, I thought gratefully, when another voice called out, 'Dad, a paper cup isn't big enough . . .' (Please note, I know who it was, but I'm not saying!)

It was past 10 p.m. when the RAC arrived: our directions had been rather vague, they said. A powerful beam illuminated the problem. The alternator had gone. 'Look, I'll charge the battery, that should get you home, but not tonight with no lights. Wait until dawn, then take it steady all the way,' we were advised by the mechanic.

We settled down as comfortably as we could, put our coats on and hoped for the best. John and I slept but fitfully. Gentle snoring from boys and Billow, then we shook with stifled laughter, as we heard Billow lapping water. From the goldfish bowl . . . I hope he doesn't swallow Goldie, I thought.

We were stiff and cold in the early morning, but the boys managed to shift the furniture in the back to open a side door, and stepped down to take the dog for a run in the field beyond the hedge where we were parked. Tiger had to make do with a litter tray in case he stalked off and we couldn't find him quickly. We were relieved the goldfish had survived the dog's thirst. Maff and Katy appeared to have had a good night's sleep!

We drank tepid tea and ate the ham sandwiches we'd reserved for breakfast in our new abode. But none of us were able to wash.

Well, we coasted carefully along and there were more mini-crises along the way, but I'll draw a veil over those. John had to phone the haulage company first thing to let them know we would not be in residence until late afternoon. They were not sympathetic, having planned to unload us early and then reload for another trip, later in the day. We were told we would be penalised, but were past worrying about that.

* * *

We arrived in Kent, travel-stained, and it was just starting to rain, as we looked out at our chapel, an imposing red brick edifice, built by local Methodists in 1884. It was surrounded then by a meadow starred with daisies, (where later a new estate would be built) with a village football pitch beyond – our boys would love that! The main feature at the front was a beautiful round stained-glass window which we discovered beamed rainbow light to the gallery. John wisely didn't mention then, that along the far side was a graveyard, but all the ancient memorial stones had been laid flat, and this area we were bound to grass over. The windows along the chapel walls were typically ecclesiastical, long, curved, occluded glass, but difficult to curtain adequately. The entrance was not what we expected; John would make a splendid new door a priority.

The haulage men had decanted our furniture into the front garden, to pay us back for being late, and there was an overflow on the pavement, now getting wet. Our new neighbour came out to help.

'Your girls are waiting in the kitchen,' he told us. 'We had a key, so let them in. They've been worrying about you all day!'

We hadn't expected them until Sunday, so this was a wonderful surprise. Jo and Ginge had the kettle on and they'd been to the shop for milk and tea. It was quick hugs all round, and a chorus of Happy Birthday! to Ginge who was eighteen today, before we got down to business. 'We'll celebrate tomorrow,' we promised our lovely daughters.

The previous occupants had obviously departed in a huff judging by the terrible mess they had left behind. There were numerous letters (opened but thrown in a heap on the floor in the main room) from their bank, unpaid bills and threatening letters from the suppliers. I pounced on bottles of sleeping pills and anti-depressants and put them in a safe place; worse was to be revealed. There were two bedrooms downstairs, designated for the girls (when home) and the three boys. There was a bathroom downstairs, and another upstairs – two more bedrooms led off the gallery, under the eaves, for John and I, Katy and Maff.

The girls' bedroom was filthy – our neighbours told us that our predecessors had kept two large dogs and eight puppies in there! We located the Dettol and cloths – fortunately the girls had turned on the immersion heater, so there was plenty of hot water. It was going to be another long night . . . Then in walked dear Jonathan who'd driven from Suffolk, where he now worked, to offer both moral and physical support. He is always so positive and cheerful!

The kitchen was the only room which had been fitted out properly. The drawback was the uneven floor. The dog owners had dug up a lovely brick path which encircled the chapel, and cemented all these bricks in place. We got wet muddy feet from trailing round outside, bringing in our goods.

Had we exchanged one disaster for another, we wondered?

Then I saw something which gave me hope for an uncertain future. There was a small room, which we thought would make a cosy dining room. With the long table, the settle, chairs and small dresser in place, this room would prove our refuge, and the sanctuary where I would write many stories. As we brushed away the cobwebs, gold lettering was revealed on the wall. This message must have comforted so many in times past. It read:

HIS MERCY IS EVERLASTING

PART 5

WHO STIRS THE PORRIDGE IN THE POT

Mid-1970s–1990s

CHAPTER 51

Who Stirs the Porridge in the Pot?

It was impossible to transform our living quarters overnight, we soon realised it would take us weeks, months, probably years to do so. But our new home in Kent, a mid-Victorian chapel, was a refuge, and once we got to grips with clearing the debris left behind by 'the wreckers' who had ripped out the heart of the place, the family became optimistic over the possibilities. We were helped considerably in our endeavours by the acquisition of an industrial cleaner – a large drum on wheels which could suck up rubble and even water. We needed ear muffs because the whirling drum rattled and crushed the contents and threatened to regurgitate them. Fortunately, the chapel walls were thick, so we received no complaints from neighbours.

The children loved all the space; but initially, the only place where I could relax was the cosy former vestry, the one room with doors, where I could shut myself off from the chaos occasionally. As mentioned, I found the illuminated message on the wall of my sanctuary very comforting. It told me: *His Mercy is Everlasting.*

Rooms were given names, and Katy, when asked to describe her unusual home by her new teacher, proudly boasted of our 'dog hall'. This was situated beyond a side door to the chapel which was never used, or you would have stepped out on to flattened tombstones. Billow, our Old English cross, had his quarters here, outside the boys' downstairs bathroom, which was designated for their exclusive use because they quickly acquired weekend jobs on local farms, so that area had a pungent smell of manure from their discarded boots.

John placed a notice, No Boots Past This Point! on the door of the little dining room which led to the lofty sitting room. (Some time later I was embarrassed by the sight of one of our young clodhoppers' girlfriends obediently removing high-heeled, high-fashion boots, before joining us in the other room.)

This vast room was dominated by an enormous chimney breast which John was in the process of building for several years. (It never actually got through the roof.) There was rudimentary central heating, but only the kitchen, the dog hall, two downstairs bedrooms, plus the small living room were cosy in winter. The sleeping bags from our camping days came in handy now, we huddled under these on settees and chairs. I was conscious that visitors, when invited by the young ones to 'dive under', sometimes wrinkled their noses, because these comforters were not too often in the wash.

That first chill winter we thought we might be warmer up on the gallery, that's if heat really did rise as John often reminded us. He hung a thick sheet of plastic from the beams to hopefully deal with the draughts. The boys obligingly hauled up a settee and armchair and the TV. We positioned a massive plant pot in a corner to make it look more homely. Unfortunately, one evening we had a visitor. A mouse ventured out from under the eaves and ran up John's trouser leg. The girls screamed and jumped on the settee which rocked and almost went backwards through the plastic screen. John shook his leg, the mouse dropped out and disappeared double quick, to more screaming.

John said: 'Why did you make all that fuss? It was my leg, after all.' We moved all the stuff back downstairs again, except for the plant. It thrived up there and almost went through the roof, unlike the chimney.

The boys didn't mind the odd mouse. They turned the gallery into a games area, with Scalextric buzzing at one end. A snooker table was much in use at the other. They didn't worry that the gallery was not railed off. In time, toddling grandchildren sat in safety, in the middle of the green baize. They sometimes left damp patches. Those waiting their turn with the cue fashioned paper aeroplanes and let these flutter down from the gallery on to our heads as we sat below. These paper planes were often minor works of art!

The beautiful oriel window cast glorious hues over the floorboards. To one side of the gallery, there was a spare bed, curtained round for visiting friends. We needed to remind them to duck beneath the beam at the top of the stairs; the younger children were happy when they hit their heads on this because it meant they were now taller than five foot! One Swedish visitor said gallantly, 'I had a good night's sleep, I was knocked out and knew no more until morning . . .' He had also forgotten to dress before finding his way via the vestry dining room to the House of Horrors (the boys' bathroom), but we concentrated on our breakfast porridge and averted our gaze.

John and I, Katy and Maff had bedrooms under the eaves. We had our own bathroom, thank goodness! Even this had its gremlins: we were kept awake for hours one night by what we thought was a drumming session by our neighbours' boys, but eventually twigged it was 'knocking pipes'.

* * *

The first two weeks in the chapel, the children were upbeat, liking their new schools, and exploring the surroundings. John and I, however, were suddenly overcome by the enormity of what we had done. We'd returned to familiar territory, it's true, but John had to find a job, and money was dwindling rapidly. I had to 'stir the porridge in the pot' – and scour the saucepan later. John's forte had always been the perfect English breakfast, but we needed to economise. He didn't feel like going out and meeting people, nor did I, but after the three boys and Ginge had left to catch their buses in the morning, it was up to me to walk the two youngest to primary school and later to collect them in the afternoon, for we now lived in a much bigger village and there was a busy road to cross to the school.

We missed the older children a lot. Soon we would be a family of seven, not eleven, I realised, when it was time for Ginge to go to college in Bromley. I blinked back the all-too-ready tears when I thought of our diminishing numbers.

One afternoon, John was poring over papers spread out on the kitchen table.

'Any letters to post?' I asked hopefully. I had typed out for him a batch of CVs, but we'd had no luck so far.

'No,' he replied, not looking up.

'I'm off to meet the children then . . .' I wanted to add, 'Would you like to come with me?' but I guessed he wouldn't.

This was a prosperous Wealden village and along the main street on my route, there were distinctive old houses, with newer dwellings in between. On the other side of the road was a discreet small development of family homes built on land which had belonged to the old mill, which sadly had been dismantled not many years ago. The whiteboarded mill cottage had a lovely, rioting garden – I wondered who lived there. Someone special, I hoped, because of the history. I would not be disappointed.

I passed the village hall, where so many activities appeared to go on, and came to a quaint little wooden property called *Evergreen*. I half expected to see and hear Jessie Matthews, the musical comedy actress, serenading me over the picket gate. From avid reading of my aunt's pre-war film annuals as a child, I recalled that Miss Matthews had been in a show called *Evergreen* in the thirties. In the minute front garden, and it was the end of October now, an elderly lady sat facing the street, from a deckchair. She wore a floppy sunhat, a cape and stout boots over thick, ribbed stockings, and she appeared to be snoozing. But the moment I attempted to tiptoe by, her eyes opened wide, and she greeted me, 'Good afternoon' in clear, ringing tones. She had introduced herself the first day I did the school walk, as 'Miss Bough, pronounced Boff – my friends call me Boffy.' That was the extent of our conversation so far.

Further up the street, set back out of sight, was a manor house in secluded grounds, a dairy farm, the cricket field, and opposite a splendid village green where the bus stopped, a thriving general stores. I had to cross over the road at this point to turn down the church hill. The Saxon church looked out on to a delightful small school. There was the post office stores just before the school, where the waiting mothers congregated. The crossing lady would shortly arrive with her lollipop, to usher them back over the busy road. Most of them would go in the opposite direction to me, past the big shop to the council estate, again a well-thought-out extension to the village, with excellent housing. This was on the far side of the green, tucked away behind the church. The mums, some with pushchairs, prams, or with toddlers on reins, glanced at me curiously, as I walked quickly past and down to the school gates. There were two or three mothers already there, ready to collect their children from class one. Matthew was in class two, which was let out ten minutes later. They departed, with a smile and 'hello' to me, then I stood there alone.

The class two children emerged, and scampered up to the shop with pictures in hand, and socks at half mast, to join their parents. I didn't realise then that only the youngest children were supposed to be picked up directly outside the school.

Matthew, the last out, was coming towards me now, dragging his feet. I glanced up as I became aware of a big vehicle arriving outside the shop. A man jumped down from the cab, leaving the engine running, and went inside.

I noticed that it was an oil tanker. Even as I felt Maff slip his hand in mine, I became aware of a voice shouting above the roar of the engine.

As if mesmerised, I stared at the tanker, rolling downhill towards us. A woman was waving frantically at me. '*There's no driver!*' she yelled. The other women were frozen to the spot, like me. With them was the driver of the tanker, clutching a packet of cigarettes.

I was suddenly galvanised into action, 'Run!' I cried to Maff, pulling him with me. The ground seemed to come up and hit us as we tumbled over and over.

The next thing I knew the tanker veered and demolished the metal barrier outside the school gates. The engine cut out, and as I struggled up, I saw my little boy lying between the great wheels. I tried to call him, but I couldn't. The mum who had saved us by her quick thinking, arrived, out of breath, but lifted Maff up and dusted him down. 'He's still in one piece, thank God, but he's in shock,' she assured me. There was a helping hand for me, too. The headmaster was holding back the next batch of children, which included Katy, but her teacher, a small, dark-haired Welsh woman, whom I had thought to be strict and not tolerant of fussy parents, couldn't have been kinder. She and my saviour, who I learned had a daughter in Katy's class, took Maff, Katy and me into the school, and Meg, the teacher, my good friend from that day, quickly provided hot, sweet tea. Then she rang John to ask him to collect us. Amazingly, neither Maff or I had sustained any physical damage, though my best coat was muddy and ripped.

The poor Head was in shock, too. He kept saying over and over, 'It's a miracle . . . it would have been a massacre, if the other children had come out then.'

I really have to end this chapter here. After all these years, it still affects me . . . I will just add that it came to me too, that it was a miracle. We had been saved despite the odds. Life was worth living after all. I vowed not to feel sorry for myself again.

CHAPTER 52

Happy Days are Here Again

'Hang on a minute,' I said to the children as we were about to go out of the chapel. I dashed upstairs to the bathroom and knocked on the door. It opened, and John stood there looking comical with one side of his face razored-clean and the other side smothered in shaving cream.

'What's up?' he asked, surprised. 'I thought you'd be halfway to school by now!'

'I just wanted to say good luck, once more!' I replied, bestowing a kiss on his smooth cheek. I was over the moon with excitement because this morning he had been summoned back for a second interview for a job.

As I re-joined the children, Katy said reproachfully, 'Mum, the White Rabbit's beaten us this morning.' She pointed ahead to a small, hurrying figure, wearing a distinctive white fluffy beret, with a reluctant large child in tow. We couldn't hear what she was saying, but we guessed it would be the same lament as every morning. 'We're late! We *must* be late!' I know it was naughty of me to have thus labelled this harassed mother, but it is a family quirk inherited from my dad and his family. (His sister, when unexpectedly presented with a sulky young relative, promptly referred to her as 'the impossible child'.)

'Last ones this morning,' Cissie the crossing lady said cheerfully. 'Lucky I spotted you coming. The cuckoo's only just gone over.'

'The cuckoo?' I said, then the penny dropped. So, others did this, too, I thought – I wondered what my nickname was . . . Oh well, whatever it was, I no doubt deserved it.

Cissie paused on the far pavement for a moment. 'It's the W.I. this evening, in the village hall. Seven-thirty. Why don't you come?

You'll get to know people then. Mostly the posh lot from the big houses down your way. We could do with a youngster or two to liven 'em up.'

Youngster! I was flattered, being now in my early forties!

'Will you be there?' I asked. Meeting new people was still rather daunting.

''Course I will. Bye then!'

* * *

'No, I haven't joined the W.I. yet,' Meg told me, as she shepherded the children into school, having been on the look-out for latecomers. 'I'm waiting until I retire! Too many other things to do after school, like marking books, preparing lessons and refereeing netball matches. I wonder if they all turn up in hats still? Mind you, they were jolly good at making all that jam in the war. Millicent plays "Jerusalem" I gather, and dear Mrs Burton does the refreshments, as she does for all the other societies in the village.'

'Is she the lady who rides that big black upright bicycle?' I asked.

'She is indeed. And Millicent is our part-time music teacher. Has Katy a recorder? She'll need one, for the Christmas concert.'

I didn't like to say that after the boys' early-morning practice on the recorder in the past, their father had said he considered it an instrument of torture.

That evening we had two things to celebrate: John felt he'd had an excellent interview, and for some reason the whole family was excited that Mum was going out! My one and only lipstick surfaced from the dressing-up box, the only problem was I didn't have a hat, apart from the woolly pom-pom on top variety for when it snowed. However, Ginge lent me a sparkly hair slide to adorn my hair and I chose court shoes and nylons, rather than the coloured tights and ankle boots I wore as a rule. The village hall was only a hundred yards up the road, and here we had street lighting!

Busy ladies were putting out hard wooden chairs, facing the table for the President, Secretary and Treasurer, which was positioned below the stage. Rather dusty curtains were drawn across this, and Cissie, who had greeted me at the door, whispered: 'We used to put on plays at one time, but not nowadays. We also had a darts team, and played in the local pub, but the new committee disapproved of that.'

The committee didn't look new to me, they were all ladies well over middle age, but at least they didn't wear hats, though some wore silk head scarves to protect their newly set hair. The hairdresser obviously had a busy day when it was W.I. time.

I noted the hatch was up and I could see Mrs Burton counting out the cups on the table and a mouth-watering display of cakes. All for 5p! Mrs B was round, short and rosy-cheeked with bright blue eyes and plenty of laughter lines. I had been informed that she had the prettiest council house garden, that she entered into every aspect of village life with gusto, and was the village wise woman, loved and respected by all.

When it was time for the speaker – and I can't recall a thing about a very dull talk – Mrs B pulled down the hatch smartly, which showed what she thought of *him*, and not a single W.I. member said a word.

First there was "Jerusalem", and Millicent struck the keys of the piano gamely, while muttering that it needed tuning. She was a handsome woman, with a mass of silvery hair, and taught singing as well as piano. I suspected she preferred younger, more enthusiastic pupils, judging by her reproachful sighs at our wavering rendition. Then came The Minutes of the Last Meeting, followed by The Business, which involved every word of every letter or leaflet being read aloud, whether important (or so it seemed to me) or not. The president had a little cough every other paragraph and scanned the audience to see if they were listening. 'Any other business?' she enquired, at last. When answer came there none, there was a united soft sigh of relief, until the speaker began shuffling a sheaf of papers.

The Secretary was, to my delight, Miss Bough. She was busy taking notes throughout. When she hadn't nodded off, that is. I would discover that it made absolutely no difference when she read them out next month. There were never any puzzling gaps. Again no one said a word about her little 'absences' or nudged her awake.

I thought, these quiet, restrained ladies are actually very nice. They respect others' eccentricities, and they obviously care about the community they live among. They smiled at me, and I smiled back. One of the committee approached me in the break to say, 'What lovely little children you have!' which, naturally made me warm to her. She added: 'I do hope you will want to come again, it's nice to see new faces – and, familiar ones too – Millicent used to provide the music for all our dances here during the war. She worked hard in the land army all day, but she was never too tired to oblige on the piano . . .'

'And Mrs Burton?' I queried.

'Oh, she was a busy young mother but she could still get twenty cups of tea from a pint of milk and a quarter of tea! She was a wonderful cook even then.'

Millicent, primed by my friend Meg at school, fetched my tea and a large slice of fruit cake. 'This is only my second time,' she confided. 'Cissie said they could do with a bit of insubordination . . .'

'She hinted at that to me too,' I said.

'I could hear you singing in the front row,' Millicent told me.

'Oh dear! I know my voice carries – it has to, with so many children to call to attention!' I thought I would make sure I didn't sit in the front seats again; if you twiddled your toes, so to speak, you received reproachful glances from the hierarchy at the table.

'My dear, I intend to find a choir amongst this lot—'

'I don't think I'd be suitable,' I said quickly, before she could suggest I be a part of any singing group.

'Nonsense! You have a good soprano voice,' she said firmly.

Wait 'til I tell the family that, I exulted – no more requests to 'could you please not sing so loudly Mum, everyone was looking at you!' from most of my children in turn, when I attended a school service.

We were shushed as the competition was judged. This was a display of matchboxes, and the winner was the member who had managed to pack the most small items into a Swan Vestas box. I thought this would make a good game for a rainy day when the young ones were bored at home.

'The winning box had *six* pins – you can't get much smaller than that; it's not in the rules,' Millicent said sotto voce. What rules? I wondered.

I overheard a couple of other grumbles. The W.I. were certainly competitive!

I had something else to tell them when I got home: 'There's a jumble sale on Saturday, and I've been asked to help!'

'We'll all go,' Ginge said. 'So will the girls, if they're home then.'

'We won't!' cried Dad and the boys.

* * *

'Young and able, carry table.' Mrs. Burton winked at me. 'You get away with a lot if you're grey and feeble.' She indicated her own thick grey bob of hair.

I grinned back and unfolded the legs of the trestle. It was quite a tussle. 'You're not feeble,' I told her. 'You set us all an example!'

She tossed me a starched white cloth. 'I've got the best job, overseeing cakes and produce, plus refreshments as usual. Put that large cake to one side. That's for Guess the Weight. 10p a go.'

'Glad it's not guess the number of currants,' I joked. 'You don't spare the fruit, it looks yummy! Can I help you on this stall?'

'Sorry, dear, Millicent's asked for you to be with her on the underwear stall – that's very popular, you'll see.'

I didn't fancy that, but I guessed new members drew the short straw.

I cast a regretful glance at my favourite stalls, the bric-a-brac and the books, as I made my way to the end of the hall and a table piled high with mainly white (or sometimes off-white) garments where I was needed to help with the sorting. I knew from past experience that buyers would ignore the neat heaps and dig deep, that garments would land on the floor and be trodden underfoot when the doors opened and the masses rushed in.

Miss Bough was already ready and waiting. She had a small table next to ours for the raffle. She'd sold two books of tickets in advance.

'D'you mind if I have a quick look, dear? I don't suppose I'll get another spare moment until they do the draw . . .'

Millicent compressed her lips but said nothing. She gave a little shake of her head at me. I chose not to see this. I held up two soft, new vests with sleeves: 'Are these any good to you?' I asked.

'I prefer the Opera top,' Miss Bough said. 'Any nice corsets?'

Millicent couldn't contain herself any longer. 'You must wait until after two o'clock,' she insisted. 'If I find such a garment, I will put it to one side for you.' She gave a slight shudder as she thought about it.

'Thank you, Millicent,' Miss Bough said, sitting down heavily on the chair thoughtfully provided behind her raffle table. She began to rearrange the boxes of chocolates, the writing paper, unwanted gifts like men's sock suspenders, and a solitary bottle of someone's home-made elderberry wine.

The doors burst open and the battle, for it was that, commenced.

It was a chilly day, but underwear wasn't the best-seller of the day. (Although my girls looked pityingly at poor Mum knee deep in Chilprufe vests, they patronised the more colourful stalls.) Alas a pair of corsets didn't surface, and there was a growing pile of single socks, but someone nicked (or maybe they paid for) Boffy's stick, which she'd left lying on our table. Fortunately, Chrissie, on the door, recognised it and managed to return it.

The cry went up, 'The gypsies are here!' However, unlike some of the jumble hunters, who I was assured were not locals, they paid up, even if they struck a hard bargain.

When the crowds thinned out after an hour, I escaped to turn over the books and made two more friends, husband and wife. He was wheelchair bound following an accident on the farm they had proudly taken on as newlyweds. I would learn later that Ian had realised a great ambition as a young lad – he had travelled abroad in a banana boat, working as crew, and eventually ended up as a cowboy in the Falkland Islands! It turned out that he was a fellow writer. His wife, Judy, helped with the Brownies and Guides, and illustrated her husband's articles and stories with beautiful pen and ink drawings. Ian had many books to personally recommend. This couple were very involved in village life. They lived in a property behind Miss Bough's.

I went home, weary because 'young and able, collapse and put away table' . . . All dozen of 'em. Swept up, stacked chairs, sorted the leftovers, oh, it had been fun, but . . . Still, I had my bargain buy. It hadn't sold on bric-a-brac, but I was offered it for 2p. A tiny statuette of a ballerina, about three inches high. I didn't know it then, but she was art deco. She dances now in our display cabinet. I'd never part with her.

CHAPTER 53

Feathers Flying and Adorning

John was back in the working world; he was now manager of an oil depot. It seemed like poetic justice after the episode of the runaway tanker. The only drawback was that it was a fair old drive away, but he had a company car. This was a great relief to him, to me and the family, but it was coming up to Christmas, and the coffers were still low until the pay cheques rolled in. So, I looked around for a seasonable, reasonable, job. I didn't realise that these two requirements don't always go together.

A notice appeared in the post office window: TURKEY PLUCKERS WANTED. Being of a squeamish disposition despite having a large family and having lived for years on a smallholding, I hesitated, then read on. What could be easier or more convenient? The farm was near the school! The hours would tie in very nicely. There would also be a turkey at the end of the stint at 'a special rate' for the workers. That clinched it for me.

I was primed by a regular worker at the farm. 'Wear your oldest clothes, wellington boots and a woolly hat. It's freezing in the plucking shed. You need rubber gloves, a cheese knife and a fine needle and white thread.'

I couldn't imagine what sewing was needed; I have never been a dab hand with a needle, and rubber gloves are cumbersome. Chris had taken over in that department, narrowing all the legs of the boys' jeans, sometimes disastrously, on the sewing machine. They were becoming followers of fashion, with their great Doc Marten boots which took forever to lace up. (The Pixie Boots were yet to come.) Ginge still sewed beautifully by hand, the patches on her jeans were works of art. She was custodian of the sewing box. She'd provide the right needle.

Cheese knife sounded hopeful, I thought: I visualised a large round cheese on a plate appearing at elevenses, and the workers cutting off a generous slice. I wondered if they supplied nice crusty rolls too . . .

My informant added: 'A magnet is useful (she didn't say what for). She cheered me up with the next statement: 'You get warmed up as time goes on, when the feathers get deep.'

Fortunately, she didn't tell me I'd be a pariah after a couple of days because turkey pluckers had a distinctive smell, or about the possibility of developing tennis elbow. Or about the bout of turkey flu I would no doubt succumb to and have to struggle through. (After the first picking season, the pluckers were mostly immune to this.)

The post office, despite encouraging us with their notice to join the legion of turkey pluckers, now put up a much bigger sign: NO TURKEY PLUCKERS ALLOWED IN THIS SHOP. *This doesn't mean just the aliens from other villages, it means YOU*, was unwritten, but I soon realised that this was a fact.

So I joined the boys' boot brigade, but I left mine out in the coal hole as they were even more odorous than our sons' farm boots.

'Turkey plucking – oh dear!' was the opinion of the mums on the school run when they saw my get-up. They couldn't dampen my enthusiasm. That came later, when I was ushered into a dark, draughty shed, where the only light on a dull grey morning came through the gaps in the building. The floor was hard-baked mud, there were a few chairs and a large table in the middle. Off this unattractive place (I had visualised a barn with lovely old beams) was another section, from which I could hear the muffled gobbles of turkeys. I nearly turned to make a dash for it, but there was a crowd of us now, jostling for the best seats, away from the worst slits in the wall.

It would be several days later before any of these experienced workers would deign to speak to me, the interloper. I was given some basic instructions by a Scottish girl, which was the only help I received. Jeanie very kindly helped me to fold back the rigid wings of my first turkey, which was the only one I managed during the morning. 'Do those first,' she advised. The cheese knife, I learned, was for quilling. You placed your plucked bird on the table and went carefully all over it to remove any remaining quills or stubborn feathers. The needle and thread was for sewing up any tears. I don't know about tears, I had *tears* in my eyes and my nose kept running while I did my cobbling-up. Unexpectedly, the red rubber gloves saved the day, I couldn't have coped otherwise. I only managed five minutes' break for my lunch, no time to trek across the farmyard to the privy. You couldn't leave a job half-done.

That afternoon, young Katy went in the shop on my behalf – the shop assistant let out a little scream when she saw me hovering outside. 'You're not allowed in!' My fellow mums kept a wide berth. I staggered home, aching in every joint. I decided to use the boys' shower, because I wasn't sure I could make it upstairs . . .

The dreaded turkey sniffles struck me on the third day. I was committed to my work, so I took a man-size box of tissues with me and hoped for the best.

Then the snow began to fall. It drifted through the cracks and blew through the shed door whenever it was opened. We were all coughing now. On a couple of occasions, a visiting daughter came to my rescue, and helped poor old sick Mum with her task. Sara was great at repairing any mishaps and Jo somehow managed to swap my giant half-plucked monster with a smaller version left for a few moments on the table by one of the pluckers. He looked at it suspiciously on his return, but took it back to his seat with a sigh. At least our feet were warming up as promised, in the feather bed around our wellies. We didn't lose our needles in a haystack, rather a mound of feathers. The magnets weren't much help. When scissors, knives and even a wedding ring were seemingly lost forever, someone brought in a metal detector. They found the wedding ring, which was the most important.

I was on my third pair of Marigold gloves when the cry went up, 'We've done it!' We peeled off our gloves and went home. I was able to return to the school to pick up the children, smelling of lily of the valley perfume and wearing decent attire. But it took some days before I felt back to normal.

We were to be paid just before Christmas. I joined a long queue outside the farmhouse, one frosted white morning. We shuffled this time through thick snow, and we were only allowed into the pay office, i.e. the kitchen, one at a time. No mince pies or mulled wine were on offer, not even a nice hot cup of coffee. I accepted my wages with numbed fingers and mumbled my appreciation. The list was checked, and I was asked to pay for my turkey, which could be collected a few days later. Despite the concession, I had only a few pounds left.

The twenty-five-pound turkey hung in the hall of the chapel until Christmas Eve. Katy recalls looking at it fearfully, but Ginge immortalised it in a painting. One of us, I can't recall who, offered to hang it on their wall.

Those turkeys were beautiful specimens, and because I had seen the excellent conditions in which they were kept on the farm, and was aware they were humanely despatched when the time came, I felt I had achieved something in that shed . . . Some years later, I would actually become a champion turkey plucker – and that was quite an achievement, I can tell you!

* * *

There were more exotic feathers adorning a magnificent headdress. I was learning more about Boffy by the day. She was the younger, only surviving daughter of a suffragette, and her sister had been a well-known dancer in her day. Boffy had inherited all her stage costumes, and these came out in turn for the W.I. Christmas party, whether fancy dress or no.

This year, Boffy wore a Minnie-Ha-Ha dress with a Hiawatha head band, with gorgeous coloured feathers. From this were suspended false black-wool plaits. She had beaded moccasins on her feet. Who could possibly upstage that?

The staid committee ladies became flushed and sang and danced to the constant flow of tunes emanating from Millicent's flying fingers on the piano. I got over-excited (on cups of tea) and was looked at reprovingly when I encouraged an elderly member to 'peel off!' during the Happy Ho Down. 'What *do* you mean?' she asked. We played silly games with pencil and paper, and dear Mrs B muttered away behind the hatch and kept the urn bubbling. She had a wicked sense of humour, and I enjoyed her little 'asides'. I also discovered that she had a lovely singing voice. We all stopped in our tracks once to listen as she serenaded the tea cups.

My friend Meg had received an invitation, and she confided that she might change her mind, join the group sooner rather than later. There was another guest, the newly retired district nurse, and Girl Guide Commissioner, who had recently moved to the Mill estate. She and Meg were joint winners of the quiz game where the names of local places were scrambled – I suspected they might have played the game before, with the school children or the Guides! Beatrice was another large, comfortable lady with a booming voice and she still had the health of the village at heart. She issued advice freely, which was not always appreciated. She had a hearing aid which emitted whistles at inopportune moments, like when she was in church.

It was no surprise when Beatrice was elected President at the next W.I. AGM. She and Boffy were a perfect team, even though they rubbed sparks off each other, being two strong-minded single ladies. I was voted to serve on the committee as Press Secretary, much to my surprise, and I was pleased to learn that committee meetings were often held at Mrs B's house, where her nice husband waited for a lull in the conversation and then appeared with a loaded tea trolley! Oh, those feather-light sponges oozing with home-made strawberry jam . . . Alf cut such satisfying slices.

CHAPTER 54

You Can't Teach an Old Dog New Tricks

(I don't mean Billow, I mean me . . .)

It was spring, and I was ready for a new challenge. I was approached this time by two long-time field workers who said they admired my fortitude in the turkey plucking shed! Would I like to join them in hop training? They assumed I was keen on gardening; well, the truth is I know how lucky I am that John and most of the children have a love of the great outdoors, and growing things. Wherever we have lived, John has made beautiful gardens, some large, some small, and I have appreciated them all.

I am inspired by rural pursuits in general. A group of us in the village met for the midweek church service, taken by a lovely ancient retired vicar, full of fun, who confided that he used a black felt pen to 'fill in' the holes in his socks: 'My dear wife thinks it's a splendid idea!' We went afterwards to a grand house with a stream and a punt in the garden, and had a shared lunch there before embarking on various handicrafts. Every Christmas, John slyly brings out the snowman I made then from a cardboard tube and a long strip of bandage, and a rather wonky fairy fashioned from felt . . .

However, I had only a romantic view of 'hopping' days past. My good friend Liz actually made it sound idyllic. 'Each family had its own hut, and we little ones helped in our own way. We had sing-songs around a camp fire and sausages cooked on sticks held in the fire, for supper . . . We slept on mattresses filled with straw, and woke to the heady smell of hops and the prospect of another sunny, busy day . . .'

Liz's gran's had been one of the many families from the East End of London who spent their holidays in Kent picking the hops. She married a local lad and never went back.

So, I rashly said yes. My old clothes were clean and ready, my boots just needed a hose down. 'Hop garden' sounded just the job in fine weather.

I can't say to this day where the farm truck took us. I was picked up on the corner of Church Hill after the children were safely deposited at school. They moaned a bit because they were not going along for the ride and 'the picnic' Mum would undoubtedly enjoy later after a leisurely spot of *Firsting*, i.e. training the tender shoots up the strings.

The truck had obviously been used for transporting pigs recently. Sacks were spread over the grubby straw for the workers to sit on as the truck lurched along narrow roads or jerked to a stop when confronted by a tractor. I was 'all shook up' and wondering if it was too far to walk home, when we bumped down a rutted lane for what seemed like a couple of miles, to a forest of hop poles. Our party of six descended from the tailboard on wobbly legs.

I longed for a cup of tea, but it wasn't yet 9 a.m. A stocky man told us tersely that we were on piecework, which was bad news, only he didn't say that, of course, for beginners like me. 'You will be paid by the cant,' he added. What on earth was a cant? At least it was downhill all the way, I thought: my eyes glazed over at the endless marching poles. Where were the hops? Seeing my indecision, the foreman knew he had a rookie. He led me to my first pole. The four strings reminded me of a harp – would they twang if you plucked them?

'See these shoots? You train the strongest ones, two together up each string . . . The weaklings need to be pulled up, to give the others the best chance.' He then demonstrated the sequence to me, but his twirling of the shoots was so swift, I wasn't sure I could master the technique. 'Well, I'll leave you to it,' he said, and he rattled off in the truck. My companions were disappearing fast along their poles. I had no one near enough to call on for advice.

How I wished John was with me. He was used to training runner beans, this would be a doddle for him. I took a deep breath and got down on my haunches – I already knew this was going to be back-breaking labour . . .

Well, I twiddled those darn shoots some one way, and some the other, whichever they seemed to prefer. The foreman hadn't told me they should be trained in a clockwise direction. Any good gardener would have known that, wouldn't they?

Around eleven, my legs were giving out. I collapsed on the ground. The sun beat down mercilessly on my head. I had retied my kerchief (we all wore them then; they were scraps of silk or cotton, brightly patterned) round the back of my neck to prevent sun stroke. I fumbled with my back pack, pulled out a banana and was just taking a bite, hoping it would give me the energy to carry on, when a booming voice startled me: 'Not time for a break yet!' I looked up to see a face glaring down at me. One of my fellow workers had spotted me and run over to reprimand me.

'Sorry ...' I murmured faintly, struggling up and managing to crawl forward on my knees. Didn't they label workers like me 'Blacklegs'?

By the time I reached the bottom of the hill, I realised I was on my own. The others were enjoying their lunch, back at the top and were about to move on to pastures new. Literally, because the truck would pick them up and take them heaven knows where.

'Hurry up, Sheila!' came the call. I hadn't time to eat lunch, so I poured myself a cup of tea from my flask. Again, I looked up to see that I had broken an unwritten law. The foreman had been checking my progress.

'*You* ain't going nowhere,' he said brusquely. 'You've jiggered most of 'em up the wrong way!' He didn't say 'jiggered' either. 'You'll have to go back to the beginning and jigger 'em all the right way. Well, we're off. I'll pick you up at three o'clock, you should have finished by then.'

In fact, I never went back. I don't suppose they would have asked me to, anyway. No *Seconding, Thirding* and *Twiddling* for me. Having no head for heights, I couldn't have managed the last procedure, which entailed climbing a ladder and using a wand with a prong on the end to do the final twiddling of the full-grown hops. I wasn't sacked, but you can still feel sorry for me, because the next morning both our young ones were poorly. They had gone down with chicken pox. They didn't have it mildly, as the older children had, in our orchard days, when, though in quarantine at home, they had enjoyed recovering mostly outdoors in the sunshine. Katy and Matthew had those horrible blisters mostly inside their mouths and throat – it was a virulent strain that year . . . but I heard later it was a good year for hops.

Well, before you think what a wimp I am, before too long, I gained respect for my endeavours in an unexpected way.

I met a young red-haired mother with two little boys in the shop one day, and we got talking. She had only just arrived in the village and was feeling lonely. She invited me over to her house nearby for a cup of tea. She was a few years younger than me, but I've always had friends across the generations – age doesn't come into it.

We sat in the kitchen and I couldn't help commenting on the lovely smell of newly baked bread. Along the counter were stacked several loaves, mostly wholemeal, with crusty tops, and a tray of rolls, twisted into attractive shapes.

'When we married, we decided to take on a bakery and make *real* bread,' Sue confided. 'My husband started work before dawn each day, to make and prove the dough. I went in later to make the cakes. We both worked until late afternoon, we didn't close the shop until the shelves were empty . . . We made a good team and we were doing really well. Then the babies came along, and I couldn't do all I did before to help him. He was so tired all the time, and we lost heart in the business. We had an offer for the bakery and the shop, and we decided we'd had enough. We still love baking—'

'I can see that,' I said, looking at the tempting loaves.

'But, we knew our marriage would suffer if we carried on. The children hardly saw their father, he was always working. So we came here because my husband is now a sales representative for a big firm.'

'Are you feeling better now?' I ventured.

'We're getting there . . . I was disappointed to find you have no playgroup here – it would be a good place for the children and me to make new friends. I've been looking into starting one up, but I can't do it on my own. I was a teacher before I married, but of secondary-school children. *You* have plenty of experience with younger children, I'm relatively new to dealing with toddlers – would you like to be involved?'

I thought about it. Then I said, 'When we lived on the smallholding and all the children were young, there were always other children round to play. My friend's two little girls almost lived at our place, she said she trusted me to look after them while she was working. The more the merrier, was my motto.'

'How about you and me working together? We could hire the village hall twice a week and do some fund-raising for equipment—'

'We'd need to canvass the village first, see if that's what they'd like,' I said. 'And wouldn't we need training?'

Sue nodded. 'I've already been into all that. You join the Preschool Playgroup Association and do a course. You have to have a police check, and a health check too. You need a certificate in first aid. It'll take a few months to set up, but we'd have to do it properly. When it's up and going you need a team of volunteers to help – and really, we could do with someone like a nursery nurse or an ex-teacher in the team.'

'I'll ask around, as I know more people than you, from the school run,' I offered.

'I don't think there will be much possibility of being paid ourselves, does that worry you, Sheila?'

'Some jobs you do for love,' I said.

I went home, walking on air, with a warm loaf of bread in my bag. Training toddlers was more my style than training hops, wasn't it?

CHAPTER 55

Boys and Girls Come Out to Play

We began with notes through letterboxes, coffee mornings and mum's meetings, and it seemed to us that there was a real need among the local children to get together to play, learn and have fun.

Sue had done her homework: as prospective supervisors we had to be thoroughly vetted by the local authority; the village hall had to pass a stringent fire hazard test and we embarked on fund-raising for equipment. We also joined the Pre-School Playgroups Association.

There was now a third member of our team, Marcia, who was taking a sabbatical from teaching science in a comprehensive school. I was to add to their expertise my experience of bringing up and amusing a large family, and I suspect, to add the motherly touch – you know, taking children to the loo, or coping with Lolly, who's been screaming blue murder since her mum went.

We had great fun, once a week, planning our two sessions. Children thrive on a mix of familiarity, stimulation, firmness and, importantly, in my view, imagination. We adapted, modified and approved our ideas as we went along. It was physically hard work as some of the play equipment was heavy and had to be stored in what was usually an inconvenient place. Try lifting from a height a plastic pit filled to the brim with soft, golden sand – and buried treasure!

Everything had to be put away neatly at the end of each session, too. We hopefully issued a rota of helpful mums at the start of each term, but it was surprising how it always seemed to be the faithful few who kept turning up.

'Most mums,' Sue said, 'open the hall door, shove their children inside and beat a hasty retreat!' They claimed that if they lingered longer, the children just clung tighter. They had a point! However, we didn't really mind. Some of them obviously needed the break.

I will now give you the lowdown on a typical playgroup day! Around this time, I was writing a series of articles on family life, the highs and lows, for *My Weekly* magazine. I've just found a cache of these mags. They read like a diary, in the present tense. I am happy to say that it really was as I recall it now, so I'll continue in the same vein . . .

It's 8.45 a.m. Family has departed, washing-up is done, beds pulled together, dust on the mantelpiece ignored, ditto overflowing wash basket, and I have seen Katy and Maff into school. I have a bagful of playgroup paraphernalia, along with the register and hall key.

At 8.55 a.m. I collect four pints of milk from the hall step and open up. Then Marcia arrives, sensibly attired in her uniform of ancient jeans and baggy jumper which, she proudly informs me, is the only thing she has ever knitted – fifteen years ago, in her teens! She really doesn't look much older than that now, being small and slight, I think. We work very well together. We arrange the tables and chairs around the hall and unroll a large gymnastic mat.

Into the tiny corner of the storeroom we venture at 9.10 a.m. We select the table activities of the day. Whilst Marcia puts out the building bricks, jigsaws, blunt scissors, crayons, paper, old wallpaper pattern books, I arrange the book corner, with little chairs circled invitingly around. Then we mix up plain flour, cooking oil, colouring, salt and water into a lovely pliable lump of play dough.

The first children arrive along with Sue and her own two little ones, at 9.20 a.m. She assembles the slide and small chute, tumbles bricks out onto the mat, spreads a large sheet of plastic to hopefully catch the drips from the painting easels, goes into the kitchen to put on the kettle, sets out the coffee cups and mixes more paint.

We know it's 9.30 a.m. when the door is flung wide, and in they all troop! Sue copes with the register and money. Marcia greets any newcomers and I unbutton coats, stuff gloves into pockets, slip plastic aprons over often-protesting heads and peg up painting paper. One or two mums linger, nostrils twitching at the aroma of coffee.

In the winter, we're in the hall from 9.30 until 10 a.m. but if it's fine, we go outside into the small garden, with the sandpit.

The older, bolder children move from table to table. Ruth is the exception. She concentrates on the jigsaws, sometimes assembling them upside-down, but doesn't socialise with the other children. Toby gets in a sly dig with a pencil at Ben. Ellen gets her long hair tugged.

Rosy, blowing into a mixture of paint and washing-up liquid in a mug through a straw to make bubbles, sucks by mistake and splutters!

The more boisterous children queue impatiently for the chute. This, and the mini-trampoline, need constant supervision. When tears and tantrums develop, I suggest music. Marcia puts her hands over her ears and wears a pained expression. I fetch out the elderly record player, our few records and the musical instruments – some home-made.

We twang an elastic band across an empty tissue box, rub sandpaper blocks together, rattle lentils in a plastic bottle, play a comb-and-paper and bang a sweet-tin drum. After ten minutes of cacophony and dervish-twirling I confiscate the instruments of torture and decide to remove my lot farther down the hall for some play-acting.

Sometimes we go the moon, 'Pull on your boots, zip up your spacesuits, fasten your seat-belts – three, two, one, blast off!' But today we fancy a visit to the old witch of the woods.

'Tie up your horses,' I say, when we've galloped over to the clearing where the old witch is stirring her cauldron and making spells. We stir vigorously, too, and chant, '*Iddy, Oddy, Idey, Og*, let's all become a hopping frog!' We hop about and get into trouble for knocking against Toby's castle of bricks and demolishing it.

'Time to clear up!' Marcia calls. We all stack the table-toys, admire the paintings and lay them out to dry. We always feel sorry when impatient mums can't wait to take home the latest 'Picasso'.

By 10.45 the tables are formed into an L shape. The children drink their milk and munch their biscuits. We sing 'Happy Birthday' to Giles, who is four.

Now for Marcia's speciality. On an easel she has pinned a picture of an old, sad-looking woman, wrapped up in a shawl and wearing a huge apron with a pinned-on pocket. 'What do you think we are going to sing?' she asks brightly.

'There Was an Old Woman Who Swallowed a Fly!' someone shouts and they trot up in turn to deposit the various unlikely objects they sing about into the bulging pocket. Until – 'She's swallowed a horse!' – and Toby shouts in relief, 'She's dead, of course!', because he can't wait for Big Toy Time. Another song follows, this time 'Five Little Spotted Frogs, Sat on a Spotted Log'. It's a great favourite, and we illustrate that too, with a super picture painted by Ginge, as part of her teacher-training course.

It's 11 a.m. now, time for the Special Activity! If a big occasion looms up like Mother's Day, we get out the glue and make sticky cards with coloured paper or tissue, sticking on feathers or pasta. Sometimes, we make something to illustrate a song, perhaps cut out Nelly the Elephant, poke our fingers through the hole in the face, wiggle them for her trunk and then dance and sing around the hall. Or I am asked: 'Please can we have one of your tapes, Sheila?' Several of my short stories for small children are on cassettes produced for playgroups. An added bonus is, I receive free tapes for our own group. Their favourite (and mine!) is *Toffee Cakes on Tuesday*, to which the presenters have added a catchy song. (I sometimes wonder if any of my earlier bedtime stories for the Hull Telephone Company, for which I received 7s. 6d. each, were ever recorded . . .)

However, today we have a Great Activity planned and several mums have been enlisted to help. We're going to record our footprints!

One mum supervises the taking off of socks and shoes while another mum lines up the children. Little ones first, they can't wait . . . In a tray Sue has poured some bright blue paint, Marcia and I unroll a long, long piece of lining paper, Toby's mum is poised with a marking pen, and finally a mum crouches over a bowl of soapy water, with towels nearby.

Tina steps in first. A tiny footprint is recorded. Minnie's next, red-eyed and runny-nosed because she is not No. 1. The line is fairly well-behaved, but there's some shoving from the rear. George dives for the tray of paint, slips up and rolls in it. He's smothered in blue from head to foot. George's mum gathers him up and rushes him to the kitchen sink. The bubbles soon turn blue, and suddenly the fun's gone out of the whole affair. Marcia goes to help. The rest of us send the remaining children smartly through the process, clear up and sigh with relief.

It's now 11.25 a.m. and the hall's cleared. From the grubby recesses beneath the stage, we bring out the big toys. Most children get the car, bike or rocker of their choice, and the milk-float, as usual, is the most popular.

'Three turns round the hall,' we say firmly to Lolly. 'Then give it to Toby.'

Two of us supervise, while the other clears up the kitchen and begins tidying away. The noise level is horrific – but they all look so happy!

Story time follows at 11.45. It's Sue's turn today. Like little angels they sit quietly in a circle, listening. The first mums tiptoe into the hall, and listen, too. The story is an old favourite, all about a giant jam sandwich which captures a plague of wasps. I start to feel hunger pangs. We then button up coats and buttonhole mums.

'Don't forget we're going swimming at the Sports Centre, next Tuesday. We need helpers for the walk to see the lambs the following Tuesday. Yes, I know we have to negotiate that dangerous stretch before we turn up the lane, but we've got a length of rope. What for? Oh, well, you'll see, but it works I assure you! Bye, bye.'

Then it's just us three and it's noon. We sweep up the hall. 'Look at all those cigarette ends,' Marcia says indignantly. 'That's not us,' and 'Ugh! More chewing gum! I had to take some out of Rosy's mouth. She told me she found it stuck to the radiator. The Youth Club make more mess than our little ones do!' 'Did you tell Rosy's mum?' 'Er. No, do you think I should have?' We forget it.

I go home to my bread and cheese. I can't wait for liver and onions. But as I unwind, I think: I had a great day – despite George's slip into the blue!

* * *

Well, Marcia and I continued to enjoy the challenges and catastrophes for over four years, after Sue and her family moved away a year after we set up the playgroup. We had great support from a regular team of mothers, including one mum with a small daughter who was 'doing it all again,' she told us with a smile, as her elder daughter was sixteen and her son a teenager when little Nicola was born. This was June, who has been my dear friend since those days, as you will see from the dedication to this book, and later chapters . . . Time for a new team.

Out of the blue, I was offered a new challenge – you'll hear about that later!

CHAPTER 56

Wedding Bells

There were eleven of us in the minibus, just like old times. Not J.P., as we were joining him in Suffolk, for he and Di were to be married tomorrow, but we had collected his best man, Graham, en route. We travelled on the Friday evening, after work and school. I had to call the boys in from the football field when John said it was time to go. They had their own bags ready packed. I should have checked that Roger had included his new black shoes to go with his best clothes for the wedding. Halfway through the journey he realised that the shoes were still in their box at home, and that he was wearing disreputable old trainers. 'I didn't say anything then, as it was too far to go back,' he confessed on our arrival. We would need to go out early next morning to buy him another pair. We were miles from the nearest town, so had to pin our hopes on the local Co-op.

Some of us were staying with Jonathan in the cottage which went with his job on the dairy farm, but the girls, including Katy, who were to be bridesmaids, together with Di's younger sisters, were staying nearby with the same dear aunt with whom we lived during the war. We had Billow with us. He was our only pet at the moment, as Tiger, our ginger cat, had 'faded away' quietly last summer at fifteen years old.

J.P. and Di had been very busy in their limited off-duty hours – Di was a nursery nurse. They had decorated their Victorian cottage and begun to tackle the wilderness of garden. On the kitchen wall Jonathan had painted his own version of the popular newspaper cartoon, *Love Is* . . . They were our own ideal young couple, we thought fondly, when we saw this tribute to his bride. Di had filled the shelves with pottery – she was already amassing a collection of china cockerels with bright plumage, also cooking pots – even then, she was a splendid cook.

They had big plans for the garden, we just knew that some time soon, a menagerie would appear, just as it had with us, in our orchard days!

Three very important family members would be missing from this happy celebration. John's mother had sadly passed away a year or so back. It was a great loss to us all. I always say I had the perfect mother-in-law. My own father was very frail at almost ninety, and now bedridden following a stroke, and my mum could not leave him. J.P. and Di had decided that their wedding should be on Oz's (that's what I called my dad) birthday in March.

None of us guessed how cold it would be on the east coast, with bitter winds blowing. Di's mum had to rustle up enough jumpers for the girls to wear under their pretty bridesmaids' frocks. Not quite the spring wedding we had visualised.

The boys had spent the night in their sleeping bags in the living room. They went out with J.P. at dawn to watch him milk the cows and to help with the feeding. Matthew and Billow reluctantly stayed indoors with us. The farm chores still had to be done, but J.P. was being allowed the rest of the day off! John cooked bacon and eggs all round. The fire was lit, but it was a dark, dank morning.

After breakfast, John, Matthew and I took a reluctant Roger shopping. The only acceptable (in Roger's eyes) footwear available was a pair of white trainers. Hardly the shoes to wear to a wedding, but preferable to the now muddy ones he had on. We were running short on time, and parted with a fiver for this bargain.

Chris and Michael were actually spruced up by the time we returned to the cottage. Graham had taken them in hand, as Jonathan was nowhere to be seen. He'd been called back to the farm to help deal with an emergency, they told us. We learned later it was a calving.

There was less than an hour to go before the wedding. John and I tried to keep calm, but there wasn't anything we could do, except get changed into our finery. Graham was hovering in the background. Poor chap, I thought; all this family stuff must be a shock to the system.

With half-an-hour to go, we had to leave for the church. We knew that the girls had been fetched earlier from my aunt's and taken to the bride's home. They would be well looked after by Di's lovely mum, Daphne. Graham waited for the bridegroom and promised us they'd arrive at the church before the bride . . . Fortunately, as we settled in the minibus, Jonathan appeared. From the look of him he would need a good bath. Had he got time for that? We waved at him, laughing in relief. 'Good luck – see you in church!' we called, crossing fingers.

All the guests had arrived, despite the weather. We hurried into the little country church tucked away 'in the middle of nowhere', and John and I and Maff were shown to our pew at the front. The organ was playing and the bride would shortly arrive, but there was no sign yet of the bridegroom and the best man . . . I got down on my knees and said a fervent little prayer.

'They're here!' the whisper went round. There was a palpable sigh of general relief. John squeezed my hand, he guessed I had tears in my eyes.

Then I almost had a fit of the giggles, because as our son stood waiting with his back to us, I saw that his wet hair was dripping on his collar. He hadn't had time to dry it.

Heads turned, the organ pealed, and Diane, in a beautiful white gown made by her mother, with auburn ringlets tucked under her veil, came slowly down the aisle on her father's arm, followed by her six bridesmaids in blue. Di was only nineteen, Jonathan was twenty-two, and their faces glowed with happiness. Somehow, we all felt warmer, despite the weather.

Later, after the photographer had done his bit, we all repaired to the village hall and to a veritable feast, crowned by a wonderful wedding cake. I can't tell you what we ate, because the rest of the afternoon seems like a dream. It all went smoothly, despite the early-morning setbacks.

We returned home to Kent that evening. The bridegroom, after Sunday-morning milking, and his bride left to spend their honeymoon in Surrey staying with my parents. Apparently, they took their cases upstairs and changed into their wedding clothes. Mum and Dad were thrilled and touched to see them just as they had looked the day before, and dear Di presented my mother with her wedding bouquet.

At the time of writing this, my mother is 101 years old! J.P. and Di are still very close to her, in fact J.P. visits her every day after work and does her shopping. (She moved back to her native Suffolk after my father died.) They have now been married thirty years – it hardly seems possible!

* * *

A year and a half later, in September, there was another celebration – our Silver Wedding Anniversary! We made the traditional cake and were so excited we found ourselves telling everyone, 'Open House!'

Boffy heard about the party on the grapevine – courtesy of Katy and Matthew. They ran ahead of me as we wended our way home from school each day to hear all the village news before I did. Recently, she'd held out a glass Kilner jar containing some unidentifiable black objects floating in what looked like brine. 'Found this jar lurking in the cupboard under the sink,' she said, 'I thought it was time it was used up. I might have the contents for my supper . . .'

'But, Boffy – what are they?' *Botulism*, I thought.

'Could be tomatoes, could be plums – luck of the draw, m'dear. I just need you to unscrew the top of the jar for me. I asked the man working over the road, but he wouldn't do it.

'Go on, Mum!' chorused my offspring.

Naturally I didn't try very hard, and suggested she dispose of it. A few days later, Boffy told me triumphantly, 'I got it open!'

'You didn't . . .' I asked apprehensively.

'I had them, whatever they were, on toast. Very nice!' Boffy said. (I couldn't resist using this little story, much later in my book *A Winter Hope*, previously *The Family at Number Five*!)

Now, I confirmed that she would be very welcome to pop in like other village friends 'for a piece of cake, and a toast.' The other new friends took us at our word, and did just that; we were pleased to see them, but the chapel was overflowing with our extended family, including uncles, aunts, cousins, some with small children, and our siblings with five nephews, and our niece, Penny, newly married herself. There were old school friends with us, too.

We had a running buffet all day. The boys operated the soft drinks soda stream, wisely hiding Boffy's home-made ginger beer, which Roger had sampled and then exclaimed, '*Poison!*' John sliced a whole large turkey and home-cooked ham. I'd invested in two giant glass bowls for our favourite raspberry trifle. Roger had presented us with a huge silver-coloured teapot, which needed a packet of tea every time we brewed it. We had to buy a display cabinet for all the silver trays, magnificent tea set and other items we were given. Quite a contrast with the twenty-two tablecloths we'd received as wedding gifts, but then times were still austere, ten years after the war.

Mum and Dad were, of course, unable to come, and we planned to visit them shortly and have a mini-celebration with them then. I'm so glad we did, because we lost our wonderful Oz three months later, on Christmas Day.

However, on our anniversary there were several elderly relatives who could not recall meeting each other before. I remember John's Uncle

Tom joining the long queue for the toilet facilities and his cheerful cry of 'Make way for the walking wounded!' And a cousin telling us, 'I have just had a very interesting conversation with your marvellous old aunt – the one in the sunhat – d'you know I couldn't for the life of me remember her name . . .' We saw the lady referred to, holding court in the garden. It was our friend Boffy, dressed up for the occasion in magenta satin with a lace jabot. (I was not quite so grand, but very pleased with the pretty pink frock presented to me by Jo.) Boffy had been among the first arrivals in the morning, and this was late afternoon.

Too soon after our arrival at the chapel, a new estate had sprung up in the wilderness around us, although fortunately for the boys, the playing field remained sacrosanct. Although we missed the daisies and dandelions and the long grass beyond our plot, there was a car park adjacent to the side of our garden, beyond the stout fence we had erected. Chris was now living away from home on his second farm placing before going to agricultural college, and Michael was doing well at his engineering apprenticeship in the nearby town. Both boys had their first small cars, so the car park was good news for them! On this day, visitors from afar were also glad to have somewhere to park off the road. (There's usually a silver lining to a drawback, isn't there?)

It was such a happy day and the chapel was the perfect place for a big party. The last pot of tea was made and dispensed among the remaining guests after the cake had been cut. The crowd thinned out, and the washing up and filling black sacks with paper plates and crumpled paper napkins began. It was getting towards dusk when we decided the garden would have to wait until the morning. We were all ready to fall into bed after a day which had been busy since dawn. Glancing out of the window, I exclaimed: 'Oh, no!'

'What's up?' John asked, yawning. 'You're not going out there again to tidy up. Enough's enough.' He was already in his dressing gown and slippers. The family had all retired to their rooms.

'No, it isn't,' I said faintly, pointing at a shrouded object in the gloom. 'Boffy is asleep in the deckchair – didn't anyone notice?'

'There's going to be a moon,' he said hopefully. 'We put a rug round her knees earlier when it got nippy. Don't you think—'

'No!' I said. I saw he was grinning. He didn't mean it.

'I'll get dressed again, and take her home. You win,' John said.

He guided her gently up the road, opened her door, switched on the lights. 'Goodnight, Boffy. Off to your bed now, eh?'

'It was a lovely party, thank you. You made my day,' she said.

Dear Boffy, you made our day, too, bless you.

CHAPTER 57

No Cup of Tea for Rosy Lee?

A big fete was planned to take place on the village green one August to raise money for the village hall refurbishment and the coming 800th celebration year of our parish church. Representatives of the many village organisations were roped in on the committee. Marcia and I represented the playgroup and John and Bill were involved too. We were a large committee, all eager to contribute ideas, so it was fortunate that Ian, the ever tactful but firm chairman, was in charge.

A fancy-dress parade for the children, suggested Meg. Here, Boffy suggested brightly, 'Couldn't we all be in costume?' It was hastily agreed that this should be optional. The local Music-makers quartet was mooted by Millicent. She was the only female member, and was firmly established as their leader. The village policeman liked the idea of a motor-cycle line-up. (A chance for him to check local lads' machines?) Ian's friend Ben volunteered to run a hot dog stall. That brought the suggestion of a dog show. John and Bill offered to take turns in a dancing bear costume with a hurdy-gurdy. They didn't take into consideration that it might be a hot day and a fur suit could be claustrophobic. Mrs B was, as always, put in charge of the tea tent and cakes. Suddenly, the attention turned to me. 'What about you, Sheila?' was the challenge. A pause, then came inspiration (or was it?). 'I told fortunes once – oh, years ago–' I said. The committee were enthusiastic. I was promised a small tent, a goldfish bowl (empty) as a crystal sphere, and the costume and the spiel were up to me. It was decided, just like that . . .

Katy was really excited when she heard about it. 'Oh, Mum, I'll do your make-up and help you dress up – me and Maff will make you a chart, so you can look up all the signs, Gemini (this was her birth sign) and that.' 'They are all in my comic, this week!' She was right, there was a double-page spread. I also recalled the long-ago summer when my cousin and I found a well-thumbed paperback on palmistry and tea-cup reading, 'for afternoon tea parties', which we pored over for hours, and then practised by 'reading' the palms of willing, or unwilling, relatives and school friends. We both had a talent for telling stories, so no one believed us.

Everyone will know it's me, I thought, and I'll only say nice things. It must be 'just for fun'. (Here I have to admit that a traveller friend once told me I would be famous when I was old, so I've always had hopes, but it ain't happened yet! Well, getting older has, but not worldwide acclaim.)

John and Bill put up the flags around the green. They helped erect the tents. John had made a hurdy-gurdy box with a handle to turn, and concealed a cassette player inside. The tape played real hurdy-gurdy music. The bear costume was very realistic, and yes, stifling to wear. They were both over six feet in height, so with the bear head on top looked even taller. They planned to take half-hour stints inside it. By eleven o'clock in the morning of the Big Day the smell of frying onions from the hot dog stall and drifts of smoke pervaded the village, and sent folk hurrying for the midday opening.

The fete was opened by our very own Beauty Queen, Ian and Judy's gorgeous daughter. There was a rival attraction in the Strong Man, who had once been in Meg's class. He'd developed muscles since then and a crowd of admiring girls soon gathered round him. Meg observed drily in my ear: 'I was stronger than him in those days!'

In the cool, dark interior of my tent, I tried to memorise my astrology. I could hear the music and the laughter and was aware of folk brushing past my tent, and the aroma of onions and hot dogs grew stronger as a breeze wafted these in my direction. For the first half-an-hour I had no customers at all. I considered retrieving the sign, Rosy Lee and her Crystal Ball. Consultations 50p, and amending it to 30p a session.

I hope I looked the part, with my long hair plaited, gold hoop earrings (curtain rings – I don't have pierced ears), a shawl, an embroidered blouse and one of my Indian cotton skirts. Marcia had actually done my make-up as she had a box of greasepaints. I hoped I was unrecognisable, like my husband sweating away in his hired fur costume. He and Bill already had a satisfactory jingling in their collecting box for the day's good cause. The Quartet played valiantly, seated in a circle rather too near the dog show, so had to compete with a chorus of barks. The bobby tut-tutted over the motor cycles and offered advice. Our neighbour had turned up in fancy dress, rather puzzling, for he was wearing swimming trunks and wellington boots, or maybe he was just catering for both sunshine and showers . . .

I was longing for a cup of tea, when the tent flap parted and in came my first customer. I had seen her picture in the paper recently. I knew she had a title, that she had a holiday mansion on the outskirts of the village, but that was all.

She smiled at me. 'Would you like to read my palm?' She held out a beautifully manicured hand, with a diamond ring sparkling above her wedding band. My own hands contrasted with hers. The old palmistry book had the low-down on hand shapes. Mine were not artistic (although I fondly imagined I was) – I was disappointed to discover that I had 'mechanic's hands'. My family would dispute that! The hand I now gazed upon would have fitted the 'lady' category.

Her voice was soft and sweet, with a captivating accent. Her blonde hair gleamed and her face was reflected in my crystal ball.

'You do not come from round here . . .' I began. I knew that much from the article in the paper.

'Ah, you know who I am?' she queried.

'I believe so . . .' The words spilled out from my sub-conscious. 'You were a dancer?' (I certainly had not read that information.) 'Ballet,' I continued.

'Yes, but that was a long time ago,' she said. She sounded sad. 'In my own country.'

She nodded in agreement at every statement I made. 'This is true.'

It was an uncanny experience for me too. She smiled and said, 'Goodbye and thank you.' I had earned my first fifty pence.

I was still bemused when I became aware that there was a long queue outside my tent. They must have been attracted by my first client, certainly not by me! I snapped into action and enjoyed the next couple of hours or so. Giggling girls and red-faced boys, stout matrons and twinkly-eyed grandfathers, including my neighbour, still in his peculiar get-up. The music had ceased: I emerged at last from my tent and discovered that the stall holders were packing up, the crowds going home to tea. 'Sorry, one of the dogs ate the last sausage . . .' Ben said as he dismantled the hot dog stand and scattered a broken bap to the ducks on the pond. The tea urn was likewise empty. 'My dear,' Mrs B said, concerned, 'Didn't anyone bring you a cup of tea?' I shook my head wearily. I looked around for the Russian bear, but he and Bill were counting their takings. Our children had gone home with their older siblings, to feed Billow and to have their own tea. Billow had not been dog show material and had wisely stayed in the chapel.

My friend claimed the crystal ball, and I rolled up the astrology map. You won't be surprised to know I have it still. I handed over my glass jar with the slit in the cover. It was crammed full of silver pieces.

That was the beginning and end of my brief career as Rosy Lee. You see, I couldn't help wondering why it was I had been so accurate in my predictions ... something not to meddle with, as my dear old dad would say. It made me think of a story he'd told me once, and what happened when we delved deeper ...

Dad's mother was the grandma-I-never-knew. I felt I did, because Dad told us so many stories of his unconventional childhood, first on the Isle of Sheppey (his father was in the Navy) and later when his mother ran a theatrical boarding house in Brixton. Oh, those wonderful music hall characters of the late Victorian and Edwardian era! My grandma sighed over moonlight flits by boarders who couldn't pay the rent: some left goods in lieu of this, like a violin, an oil painting, a trunk full of costumes, but she didn't bank on a pair of toddlers left in her care, whom she cared for over many years, until they were grown up. Jane, my dad called his mother fondly. So I felt I knew her, and she is very much part of my first published novel, *Tilly's Family* (now *The Nursemaid's Secret*). I have her household remedies books and recipes from the turn of the last century until the 1930s and they are invaluable when I am writing of that era.

Jane was considered to be 'fey'. She had a Spanish grandmother (like Jane, and Dad, I have inherited her dark eyes and so have five of our children and many of the grandchildren) and the family home had been in Cornwall. Dad had visited there as a boy and remembered it well. When we were in the West Country ourselves, he asked us to find out if the farmhouse was still there. He told me that Jane had experienced a vivid dream once about 'hidden treasure' buried in the garden there, in the eighteenth century, 'near an oak tree, with a rope swing.' He wondered if this had ever been verified ...

Well, we found the farm, and we also discovered that the old churchyard was full of Jane's ancestors, including one with the intriguing Christian name of Arminal! A lovely elderly couple, now retired from farming, told us they had lived there since their marriage. Over cups of tea and hot buttered scones, I mentioned the mystery.

They took us out into the garden. There was the ancient oak, and the now frayed ropes of a long-gone swing. 'Our son was digging here, when his spade struck something hard,' the old farmer told us. 'It was an enormous stone slab and he couldn't shift it. The grass has grown over it since.' He poked about with his stick. 'We heard the rumours, but thought it was best not to try to find out.'

We agreed, but it was uncanny to think we had found the place in Jane's dream. Actually, John probably hit on the truth when he said later to me, 'I think it was actually an ancient cess pit. In that case, who would want to shift that great stone?'

I didn't say, of course, but I believe Jane would have wanted to gaze into the depths, and yes, in a holding-my-breath sort of way, so would I.

CHAPTER 58

'Gorillas', Grapes and a Ticket to Rye

Time for you to meet June! We were in a lush part of the Weald of Kent, overflowing with cherry and apple orchards, hops, and yes, strawberry fields. We were also not far from the coast and quaint little towns like Rye, with its harbour and fascinating shops. This was H.E. Bates country, not too far from where the Larkins had their genesis. H.E. is still one of my favourite authors.

June's youngest, Nicola, called Nik, had just started school, so June and I teamed up for a holiday (or so we thought) in the sun, picking (and eating) strawberries just a lorry ride away from home. We had a lot in common: her elder daughter was an artist, like Sara and Virginia. ('What about us?' the rest of the family might well remind me. They are certainly creative too, as you may have gathered from their proud mum! It's in the genes, as they say.) June's Debbie had already drawn the captivating little bear who featured in the *Forever Friends* cards and spin-off stationery. June loved books, like me – she had worked as a librarian before she married.

Neither of us were natural field workers, but gave our utmost to the cause for little reward. That sounds sanctimonious – sorry! But we did do our best, honestly. June is now an accomplished gardener, while I like looking up from the keyboard and gazing out at the flowers with pleasure, from time to time.

We had what appeared to be an interchangeable wardrobe of ancient trousers, drab anoraks and wellington boots. As we both wore glasses, had fair hair and burned in the sun, we even looked alike. We were not the sort of strawberry pickers who stripped down to bra and shorts, but then none of the team were remotely like that either. There were ancient pickers, surprisingly nimble, and skinny girls who loped along the rows and filled their punnets with the biggest and best fruits. There were young mums who grumbled a lot and took cigarette breaks under the hedge when the farmer wasn't looking. June and I suspected that a couple of these women 'lifted' a tray or two from the piled-up boxes at the end of our rows, while we were toiling at the far end, but we couldn't prove it. The mums also had small children in tow, some still in nappies, not always well behaved, but then they were not allowed to play hide and seek among the rows and were bored. '*Shut up!*' was the clarion call.

The rows of strawberries stretched out of sight and by midday we were down on our knees, crawling in the straw. After the first day, I took a cushion. My knees were flattened and raw. Once or twice we fell among the strawberries and felt like lying there until we were missed a week or so later. It was cooler among the green foliage, though the straw pricked our arms and legs, and we squashed a few berries to the horror of the man sent to see what we were up to. He issued a warning. I actually retaliated with, 'We can't be expected to work in these conditions. The toilet is disgusting.' The shed which seemed to be miles from the field housed a bucket with a plank over it. The man scowled. 'You're not supposed to go there, unless you *have* to,' he said tersely. We were speechless.

We knew the technique, brushing a hand among the leaves, feeling for clusters of fruit; only picking the reddest and mixing small berries with large. Any we 'plugged' – well, we ate the evidence. The problem was, this was a new variety of strawberries, delicious but huge and hard with stalks which we had to wrestle with, between finger and thumb, before they snapped. We were told by one of the overseers that these were 'gorillas'. Well, that's what it sounded like, began with a G anyway. But gorillas they certainly were, and our fingers were really sore by the end of the afternoon. They were stained too, and I had to buy a pair of white gloves to wear to a social occasion at John's head office. Have you ever tried eating 'nibbles' with gloves on?

Things did improve, and so did the weather. We actually made cotton squares into halter-neck sun tops and wore floppy hats like Boffy. We were still glad of something to kneel on, for the straw was harder and more brittle by the day. We felt proud that our strawberries were destined to be eaten at Wimbledon, and we topped each punnet with the biggest and juiciest of all, with perfect green 'caps'. When Sara wrote to tell us that she had spent her birthday queuing for hours with fellow students from the art college to watch the tennis, and that they had a celebration lunch of strawberries and cream, I wondered if they had been 'our' gorillas ... I should have hidden a little note in the punnets, rather as women did who knitted socks for soldiers: 'Picked by Mum x'

We were accepted by the gang, and told that, unofficially, we were allowed to fill our empty lunch boxes with small strawberries to take home for our family. 'But you must only do this in your lunch break, when you aren't paid to pick.' I was very popular at supper time at home. Good old Mum! I did spend much of my earnings on cream from the farm, though. The strange thing is, I had been allergic to strawberries as a child, they brought me out in hives, but eating them fresh like that I was fine. I liked them best without sugar and cream.

I recovered from my initial dismay at the conditions I was working under, though neither June nor I would join the others 'hopping behind the hedge'. We just tried not to think about calls of nature. It was so different from the *Knee Deep in Plums* days when I'd so enjoyed picking strawberries in a small field up the lane, with Katy in her pram under a canopy, and five-year-old Roger filling the trays with punnets for me. I was among friends there and I could pop home when necessary. Here, though, I was doing a real job, I was fitter and tanned at the end of it, and my hair was bleached blonde at the tips. We were also invited to pick the plants clean at the end of the season, for free! Then I was stirring strawberry jam in the pot. A whole army of jars marched along the kitchen shelf, but I knew the family would soon thin out the ranks.

* * *

Later in the year June and I joined the grape pickers. This was a model vineyard, with proper loos and respect for the workers. Lunch breaks were leisurely affairs, because free bottles of wine were dispensed by the owner. As non-imbibers, it amused us to see the soporific effect this had on some of our fellow pickers. We were paid by the hour, so although we worked steadily, there was no sense of urgency.

We moved along the vines, secateurs in hand, and the laden sprays of grapes nestled in the buckets at our feet. Every now and again, a nice man, bent almost double under the weight of a huge bin strapped to his back, paused by each picker to request: 'Would you be kind enough to empty your bucket into the bin? Thank you very much.'

We couldn't eat the grapes because they had been treated with what looked like a fine white powder. We wore gloves so that we didn't come into contact with this. We were shown the various processes, where the grapes were washed and then crushed. June and I wished we could tread them as they used to do in France!

One day a TV camera crew arrived to film us. A single mum who worked with us, was terrified she would be spotted by 'the powers that be'. She lurked in the loos (clean, sparkling and sweet smelling) until the crew had gone. We felt for the poor girl, trying to hush her children.

This really was a break for us, and we thoroughly enjoyed the grape picking. At half-term Katy, Maff and little Nik came along with us, and they had a great time, too. My two played with the small girl on a lovely lush spread of grass under shady trees. Children were welcome here. The vineyard folk were great. Matthew recalls that the youngsters were invited to pick juicy Spartan apples from the trees in the meadow, and take some home, too. Scrumping permitted – wonderful!

Before they went back to school, I had time at home with the children. Roger usually came in for lunch, but today he would be invited into the kitchen of kind Mrs Greengrass, the farmer's wife. She made chocolate cake especially for his elevenses. He had stepped into brother Chris's shoes, well, boots, on a local farm with the intention to follow him in due course to agricultural college.

Katy, Maff and I took the bus along the winding lanes, past oast houses and white boarded cottages, through all the little villages in a roundabout route to Rye. It was a special excursion ticket – we picked up passengers at every stop – and a lovely day out. We came at last to the harbour, where Rye's fleet of fishing boats was moored, bobbing in the sun-dappled water by the Salts, grassland which in times gone by was purposely flooded with sea water, Following evaporation, salt deposits were collected and used in preserving the catches of fish. Time to disembark! We took the short cut into town, mingling with the crowd from the bus, then dispersed in various directions.

Rye is so soaked in history with tales of smugglers, like the Hawkurst Gang who frequented the Mermaid Inn, with loaded pistols at the ready beside their tankards of ale. We toiled up and down the steep cobbled street, peeping in the leaded windows of the inn and looking across to The House Opposite, aptly named, as was The House With a Seat (in the porch), which was next door to The House Without a Seat. The children loved all those names. It was like stepping back into medieval times, we always had an eerie feeling in Mermaid Street.

We couldn't see all the sights on one visit, but we admired the Landgate, the remaining entrance to the town. Our guide book told us that this was built in the fourteenth century and restored and strengthened after the French sacked and burned all the wooden structures in the town in 1377. Rye, we were aware, was one of the Cinque Ports and played a vital role in the defence of the coast from attack by the French. We saw the old grammar school, now a private dwelling, 'It couldn't have had many pupils,' observed Maff. From the outside, it appeared that the rooms inside were tiny.

They were keen to spend their pocket money, so we visited the Rye Pottery. The china was beautiful, but all we could afford was a blue-and-white egg-cup apiece! Another fascinating shop was packed with ephemera. Bags of marbles, amazing working models and old-fashioned toys which we took time to enjoy and select. I bought a clockwork mechanism for a musical box for John, the haunting Harry Lime theme.

We had eaten our packed lunch on the bus (I was as bad as the children) and were feeling thirsty. The restaurants were packed with tourists, so we kept walking. 'Can't see any shops along here,' I began, as Katy suddenly decided to descend a flight of steps towards an open door. 'What are you doing?' I called. Maff was close behind her, but he turned and pointed out a notice, before they disappeared from sight.

ALL FRIENDS WELCOME FOR COFFEE AND CAKES. SAY FAREWELL TO THE OLD DOCTOR.

Oh, no, I thought, they don't mean *us*! I entered the portals. I guessed that this was the waiting room off what had been the doctor's surgery. There were tables and chairs, balloons, and the Guest of Honour, opening his gifts at the top table. My children were already seated, and beckoning to me. 'Come on, Mum, we've told the lady you prefer tea, and that we're not allowed coffee!' No one seemed to mind that we were strangers at the party. The helpers were all smiling. They had made me tea instead of coffee: 'Oh, no trouble, dear!' The cakes were mouth-watering and the children had long glasses of iced lemonade. It was cool in that room and we were grateful for the rest: cobbled streets are hard on the feet.

We slipped away after the speeches, whispered our thanks to the lady in charge, and ran to catch the bus home. Downhill, thank goodness, so we made it just in time.

In a year or two, there was a similar incident far from Kent, but that's another story.

CHAPTER 59

The Bash Street Lot

Our W.I. had long standing links with an East End settlement. Every summer a coach-load of Londoners arrived at the village hall for a summer treat. Our President, Beatrice, referred to them irreverently as The Bash Street Lot. I soon learned why.

Mrs B had organised the meal. We all contributed to this. We lesser mortals made the tables look pretty with starched cloths, paper napkins and vases of flowers. The welcome party waited at the hall gate in the garden. We all had our appointed tasks: loo patrol, not easy, when they all wanted to go at once; seating guests, or offering a glass of sherry. We were also looking forward to the entertainment which Meg and Millicent had arranged. This had been voted on by the committee, of course. On this occasion Millicent was supplanted at the piano by a distinguished-looking man who had a vast repertoire of old-time tunes. We also had a puppeteer as the main attraction. Unfortunately, none of us had seen this chap in action, just been impressed by the fulsome literature sent out by his agent, claiming 'Of TV and radio fame.' Perhaps *radio* was in small letters because how can puppets be presented in that medium? The older ones amongst us had the answer – 'What about Archie Andrews? Peter Brough's naughty schoolboy, was very popular on the wireless in his time. Wasn't he in a programme with Petula Clark?'

After the sherry, lunch was served. It was a cold collation – ham, chicken drumsticks, slices of pork pie, and buttered new potatoes. There were giant bowls of fresh salad, pots of homemade chutney, potato salad and, unfortunately, crisps. Most of the latter crunched noisily underfoot – the hall caretaker would not be amused. There were also baskets of bread rolls. Another mistake.

I was beckoned by a very old man in a Fair Isle pullover. 'Ain't you got no sliced bread, love? 'Ow am I supposed to eat them rolls with no teeth?' An echo of 'no teeth', went round the table. As most appeared to have a full set, false or otherwise, when they arrived, we guessed that dentures were now in pockets or handbags, wrapped in the dainty paper napkins we'd provided.

'I came prepared,' Mrs B said calmly, when flustered, I ran to her kitchen for help. 'Just in case they wanted sandwiches for tea.' She produced a *Mace* cut loaf from under the counter. By the time I got back to my waitress duty, the bread rolls were doing just that, being rolled across the table by several of the Bash Street 'Boys', Also, the little dishes of butter were empty – applied to the already glistening potatoes, or eaten with a spoon, I suspected. Back I ran to the kitchen for the Flora, which had been intended for the sandwiches. They dug enthusiastically with their dinner knives into the big tub of margarine.

'It'll just be strawberries and cream for tea,' Mrs B warned us. 'They had the fairy cakes with the sherry, said they left home before breakfast. That sherry is responsible for the boys. Beer would have been better.'

The Bash Street 'Girls', in their best frocks, with newly set hair, were merely flushed from the sherry, and very appreciative of all our efforts. 'Lovely ham, dearie. You done us proud. Sorry about the lads – can't take 'em anywhere, eh? Worse'n kids!'

The pianist had been playing gentle background music all through the lunch hour, and I recall his pleasant tenor voice singing: 'I'll be seeing you, in all the old familiar places . . .' All the chairs were now assembled at the other end of the hall, so that he could continue to entertain the visitors while we dealt with the mess left behind on top of and under the tables and 'cleared the decks' for the puppet show.

I have to commend the Bash Street Girls again; they chattered a lot, but they didn't get up to mischief like the Boys. They sang along to all the tunes. They put their teeth back in, too. The boys were restless, and then one called out "Ow about requests?'

The pianist looked apprehensive. 'By all means.' He had discarded his dinner jacket, and poor chap, his shirt was damp with sweat. Rivulets ran down his cheeks from his forehead, as he couldn't pause to mop his head with his handkerchief.

There followed the most ribald songs I had ever not heard, if that makes sense. Most of the W.I. retreated to the kitchen, where we fell about laughing. There were one or two murmurs of 'disgusting', but I saw that Boffy was tapping her stick in time.

Our pianist called it a day and departed. The puppets, I'm sorry to say, were just as naughty as the Bash Street males. We didn't know what to do, except smile weakly, and pray it would not be a long ordeal. It was a very saucy show indeed. The entertainer retorted later, when we told him off, 'I only gave them what they expected. They loved it.' Well, we had no answer to that.

They grumbled about the strawberries. 'We had 'em yesterday, on another outing. We're not supposed to have real cream, clogs you up.' We looked at each other. What about all that farm butter?

'Hurry up with the teapot, Missus,' they called to Mrs B. 'We're going on somewhere else after this, for a fish and chip supper!' First there were long queues for the loos . . . tea is obviously unwise immediately before a journey.

That was the last straw. Meg had a suggestion. 'Next year, let's have the disabled youngsters from my nephew's special school here for a day – we can take them to the farm, visit the donkey sanctuary maybe, play games and have a picnic – what d'you say?'

We said, '*Yes!*'

* * *

The W.I. accounted for most of my social life in those days. Every one of those ladies was special in their own way. They were all my friends, I can't mention them every one by name, but I specially appreciated Boffy, Meg, Millicent, Judy, Eileen from the Mill Cottage (more of her later!) and a newer member Pam, who had moved next door to Beatrice.

Pam was now treasurer (she would later become secretary) of the W.I. We had a special bond because Pam as a toddler had been trapped in her pram by a runaway lorry which had mounted the pavement. Fortunately, Pam had no personal recollection of this event, but it had blighted her mother's life. She had been overprotective of her only child. Pam's father (she obviously inherited her sense of humour and fun from him) was a naval captain. Pam had cared for both parents in their nineties, and had to wait to marry until she was in her mid-thirties. She brewed what she called 'naval tea' – very dark and strong – for her friends, and we listened entranced to her stories of being a magician's assistant and 'sawn in half' on occasion at Toc H shows.

A talking point in Pam's house was a wonderful carved ebony statuette on the banister of the stairs which went up from the hall. This had been fashioned by her father while on a long voyage and presented to her mother. It was a magnificent specimen of a male nude. The captain had been forced by his shocked wife to provide his work with a loin cloth.

The captain had also made a chiming clock, which chimed off-key, part of its charm. His ceremonial sword was fixed to the wall, and was the first thing you saw when you entered the house. Pam's husband had a similar dry humour to his late father-in-law. Pam was a feisty lady and she and her beloved often had spirited discussions, but they were a really devoted couple. Sadly, she was widowed just a few years after they had set up home for the first time on their own. They had no family so generously asked Boffy to join them every Christmas, as she had no close family either. Later, Pam herself was 'adopted' by a neighbouring young couple. They look after her to this day, now she is very frail. Hilary, whom Pam looks on as a daughter, told me that Pam, who has suffered a stroke and is in a nursing home, said one day, 'I wish I could manage to visit my dear friend Sheila . . .' I was very touched by that.

W.I. members volunteered to give the vote of thanks to the speaker. One memorable occasion was when Boffy decided she had a very special reason to do so. Our speaker had been with the Metropolitan Police before retiring to this area. He told of us his London beat when he was a young bobby and of Lord Mayors' processions and Royal occasions. Boffy was obviously eager to say something at the end. After all, she had been a courier on a tourist bus in London after she retired from her high-powered job doing the same, only abroad. She'd talked to the group about those days.

Question time, and this proved very lively. Then Boffy rose and addressed the speaker in her carrying voice. 'I imagine,' she said, 'this is the first time you have received a vote of thanks from the daughter of a woman who went to prison for assaulting a police officer. She knocked off his helmet with this' – she brandished her stick.

'Er, no,' muttered the ex-policeman. The stick was waved in his direction, and he shifted his position, for he was within striking distance.

To our relief, Boffy continued: 'My mother was of course a suffragette. She was on hunger strike in Holloway and force fed. Unfortunately, I was only a child and couldn't join her, but my sister did. I am very proud of them both.'

'So you should be,' the speaker said fervently. He looked at his watch. 'Would you excuse me – I promised my wife I would be back home by ten. You have been a lovely audience. Thank you.'

The applause was deafening, very gratifying for the speaker, but it was also meant for dear Boffy.

CHAPTER 60

On the Leslie 'Gateau' Trail

The year 1980 was a great one – our first grandchild was born in March, a little red-haired boy, named Matthew after his youthful uncle, so, naturally he was soon known as 'Little Maff'. We visited J.P. and Di in their new home near Banbury, where J.P. was stockman on a dairy farm. We were all thrilled to bits with the new member of the family. He slept in a rocking cradle which had been used by generations of our family. They also had two dogs by now, an Old English named Elsa and a collie cross Lab, Leo, both very good with the baby. Di and J.P.'s favourite film was, of course, *Born Free*.

This was also the year I became a Romantic Novelist! I was a runner-up in a short story competition, *Friday's Child* was published and I earned the grand sum of £10! I continued with my family anecdotes in magazines, and children's stories, but soon I was writing regularly for *Woman's Realm* – a magazine full of super stories each week – I was thrilled to be among their authors! It was the *Realm*'s fiction editor who urged me to write my first novel: that one was seven years in gestation, but the books have flowed, one a year ever since . . .

Ginge was in her last year at college and itching to see more of the world like her elder sisters, both of whom were already seasoned travellers. The previous summer, Jo went to Israel to work as an au pair for a few months, and, later, to a kibbutz. She travelled on her own, which worried us, but she proved up to the challenge. However, we were very thankful when Nigel (soon to be her husband) joined her there, and brought her safely home, just in time to help us celebrate our Silver Wedding. Sara's watercolours were a map of her artistic ventures far afield, too, but she always travelled with a group of friends. When she brought any of these fellow students home, Katy and Maff always seemed to have fits of the giggles as they listened in to earnest conversations, and had to reprimanded. Sara said crossly: 'Mum, they are – *gooseberries!*' Though Jo found Katy useful in pulling off her tight boots, even if the poor child was propelled backwards across the room clutching the boot, and red-faced from the exertion.

This summer, Jo, who had been temping meanwhile, and living at home, was off again to work on a summer camp in the States!

The boys had already been on holiday, camping in Wales, cheerfully pushing the old banger (the one which was passed down the line for several years, and changed colour frequently) up every minor hill they came to. John and I were missing the earlier family camping trips we had so enjoyed, forgetting all the drawbacks of thistle-thick fields and sheer cliff tops, cold showers, getting bogged down in foulsmelling ditches and shivering in the early-morning dew; mislaying the pegs so that the tent had 'lift off' in a bitter wind. We recalled lovely sunny days, the smell of bacon and eggs as John stood over the little cooker in the back of the minibus.

'Let's have an adventure,' John said. 'You, me and the young ones. We'll look out for a second-hand caravan and go to Scotland – to where I was as a boy during the war.'

We were enthusiastic, having been enthralled by all his stories over the years, especially those about his friend Leslie Catto – a name converted to 'Gateau', by the children – whom he hoped to see again.

We acquired a Sprite four-berth caravan, a veteran it's true, but just what we were looking for – still sound, and although basic inside compared with today's splendid mobile homes, comfortable. We could tell it had been well looked-after by previous owners. We enjoyed buying pots and pans, gas cylinders, a hammock bed for Maff to go over Katy's single bunk, a Portaloo with a large container of 'blue', a water carrier and new sleeping bags. We added a battery radio and serviced the fridge. John fitted a tow bar to the car. He had a practice run or two; we planned our trip to take in places of interest and were ready to go the last week in August. Ginge would be home to oversee the boys and look after Billow. The latter, of course, was a doddle compared to the former! Though, Michael and Roger had their bantams to see to.

Katy and Maff were just the right age for this venture; she would be off to the comprehensive school in September. She was now an enthusiastic Girl Guide, although as she was so petite she wore her blue blouse as a dress, with a belt round it, and didn't need a skirt! She could have tucked her long golden hair in the belt, we said. Maff, now boyishly short-haired but still with the white flash on his crown, which had given him the alternative family name of 'Plume', didn't take to the Scouts, unlike his brothers before him – Jonathan had difficulty at the end to find a spare inch of shirt to sew on all his badges! But both Maff and Katy loved the outdoor life. They explored all the country lanes round us. Katy was small and light enough to ride a friend's Shetland pony but Maff cycled alongside her, to make sure she was safe. He is still a very caring chap. His main hobby then was his two pet goats, which he kept in a local field. We benefited from the milking later – except for the time they unwisely ingested bulrushes . . .

As in the past, we couldn't wait until the Saturday morning to set off on our epic journey. We left on the Friday, early evening, planning to make our first stop before dark. We didn't reach a camping site before dusk. After we came off the motorway, we made for a service station on the outskirts of Birmingham, only to find the car park too full to accommodate the caravan, so we had no alternative but to spend the night in the lorry park! It was quite unnerving, parked in the midst of all those giant articulated vehicles.

We lit the gas lamps in the caravan. Pulled the curtains. At least we had plenty of food and water, and, most importantly, a loo in a cubbyhole. The kettle hissed on the little stove and I asked Katy to pass the teapot.

'You forgot to bring it Mum!' she told me.

'You know I can't stand teabags,' John said unreasonably.

I thought it wise not to admit I hadn't any loose-leaf tea either . . .

I'll draw a veil over the roar of engines and loud voices, as lorries departed before dawn. We were on our way too, as soon as it was light, after I dunked the tea bags in mugs, but no one said a word.

I'm a bad traveller, though unfortunately for John I can sleep when I should be navigating, though this annoying habit of mine can be a boon. It's a relief if I can manage to snooze away many miles of motorway, but I do endeavour to keep awake along the scenic routes.

'Thank goodness!' John said, with feeling, after we'd driven through the Cheviots, and I perked up, eyes open at last, feeling thoroughly refreshed. 'We've been on a regular switchback ride – I thought the caravan would jack-knife! "Don't you two dare wake Mum!" I said.'

* * *

The second afternoon we arrived at Loch Ness. It was a gloomy spot, with looming trees, unexpectedly deserted. While I rustled up refreshments, the children amused themselves and let off steam by rolling and whooping down a grassy bank. 'You'll frighten the sheep,' John said. The sheep were significant, as you will see, later. We made up our minds to travel on to a camping site a few miles on. Both Katy and I felt too nervous to stay where we were, in case the monster reared its ugly head. I don't think that Maff and John were too keen either, other-wise why didn't they try to persuade us to stay there?

The camp site was a very superior one, expensive too, owned by a Lord, no less. There were rules and regulations and we were chided for not belonging to the Caravan Club. (We joined the next season.) Here John ran the car battery flat by connecting the radio. While he charged the battery, we enjoyed the luxury of hot showers, despite the warning: YOU WILL BE PROSECUTED IF YOU STEAL THE TOWELS.

I privately thought you wouldn't be tempted to do any such thing, because the towels were worn and skimpy. We were still damp and needed to struggle back into our clothes.

This was a working farm, and we enjoyed fresh milk and eggs from the little shop. Top prices. Aristocratic hens and cows, we decided.

On we travelled, and at last reached our destination. John's war-time journey as a small boy with his family by train had been very different to ours. They had boarded the train during an air-raid at King's Cross. Stirred by the story, I later wrote *The Spirit of Millie Mae*, which was retitled as *The Girl by the Sea*. I will let you into a secret . . . the young boy in my book, Barney Rainbow, is based on the character of John, and the setting in Scotland is the very same fishing village.

We had driven along the coastal road with tantalising glimpses of the glistening sea and stretches of silvery sand below towering cliffs. The old railway track for local freight which John remembered had gone: in its place was a small private caravan park. It was just a few steps over a track to the beach, a perfect site for a holiday.

The next morning we were impatient to climb the steep street with grey stone and slate cottages which overlooked the harbour, to find the place where John and his sisters and his parents had stayed during the middle years of the war. John's dad was a contracts manager for the building of new runways at the aerodrome at Lossiemouth, and where he went, so did his family. His two older sisters had just left school and secretarial college and took jobs in Elgin, the nearest town. John and his younger sister Pam went to the local school and endured some tough times. There were a couple of other boys who were not local so they stuck together and stood up to the real bullies. The head teacher was very stern and the tawse, a strap, was often employed for minor misdemeanours.

John sniffed the air: 'There was always an all-pervading smell of fish soup then – our landlady cooked fish for us most days! I used to go with the local boys in the late afternoon and watch the fishermen sorting their catch. All the children except for my friend Leslie, the Minister's son, spoke Gaelic when out of school. We stood back from the crowd, not fitting in.' He conjured up for us the black-clad women, knitting busily with one hand, with the second needle thrust in their belts, as the fishermen threw the undersized cod and herring to the boys. The test was to see which one could achieve the longest string of tiny silver fish, as the lads threaded them through the gills.

'I learned how to prepare them for my mum, by watching the younger women gutting them with their sharp knives, quick as lightning, they were. As their fingers were all scaley and fishy, they only ate the middle of their jam sandwiches.'

'Is that all they had?' asked Katy in disbelief: '*Jam* in their sandwiches?'

'Yes, so did *we* often during the war!' John and I agreed.

We went downhill to the harbour but there were no fishermen or boats to be seen, nor young lassies gutting fish. The smoking huts were deserted. The rainbow-hued combinations, all-in-one undergarments, knitted by the grannies from scraps of wool, which kept their men folk warm in bad weather, no longer fluttered on the washing lines. That was a disappointment, too.

However, it was still a fascinating place. The soft sand stretched for miles. Cormorants zoomed low over our heads as we walked along, and pigeons and herring gulls chattered and swore in the clefts in the sandstone rocks. The children paused at the rock pools, exclaiming over the hermit crabs in their protective whelk shells which disappeared under the trails of glossy green seaweed. We came at last to the blow-hole, a huge rock with a hole in the centre. The sea rushed furiously at the rock, just as John had said it would; the spray smacked our faces as we stood gazing at the spectacle while the water burst through the blow-hole with a roar like thunder. It was awesome and exhilarating.

There was a bakery where we purchased soft baps and lardy cakes for our daily picnics. We were on the Leslie Gateau trail, and he was very elusive. The assistant in the shop remembered his family. 'Aye, they moved on when the Minister retired. I heard they went to Edinburgh . . . Young Leslie became a doctor, they say.'

We needed to adjust our mental picture of Young Leslie. John's memory was of a lively boy, the youngest of four brothers, who'd told his friend, 'If you have a good wash at nights, you don't need to bother in the mornings!' (John's mum didn't agree with this theory!) They'd had great fun cycling in and out of a box-hedge maze in the manse garden. We all wanted to meet Leslie, but Edinburgh ... the festival was on, and it seemed impossible. I think I must tell you now, that we haven't found him yet. Does anyone out there know Leslie *Catto*?

* * *

It was lovely weather, and one day, when Katy was wearing a brief sun top, Maff observed: 'You've grown a jelly mole on your back, Kate!' She tried to see it, but couldn't and I was called to give an opinion on this phenomenon. 'Ugh!' I cried. 'You've got a horrible *tick* on you!' We'd had to deal with these on Billow before now. John said she must have got it when she rolled downhill among the sheep at Loch Ness.

The nearest doctor, we were told, was at the next village along the coast. We drove over there immediately. A friendly local directed us to the surgery: 'The house behind the yellow car, see?'

The door was open, and Katy and I ventured shyly inside. The waiting room was an ordinary sitting room and there was only one elderly lady in a wheelchair waiting her turn. We sat down beside her, and she seemed pleased to see us and talked a lot, although we couldn't understand everything she said. Half-an-hour went by, then I asked her: 'Isn't the doctor here yet?'

Our companion laughed. 'Oh, this isn't the doctor's house. That's two doors further up! This is my house, but I'm glad to have met you.'

We hurried along to the surgery. Another open door into a sitting room. It was full of patients, who stared at us then ignored us. I heard one say to another, 'Tis the visitors that gave us this terrible cough ...' We kept quiet in case they pointed an accusing finger. Prominent in the room was a piano. There was a large notice propped on top. It read: WILL PATIENTS KINDLY REFRAIN FROM PLAYING THE PIANO.

'Oh blow!' whispered a disappointed voice in my ear.

'Shush!' I warned young Katy.

When it was our turn, she jumped up on the couch, still wearing her little red wellies, which she said were a protection against jelly fish when paddling. The young bearded doctor was a ringer for Doctor Finlay (as in his casebook) and just as charming. He tweezed out the horrible tick while telling us a lighted cigarette was quicker, while not recommended. Relieved of the jelly mole, Katy danced out of the surgery, all smiles.

Maff and John wanted to know where on earth we had been. This was a wonderful holiday and we enjoyed almost every moment (except for the tick, of course). On our way home we went to the airport to collect Jo, and heard of her travels on the Greyhound buses.

CHAPTER 61

A Family Crisis, Followed by
Two Summer Weddings

The late-night phone call from J.P. had us reeling with shock: our dear little grandson was critically ill in hospital. He'd seemed off-colour, that was all, but after Jonathan had gone to work that morning, the baby had turned blue and become unconscious. A neighbour summoned an ambulance and Di went with him to the hospital – neither of them would return home for several weeks. Young Matthew was not yet two years old, and Di was pregnant with their second baby.

An emergency operation revealed that from birth one of his kidneys had been unable to function properly because of stenosis; the baby had been poisoned by the build-up of toxins unable to escape in the normal way. It really was touch-and-go, and the little boy was in intensive care for some time.

* * *

At last we had good news – they were coming home! We drove the long miles between us to see them reunited. That small chap was actually bouncing about and laughing when we walked into their living room, but I shall never forget poor Di's pale, wan face and her obvious exhaustion.

Throughout his childhood, young Matthew was often in hospital, for smaller operations, but has always been serene and positive. He is in his twenties now and keeps fit and healthy, enjoying rock-climbing, so there was a happy outcome. He has always been studious, and deserves the success he enjoys in his working life. We salute you, Matt!

* * *

Two weddings, two weeks apart – we took it in our stride! Two wedding cakes, one with yellow ribbons, the other with pink. The first to be married were Ginge and Allen. She had been working in Denmark for a year, caring for a small boy – this was after a short period as one of a team of carers for quins born in Kent! She'd met Allen at college, and he was already teaching. The children in his class called him McEnroe, because of his similar hairstyle – however, he had – has – a sunny laid-back temperament, and plays drums in a local band! As for sport, one of his wry stories was of being a marshal in a cross-country race and somehow directing the runners in the wrong direction! Well, he was engrossed in a book at the time, was his excuse.

Their reception was held in the half-acre garden at Allen's parents' house in a village near Sittingbourne. We helped to clean an old barn and set up trestles for the wedding breakfast. John and Jack, Allen's dad, donned striped aprons and carved turkey and ham with aplomb. It was a beautiful day, we sat in the garden soaking up the sun and even cut the cake out there. It was all very relaxed and it was definitely an occasion to store in the memory.

Sara fashioned beautiful fragrant bouquets for her sisters, to match their dresses, in turn. She picked the flowers from Allen's parents' garden for Virginia, who wore a floaty, Indian cotton frock in pinks and purples: with her long, dark hair and sandals she was the perfect outdoors bride. Allen, who is not one for suits, but feels (and looks) right in comfortable casual clothes, borrowed a grey suit from his dad! Young relatives, including little Maff, climbed trees and older ones relaxed – we still had speeches and toasts to bride and groom, but the informality of it all was great.

Katy was bridesmaid, and repeated her role a fortnight later for Jo and Nigel, who were married in our local church. They had been sweethearts since they met in the heatwave summer of 1976. Jo wore a jade green silk dress, and in the centre of her posy was a perfect peach-coloured rose from the chapel garden. This has been known as Joanna's rose, ever since.

Michael, being the proud owner of a new white mini, provided the wedding car for the bride, his little sister and their father. It was a ten-minute walk to the church, so most of the other guests went ahead, to join the groom and the best man. Nigel's mum, Mary, and I thought we were being collected later, but as time went on, we decided we'd have to make a run for it to be there on time! We needed to be speedy, for it had begun to rain. Panting, we arrived, just before the bride, who had been touring round until everyone was safety in the church! I guess we looked a bit bedraggled, but then, all eyes were on the bride!

It was unexpected when our dear Jo walked down the aisle to the strains of 'All Things Bright and Beautiful' – difficult to match your steps to, as she said later, but it was her favourite hymn. Katy, naturally, skipped behind the bride and her father.

This time there was a thunderstorm and there was a power cut, so the organ ceased in our mid-hymn singing. We rushed back to our chapel for the party, where John, thinking everyone would need a cup of tea, brewed it in the caravan in the drive! He remarked ruefully, 'I didn't think about the wine glasses lined up at the ready!' He was soon busy carving yet another turkey and ham, and I put out proudly the big bowls of special trifle, just as I had on our Silver Wedding Day.

Another very happy time, with extended family and old friends congratulating the newlyweds. Both girls had requested simple, family weddings, and were very contented with their lot.

* * *

Following the weddings, we had visitors from America. Mollie and Laurance were cousins of my mother. Mollie's father had emigrated to Canada in 1910 to a place called Moose Jaw. Mollie's mother sang in the church choir (she was from Lancashire) and they met and married there. He built his own wooden house; he'd trained as a carpenter on a big estate in Suffolk. Times were tough, conditions primitive, but the pioneers thrived, as their family grew. Eventually they moved on to North Dakota, where Great Uncle Joe became a wealthy man.

We had already met Mollie's lively sister Jean a year before, when she embarked on a whirlwind tour of 'the old country.' She and Katy immediately bonded, as they were alike in many ways – small, and live wires! Jean had obviously been the Katy of her day! Maff and Katy stuck to Jean like glue, and reported to us: 'Jean has what she calls a *bosom buddy* – it's her wallet and she buttons it up inside the front of her blouse!' I can picture them giggling when Jean, who had unwisely taken them shopping, had to unbutton herself to extract a traveller's cheque! We took Jean to Ellen Terry's cottage, at Smallhythe Place, and she couldn't resist touching things, which alarmed the custodian. 'Just think, the great actress must have loved this – or that—' she cried, in her excitement. I almost felt like pretending I wasn't with her and my children!

Mollie was tall and beautiful, and much quieter. Laurance was the ebullient one of the two. They were over here for a year, renting a tiny cottage at Sevenoaks. They were recently retired from teaching English and music. Both had lovely singing voices.

That year, during Christmas week, we invited them to join us at our local church to listen to the Canterbury Singers who were in concert there. It was a chilly evening, but we wrapped up warmly and stepped out smartly together to the church. Bells rang to welcome us inside. Latecomers reported, 'It's beginning to snow!' We sang all the lovely old carols, and enjoyed the anthems by the visiting singers. John's cousin was among them. There was a bird fluttering above the choir's heads, disturbing their concentration. The verger attempted to prop open an overhead window to allow the bird to escape. What happened next was that snow poured in through the window, which the verger was unable to close, and cascaded down the necks of the unfortunate singers. To their credit, apart from the initial gasps of surprise, they carried on with their repertoire. In the front pews, we were now all shivering with cold, too.

However, when we came out of the church and found a white world, it just added to a magical evening. We linked arms and trudged back to the chapel singing: 'Show me the way to go home . . .' Our relatives were worried about driving back to Sevenoaks in a snowstorm, so we set to, to make up spare beds and moved family around.

Mollie often reminded me of that happy evening, and the giant dish of macaroni cheese we conjured up for supper, followed by a large treacle tart! Simple things taste good at such times, don't they?

During the Christmas break, Katy and Maff went to stay with them for a few days – again it snowed, and they had to journey home by train. We didn't worry, because dear Maff was so sensible and looked after his big (little) sister . . . Katy came home in a new warm dress, run up from a tartan curtain by clever Mollie – well, she was the daughter of a pioneer! She'd learned to sew as a child when her mother boiled up sugar sacks and Mollie joined a group of churchwomen who made (beautifully embroidered) muslin nightgowns for babies, pillowcases, and other useful items. Jean was given a pair of tea towels when she married Del sixty years ago, which she treasures in her memory box.

Each December, we festoon our tree with white frosted lights which Mollie and Laurance brought with them from America and then gave to us, when they returned home. They both passed away recently, but my book, *The Watercress Girls*, later retitled *The Meadow Girls*, was inspired by the five Mackley girls, as they were known, and I'm glad Mollie knew I had written 'their story'. Jean, the younger sister, helped greatly with the research of this novel.

CHAPTER 62

Well, There's Kids – and Kids . . .

'Would you come and help with reading at school?' Meg asked me. I guess she thought it was about time I had a new challenge. I'm not sure she approved of me typing furiously away at my stories on the dining-room table. That was too introspective in her view.

So I spent afternoons with Meg's juniors and it took me back to when I was ten years old and along with a couple of other children was given the task of coaching slow-readers for the term before they went to secondary school. Only recently, my old friend Anne, who had been a fellow pupil-teacher, told me of the shock she'd felt when she learned that the boy she had helped was killed when a flying-bomb hit his house. She never spoke of it, at the time.

The books were more lively and entertaining than they had been then. It was good to see the children growing in confidence, and fluent in reading aloud.

There was a new headmaster, and one day he had a request, too. Would I read to a group of children in his study for an hour on Friday afternoons? These were children who often disrupted the quiet reading sessions which all the teachers took in turn; they fidgeted and annoyed the better behaved. This was a challenge indeed! Was I up to it?

I sat within the circle of nine- and ten-year-olds, more boys than girls, and opened the Puffin book with some trepidation. One of the girls was shifting about in her seat, and held out her hand. 'Look Miss, I got an engagement ring in Play today. D'you think he got it out of a cracker?'

'Very nice,' I said lamely, ignoring the question, in case the boy concerned was offended. Then I took a deep breath and began reading that wonderful children's classic, *The Silver Sword* by Ian Serraillier. It was a book which Virginia, I recalled, had loved at this age. But these were not avid readers, they were restless, they would rather be outside, kicking a football around. This was the story of three young Polish children, two sisters and a brother, refugees during WW2, who travel across Europe to find their missing father. He has escaped from prison and made his way back, to find his home in Warsaw in ruins and his children gone. Jan, an orphaned lad, befriends the family and this resourceful boy helps them to survive and to be reunited eventually with their father.

I read on and on, as absorbed in the story as the children. They sat quiet as mice, and listened. I didn't hear the bell announcing time to go home, neither did they. Had I really been reading aloud for an hour?

The headmaster looked in at us. He smiled. 'Did you enjoy the story, children?'

A concerted chorus of 'Yes, Sir!'

They were not the only ones who went home with their head in the clouds.

Some time later, there was a vacancy for a dinner lady, and I was asked to apply for the job. Matt (he preferred that now to Maff) had joined Kate (she preferred that to Katy) at the senior school, and told me the school dinners at the old school were great – and that convinced me! A free dinner was part of the deal. The hours were from 11 a.m. until 2 p.m. – we had our lunch, served the children, then went into the school field or playground to supervise them, while the teachers had a well-earned break. After a few months, another helper and myself were asked to be classroom assistants for an hour in the afternoons, which we both enjoyed. The meals were indeed very good, for the school cook was the daughter of a London chef who had taught her to cook when she was young.

I am now going to dip into *My Weekly* magazine again to catch the flavour of what happened one day while I was at the school 'on field duty'. The article was entitled, 'I'm Frightened to Guess Who's Coming to Dinner!' The magazine commented: 'There's something different served up every day . . .' True words, indeed. They were written in the present tense, and do you know, it still feels like that, all these years later!

As I turn the corner and hurry down Church hill towards our little Victorian village school, my mouth begins to water.

To me, who so dreaded school dinners as a child, the aromas wafting from the kitchen are heavenly. I remember, with a little shiver, those loathsome, dark green greens and the Terrible Twins who would 'oblige' – for a price – with my pud! We had ledges beneath our trestle tables where lurked little paper bags, grease spotted with gristle, waiting to be furtively removed and planted in the school garden. We were 'digging for victory' then, and I suspect the teachers added their contributions, too!

'Hello, Sheila,' says Clare, our cheerful cook. She has performed wonders with the temperamental old cooker as usual and when we've got the kettle on, filled the water jugs and set the trolley, we sit down to our lunch at 11.30 a.m.

Zoe, my fellow dinner lady, takes a peek at the sweets. Whatever shall we have? Every day there's something tempting – and often celebratory. The whole school clapped the Easter gateaux!

'I've made some meringue nests – they freeze well, Clare tells us. I'll fill them with fresh strawberries, do you think the children will approve?'

'Oh yes, and so will we!'

Health-conscious parents need not worry now. School dinners are delicious, nutritious and well balanced. Clare uses wholemeal flour and not too much fat. Fresh fruit and crisp salads figure prominently in the menus.

Replete, Zoe and I trundle the trolleys into the adjoining hall. This lofty, once grim and depressing room has been transformed by the energetic staff with the help of parents. White walls and lipstick-red paintwork are embellished with the children's colourful and imaginative paintings and poems. We move in smart rhythm down the length of the hall, clattering knives and forks into position, placing water jugs, salt and pepper pots, plastic beakers and chairs for the staff.

As Clare unplugs the heated trolley in the kitchen, the first children come eagerly in.

'What's for lunch today?'

To me: 'I like your shoes – the man who lives in our house has got a pair the same!' (Dubious compliment, don't you agree?)

'Tell him off! He pulled my jumper!'

'Did you watch the horror film last night?' No, I was in bed asleep!

'My mum had a new baby in the middle of the night. When I woke up my granny was there and she told me.'

'I got two house-points for my story – look, it's on the wall.'

'I put a sheep's skull on the nature table. My teacher was very surprised.' (I bet she was.)

'I don't want any dinner – sniff! I've got a tummy-ache.'

'Look at my fingers! My brother done it.' (Pulls back plaster to reveal miniscule injury.)

The children settle down, and hands are demurely folded, eyes downcast (except for Terry's) as the teacher on duty leads The Grace.

Today it's my turn to help dish-up. Zoe pours water, cuts up the little ones' food, listens to the latest news, and keeps an eye generally on the children.

Normal – Medium – Spot are the menu sizes, but now and again, a large, hungry child will request, 'Gigantic, please!' or a nervous newcomer will whisper, 'Do I have to have any?' We encourage them to 'have just a little', which is invariably tried and eaten. Soon hands are shooting up eagerly for seconds. The 'Custard King' has been known to consume four platesful!

Zoe is first out in the playground with the children. In winter we feel restricted as balls whizz around our heads, marbles are disputed and every tumble necessitates first-aid.

Boys disappear round the shed, crawl under the mobile classroom, climb on to the oil-tank wall. Girls tend to creep back indoors to lurk in the toilets, or join forces with those legitimately pasting and cutting for the babies' class.

There is the occasional joy of snowballs – provided you've brought your wellies – but how we long for the weather to improve so we can have a Field Day!

The large school field rolls and rollicks downhill and the views of farmland, trees and church are magnificent. The football pitch and running tracks are marked in the spring and our teams soon become used to the vagaries of the turf.

Today, cartwheels, handstands and headstands are practised on the springy grass. Little boys make clouds of dust fly in the ditches as they zoom their model cars, and Zoe and I are soon clutching bunches of daisies and clover. Our pockets bulge with discarded recorders and dolls as we keep a watchful eye on the far corners.

A cluster of boys looks suspicious. I wander down to take a look. Do they, like me at that age, have secret bags of food to dispose of?

'Watch out! He'll bite you!' I hear.

I quicken my pace. Little Jenny had mentioned a snake to us yesterday. Probably a worm, we'd thought – or a figment of her fertile mind. Am I seeing things, or is that a *goat*?

It is! Lydia has her arm slung familiarly round its neck. The bearded mouth snaffles the last crisps and its tail swishes with pleasure.

'Look! Isn't he lovely? He must have got through the hedge!' Or was he enticed?

'She,' I correct her, thinking . . . I recognise that goat . . . it's either Lucy or Drusy – my son Matt keeps her in the farm field beyond.

Zoe and I examine the hole in the hedge. 'That's where that awful Barnaby escaped last year, d'you remember? It was the last day of term. When he got found out, he said we'd given him permission.'

Lucy/Drusy doesn't want to return that way – in fact she won't budge. She likes the children, she likes the cuddles – and she's nosing in pockets for more tidbits.

I sprint back to the school. 'Help!' I cry to a passing teacher. She finds a long coil of rope.

It's easy enough to catch a docile goat and to thread rope through its collar, but it takes the whole football team to urge her up the field. Then she clatters crossly across the asphalt, has an inspection of the staff's cars and reluctantly accompanies me back to the farm. The children are very disappointed to see her go.

It's a hot day and I'm perspiring. I thought our old dog pulled, but he's nothing compared to this goat.

Luckily for him, Matt is not about! I pen the goat up. Then – Where's the other one? Drusy/Lucy has vanished, too!

I hack my way through the nettles and thistle towards the dividing hedge. There's the hole – and there's Drusy/Lucy investigating its possibilities egged on by the children on the other side.

Drusy/Lucy is not as friendly as her sister. She shows her teeth at me and kicks my already nettle-stung ankle. I hop back, hand through her collar, chanting endearments, but thinking blue murder. As I give her a helping hand into the pen, I hear the whistle.

I stagger back uphill and puff along the playground. The children, filing back inside the school, greet me excitedly.

'Cor, your face is all red!'

'Can't you bring the goats in to play tomorrow?'

'Aren't you lucky having goats in your family!'

I smile weakly. Wait until I see my son tonight!

We supervise the babies in the washrooms and then see them back to their classroom. Like magic, the noise subsides, and they sit quietly on their mat to listen to a story.

I still have a car in my pocket, and the handle of a skipping rope. Clare is washing the floor of the kitchen.

'Had a good lunch-hour?' she asks.

'We've had a *Field Day!*' I say, with feeling.

CHAPTER 63

Putting on Our Parts

We were having our W.I. committee meeting at Millicent's house. She lived in an old lodge within a secluded, lovingly-tended garden, with her two aged dogs. 'From the same mother, would you believe it,' she said. Well, they certainly didn't look like sisters. The bigger dog, which resembled a golden Labrador, was named Beauty; the tiny, scruffy, whiskery one was black – no, she wasn't called Beast, for she had a very sweet nature, was the more intelligent of the two – and answered to Tuppence.

Millicent's house was a reflection of her artistic temperament – she was obviously multi-talented. She had been brought up by an eccentric aunt and uncle. She told us stories of her unconventional childhood, how she'd gone along with her aunt to Ellen Terry's cottage where her aunt was hanging new curtains she had made for the actress. Millicent was fascinated by the bed, which was chained to the wall, because of the sloping floor. She thought Miss Terry would have had much more fun careening down the room in it.

Besides being a musician, choir mistress and enthusiastic gardener, Millicent also painted and potted: she constantly took up new crafts, and was busy with several projects at the same time. There were half-woven baskets, glowing tapestries folded over chair arms – 'Watch out for the needles!' she reminded us cheerfully. Her pride and joy was a grand piano, with piles of music scores, some of which she had composed herself.

When we had completed the 'business', she bustled into her kitchen, colourful with tiles she had hand-painted, and made a big pot of tea. We enjoyed her buttered scones (she was a good cook too) and drank tea from bone china cups.

'Let's have a sing-song,' she encouraged us, as the dogs hoovered up our crumbs. She sat down at the piano. We awaited her command.

Unfortunately, our singing upset Beauty, who lifted her head and howled, very loudly indeed. Tuppence joined in with a 'woof' or two. Millicent had arranged us in a circle of chairs around her as she played. The dogs were in the middle of us. Catastrophe! Beauty produced an enormous puddle, which lapped round our feet. Singing faltered and our pianist swivelled round crossly: 'Why have you stopped!' Then she realised that we were all sneakily abandoning ship – well our seats anyway. She sighed, went into the kitchen and came back with a large saucepan and a dish cloth. The more genteel members blanched at the choice of mopping up utensils. Millicent was obviously expert at this task. Poor Beauty hid behind the settee.

'Now you're all here,' Millicent said, surprised that we didn't want a second cup of tea or another scone, 'I have a bright idea ... We should put on a village pantomime, as we used to in the old days. Sheila can write it for us, I'll compose some music, and produce it, of course. All agreed? I'll have a casting session here next week.'

So that's how I began my pantomime career. Millicent produced a tattered script, all of three pages, and commanded: 'Enlarge it!' How could I resist *Cinderella*? Before I knew it, I was an Ugly Sister, too. I never revealed that I had written my first pantomime at nine years old in primary school, and also appeared in that as Puss in Boots, in a costume fashioned from our old blackout curtains! Millicent had suspected I was a thwarted actress, and she was right. Mind you, the Sunday school I attended when six or seven had a job to find a Joseph willing to play opposite my Mary in the Nativity play. Eventually, the undertaker's son obliged, but I'm afraid I had to whisper his lines to him. He mumbled a threat or two through his grey woolly beard. Looking back, I guess it was my enthusiasm that put them off. Later, when we studied Shakespeare in English lessons and acted in front of the class, I was Lady Macbeth, 'Out damned spot!' I cried; then I was Shylock – I enjoyed the character parts – I wasn't so keen to play Henry V's Queen. Perhaps it's time to reveal that I was shy and quiet when I was young, but I surprised my family and friends when 'throwing myself' into a part!

Every single member of the W.I. was roped in for that first panto. Judy painted backdrops and designed posters, tickets and the programme. She and Alice made wonderful props, like the coach in which Cinderella went to the ball, and an enormous pumpkin from vacuum cleaner bags. Molly, Boffy's neighbour, designed 'wings' on stage from old curtains. Boffy advised on costume, of course. Pam sat in the prompt corner. John's sister Betty came up with some lyrics for Millicent's new music, including Cinderella's song.

Millicent arranged the footlights, trained those who didn't wish to act to produce special effects, and produced songs and music which were a challenge to us all. Cinderella, our youngest member, looked the part, but refused to sing. Mrs B, in the wings, provided the voice, pure and sweet, as Cinderella mimed the words. Buttons, on the other hand, could sing, and was a champion tap dancer! I had a great partner in Joan, the guide captain – she was the bossy Ugly Sister and I was the Put-Upon one – we were both after the Prince, but our feet were too big for the glass slipper. All the cast were dedicated, and again I can't mention them all, but one who stole the show was a tiny lady, known ever after as Fairy Maud!

Also, there was Eileen, from the Mill cottage. Eileen played a minor role on this occasion, but later she had the plum parts, like Wishee Washee in *Aladdin*! She was another small, dark-haired, slim lady, who had been born in South Africa and married an Englishman during the war. She loved cats and we heard all about Rhubarb and Custard, the current pair. We also learned that she had a famous daughter, a delightful actress, Linda Bassett, who came with her friends to all our shows, and applauded us enthusiastically from the front row. Linda obviously got her gift for drama from her little mum!

At the dress rehearsal, we were joined by Millicent's quartet. The music made all the difference. 'You don't need a microphone!' Millicent cried to the faint-hearted. 'Just project your voice!' We learned to come front stage and to involve the audience.

Children from the local dancing school, dressed as mice, provided the 'Aah!' element. We wore our costumes for the first time, too.

Joan and I had our best moment when we had a tussle on stage. Alice made me a 'pull apart' dress. When Joan grabbed me from behind as I displayed my finery to the audience, she declaimed: 'Your frock does nothing to camouflage flab. That pink makes you look like an overdressed crab!' I was revealed in outsize bloomers and long-sleeved vest. We were expecting laughter from the audience, but to my astonishment, the overwhelming reaction from them was sympathy for poor downtrodden Aggie. I felt like a born-again actress – it was heart-warming! I realised the audience *liked* me! Linda gave me a hug and said I had missed my vocation! I've been a great fan of hers ever since. I loved her performance in *Lark Rise to Candleford* on TV.

Year by year, the pantomimes continued, and other groups asked if they might borrow our scripts. Millicent, Meg and I got to see most of these productions! The tickets were invariably a sell-out, and we gave all the money raised to charity. By now, most of us were tap dancing along with 'Buttons'.

In mufti one afternoon, walking along the village street, I was hailed by a passing stranger on a bicycle: 'Why, it's Mother Goose!' I knew then I couldn't hide 'behind my character'!

We also began to tour round residential and nursing homes at Christmas with shorter, slicker versions of the pantomimes – I called these 'Potted Pantos'. Just a few props, and quick changes of costume, and Millicent on the piano. We had an amusing if rueful experience once. We had been invited to another W.I.'s Christmas party, as the entertainment. Millicent previewed the stage and facilities, and told us, 'They have an excellent piano, thank goodness.' What we didn't know was that the 'resident' pianist, who had fought long and hard to get that instrument, wasn't about to let us or rather Millicent, loose on it. She got the caretaker to move it to a hiding place behind the stage, and to put the old piano in its place.

We began on a high note, literally, for only the top keys functioned, most of the rest were dumb. Millicent bashed at them furiously, to no effect, and we squeaked our way through the songs. A quick glance at Millicent's quivering back, clad in shiny black satin, made us quake. Afterwards, we bolted down our cake and made for the exit without the usual pleasantries. Millicent never forgot – and certainly never forgave the perpetrator.

*   *   *

So now, rather as I had been in the old days when we were knee deep in plums, I was the village scribe, though then I was writing letters for the traveller community. I wrote for the local paper, for the church magazine, and I penned more plays and pantomimes for the school. This reduced the time I could devote to paid writing, but I was still busy with articles on family life and romantic stories set in the past. I wasn't the only one researching and typing at the rate of knots: Marcia and Ian were involved with a book about our village. Judy, Ian's wife, produced lots of her delightful pen and ink drawings, an example being a pair of oxen pulling the plough. I was asked to edit the book for them, which meant I had the privilege of reading it before most of the village. It was a labour of love for the three of them and a job well done.

I have told you something of some of the folk I knew then, but there were others with interesting stories which they longed to share.

Mostly single, elderly ladies who would surprise and delight us all. I was asked to write a series on Village Voices for the Parish mag. Beatrice, the retired district nurse had a great deal to tell. She had trained as a Norland Nanny and when she was in college, her father visited her one day. She was told in no uncertain terms that men were not allowed on the premises. 'He's not a suitor, he's my father!' Bea protested. But the rules could not be bent. She became nanny to a famous film star's family and enjoyed it very much. At the beginning of the war, she retrained as a hospital nurse, and was in London throughout the Blitz. There were tales of her early 'district days' – of working in slums but how her impoverished clients always made her a cup of tea, and one dear old man covered each step of the stairs to his flat with old newspapers to protect her shoes, and also placed a paper on the seat of her chair. She remarked that there was dignity in poverty. When a child saw her coming up the stairs with her black bag and exclaimed: 'Blimey, I 'ope you ain't got a new baby in that!' Beatrice opened it to prove she hadn't. 'Just come to cut Grandad's toenails,' she said. She took her Guides to Norway on camping holidays, and sewed her money bag to her underwear for safe keeping.

There was another lady of the same vintage who had connections with the film world. She had been engaged at twenty to a young actor. Her father wouldn't allow her to marry him, but Kay followed his career avidly, and was glad he married happily and had a family. She respected her father's wishes, she said, and never contacted him again. She had worked for a well-known firm of cotton thread and embroidery silk manufacturers. Kay was a secretary in the office, but over the years she collected samples of all the colours you could imagine. She embroidered pictures on linen as gifts, from her own designs. Another hobby, besides her real passion, gardening, was writing jingles for greetings cards, and she was very good at this.

These thumbnail sketches, led to me being asked to write tributes to be read at funerals. I also wrote, at his dictation, the life story of an elderly farmer who wanted copies for his family and friends. I called it 'Give him the best, but in a smaller glass', words spoken by his own father, when he was a lad, and allowed his first taste of beer. It needed tweaking and some tactful editing (he'd had two wives and two families!), and it bore his name as author, of course, but he was very pleased with the end result. Extracts were read at his funeral, as he wished. Most of the congregation, including us, had been privileged to attend his eightieth birthday celebrations not long before. We all said he had enjoyed every minute of it, and that was a good feeling.

John and I were very proud when we learned from the farmer's wife that her husband had remarked, when in turn, our sons gained a good grounding working at weekends on the farm while they were still at school: 'Those boys are a cut over other boys.' This was praise indeed from one who did not give it lightly.

CHAPTER 64

Merv the Midnight Grocer

Marcia and her family were enthusiastic about a wonderful holiday in a narrow boat on the Mon and Brec (Monmouthshire and Brecon) Canal in Wales. 'Why don't you take your children – they'd love it! The dog, too.'

Kate and Matt were teenagers now, and they thought it was a great idea. We arrived at Gilwern, at the offices of the Princess Line, and were taken aboard to learn the ropes.

The long boat was traditionally decorated with larger-than-life exotic birds and cabbage roses, predominantly in scarlet, green and gold paint. All that was missing was the horse: the *Princess* was powered by diesel fuel, but she moved along the mysterious dark water of the canal at no more than walking pace, which was perfect for our enjoyment of the countryside we would journey through.

The interior of the narrow boat was just as nostalgic. There was the dresser, with its painted knobs, and the display of blue-and-white willow-patterned china from the local market – probably not so cheap as it had been a century ago, but certainly just as cheerful. Cups dangled from hooks along the dresser shelves. There was a modern stove, and a shining kettle, not the black, sooty one I had fondly imagined. There was a lucky horseshoe fixed above the windows, along with polished brass ornaments. Storage was inside the bench seats, not plain hard wood as in the old days, but comfortably upholstered, for at nights, they doubled-up as bunks. There were more bunks in the hold, which were bagged by the young ones. The smallest room lived up to its name: you had to enter sideways on and double up under the shower. The toilet would, we were advised, need regular emptying at designated places along the route, where we could also take on fresh water.

The boat was well equipped. In the hold there were mops, brushes and buckets; life jackets; a boating hook (to fish things out of the water – hopefully not 'man overboard!'). Also, a coil of rope and a can of diesel. In the dresser drawers were maps and brochures detailing places of interest. We were provided with sleeping bags with inner linings (difficult to struggle out of, when midnight visits to the loo were required) and pillows. Lighting and cooking were by bottled gas.

We were off! The young ones untied the boat, scrambled aboard and decided to sit up top so that they could see all. John was at the wheel, and Billow lay beside him enjoying the afternoon sunshine. I was down below, unpacking the provisions we had bought in the village. A story was already unfolding in my mind; the resulting book would be called *The Summer Season* and later retitled *The Canal Boat Girl*. I would set it in the past, in the heyday of the canals, I mused. I even had a name for my heroine, Ruth Owen, one of the Singing Barleys . . . She is a favourite heroine, to this day.

(The following sentences, which appear in my novel, were recorded the next morning, as I looked out of the window, upon waking.)

'In the clear early light of that June morning, damsel flies, tiny, translucent, bluey-green, flickered along the lush reeds below the towpath. Fish moved mysteriously, occasionally rippling the clouded waters of the canal. A cluster of ducklings, anxiously tailing duck and drake, sailed close to the narrow boat.

On the bank, wild flowers grew in sweet profusion: poppies, forget-me-nots, tall, swaying yellow flags. Below the tangled brambles, the meadow sloped away to the river. Like a painted backcloth, reminiscent of the ones before which the Barleys had so often sung, was the great mountain, brooding over all.'

The *Princess* glided smoothly along through tranquil light and shade. We marvelled at the amazing reflections of enormous trees in the water. We were experiencing life at a slower pace: we took it all in, the wild life in the fields, a flotilla of swans mirrored in the canal. We passed a boathouse which seemed to be floating on the surface of the water, a cottage or two, then a large white-painted house where the turf rolled green down to the water's edge, and stone steps up to a grand entrance were flanked by mossy, submissively crouching statues. As we meandered past, the upstairs windows were flung up, one by one, the drawn curtains billowing out in the breeze. My pencil raced across the pages of my notebook. (*Ty-Gyda-Cerded*, the house with all the steps, as I later named it, was to feature in my book.)

We saw long-tailed black sheep; encountered a three-legged dog, explosively defending the next bridge. Billow had been sneaking out onto the towpath on occasion, then scrambling back aboard, but now wisely he laid doggo. The lock-keeper's cottage came into view and we were about to tackle our first lock.

When I say 'we' I expect you guessed that while I was still day-dreaming of coal barges lining up to go through the lock at the turn of the century, John and his young team were ready and eager to set to.

'You stay below with the dog,' John suggested kindly. 'We can manage. The lock-keeper's looking out, as we're new to all this.'

I watched, bemused, as Kate and Matt wound the paddles while John held the boat steady. The *Princess* rose high on the swell of water. The youngsters dashed to the far end, to operate the paddles there, so that she could float through the open gate. The crowd, mostly from the following craft, who had gathered on the bridge to watch, let out a resounding cheer.

All aboard – 'Cup of tea coming up, Mum?' was the cry. The lock-keeper waved a cheery goodbye.

We went through another lock later, but although I looked forward to a repeat performance, I felt the urgent need to 'just close my eyes for a second' as we made the approach. I blamed my narrow bunk, which befitted a narrow boat, but caused fitful sleep at night. Kate said reproachfully afterwards, 'Oh, Mum, it was awful! There were even more people watching than last time, and you slept through all that rushing water, and they were peering in at you as the boat finally came up – how could you?' Very easily I'm afraid.

I also missed the unfouling of the screw when we became bogged down at Pontypool and the boatman waded in to our rescue. I awoke only as we puttered gently on our way! In the meantime, Matt and Kate had been to the local leisure centre to pass the time, and joined a class of infants in the junior swimming pool. They reported ruefully that there was a dragon of a teacher in charge who watched their every splash.

I wrote this piece of doggerel – there were several more verses, but I'll spare you that: 'Oh we're the water boatmen; we hardly ever wash, or comb our hair, unless we're feeling posh. In my dreams I call out loud, how *can* we pass through all those locks, If we are fast asleep? While our narrow boat just rocks . . . Apples mixed with grubby socks . . .'

We made quick sketches to capture the memorable moments.

Every now and then we saw a sign on the towpath. When it read SHOP, an arrow indicated that if we moored up, and trekked across a footpath, we would eventually come to a shop, and sometimes a village, with a church and a pub, not just an isolated hamlet. There were also farms which sold eggs and milk. One morning, a farmer told us about his friend Merv the Midnight Grocer. 'We call him that, because he opens and shuts the shop when he thinks he will, and he usually delivers after dark, sometimes in the early hours. If you can catch him in the shop, you'll find he sells absolutely everything.'

We followed his directions. We had to climb a craggy wall, we heaved the old dog up between us – his leaping days were over – and when he was safely on the other side, we landed in turn with a jarring thump on the grass verge of the steep hill which we now had to climb to the village. The canals of course are low down so it is always puff-and-blow when you visit a settlement on foot.

As we reached the crest of the hill the view of the valley below was quite breath-taking. Sheep in clusters, and cottages in the dips, with purple-slated rooftops. The sun was warm on our backs, there was a further track leading up to the distant pub. Did the patrons roll downhill after closing time, we wondered? We turned left into a square, with a level path, where the shop was flanked by cottages. As the farmer had warned us, the blinds were still down. I fished in my pocket for my notebook and scribbled the following, resting the book on John's back.

'There is a cobbled courtyard before a stable door with a hitching post for horses and a water trough. A barrel cut down for the planting of flowers and a pile of folded dusty sacks waits on the step, obviously returned by an earlier disappointed customer who failed to rouse the midnight grocer. Ivy twines through the letter box . . .'

(Before we even met him, I knew I would 'transport' the Midnight Grocer back in time in my story. He is Eli Pentecost in the book.)

Another customer joined us, and took up the yard broom when our knocking went unanswered. She tapped an upstairs window smartly.

The occupants of the nearby cottages opened their doors to see what was happening. The bolts shot back, the top half of the door swung open, and Merv leaned his elbows on the lower half and poked his head out. He smiled at us. He had a round, jolly face and a mop of hair. 'Shop was it?' he asked sleepily. Then he beckoned us to come in, while he went behind the counter.

It really was a shop which sold literally everything and anything, from sacks of potatoes, jars of sweets, mousetraps, matches and mothballs. There was not much room to manoeuvre between boxes piled on the floor. Under a glass dome on a piece of marble, on the counter, reposed a great slab of yellow saffron cake labelled 'Mother's Cake'.

I was itching to make more notes, and later on the boat, I wrote:

'Squeezed between the barley sugar sticks and blue bags of sugar was a stack of hard-crusted loaves which looked as if they would snap the consumer's teeth . . . with a pencilled card: "Mother's own Bread". Along the shelves, next to jars of cloves and whole nutmegs, were pickles and jams, red, gold, green and rich brown declaring themselves to be "Mother's Gage", "Mother's Mustard Pickle", "Mother's Bramble", "Mother's Relish" . . .'

Now, Merv observed: 'On the boats, is it? Let me take your order and I'll deliver later, wherever you are moored up for the night.'

'Er – we'll take the groceries with us now, if we may!' I said quickly.

We were all thinking his mother must be quite old but still busy with all that baking and stirring, when she appeared through the back entrance to the shop. She was not a little old lady at all, but an attractive blonde woman probably in her mid-thirties. Like Merv, she had the appearance of one who had risen from her bed in a hurry.

'Meet Mother,' Merv beamed. We were none the wiser.

Mother packed our basket with her bestselling lines, a loaf of her bread, a large piece of her cake and a jar of her greengage jam. She took from the meat safe chump chops which she wrapped well in newspaper, likewise Mother's bulging, herby pork sausages.

Merv plucked the stub of pencil from behind his ear, and added to our list.

'Oh, you must try my cream cheese!' Mother told us. This looked like clotted cream in its dish. I prefer cheddar, and John, Stilton, but we couldn't say no.

We said goodbye and thank you, and as we departed, the sign on the door was turned to CLOSED.

'They're going back to bed, I shouldn't wonder,' I said.

'Wouldn't you, if you'd been rowing a boat full of goods most of the night?' John replied.

'You're not supposed to travel along the canal after dark.' Matt had read all the rules.

'Precisely,' his dad said.

* * *

Our camera was constantly clicking as we journeyed on. Matt and Kate hugging the trunk of a giant tree, impossible to circle with their arms, so they peep out on either side. This tree had its roots seemingly (impossible, surely?) embedded in a great rock; just as well, because it leaned alarmingly toward the water. A tall, deserted mill, with shattered windows – who had toiled there long ago? The lock cottage, now a museum, furnished simply as it had been in the past; tiny rooms. We spent some time there. We walked to the nearby river. The water here was clear and ran cold over amazing pink rocks. We all had a paddle, including Billow.

We saw a large rowing boat, with an awning, full of children wearing shorts and plimsolls, with bare brown bodies and tousled hair. They were laughing and scolding at the same time, as a couple of spaniel dogs were shaking water over the family, after an energetic dip. This family were camping on their boat and having a wonderful carefree holiday.

We came upon a film crew making a documentary for a schools' TV programme. The cameraman had obviously run out of socks, like us, and we couldn't help noticing that he had the largest, filthiest feet we had ever seen, but he gave us a little talk on the rekindled interest in restoring the canals for leisure and pleasure.

We were disappointed that the tunnel was closed for repairs on this first holiday (we made up for that on later canal trips), but we pictured the leggers hanging perilously either side of the narrow boat, pushing with their feet on the slimy walls in the dark . . .

Another vivid memory is ascending a steep street one Sunday morning when the sun was already scorching down on us, and seeing on the front windowsill of a little terraced cottage plates of Devils-on-horseback – bacon wrapped round little sausages – and us conjecturing the reason why: a wedding feast? A party? The 'devils' wouldn't need cooking, because they were already sizzling in the heat through the glass!

This was a holiday we would never forget, and it inspired me to write full-time. *The Summer Season* was actually the fourth book I had published, because first I had a promise to fulfil in memory of my father . . .

CHAPTER 65

A Writer's Companion

Now that Kate was at college, and Matt was in his last year at school, John encouraged me to write that first book. I had worn out my little portable typewriter which had succeeded the cumbersome long-carriage machine I had used for my early stories back in the orchard days, and this was replaced with my first electric typewriter. This was also a heavy machine, but needed the lightest touch, and I was used to hammering keys which often stuck together in mid-air in protest. I practised, panicked and practised, and gradually mastered the new technique.

It was quite a wrench to leave the village school, but the staff and pupils gave me a lovely send-off, with speeches, flowers and the latest copy of Roget's Thesaurus. I left with a bundle of thank you letters and drawings from the children. The goats were featured in one picture!

Twice a week I spent a day in the county library, researching the era I was writing about, 1890–1920. I sat in a quiet room upstairs, with other students, and Linda, the librarian, found me all the relevant books. I wrote letters too: no internet browsing for me then!

I gained several pen pals in the process, and much valuable, generously given, information. There was Dick Playle of the Music Hall Society who also knew the Isle of Sheppey well, where the first part of my novel would be set. He wrote in beautiful copperplate, and it was a pleasure to read his letters. Another new friend was Pino Maestri, the historian of London's Little Italy, who kindly sent me masses of material. I named a character in the book for him! Sheppey library provided copies of local newspaper cuttings of the time, which, written in old-style journalism, vividly brought the past to life. I also had letters my father had written about his childhood in Sheerness, his encounter with a suspected German spy, a photographer, and the terrible winter of 1895, when the sea froze, and the island had been cut off from the mainland.

It was time for us to visit the island and retrace my father's steps as he explored it with his brother and sister so long ago.

Dad was born in 1890 in 'a little cottage under the sea wall' in Sheerness. 'We opened the back door and looked over the wall at the spuming sea.' The children hardly ever wore shoes but ran barefoot over soft, clean sand – it sounded an idyllic childhood. Dad's father was in the Navy and away for long periods – his mother was a wonderful cook and was steadfast in adversity. She brought her children up to be resourceful and to work hard at school. They called their mother by her Christian name, Jane, and their father was nicknamed Petty, because, as Alice, my aunt said, 'He is *un petit homme* – a little man!' He was also the ship's doctor – I'm not sure he was qualified, but he was very knowledgeable and highly regarded for his skills. He had also studied Latin at grammar school.

Well, the house was still there, under the sea wall, as Dad had said. It was actually up for sale, and we did think of asking to see over it, but decided not to. Amazingly, the neighbours, when hearing the family name, had heard stories about the three mischievous children who'd lived there at the end of the nineteenth century!

We made several visits to the island, and I wrote a short story entitled *Running with the Wind in Her Hair*, with a heroine who helped a band of smugglers in the eighteenth century. I took copious notes for the proposed novel, jottings like: 'Blue Town was so called originally because of the availability of Admiralty paint, which brightened up all the old buildings . . . It was "blue" for another reason, and it was out of bounds for children and respectable folk . . .'

The museum was a wonderful source of material. Oil paintings of the Great Flood, the inevitable consequence of the Great Freeze after the thaw finally set in, when folk rowed boats along the main streets. Before that, water supplies had been rationed for many months! Hard times, but determined islanders.

We walked for miles, as this was the way we could absorb the atmosphere and discover the past. *Tilly's Family* (later *The Nursemaid's Secret*) was slowly, but surely, coming together, but it would be some time yet before it was published by Piatkus. The catalyst would be the acquiring of an agent, and wise editor, Judith. She had faith in me. Thank you, Judith.

All this time, I continued writing my short stories, and receiving heart-warming feedback from readers. Sally, my editor at the *Realm*, encouraged me with my novel research, too. I was still busy with pan-tomimes and the W.I. but I missed our children at home, and those at the school. June, my fruit-picking friend, who was now working part-time in the local stores, asked me if I would keep Nik, her daugh-ter, company in the school holidays; it was the perfect solution – Nik and I were already friends – she reminded me of Ginge as a small girl, dreamy and studious, always with her head in a book – like me, too, I suppose, at that age! While I encouraged Nik in her reading, and we talked about books and writing, I decided we would both benefit from going out and about, and fresh air! Nik recalls that she visited 'Sheila's old ladies' and was made a great fuss of, and shown their treasures. Nik is a true friend to this day, despite the disparity in our ages – we went to her wedding, and now she is a young mum to Izzie, she works part-time in the University library, like June before her.

As for elderly ladies, I also volunteered to help with bathing duties at the day centre. Boffy had at last been persuaded of the benefits of attending the centre, after a few weeks of being collected by the special bus two mornings a week, when she disappeared after arrival while the driver was busy with wheelchairs and walking aids for the less able-bodied. Boffy was off into town to do her shopping. She reappeared when it was time to go home. The staff caught up with her one day and persuaded her to go back to the centre for a bath, to have her clothes washed and then to have a hot lunch. Dear Boffy looked lovely afterwards – she chose a new outfit from a rail of clothes, her hair was soft and silvery and set in curls, and – shush! – she was a shade lighter . . . We loved her as she was, but now she was too frail to care for herself properly and too proud to ask for help.

Well, Boffy told me they needed volunteers and could she mention my name? Some of my friends were already helping with other aspects of eldercare, so why not me, I thought.

There was a special bath where the side swung out so that the one being bathed could enter easily and sit on a seat inside the bath. This 'open and close' method reminded me of the bacon slicer in the shop. As one or two of the ladies were amply built, I was always secretly worried I might unwittingly 'slice' when I closed the door . . . Fortunately, my fears were groundless. It was a very onerous task, and I usually got very damp. One lady, after I had been forced to change my dress for a bor-rowed flowery crimplene from the ever-obliging rail, looked at me and pronounced: 'You usually look so drab! You look much brighter today!'

I only ever bathed one man, and I'm afraid that was the end of my career as a bath attendant. I won't go into the reasons, but I think others had refused to bath him before me. It took ages to clean the bath . . .

We had reluctantly decided that we should move. We were rattling around in the chapel now – it was too big for us. We looked for somewhere nearer town and the school, a couple of miles away. We found a nice house with plenty of room for visiting family and a lovely mature garden.

'We'll be back all the time,' we promised our village friends.

But before we left, dear Boffy passed away. On Saturday afternoons, she always made her way up to the shop before it closed, to collect her regular order, two cream cakes. It was dark in the evenings now. Several people, in retrospect, mentioned that her cottage had been unlit all evening, but they had assumed Boffy was at a friend's.

Her good neighbour, Molly, raised the alarm first thing the following morning. Boffy was discovered lying unconscious in her hallway, still clutching the precious paper bag containing her treat for tea. The ambulance took her to hospital. Molly asked me what she thought Boffy would want to have to hand when she awoke. We decided, her King James bible, worn from her daily readings (she was a Christian Scientist) and a photograph of her beloved sister. Molly took them into the hospital later, with flowers. I'm sure she knew, even if she couldn't speak. Her passing was very peaceful.

Her only relative was a distant cousin, but it was very fitting that he was an actor, we thought. When the little house was cleared, Judy and Ian bought it at auction for their mother, for it was after all, in their large garden.

Most of the village turned up to Boffy's funeral, and her cousin gave a résumé of her life. She was a fascinating character, and in my mind's eye I see her still.

* * *

It was a week before Christmas, we had just moved in to our new abode, and Sara and Phil's wedding was the following weekend! We were a full house and in happy chaos. My mother and aunt had arrived and been taken to stay with our friend Pam, who looked after them splendidly. This was after taking in John, Matt and me (and the dog) for six weeks when the chapel was sold, but we hadn't completed then on the house! Our furniture had been stored over at another friend's smallholding, as Alice had barn space. The boys coped with the moving of same from place to place!

Sara married Phil, back at the village church. She looked beautiful in an Edwardian-style dress she had designed herself. This time the smallest bridesmaid wasn't Kate, but Jo's three-year-old Carly, our first granddaughter. We had five grandchildren now, but Di was expecting her third child, which would be another granddaughter, Hannah, in February next year.

It was a very cold day indeed, with a real threat of snow, but nothing could spoil a very happy occasion. Though I'm glad our goose pimples didn't show on the wedding photographs! Sara and Phil both love the sea, and had chosen as one of their hymns, 'For Those in Peril on the Sea'.

They had already found their dream home, a house on a hillside, fittingly called 'Bali Hai'. This was in the Mumbles, South Wales, and they have lived there ever since. Sara has organised Sculpture on the Beach for several years, and is artist-in-residence at several local schools. Phil is a wildlife and surfing/sports photographer.

The reception was held at a local hotel and the proprietors kindly voted the wedding cake made by John and me as the best they had ever tasted! (This was before they saw the lipstick markings on a statue in the garden, and we are still wondering which of the under-fives present was responsible!)

We had our usual happy family Christmas meal around the big table. I guess the new family in the chapel were doing the same.

* * *

In the new year there was sad news of another old friend. Dear Mrs B, whom I had first met in the W.I., had died very suddenly. Meg came round to tell me. 'She was sitting at her table, with her Christmas cards spread out to choose and sign, and when I touched her shoulder, I realised she had – gone . . . I couldn't tell you until after the wedding and then Christmas.'

We had to carry on with the pantomime without our best singer in the wings. But we all 'felt' her presence; she was that sort of person. The W.I. put a plaque up over the kitchen hatchway in the hall, in her memory. She was also much missed by the cricket club and the horticultural society – they present a cup at the annual show named for both Mrs B and Alf.

This is, I think, the right place to end this particular chapter in our lives. I hope you have enjoyed it – it has given me much pleasure to write about our chapel days.

I would just like to give a hint of what follows – two more marriages, in Kent, then retirement to Suffolk, where I was born, many more books written, and now, a total of twenty-two grandchildren, who range in age from almost two years old to twenty-nine! Later weddings, all our family are happily settled with good partners in life, and the first of the younger generation, Hannah, will be marrying next spring. And John and I, of course, who have already celebrated our golden wedding, are still together and enjoying new, if smaller, challenges.

SHEILA'S LIFE POST-MEMOIRS

Sheila and John retired to her beloved Suffolk where she was born and where she spent her World War II evacuation years. She was reunited with her mother and aunt. Sheila formed a writing group and was involved with the local church. Wherever she was, she loved being part of the community and being helpful to others. John continued to help with book research. He bought a boat and enjoyed sailing on the Suffolk coast.

In later years, Sheila was in her element when surrounded by her children, grandchildren and great-grandchildren to whom she recounted family stories and inspired them all to be creative.

Sheila continued writing and publishing books until the end of her life. Her love, kindness and presence is still felt amongst her proud family.

Sheila aged about 4 with her parents at Jaywick Beach, 1935

Sheila aged about 11, 1942

Sheila aged about 16, Thornton Heath, 1946

Sheila aged about 16, 1947

Sheila aged 17 on holiday at Jaywick, 1948

Sheila aged 21 and John on their engagement, Thornton Heath, 1952

Sheila aged about 21 with her dog Waggles, Thornton Heath, 1952

Sheila and John with her parents in London, 1954

St Margaret's Bay, Kent, 1960.
From left to right - Ginge, Jo,
Sara and JP

St Margaret's Bay, Kent ,1961.
From left to right - Ginge,
Sheila with Jo, John with
Chris, Sara and JP

Kent, 1962. From left to right -
Sara, Jo, Ginge, Chris and JP
with their Scottie dogs Hattie
and Seamus

Crabapple Cottage, 1962.
From left to right - Jo,
Michael, JP, Ginge, Sara,
John and Chris

Family photo of children in the orchard with aunts and grandmother, 1962

John, Jo and JP and their uncle and cousins in the orchard, 1963

Sheila with children in Kent, 1963. From left to right - Sheila, Roger, Michael, Ginge, Sara, Jo, Chris and JP

John and Ginge making a seesaw out of an apple tree branch, 1963

Grandparents and children in the orchard, 1965

Family photo in the orchard at Crabapple Cottage, 1966. From Left to right - Ginge, Roger, Sara, Jo, Chris and Michael

Camping trip to Wales in the Comma van, 1971

Holiday in Devon, Mothercombe Beach, 1971. From left to right - Ginge, Maff, Sara, Katy, Jo, JP, Chris, Michael and Roger

Family group including grandmother and aunts in the orchard at Crabapple Cottage, 1972

Katy with Billow, 1974

Matt, Katy and Jo outside The Chapel, 1977

Roger, Ginge and Sara on the Mere, Suffolk, 1979

Sheila (far left) in panto, 1980s

Sheila and John in Suffolk, 1994

Sheila amidst flowers in Suffolk, 2018

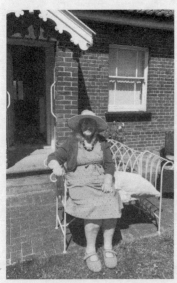

Sheila at her retirement home in Suffolk, 2019

Sheila at home in Suffolk, 2019

Enjoy heartwarming fiction from Sheila Newberry

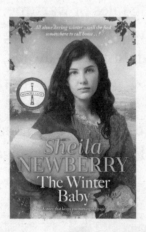

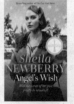

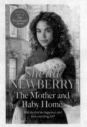